H
C
C
S

Harvard Contemporary China Series, 7

The Harvard Contempory China Series, now under the editorial direction of Harvard University Press, is designed to present new research that deals with present-day issues against the background of Chinese history and society. The focus is on interdisciplinary research intended to convey the significance of the rapidly changing Chinese scene.

From May Fourth to June Fourth

Fiction and Film
in Twentieth-Century China

Edited by

Ellen Widmer

David Der-wei Wang

Harvard University Press

Cambridge, Massachusetts

London, England 1993

This book is printed on acid-free paper, and its binding materials
have been chosen for strength and durability.

Library of Congress Cataloging-in-Publication Data

From May fourth to June fourth : fiction and film in twentieth-century
   China / edited by Ellen Widmer and David Der-wei Wang.
      p.   cm.—(Harvard contemporary China series; 9)
   Includes bibliographical references.
   ISBN 0-674-32501-X (cloth : acid-free paper).
   ISBN 0-674-32502-8 (pbk. : acid-free paper)
   1. Chinese literature—20th century—History and criticism.
   2. Motion pictures—China—History. I. Widmer, Ellen. II. Wang, David Der-wei.
   III. Series.
PL2302.F76 1993
895.1'509—dc20

92-19186
   CIP

To the memory of our colleague Marston Anderson
1951–1992

Contents

II Subjectivity and Gender

III Narrative Voice and Cinematic Vision

Preface

The papers in this volume were first presented at a conference titled "Contemporary Chinese Fiction and Its Literary Antecedents," which took place at the John King Fairbank Center for East Asian Research on May 11–13, 1990. The conference was organized around the question of whether and how Chinese literature since the Cultural Revolution (1966–1976) shows continuity with what is commonly known as "May Fourth" literature, that is, literature from 1918 to approximately 1930. Both of these literary phases sought to liberalize Chinese literature from previous orthodoxies, both looked to foreign literature for some of their inspiration, and both sought to liberate the "self" from earlier patterns of conformity. For these and other reasons, it seemed reasonable to predict that a sustained comparison would confirm the impression of continuity and identify new links. On the contrary, the findings of both the conference as a whole and of several individual papers are that these apparent commonalities need careful qualification before they can sustain meaningful comparisons and that in many ways it is discontinuity, not continuity, that prevails.

The extent of the discontinuity between two such seemingly similar eras is explained in part by the decades-long hiatus between them. Contemporary writers and critics are too young to have known May Fourth writings as anything other than history. Moreover, with the prominent exception of Lu Xun and a few other leftists such as Mao Dun, writers from the earlier period were not accessible to residents of the Chinese mainland after 1949. Though access became easier in the late 1970s, many May Fourth writers well known outside of China were discovered by contemporary Chinese writers and critics only when they came to travel abroad. Thus it cannot be said that contemporary writers were nurtured on the works of Ding Ling or Yu Dafu. As a result, the question of continuity makes a different kind of sense to foreign scholars of Chinese literature than to Chinese writers and critics, since it is only in recent times that these groups have had equal access to the full range of May Fourth writing.

Another important factor is the altered relationship of Chinese to foreign literatures between the 1920s and the 1980s. May Fourth and contemporary writers may have shared a tendency to look outside mainland China for their inspiration, but each era tended to pick what it needed from among the available foreign literatures. Moreover, foreign literatures have undergone their own evolutions since the 1930s. Even the meaning of a term like *realism* was not altogether constant outside of China over these seven decades, and schools such as socialist realism no longer held the same influence in Western countries that they once had. Another complicating factor was the shift of attention within China away from Soviet and Eastern European literatures, which had preoccupied the leading writers during the May Fourth era, in favor not only of Western literatures but of literatures of the "Third World." The role of García Márquez and "magical realism" as influences in contemporary literature is indicative of the broadening range of countries from which foreign literary practice could be absorbed. One must further note the role of Hong Kong and Taiwan, and of Chinese writers in exile, as new sources of contemporary literary ideas. The phenomenon of several competing Chinas was in no way part of the May Fourth landscape, but it has proved a vital conduit to the mainland of "outside influences"—both foreign and Chinese.

Contrasting attitudes toward China's literary tradition make another point of distinction. Where May Fourth literature sought to make a decisive break with premodern writing, contemporary literature has long since freed itself of the "anxiety" of this influence and can treat it more matter-of-factly, as a rich, nearly untapped reservoir of artistic ideas. Like the nonnative influences in contemporary Chinese writing, traditional narrative patterns are served up in surprising new contexts and combined with one another in unexpected ways. Thus, quite unlike their May Fourth predecessors, contemporary writers might highlight areas of overlap between "magical realism" and Zhuangzi or delve into the darker side of human nature by combining Freudian psychology with traditional Chinese writings about the strange.

The political agendas of both stages of Chinese literature are another important source of difference. While mainstream May Fourth writing was born of frustration over China's political weakness, the literature of the late 1970s and 1980s grew out of the shadow of the Cultural Revolution, during which the central authority was felt to be all-powerful. Though the literatures of both periods tend to be critical of government, the type of governmental problem that concerns them is often quite different. And whereas the typical early May Fourth literary figure was a modernized, urbanized intellectual, contemporary literature shows the effects of the forced migration of authors to the countryside; it is often set in the hinterlands, features ethnic minorities, and celebrates illiterate heroes and heroines. The biographical experience of writers parallels a contrast between the literary ethos of the early May Fourth period and that of the contemporary era: one focused on what was most modern—the city—whereas the other has returned to the rural origins that the earlier modernizers had ignored. One looked at characters who pitted the "self" against family and society, whereas the other concerns itself with genealogical succession (the family saga is a newly important mode). The frequently rural cast of contemporary Chinese literature might also be seen to reflect "native soil" writings of a somewhat earlier stage of Taiwanese literature. It further partakes of a movement that began before the contemporary era, when writers like Xiao Hong and Shen Congwen expanded literary topography to include Manchuria and West Hunan. Yet it is equally the result of recent political trends.

Other significant points of contrast concern language and form. The early May Fourth writers invented the literary vernacular as they wrote it. At first highly Europeanized, this language later gave way to a more speakable, less self-conscious idiom, under pressure from Qu Qiubai and others. Today's literary language has regained some of the opacity of the early May Fourth vernacular, though for utterly different reasons, among them the effort to capture local dialects and points of view. To cite opacity as a common denominator of both periods and go no further would be to miss the complexities that distinguish one type of opacity from another and to overlook the transparency of language that dominated literature in the period in between. Relatedly, to point to the short story as a fixture of both eras and go no further would be to overlook the greater range of forms available to the contemporary writer. The difficulties of writing the early Europeanized vernacular may have put a premium on concision in the 1920s; at any rate it was some years into the May Fourth era before longer works of fiction started to emerge.

In situations such as these, the broad continuities that unite May Fourth and contemporary literature need delicate analysis if they are to serve the purposes of scholarship. They are often so general as to hold little value. And though they may be derived from sound comparisons of specific works and authors, they highlight facets of May Fourth writing that were not of that era's mainstream. Shen Congwen was not among the leadership of the May Fourth literary establishment, but it is no accident that he looms large in contemporary perspective; his interest in regionalism and in the relationship between city and country anticipates major contemporary themes. Lu Xun is a household word in both periods, but his revolt against tradition stands out most prominently in May Fourth estimation, whereas his adaptations from traditional literature may have greater ramifications in the literature of today. Ding Ling and Yu Dafu likewise take on new colors in contemporary readings, although their articulation of a "writing self" (male or female) is one of the most important antecedents of writing about writing in the literature of today. Contemporary scholarship also calls attention to those who, though chronologically part of the May Fourth era, were atypical in their artistry, such as the Shanghai writers Liu Naou and Zhang Ruogu; they prefigure a trend in contemporary writing, although they themselves were a side current on the national literary scene. Finally, well-established artistic modes of the May Fourth era take on new interest simply because they are paralleled in the contemporary era, as when cinematic melodrama stimulates a backward look at May Fourth versions of the same genre. Inevitably, interpretations of the May Fourth stage of this tradition are somewhat colored by analyses of its later stage. On the basis of any of these examples, one might well ask whether the May Fourth literature under discussion in this volume is the same as that which its own practitioners understood to have existed in the 1920s or 1930s or as that which was accepted into the post-1949 canon.

In addition to comparisons between two literary eras, the 1990 conference invited comparison with a conference, also sponsored by the Fairbank Center, that was held sixteen years earlier under the title "Modern Chinese Literature in the May Fourth Era." The two conferences were similar in composition; indeed a number of people from the 1974 meeting also participated in the 1990 one. This volume, too, harks back to the earlier conference volume, *Modern Chinese Literature in the May Fourth Era*, edited by Merle Goldman and published by Harvard University Press in 1977.

Once again, however, comparison brings out differences as well as similarities. First, the array of critical tools and modes of analysis in 1990 differed greatly from what was current in 1974, to the extent that some of today's papers might not have been intelligible at the earlier conference. One of the most important methodological issues in 1974 seems too simple today: whether to divorce literature from its political, social, and economic contexts—to treat it "extrinsically" or "intrinsically," in the older discourse. In 1990 critics were generally aware of Foucault, Jameson, Barthes, and their more complex methodologies, and the issue was to decide which of these Western theories were useful and how to apply them meaningfully to the Chinese scene. This expansion of approaches created a fruitful (if occasionally discordant) dialogue at the 1990 meeting between scholars of different generations, nationalities, and critical schools.

The number of papers shaped by questions of gender in the 1990 meeting is at once an illustration of a major new critical voice in Chinese studies and a second point of contrast with the 1974 meeting. In 1974 only two papers touched on this topic and then as much in connection with social roles and rights as with literary questions. In 1990 gender was an issue in almost a third of the twenty-four papers originally presented, and it is one of three main themes of this volume. The far larger number of women scholars at the 1990 conference should also be noted in this connection. Poststructuralist notions of subjectivity put particular emphasis on the eye of the beholder, and it is no coincidence that many of the papers by women offered feminist readings. Some articles in the volume apply gender to new settings, finding narcissism in masculine visions of the future or making space for a uniquely "female tradition" while advancing generalizations about twentieth-century literature as a whole. In other cases, new thinking about gender is inspiring reconsiderations or modifications of such previously identified themes as the realistic bent in Chinese fiction and twentieth-century literature's "obsession with China," to make use of C. T. Hsia's term.

A third point of contrast between the 1974 and 1990 meetings is that the latter dealt with a literature still evolving, whereas the former focused on a completed phase. The bewilderment of the contemporary critic over his or her choice of critical method is compounded by the need to keep up with who is writing what, not only in Shanghai or Beijing or the hinterlands of China, but also in Taiwan, Hong Kong, and the West. It is not only that the geographical origins of contemporary Chinese literature are expanding. It is also that long periods away from China make Chinese writers more aware of realities abroad. The 1990 meeting took place as contemporary literature was entering a new phase, one that will be profoundly affected by the way so many of China's leading writers have responded to the events of June 4, 1989. It is probably still too early to predict the effect on Chinese literature of the large number of them who have decided not to return home.

Despite its title, this volume does not attempt to cover all of modern Chinese literature from 1919 to 1989. To discuss May Fourth and contemporary literature in terms of each other is already a narrowing of focus. In addition, the book is restricted to fiction and film. The title *From May Fourth to June Fourth* is meant rather to denote one common feature of these individual studies, all of which divide their attention equally between the May Fourth and contem-

porary periods or focus on one period in the light of the other.
Overall, the collection aims to take a first step toward linking together two phases of twentieth-century Chinese literature, even
when the differences between them outweigh the similarities. Like
the conference, the volume is intended to raise questions as much
as to answer them. With luck, it will lead to further discussions,
controversies, conferences, and volumes as Chinese literature and its
critics continue to evolve.

Ellen Widmer

Acknowledgments

Neither the conference nor the volume would have been possible without a generous grant from the National Endowment for the Humanities. The *China Times* Foundation also contributed generously toward the conference and the publication of these papers. Thanks to these gifts, it was possible to bring together many scholars from a number of countries. The face-to-face discussions at the conference were of inestimable value in the process of revising the papers. Commentators at the conference included Bonnie McDougall, Susan Wilf Chen, Perry Link, David Pollard, Robert Hegel, Philip Williams, Ellen Widmer, Merle Goldman, Edward Gunn, Patrick Hanan, William Tay, and C. T. Hsia. Rudolph Wagner, Marian Galik, Milena Dolezelova-Velingerova, Mau-sang Ng, Catherine Yeh, Marsha Wagner, Wendy Larson, Yue Daiyun, Eva Hung, Dory Poa, and Yu-shih Chen also attended our meeting; their comments, too, are reflected in the revisions. We are further grateful to three graduate students, Hu Siao-chen, Claire Conceison, and Lin Hua, who served as rapporteurs and conference assistants.

The conference was particularly fortunate to have in attendance the distinguished Chinese critics Liu Zaifu and Huang Ziping, as well as the poet Duo Duo. Along with Professor Yue Daiyun, who traveled from Beijing to attend the meeting, this group enhanced the formal program and contributed their insiders' knowledge in a variety of ways.

The leadership and staff of the Fairbank Center played an invaluable part in making both conference and volume possible. Merle Goldman and Patrick Hanan supported the project from the beginning and gave many valuable suggestions on substantive issues. Roderick MacFarquhar, Patrick Maddox, Fran Kramer, Michelle Grant, Nancy Deptula, and Anne Denna assisted in solving a wide range of logistical problems. Leo Ou-fan Lee was also extremely generous with his advice and time, and it was through his good offices that Liu Zaifu and Huang Ziping were able to attend.

Ellen Widmer
David Der-wei Wang

From May Fourth to June Fourth

Introduction

The essays in this volume address three issues that have characterized the development of modern Chinese literature and film over the past seven decades: the dialectic of city and country, the diacritics of gender and subjectivity, and the mutual evocation of voice and vision in fiction and film. The three issues cross-reference one another, in the articles as in the fiction and the films. The landscapes of city and country are realized visions of China, providing a symbolic background against which critical questions of self, gender, and national culture are played out. The presentation of the historical dynamic is mirrored in a critical re-presentation, divided and doubled by gender and subjectivity. The national identity of China is put in question in fiction, which is then transposed into the visible language of film; at last, criticism arrives to restore China to itself by translating fiction and film into its own higher language.

Drawing on a wide range of methodologies, from formal analysis to feminist critique, from philosophical deconstruction to cultural reconstruction, these essays demonstrate that the scholarship of modern Chinese literature has become an integral part of contemporary critical discourse. But instead of submitting themselves to the allure of Orientalism, these essays "talk back" to these Eurocentered theories from a heterogeneity of moving positions. Their ultimate concern is to keep literature recentered in its Chinese contexts.

To begin with, thanks to the enormous resurgence and popularity of the *xungen* (search for roots) movement in the mid-eighties, the problematic of *native soil writings* versus *urban literature* manifests itself as one of the most prominent themes in twentieth-century Chinese literature. Returning to the customs and mores of local regions, "search for roots" fiction first appeared as a modest reaction against the increasingly formulaic *shanghen wenxue* (literature of the wounded) of the early eighties—literature openly deploring the national chaos and individual suffering of the Cultural Revolution. But at a time when the whole nation of the PRC was asked to "look forward," the "search for roots" writers' insistence on looking "backward," "downward," and "inward" took on a highly polemical stance. It is no surprise that some of the "search for roots" writers such as Mo Yan and Han Shaogong should also be among the most avant-garde writers of the eighties.

In a broader sense, the concept of "search for roots" strikes the basic note of the volume. "Search for roots" indicates a historical endeavor, assessing what is happening now in the light of what happened in the past. But such an endeavor cannot be regarded as a benign remembrance of things past. Rather, the "search for roots" questions the cultural/political motivations that legitimate the form and content of the "remembrance," (re)discovers the hidden or forgotten layers of history and memory in a rigorous genealogy of the present, and maps out the trajectories that have instrumented the current polyphony of literary voices.

Seen in strictly literary terms, the "search for roots" movement leads back to the *xiangtu* (native soil) literature initiated by May Fourth writers in the twenties. Lu Xun took note of the rise of native soil literature, considering it one of the most promising tendencies in modern Chinese literature. Rooted in the Chinese soil, as its slogan suggests, the movement vowed to bring to the fore social and political issues that concerned the majority of Chinese. Highlighted in native soil discourse are such themes as the clash between traditional, rural values and modern, urban civilization; the confrontation between intellectual-revolutionaries and peasant-conservatives;

nostalgic evocations of the past or of childhood; and so on. But native soil writings could not describe these themes without betraying certain of their own limitations: To whom was native soil literature addressed (to the natives, who would not comprehend it, or to the deracinated, whose belief might be imported and therefore inauthentic)? Where should the "native" writer/narrator situate himself (or herself) in relation to all the "insulted and injured" of history? How could a text that had lost its roots in tradition still allegorically ground itself in a "native soil"?

Vacillating between all-embracing humanitarianism and self-indulgence, between altruist commitment and elite escapism, between earthy "soil" and imaginary utopia (or dystopia), native soil literature provided a textual arena wherein different social and political ideologies could compete. The past half-century has seen many debates over the formal and conceptual adequacy of the elusive native soil discourse: Mao's advocacy of an earthy discourse suitable for "the people" in the forties; Taiwan writers' promotion of a native soil movement in the late sixties and seventies; and mainland writers' desire to search out their "roots" again in the eighties. Each started as a literary campaign, yet developed into a cultural/political battle. The debates between and about them constitute one of the most complicated intellectual strains in modern and contemporary Chinese literature.

Four essays in this volume address the phenomenon of native soil literature. Joseph Lau's and Michael Duke's essays deal, respectively, with two major figures of the "search for roots" movement, Han Shaogong and Mo Yan. One of the founders of the "search for roots" movement, Han Shaogong has been highly acclaimed for creating an allegorical landscape modeled after his hometown region in Hunan. Alongside the influence of foreign writers like Faulkner and García Márquez, Lau notes that Han shows a definite indebtedness to writers like Lu Xun when he envisions a Chinese society on the brink of total disintegration, and when he lashes out at Chinese people's moral and intellectual depravity. Lau details how Han Shaogong first started as a writer of "literature of the wounded" and then developed his own "roots"-conscious style. He also observes that

Han derives his grotesque imagination from the classical *zhiguai* (recounting the strange) writings. Though the horror of the Cultural Revolution is very much in his mind, Han nevertheless is seen to transcend immediate historical exegesis and to achieve a narrative that mixes eschatological vision with grotesque realism, myth with memory. His "visitations" of the past, Lau argues, shed eerie light upon the "cannibalistic" practices of the present.

With a long list of successful works like *Hong gaoliang jiazu* (Red Sorghum Family) to his credit, Mo Yan has been widely recognized as one of the most versatile native soil writers of the eighties. He is at his best in turning familiar hometown scenes into fantastic landscapes, and creating a unique axiological system for his new worlds. But Mo Yan is not unaware of the paradox inherent in his native soil imagination, once calling his hometown in northeastern Shandong "the prettiest and the ugliest, the most unworldly and the most mundane, the holiest and the most vulgar" on earth. Michael Duke's essay starts from this paradox. Instead of the Mo Yan who chronicles the grandiose *Red Sorghum Family*, Duke calls attention to the other Mo Yan, the sullen social critic and tendentious parodist. Mo Yan's *Tiantang suantai zhige* (Garlic Song in Paradise City) is a powerful indictment of the abuses and absurdities seen in a rural town. Duke shows, by reviving the narrative mode once endorsed by Mao and his literary cohorts during the thirties and forties, that the novel posits itself both as a nostalgic commemoration and a bitter parody of the formula.

If the literature of the eighties has "recanonized" any May Fourth predecessor, it has to be Shen Congwen. As of the late seventies, Shen Congwen was deliberately ignored by mainland scholars, on the grounds that he lacked political awareness, and he remained at best only an underground celebrity among literature lovers elsewhere. But the "search for roots" movement has made us appreciate his importance again. Both Jeffrey Kinkley's and David Wang's essays use Shen Congwen as a starting point, tracing how he inspired contemporary "search for roots" writers, in terms of style, plotting, characterization, and even "imaginary nostalgia." Kinkley's essay regards Shen as a modern spokesman of Chu culture, the ancient region characterized by spellbinding myths, occult rituals, and passionate romances. As in ancient times, this "Southern" culture has been suppressed, under the hegemony of the "Middle Kingdom" culture based in the North. But the eighties have witnessed a resurgence of Chu cultural consciousness. With Shen Congwen as their model, writers like Gu Hua, Han Shaogong, He Liwei, and Wang Zengqi have striven in one way or another to revive the vitality and creativity long missing in mainstream literature. Because they highlight regional culture, local color, private sensibilities, and subliminal impulses, Kinkley recognizes them as forming a school that manifests the politics of marginality, as opposed to a highly centralized literary canon. In this sense, Kinkley observes, the school did not merely open a different literary horizon; it brought forth a new cultural/political agenda, one derived from projects begun by Shen.

David Wang's essay takes a different approach. He argues that Shen Congwen's most important contribution to native soil writing lies not in his recollection of his hometown region per se but in his intertextual play with such a recollection. Shen's nostalgia, accordingly, is best appreciated as an "imaginary" nostalgia, characterized not so much by a representational effort to enliven the irretrievable past as by a creation of an imaginary past on behalf of the present. With Shen's *Xiangxing sanji* (Random Sketches on a Trip to West Hunan) as example, Wang shows how the myth of *Taohuayuan*, or Peach Blossom Spring, is woven into Shen's text, evoking an endless interplay between geographical locus and literary landscape, nostalgia and imaginary nostalgia. Wang then investigates the contemporary elaboration of Shen's imaginary nostalgia by three writers of different backgrounds: Song Zelai, Mo Yan, and Li Yongping. According to Wang, these three writers radicalize the discourse of native soil fiction and bring to light a modernity in Shen hitherto neglected by critics.

The survey of the "native soil" would not be complete without a reference to the urban landscape. City and country must be understood as complementary concepts or Bakhtinian chronotopes, "circumscribing" each other's territory as well as each other's socioeconomic and cultural intelligibility. The study of modern Chinese urban literature has long been neglected, partly due to the shortage of well-documented material and partly due to the negative political associations (urban-bourgeois-capitalist-decadent-depraved) it evokes. Heinrich Fruehauf's article on urban exoticism, therefore, represents a much-awaited effort in the field.

With Shanghai as focus, the article provides abundant first-hand information as to how the locale and aura of the "modern" city were first formed in the early twentieth century, how urbanites defined themselves as a distinct social class, and how urban literature and culture came to life as a result of all these developments. Fruehauf further substantiates his historical research with a theoretical framework. He points out two paradoxes inherent in city culture and literature: a "domestic" exoticism and an "Oriental" Orientalism. Cultivated by the urbanites on a familiar Chinese landscape, both give rise to the images and lifestyles of the Other, and both contribute to modernism as Chinese literati understood it. Urban culture and literature made a comeback in the eighties, as economic and political restraints loosened. But given the traditional communist dogmas cherishing the country over the city and proletarian austerity over bourgeois decadence, it remains to be seen how sophisticated city culture will become in the post-Mao period.

The second enterprise that characterizes the volume is the inquiry into the issues of self and gender as shown in modern Chinese literature. Labeled by Leo Ou-fan Lee "the romantic generation," May Fourth literati demonstrate their romantic gestures most emphatically by their iconoclastic struggle against tradition, and by their celebration of the self as a newfound subject. For all their utopian goals, however, both causes are underlain by their ambivalent negotiations or, even more paradoxically, complicity with the past as a collective form of cultural and emotional hegemony. Whereas May Fourth literati expressed their radical antitraditionalism by an ironic "obsession with China," their searches for self were completed only in negative terms, by addressing the self as an absent cause. Against the conventional wisdom, which uncritically endorses subjectivity and creativity as a May Fourth legacy, we have to rethink the issue in both historical and intertextual terms and ask: How has the "configuration" of subjectivity undergone changes at every historical juncture, and why, seven decades after the May Fourth movement, are Chinese writers still engaged in a Sisyphean quest to (re)gain subjectivity?

The May Fourth literati's advocacy of the self and subjectivity engendered one of the most exciting phenomena of that era: female writers' writings about gendered subjectivity and sexuality. The modern Chinese feminist movement rose as early as the twenties, but given its controversial causes and its volatile historical circumstances, this movement soon found itself involved in endless political debate. The conflicts between gender consciousness and class struggle, and between women's liberation and proletarian revolution, became too critical to settle amicably. The result was a long hiatus in the Chinese feminist movement—from the late forties to the late seventies. In a way, contemporary Chinese women writers have taken up where writers like Ding Ling and Xiao Hong left off in the thirties. But more than finishing what had been left undone by the first-generation feminists, Chinese women have also been writing in response to a global campaign for women's rights. Examining fiction from both male and female writers, the three essays in this section raise difficult questions: How did Chinese feminist literature develop in the thirties and the eighties? What distinguishes modern Chinese women writers from their Western counterparts in style and concern? What are favorable strategies for contemporary Chinese feminist writers and critics to use in demythifying male-centered discourse?

With Lu Xun as her point of departure, Yi-tsi Mei Feuerwerker's article deals with the problem of the representation of self and subjectivity in terms of intertextuality. Feuerwerker notices that, given the May Fourth literati's struggle to assert selfhood and subjectivity, they managed to address "the self" only in a roundabout or even negative manner, in terms of intersubjective as well as intertextual references. The meaning of Lu Xun's "Kuangren riji" (A Madman's Diary), the first manifesto of the self in modern Chinese literature, accordingly, lies in "questions of meaning, failures in communication, gaps in understanding, the ambiguities of perception." A similar case is found by Feuerwerker in Yu Dafu's "Sinking," where the nameless hero's search for identity results in hardly more than a neurotic parody of his Chinese and Western sources. Sixty years after the first outcry of Lu Xun's madman, Chinese writers were still asking the same basic questions. But the irony Feuerwerker discovers is that, unlike their May Fourth predecessors, who after all benefited from the intertextual network of a tradition they intended to subvert, contemporary Chinese writers have to do without access to such a tradition. Their quest of selfhood through opposition to "others" and "others' texts" is thus made twice as difficult. Using Wang Meng's fiction as example, Feuerwerker indicates that, literally and figuratively, Chinese writers are struggling in the Lu Xun-esque "iron house" of language and ideology. Her pensive concluding question is: whether within a new authoritative textual framework that relinquishes all claims to referentiality, the search for an authentic and continuing self is possible.

Lydia Liu's essay distinguishes the feminist discourse in Chinese literature from its Western counterparts by calling attention to the unique historical and political circumstances that both inspired and repressed, both institutionalized and downplayed women's literature. Liu compares and contrasts Ding Ling and two contemporary women writers, Zhang Jie and Wang Anyi, in terms of gender, subjectivity, and discourse. Thanks to her radical works in early days, and her legendary conversion to and subsequent quarrels with communism, Ding Ling has long been celebrated as the champion modern feminist writer in Chinese literature. Liu holds that the early Ding Ling writings, such as "The Diary of Miss Sophie," can still be illuminating to contemporary feminists. They prefigure those of Zhang Jie and Wang Anyi in a number of ways: specifically, Liu notes, the emphasis on female subjectivity, the critique of patriarchal ideology and institutions, and most important, the problematization of writing and discourse through gender experience.

Putting Liu's essay side by side with Feuerwerker's, one perceives an interesting dialogue. Whereas Liu argues that modern Chinese women suffer from being reduced to a signifier in a patriarchal sign system, Feuerwerker implies that modern Chinese men are no better off, drifting amid fragmented (male?) "textual" images in search of the "self." Perhaps the patriarchal system in modern Chinese society is itself a signifier, not an essentialized signified, as some feminists would have it. Questions of this type lead back inevitably to more "aggressive" formulations, such as those in Margaret Decker's and Rey Chow's essays. Instead of dwelling solely on writings by women, Decker and Chow enter the territory of intertextuality/sexuality, exploring the problem of masculine writers' sexual and ideological biases in portraying women. Chow's essay will be discussed below in the context of contemporary cinematic representation/erasure of women; here we will concentrate on Decker's essay.

Drawing on three stories from three distinct periods—Lu Xun's "Shangshi" (Remorse) of the twenties, Feng Zhi's "Lai fangzhe" (The Visitor) of the fifties, and Gao Xiaosheng's "Cunzi li de feng-qing" (Romance in the Village) of the eighties—Margaret Decker questions whether women's social status and search for love and identity have undergone any changes in these different cultural and political contexts. All three tales highlight a male character said to be in deep remorse over his beloved's suffering (or death), resulting from their unwedded cohabitation and eventual separation. Decker takes issue with this posture of remorse. Her reading of the texts shows how a woman's desire for independence and individuality can be easily subverted by the lover, and how narrative "consensus," be it feudalist or socialist, can become a hypocritical excuse for the oppression of women. Decker further points out that, by stressing their male characters' remorse, the three writers provide a handy form of redemption for their heroes. With the payment of a "retro-spective" guilty conscience, these writers might be thought to share with their heroes a condescending attitude toward women. When contemporary male writers continue to give the last word to male narrators, their May Fourth "heritage" becomes an irony, provoking questions about the sincerity of their respect for women.

These essays usher us into the third major theme of the volume, namely, the representation of social and cultural dynamics in terms of narrative voice and cinematic vision. Fiction and film rose as the two most effective cultural media in the post–May Fourth period, capable of reflecting, criticizing, and curing social and political problems. Fiction and film provided the imaginative parameters in which the vision of modern China was to be realized, while in turn they would serve as tangible signs proving China's modernization. In fact, both fiction and film are artistic genres that are overdetermined by historical motivation; they thus demand both scholarly rethinking and interdisciplinary investigation. At issue are intricate cultural interplays: between the compulsion to tell and the need to show, between narrative "vision" and cinematic "voice," between the re-presentation of history and the reinterpretation of myth.

Beginning as they must with investigations of form, the four essays included under this theme refuse nevertheless to confine themselves to structure or to style. Rather, they break with the traditional form/content binarism and examine how form, as a symbolic social activity, manifests cultural/ideological being. They call attention to such problems as who authorizes the voices and images in the fictional/filmic text, how a text derives from other texts, what narrative features best define the "Chineseness" of modern Chinese literature, and how narrative apparatus has been promoted, institutionalized, or censored at various moments since the May Fourth period, in response to changing cultural or ideological demands.

Marston Anderson's essay approaches the interplay between textuality and subjectivity by tracing how modern Chinese writers of the May Fourth and post–Cultural Revolution periods have tried to redefine the present by "retelling old tales." At the center of his discussion is Lu Xun's *Gushi xinbian* (Old Tales Retold). Anderson discovers that, at a time of political and intellectual anarchy, Lu Xun's "facetious" retelling of old mythical and philosophical tales was itself a polemical act. Different from the heavy realist fiction Lu Xun wrote in *Nahan* (A Call to Arms) and *Panghuang* (Wandering), the retold ancient tales first appear to be "weightless"; they are deliberately made anachronistic and allegorical. They represent both a (re)creation and a repetition, both an affirmation and a denial of self, both a frivolous play with the cannibalistic past and a poignant recognition of the unbearably light present. Contemporary attempts like Zhang Xinxin's, Liu Heng's, and Han Shaogong's to rewrite myths and ancient tales as accounts of reality appear to Anderson as signs of a rejuvenated tension between tradition and individual talent, referentiality and subjectivity. *Old Tales Retold* thus strikes him as a feasible model for Chinese writers in the post-Mao era through which to express their subjectivities without completely betraying their "obsession with China," and to adhere to tradition without being lured into self-indulgent nostalgia and cultural essentialism.

With examples ranging from Lu Xun's "A Madman's Diary" to Zhang Xinxin and Sang Ye's *Beijing Ren* (Peking Men), Theodore Huters' essay aims to lay out a genealogy of modern Chinese narrative voices and to establish their conceptual origins. His search starts with a question of form and ends with an epistemological inquiry into the Chinese view of reality, narrativity, and subjectivity. Huters defines the narrative voice first by looking back into classical Chinese intellectual and political tradition. He suggests that in orthodox Confucian discursive praxis, consciousness and conventions interplay, valorizing the self's conception and perception of the world. This discursive tradition disintegrated in the May Fourth period. When conventions lose their cohesive power, consciousness, as Huters argues, becomes the only remaining avenue to the reassertion of control over the chaos of phenomena. The newly powerful consciousness found expression in a central voice, which has underlain modern Chinese narrative over the past seven decades, be that voice superficially realist or romantic, prosocialist or antisocialist, male or female. This monolingual tendency is discerned even in a post-Maoist work like *Peking Men,* a book celebrated as recording a polyphony of Chinese voices. Huters' article adds a provocative dimension to our ideas on the conventions and conditions of national discourse.

Both Paul Pickowicz's and Rey Chow's essays move the issue of narrating the nation one step further to the question of the relationship between fiction and other forms of narrative. While Chow takes interest in the ideological dynamics of the avant-gardist "Fifth Generation" filmmakers, Pickowicz is concerned more with veteran film directors, in the context of melodramatic representation. He holds that melodrama is the main strength of the Chinese cinema. Though often treated in derogatory terms, melodrama is appreciated by Pickowicz for its own verisimilar system and its own cathartic mechanism. As a mode of filmic narrative, melodrama features hyperbolic figures, heightened moral choices, lurid and grandiose events, and striking coincidences, and it unfailingly climaxes with the identification and condemnation of evil. Pickowicz draws out a tradition of Chinese melodramatic movies, bringing to mind masters like Bu Wancang of the thirties, Sun Yu of the forties, and Xie Jin of the eighties. He further speculates about the political motivation behind the popularity of Chinese melodramatic films: in a chaotic society, melodrama has the function of giving security by starkly separating good from evil, light from darkness, presenting an otherwise unattainable reality.

Thus in the case of Xie Jin's *Hibiscus Town*, based on Gu Hua's best-seller of the same title, the Cultural Revolution is crystalized into a "drama" that is the Manichaean struggle between good and evil. Amid tears and laughter, the virtuous are rewarded and the wicked are punished; order is restored and "truth" is articulated. But, asks Pickowicz, what happens when Party leaders are the villains? What are the consequences when history is continuously being rewritten under melodramatic formulae? The film of *Hibiscus Town* is perhaps more subversive today than the far more complex works of the "fifth-generation" filmmakers, because it still inhabits this ancient and powerful mode of understanding.

Rey Chow's article broaches the issue of male hegemony in the culture industry, from the teaching of children to the making of movies. Her case-in-point is the much-acclaimed film director Chen Kaige's adaptation of Ah Cheng's story "Haizi wang" (King of the Children). The article can be discussed in terms of the interplay between narrative apparatus and the expression of subjectivity. But Chow's ultimate concern is the positioning of woman in the ever-changing configuration of textuality/sexuality. Echoing Anderson's thesis about the social character of the self, Chow believes that any research on subjectivity is intersubjectively oriented, and that any achievement of selfhood must presuppose the self's creative dialogue with (rather than submission to) collectivity. Recalling Lu Xun's endeavor to define Chinese national identity and culture, through an investment in figures of the powerless (i.e., his madman's injunction to "save the children!"), Chow notices that the same kind of task is still carried on today, as indicated by Chen Kaige's movie *(King of the Children)*.

What this example demonstrates is that the business of "saving the child" can, ironically, take place at the expense of the woman and the physical reality she represents. Its empowerment of the child is based on a hidden assertion of masculine interests and an ill-disguised exercise of masculine power. Not unlike Margaret Decker, Chow sees the course of modern Chinese literature as a narcissistic circle, around a center inscribed by male textuality and sexuality, from which women are subtly excluded. Only by acknowledging gendered sociality, she concludes, can the pursuit of Chinese nationality and subjectivity break new ground.

In Leo Ou-fan Lee's essay, the three issues that have preoccupied the volume—the dialectic of city and country, the re-presentation of gender and subjectivity, and the diacritics of narrative voice and cinematic vision—are brought together in reviewing the changing forms of Chinese realism over the past seven decades. Lee starts with a reconsideration of Cyril Birch's 1974 article "Change and Continuity in Chinese Fiction," in which Birch predicted that Western-style realism would recede into (literary) history along with the May Fourth antitraditional movement, and that contemporary Chinese literature would show a Great Return: a return to a more communal, more exemplary, more classical, and therefore more "Chinese" model. Chinese (literary) history since the death of Mao has proved, Lee observes, that Birch's prediction in 1974 was too pessimistic. But as Lee points out, Birch was not entirely wrong with regard to "the persistence of the communal impulse and the limited phase of realism" that underlie Chinese literary discourse even in the late eighties. Taking up where Birch left off, Lee's essay has a twofold purpose: to investigate the historical conditions that have sustained Chinese realism through various formal/ideological manifestations, and to assess contemporary Chinese writers' radical efforts to open a new horizon beyond that of realism.

Lee notices that May Fourth realism found its expression first in the form of the short story. The realist short story broke with traditional narrative discourse as well as with the value system embedded therein; it allowed writers a more subjective angle from which to record both personal and public experience, thereby exposing suppressed or repressed aspects of reality. The discovery of the gendered self by women writers represents for Lee an especially triumphant moment in the May Fourth campaign to reform reality by re-forming literary discourse.

By contrast, the appearance in the thirties of what Lee calls the "long novel" suggests not only realists writers' desire to expand their narrative landscape but also their increasing involvement in immediate social/political causes. With "sprawling narratives," huge galleries of characters, and prolonged exposés of China's sociopolitical malaise, the "long novel" brought to the fore rhetorical and conceptual conflicts from the very heart of modern Chinese reality, tensions between social/political conscience and formal coherence, between "sincerity and authenticity." Moreover, put side by side, the short story and the "long novel" drove home the real tension between "the discovery and valorization of the individual voice and vision of the author on the one hand and the demand inherent in the realist form itself . . . to somehow come to terms with a broader reality."

Lee adds a chronotopic dimension to his line of realisms by summoning the theme of city versus country. For him, city and country are more than fictional locales: they serve as temporal/spatial indices of Chinese writers' changing perception of the Real. He declares that "one can almost make the generalization that the evolution of modern Chinese fiction is a narrative of urban–rural transition— from the urban-based subjective short story to the more objective rural novels of the 1930s."

On such observations does Lee build his framework for contemporary Chinese literature. At a time when "Mao discourse" has lost its hegemonic power, contemporary Chinese literature can in general be called realist, in the sense that writers have been engaged in demythifying Maoist totems and taboos in a spirit reminiscent of the critical realism of the thirties. But Lee discerns changes in contemporary realism, changes pointing to the possibility of going beyond the limits of realism.

With a guiding problematic that separates the realism that inquires into subjectivity from the realism that celebrates communal causes, Lee sees contemporary writers as having ambivalent or ambiguous attitudes about repositioning the self in the crowd the way their May Fourth predecessors did. Just as he confronts the short story with the "long novel," Lee ponders the aesthetic and conceptual significance of the "midlength novella" that prevailed in the eighties. Appropriately, he notices how the city-versus-country debate of the thirties was recapitulated by the "search for roots" movement of the eighties, only that it had a stronger-than-ever subversive intent.

Lee's essay thus interpolates a dialogue into a text seventeen years old. In their different moments of articulation, both voices reverberate with history. Birch wrote his comment on Chinese literature in the midst of the Cultural Revolution, and Lee was speculating on the fate of Chinese literature in the aftermath of the Tiananmen incident.

Although literature and politics do not necessarily develop in parallel, Chinese fiction from the May Fourth movement to the June Fourth incident has nevertheless shown how language, style, and literature intertwine with ideology and politics. Birch in dismal 1974 projected a dismal outcome for Chinese literature, but Lee in hopeful 1990 may very well have had a reason to feel hopeful: despite relentless efforts to reimpose censorship and coercion, Chinese writers are still writing, and their voices are heard in China from as far away as Taiwan, Hong Kong, and other Chinese communities. Seventy years ago the May Fourth movement confronted modern literature and opened with a statement of its themes and variations. From our point of view, the June Fourth incident can be only an unexpected pause, not a premature coda, in the final movement of twentieth-century Chinese literature and its part in the orchestration of modernity.

1 | Country and City

1 | Visitation of the Past in Han Shaogong's Post-1985 Fiction

In the postscript to an essay engagingly titled "Is a Modern Chinese Literature Possible?" W. J. F. Jenner concedes that "were I to answer the question posed in the title today it would be with a much firmer yes."[1] Jenner wrote the essay in September 1979 and the postscript in March 1981. Presumably, some changes in the PRC must have occurred either in political climate or in actual literary production that prompted him to take a more sanguine view with respect to the possibility of modern Chinese literature becoming more "modern." Though he makes no mention of it in the postscript, it must be noted as a historical fact that then Vice-Premier Deng Xiaoping was present at the Fourth Congress of Chinese Writers and Artists on October 30, 1979, to deliver his "Congratulatory Message."[2] To be sure, the names of Marx, Lenin, and Mao Zedong were dutifully evoked in his interpretation of the function of art and literature, but Deng's "message" was nonetheless refreshing if only because it was less prescriptive than Mao's "Talks at the Yan'an Forum."

If Jenner were to comment on the state of modern Chinese literature today, he would be impressed enough with the works of Han Shaogong, Mo Yan, and Can Xue, to name just a notable few, to concede further that modern Chinese fiction is finally "modern in ways other than simply chronological" (Jenner 194). Their writing can even be considered "modernist," to the extent that "one of the word's associations is with the coming of a new era of high aesthetic self-consciousness and non-representation toward style, technique, and spatial form in pursuit of a deeper penetration of life."[3]

I mention these three writers only because I am more familiar with their works. Depending on how one judges a work to be significant, the roster of writers who are said to have made an impact on Chinese fiction since 1976 is nearly endless. For example, Li Tuo, who regards the 1976–1986 decade of achievement in fictional writing as nothing short of a "revolution in literary paradigms," comes up with this list: Ma Yuan, Can Xue, and Liu Suola for their "avant-gardism"; Ah Cheng, Han Shaogong, Zhang Chengzhi, Mo Yan, Zheng Wanlong, Feng Jicai, Chen Jiangong, Wang Anyi, Jia Pingwa, Zhang Wei, and Zhaxi Dawa for their "root-seeking" impulse.[4]

No list of modern Chinese fiction writers who have emerged on the scene since 1985 can ever hope to be representative, because new talents periodically emerge to demand our attention. Focusing on the new generation of writers who are either in their thirties or forties, Liu Zaifu also provides us with a list of names noted for their surging vitality. In addition to those mentioned in Li Tuo's roster (excepting Feng Jicai, who was born in 1942), Liu listed seven more: Zheng Yi, Shi Tiesheng, Ke Yunlu, Zhang Xinxin, Zhang Kangkang, Kong Jiesheng, and Li Rui.[5]

Liu's article appeared in 1988. If his list is taken as a "Who's Who" in Chinese fiction up to that year, it should also include Liu Heng (b. 1954), whose "Gouri de liangshi" (Dog Shit Food), in the words of Zheng Shusen (William S. Tay), "has shattered all the prescriptive formulas for peasant-fiction writing of the last thirty years."[6] One may also lament the omission of Yu Hua (b. 1960), whose "Yijiubaliu nian" (The Year 1986) has been grudgingly singled out for praise by Lei Da for its uncanny skill in depicting the "bestiality, cruelty, and madness that is incidental to human nature."[7]

Punctuated with choruses of hallelujah, Li Tuo's and Liu Zaifu's essays celebrate the birth of a literature consciously divorcing itself from the kind of socialist example in which the hero is invariably Tall, Big, and Perfect, as is Hao Ran's Gao Daquan in *Jinguang dadao* (Golden Highway). Indeed, as we see from the contents of most post-1985 fictional work, the once ubiquitous Party branch secretary who leaps and bounds on almost every literary page of earlier decades has now virtually become the Invisible Man. He has been upstaged by what Wang Dewei (David Der-wei Wang) identifies as "characters of deformity" of all descriptions. In his words:

> Throughout modern Chinese literary history, it is difficult to find a period in which [the literary scene] is peopled by so many bizarre characters invested with such complex symbolic meaning. The range of characters that emerge from the works of the New Period mainland writers include: the blind, the mute, the crippled, the humpbacked, the sexually impotent, the bound-feet fetishist, the osteomalacia victim, the "living dead," not to mention the mentally deranged and the psychotic. Suddenly the "Socialist New China" that was once glorified by such writers as Yang Mo and Hao Ran has become a dilapidated and grotesque haven filled with souls that are maimed either physically or spiritually.[8]

Among these "deformed characters," some of the more memorable have been sketched by Han Shaogong (b. 1953), and in this essay I would like to single out his writing to illustrate the genius peculiar to post-1985 PRC fiction. However, my interest in his work goes beyond an appreciation of his artistic achievement. I also want to use his case to argue that, given less governmental interference over a sustained period of time, a gifted writer can perform many wonders in self-transcendence. With Han, it is transformation from the role of reluctant disseminator of certified Party truths to that of anguished "rootseeker"[9] bent on uncovering the atavistic ills of present-day China.

Unlike his contemporaries listed in Liu Zaifu's essay who began publishing in the mid-1980s, Han's writing career had an earlier start. So that his later work, such as "Ba Ba Ba" (lit. "Father Father Father") or "Nü Nü Nü" (lit. "Woman Woman Woman") can be appreciated as the extraordinary accomplishment it is, a brief review of his early work is in order. Very much in tune with the passions of its time, Han's first story, "Honglu shangshan" (Moving the Red Forge Up onto the Mountain), appeared in 1974. It is an exemplary tale singing the praises of Red Guards for their fearless efforts to temper steel against all odds. Though he made no particular reference to it, he must have been embarrassed by the speciousness of this morality tale, as we may infer from his confession in the postscript to *Yuelan* (1981):

> With the Red Guard band on my arms, I became interested in politics . . . But at a time when only one or two cerebrums were permitted to function in a country of one billion people, political fervor could only engender dangers. If you wanted to save your skin, you had to face the tedium of doing nothing . . . To write something contrary to your beliefs, so much so that you found it unreal, was truly meaningless. Where was the way out? Darkness loomed large, and dawn seemed to be still below the horizon. I could only wait.[10]

He waited until the Gang of Four was finally "smashed" to publish his second and third stories in 1978. Both "Qiyue hongfeng" (The Torrent of July) and "Yesu Qingjiangpu" (Staying Overnight at Qingjiangpu) are at best hagiographies of local Party branch secretaries and their deputies, thanks to whose uncompromising integrity and administrative sagacity the unwarranted suffering of the people was averted in good time. Declaring himself a disciple of Tolstoy and Lu Xun rather than of Camus, Sartre, or Kafka ("First Steps" 268), Han saw himself at this stage of his career primarily as a writer whose business it was to *ganyu shenghuo* (interfere with life), an engagé spirit best expressed through the reportage writing of Liu Binyan. To this end he published "Yuelan" in 1979, a blistering indictment of the Party's disastrous rural policy, which culminated in such foibles as forbidding a family to use their own dung to fertilize their private plot, or to feed their fowl on the paddyfields.

Assessing his own work from "Torrent" up to "Yuelan," Han Shaogong allows that "they are naive products primarily prompted by a sense of indignation and a desire to 'speak out for the people.' All I wanted was to articulate the suffering and the aspirations of the people" ("First Steps" 266). Of the stories that intervene between "Yuelan" and his first major work, "Ba Ba Ba" (1985), those that bear the imprints of the *pièce à thèse* and have been frequently commented upon by Chinese critics are "Xiwang maocaodi" (Looking Westward to the Land of Thatched Sheds, 1980); "Huisheng" (Echoes, 1980); "Fengchui suonasheng" (Bamboo Pipes in the Wind, 1981); and "Yuanfangde shu" (Distant Trees, 1983).

In broad terms, these four titles along with "Yuelan" can be characterized as "Urbling literature,"[11] that is, literature dealing with the rustification of educated youths sent down to the countryside before and during the Cultural Revolution for reeducation. The *zhiqing* (educated youth) could be an unpitying zealot, like the first-person narrator in "Yuelan" and Lu Daiwei in "Echoes," who in their eagerness to carry out orders from the state invariably inflict pain on the people they are supposed to serve.

Though my chief concern in this essay is with "Ba Ba Ba" and "Nü Nü Nü," it seems to me equally important to examine briefly the "Urbling literature" Han Shaogong has authored. This examination is necessary, again, because one becomes more appreciative of Han's talent and the progress he has made if one is familiar with his lesser work. As indicated earlier, none of the New Period writers has experienced such a radical evolution—from the ventriloquist of received opinions to the soliloquist of private anxieties. In this respect, Han Shaogong offers us a good example of the possibility for growth when objective circumstances permit.

"Echoes" is a 264-page novel-size story. It relates how a good-for-nothing by the name of Liu Genman in Shuanghe County of Hunan province rises to prominence at the onset of the Cultural Revolution by virtue of his "good-for-nothingness." Sniveling between breaths, this nitwit of a rebel certainly would not have dreamed of plunging into the revolution if a Red Guard extremist had not egged him on to cash in on his undeniable political asset: his *pin-xiazhongnong*, or poor and lower-middle-class origin. Lu Xun's influence may be at work in Liu's rationale for joining the revolution, which recalls the inanities of Ah Q: "What is there to be afraid of? Not only the people in the city talk about it, even folks at Aobeichong talk about it. Why can't I talk about it? The Chairman says it is right to rebel in carrying out the Cultural Revolution. Talking won't run against the law, and we can talk about whatever comes to our mind!" ("Yuelan" 173).

Apart from "Echoes," the *zhiqing* in Han Shaogong's other Urbling fiction are cast in a more sympathetic light. Instead of being the persecutors, they are often found in the unenviable position of "straw dogs," in Laozi's metaphor: sacrifices on the altar of the Grand Cultural Revolution. Unable to wield power because of their insignificant status in the work team, they are nevertheless privileged to witness first-hand the glaring abuse of power in the hands of the leader who, but for his impeccable class origin, would be the least qualified to supervise the work of a wasteland reclamation team. Zhang Zhongtian is one such leader in "Looking Westward." Although Zhang is a veteran with the rank of colonel, as far as job-related expertise is concerned, he has nothing to offer because he is completely unread in the ABCs of agriculture. His professional ignorance is reminiscent of the peasant turned hospital superintendent in Ding Ling's "Zai yiyuanzhong" (In the Hospital, 1941), who cannot tell the difference between aspirin and penicillin. The only saving grace for Zhang is that he is basically an honest man, serious about his job. Herein lies the supreme irony, and by extension, Han's implied criticism of the ideological drift of the Party. The fact that an illiterate like Zhang Zhongtian is appointed to oversee a team of "educated youth" at work on national reconstruction is a sad commentary on the folly of a party that values background purity over professional specialty. Granted that Zhang is at heart the good man he is pictured to be, when it comes to enhancing productivity for the good of the country, the disservice rendered by a good man is just as damaging as that of an evil person.

Of course not all the *zhiqing* in Han Shaogong's Urbling stories are cast as culprits, inciters, or victims in the drama of Chinese socialism. At times they are merely bystanders, or witnesses to a family tragedy, as is the first-person narrator in "Bamboo Pipes." At other times they draw attention to the view that *zhiqing* characters ought to receive education, thus revealing the frustrations of a generation of adolescents who missed their chance at schooling as they tilled night soil in a barren land under the tutelage of unschooled cadres. Such is the fate of Tian Jiaju in "Distant Trees," a paean to the will to survival and to self-realization in the worst of circumstances. Tian Jiaju exemplifies this defiant spirit when he manages to pull himself through a statutory loophole and leave the work team to be apprenticed as a painter.

*   *   *

Had Han Shaogong stopped writing after "Distant Trees," he would be remembered as a sensitive chronicler of *zhiqing* lives in the company of, say, Gan Tiesheng ("Juhui" [The Get-Together], 1980) and Wang Peigong (*WM* [*Wo'Men*], 1985).[12] Urbling fiction, heavy in its notation of thwarted aspirations and grim realities, is generically a kind of "shanghen wenxue" (scar literature). By drawing its material from a particular political or historical context to give meaning to the text, its appeal to the audience is inherently topical.[13] When one's memory of the havoc of the Cultural Revolution is still fresh, one can be overwhelmed by fear and trembling, as in reading Liu Xinwu's "Banzhuren" (The Schoolmaster, 1977) and Lu Xinhua's "Shanghen" (The Scar, 1978). However, precisely because the interest of the *shanghen* narratives relies so much on topicality, they pass easily into oblivion once the topics they deal with cease to be an issue.[14] As a result, these two precursors of "scar literature" have become literary obsolescences, referred to today only for their "historical significance."

Han Shaogong need not be remembered only for his "historical significance." He has remolded his career yet another time by publishing in 1985 seven stories, two of which are strong enough to vindicate Li Tuo's claim that the New Period literature represents a most radical and influential revolution whose significance surpasses the evolution of *shi* poetry from the four-word to the five-word form, or the substitution of *baihua* for *wenyan*.[15] The two stories to be discussed are "Ba Ba Ba" and "Nü Nü Nü."

Anyone accustomed to the habitual concerns of Han Shaogong's early fiction would be hard put to see the two pieces cited above as the work of the same author. Notably absent in these two examples are the temporal frame and the topographical contour that allow the narrative to impart a simulation of reality. Clearly the mode of representation has shifted from the mimetic to the parabolic.

Han's shift of representational focus midway in his creative career provides an unusual example of the "double return" in modern Chinese literature. Cyril Birch has correctly identified the characteristics of post-Yan'an writing as a "return" to the world of traditional Chinese fiction that is governed by the laws of karma, retribution, and communal values. Things may temporarily fall apart, but "the

sense of social order, which may be disrupted by an ambitious scoundrel, a lustful ne'er-do-well, or a shrewish woman,"[16] will in the end
reassert itself.

As we have seen, the "worlds" of most of Han Shaogong's early
work, such as "Moving the Red Forge," "The Torrent of July," and
"Staying Overnight," operate on the same assumption: that mistakes
will eventually right themselves under the infallible leadership of the
Party. This millennialist vision of course runs counter to the basic
tenets of May Fourth literature. Again, in the words of Birch:

> If we had to characterize the overall mode [of the May Fourth
> writers], we might call it tragic-comic in comparison with the comic-
> satiric of the past . . . The old feeling of order disrupted and
> restored is gone: order itself is gone, the world is in chaos, any kind
> of happy ending unthinkable. If in traditional fiction we can distin-
> guish two dominant attitudes, one of them norm-sharing and com-
> munal celebration, and one more individual, relatively alienated
> . . . then it is the latter attitude that characterizes the May Fourth
> writers. (Birch 391)

Since Han Shaogong's early fiction was published during the chaotic years of the Cultural Revolution, practical considerations dic-
tated that he relinquish the legacy of the May Fourth writers and
steer a safe course by replacing their spirit of iconoclasm and defiance with the Marxist dogma of struggle and rehabilitation. In
terms of literary "evolution," this is surely a retrogression, a nulli-
fication of what had been achieved by Han's predecessors. What is
remarkable about him, as we shall see below, is that he has been able
to stage a "second return" and claim his place in the central tradition
of modern Chinese literature with his highly individualistic post-
1985 writing.

What is the reason for this change? Could it be that Han is no
longer interested in "speaking out for the people"? An explanation
can be found in the testimony he provides in "Wenxue degen" (The
Roots of Literature, 1985). It begins with a thought-provoking question: "I have for some time been asking myself: What has happened
to the many-splendored Chu culture? . . . When did the source of

the vast and profound Chu culture begin to break up and cease to flow?"[17]

That he should begin his search for roots with an inquiry about the health of Chu culture is not difficult to understand. Born in Changsha, Hunan province, Han is a bona fide native of the ancient state of Chu, homeland of such intellectual luminaries as Laozi, Zhuangzi, and of course Qu Yuan.[18] If he were to seek his literary roots, it is logical that he should begin with himself. But what concerns us here is not his tacit claim of spiritual ancestry with the Chu philosophers and poets, but what he regards as the distinctive qualities of Chu literature. He finds the ethos as manifested in the *ci* (songs) of Chu to be *shenbi, jili, kuangfang,* and *gufen,* or what I would lamely translate as "mystic, splendorous, uninhibited, and indignant" ("Roots" 2).

Now nearly all his pre-1985 stories are informed by *gufen,* a moral outrage against the perversities and excesses committed in the name of "serving the people." Understandably, the "messages" borne by these "indignant" works have to be expediently crisp and transparent for common consumption, thus forfeiting any claim to the "mysticism" that was a hallmark of the ancient Chu masters, whose works Han Shaogong has now embraced as the "roots" of his imagination.

Perhaps it is in this light that Han Shaogong's post-1985 fiction can be properly studied. Before we turn to "Ba Ba Ba," "Gui qu lai" (The Return) could be considered one of the seminal stories published in 1985 for the light it throws on Han's "root-seeking" impulse. This narrative reads like a *baihua* variant of Zhuangzi's famous Butterfly Dream parable. A man known to his friend as Huang Zhixian is presumably on a shopping tour to an unspecified village. Though he believes that he has never visited the area before, he finds everything he sees on his way at once strange and familiar. What surprises him even more is the warm welcome from the villagers. He should be a total stranger to them, if it were true he had never visited the place before. They address him as Ma Yanjing (Ma the Bespectacled). He protests, saying he is Huang Zhixian, but the women around him do not believe him. They teasingly remark that he still has not given up his prankish ways.

At first this "mistaken identity" does not seem to bother him. But

his equilibrium is unsettled when a man who identifies himself as Ai
Ba confronts him with the question, "I want to get this straight: Did
you kill 'Midge' Yang?"[19] He dodges the question by asking for more
wine. Ai Ba does not press him further, and the question of whether
Huang has killed Midge Yang is laid aside when Ai Ba observes that
the "two-headed snake" midget deserved his end.

Is Huang Zhixian the butterfly turned Ma Yanjing or vice versa?
We would not have any clues to the mystery if Huang had not taken
a hot bath and discovered, amid the bluish steam, that his body
seems strange and unfamiliar even to himself. As he is rubbing a scar
on his calf, which he believes to have been inflicted by spikes on the
soccer field, it suddenly occurs to him: "Maybe not. Maybe . . .
maybe it is the wound . . . eh, from Midge's bite. Did it happen on
a morning of dense fog and rain?" ("The Return" 278).

What really transpired between Ma Yanjing, or Huang Zhixian,
and Midge Yang is described in the foggiest of terms in the passage
that follows his reminiscence. Has Huang, or Ma, committed homi-
cide? "I dare not recall any further," he tells himself. "I don't even
dare to look at my own hands. Is the smell of blood on them? And
scars from wrestling a rope?" (278). But no sooner has he put his
thoughts to rest than he "determines to conclude: No, I have never
been here. Nor am I acquainted with the whoever-he-is midget"
(278). The key words in this line and perhaps in the whole story are
nuli duanding, "determines to conclude." It should be clear that
Huang Zhixian is the former schoolteacher Ma Yanjing, whose good
deeds in the past are being evoked by the villagers to reactivate his
memory.

If we give a temporal reading to the tale, we will not be far off
track to identify Ma Yanjing as a young man "scarred" by the political
fallout of the Cultural Revolution, though we are by no means sure
under what circumstances his name was changed to Huang Zhixian
when the story unfolds. Butterfly or no, Ma Yanjing is a spiritual
cousin of Chen Mengtao in "Langaizi" (The Blue Bottlecap, 1985),
whose nerves have been unhinged by the chore of burying his
co-workers in the labor camp. Just as Ma Yanjing is fated to spend
his days wondering who he actually is, Chen Mengtao is forever
searching under his bed and on the street for the wine bottlecap he

once misplaced. Both are "scarred" victims, unable to exorcise the lingering memory of a nation paralyzed by evangelical hysteria. The past often visits the present, as we shall see in due course.

Since the publication of "The Roots of Literature" precedes "The Return" by two months, it behooves us to inquire into the extent to which Han Shaogong is able to translate his *xungen* "manifesto" into practice. As noted earlier, the anguish of confused identity affecting the narrator of "The Return" has its origin in *Zhuangzi*. Other notable "roots" of the author in traditional Chinese literature are expressed in his concepts of time and space. Taking an evening stroll to the thatched hut of San A-gong, who has died of snake poison, Huang Zhixian readily engages in a conversation with the deceased old man in a matter-of-fact fashion (the "ghost" also addresses him as Ma Yanjing). This intercourse between the living and the dead and the crisscrossing of the present and the past are unmistakably attributes of surrealist writing, but they are also time-honored traditions of supernatural fiction that flourished from the *zhiguai* (records of anomaly) of the Six Dynasties and *chuanqi* (transmitting the extraordinary) of the Tang period down to *The Story of the Stone*.[20]

"The Return" is a transitional moment in the evolution of Han Shaogong's writing, signifying his liberation from the clutches of topical referentiality. He is, to be sure, as "China-obsessed" as ever, concerned, in the famous words of C. T. Hsia, "with China as a nation afflicted with a spiritual disease and therefore unable to strengthen itself or change its set ways of inhumanity."[21] What distinguishes his obsession of the present period from that of his youthful days is the realization that, as he informed Shi Shuqing in an interview, "neither politics nor revolution can solve those problems basic to human nature. From this realization I proceed to deliberate on the questions pertinent to human instincts and existence. I also take into consideration the significance of cultural background. [After these ruminations] I come to realize that my recognition of the dark and evil sides of human beings is far from adequate."[22]

This confession is crucial. As evident in "Ba Ba Ba," the "roots" he now seeks are no longer the faint echoes of the distant past, but the atavistic deformities of his benighted countrymen. In this respect,

Han Shaogong is spiritually closer to Lu Xun than to Zhuangzi or Qu Yuan, his "fellow" Chu natives, who had other reasons for playing with dislocations in space and time. Han's scalpel cuts more deeply than Lu Xun's exposition of Chinese sickness. For all his alleged acerbity in polemic frays, there are certain aspects of life Lu Xun considered unfit for his brush. As he explained in his "Banxia xiaoji" (Notes Culled from Half of a Summer, 1936):

> If someone with more defects than the average person is copied as a model in a work of fiction, he would regard it as his rotten luck.
> But he should know that it is not the worst of misfortunes, because as a matter of fact there are people in the world who are not even fit for portrayal in fiction. If such a person were to figure in it, the more realistically he comes off, the greater the damage to this piece of work.
> Take painters, for example. A painter might do a snake, a crocodile, a turtle, a nutshell, a wastepaper basket, a pile of garbage. But no painter would do a caterpillar, a boil on the head. Nor, for the same reason, would he paint snot or shit.[23]

Han Shaogong pays no heed to such admonitions. His conception of Bing Zai, the moron in "Ba Ba Ba," verges on the scatological. According to information given to Shi Shuqing, Bing Zai is modeled on a child of his neighbor when he was sent down to the countryside during the Cultural Revolution. In fictional life, however, this child-man is found in the never-never land of Chicken Head Village deep in the cloud-covered mountains. Isolated from the outside world, the life pattern in this secluded community seems to have undergone no significant change since time immemorial. And "whatever happened [in areas] beneath the clouds did not seem to have much to do with the villagers" either.[24]

As far as topography is concerned, Chicken Head Village is pure fabrication, even though we know from Shi Shuqing's interview that the general landscapes and characters in "Ba Ba Ba" are reconstructed from the author's impressions of West Hunan when he was "sent down" to work in the Miluo River region. "Despite a wealth of anthropological details," reasons Michael Duke, "the story reads, nevertheless, like an allegory of circular and repetitive historical development or non-development of traditional Chinese culture."[25] Read in the allegorical mode, Chicken Head Village is a microcosm of China, whose "nondevelopment" is suggested by the villagers' archaic expressions in their daily speech. For "stand" they say *yi* instead of *zhan,* as in standard Mandarin. When they "speak," it is *hua* rather than *shuo.* "As virtuous as the old-style [*gufeng*]" is their manner of speech, the narrator comments editorially ("Ba Ba Ba" 7).

"Nondevelopment" is a mild equivalent for stagnation and backwardness. At other times and in other literary contexts, West Hunan's insulation from the outside world was seen as a blessing in disguise, allowing a community to maintain the "natural order of things." Here the story "Xiao-xiao" (1929) by Shen Congwen comes to mind. Shen is Han Shaogong's precursor in appropriating "West Hunanese landscapes and characters to frame universal questions of life and death, love and sexuality, permanence and change."[26] Xiao-xiao, a child-bride made pregnant by a farmhand working for her grandfather-in-law, awaits her sentence to be either drowned or sold. As an orphan, she has only an uncle as next of kin. Her uncle is consulted. "By rights, she should have been drowned," the narrator tells us, "but only heads of families who have read their Confucius would do such a stupid thing to save the family's honor. This uncle, however, had not read Confucius: he could not bear to sacrifice Xiao-xiao, and so he chose the alternative of marrying her off to someone else."[27]

But no offer to take her hand is forthcoming. In the end Xiao-xiao gives birth to a son. Her husband, still a child himself, takes to the baby affectionately like a brother. And since a boy in a farm economy is future manpower, no one in the family gives any further thought to sending Xiao-xiao away.

Shen Congwen lays out no theoretical scheme on how such beatitude is to be achieved in rural China, except that he clearly has faith in the goodness of the human heart. Again in C. T. Hsia's words: Shen's "creative concern is akin to Yeats': to stress, in the teeth of a materialist civilization, the virtues of an ordered existence in rhythmic keeping with nature and the gods, filled with animal grace and pride and yet without cunning and greed" (190).

Fifty years Shen Congwen's junior, and with drastically different experiences of China, Han Shaogong appears less perturbed by the excesses of a materialistic civilization. Taking allegory to a new height, he proves to be a spiritual kin to Mo Yan, who is equally concerned about the degeneration of the Chinese people as a race. It is time to examine Bing Zai.

Bing Zai is a man-child of arrested growth, physically and mentally. Reputedly, after he was born he slept through two days and nights without feeding, announcing his arrival in the world by uttering his first cry on the third day. The first two phrases he learns after he is able to make a conscious sound are "Ba Ba" and "F—— your mother." In fact, this is the only language he masters all his life. His eyes vacant and movements sluggish, his disproportionately large head droops like an upside-down gourd. He addresses whomever he meets as "Ba Ba," meaning "father," regardless of that person's sex or age. But if you stare at him without acknowledging his friendly gesture, he rolls his eyes and grumbles, changing his greeting to "F—— your mother" ("Ba Ba Ba" 1).

Liu Zaifu is alert to the underlying significance of Bing Zai's characterization. He sees him as a prototype of Chinese psychological sickness. Vitiated by fear and an inferiority complex, Bing Zai cannot form a value judgment objectively, since his moral perception is blocked by a narrow and insecure ego. Consequently, he is apt to classify people around him into two types: those on his side are treated as the "Ba Ba" group, whereas those pitted against him are pushed aside to "F—— your mother."[28]

Appropriately enough, Liu Zaifu confesses that he cannot help but think about himself and his own past after he has read "Ba Ba Ba." His statement is worth quoting at some length: "I discover that I too have been a Bing Zai. I believe that many of us who are honest about themselves will discover that they too have been a Bing Zai. Not only do we carry the shadow of Bing Zai in us, we can even say that, judging from our mode of thinking, we have lived our lives in as simplistic and vulgar a way as Bing Zai" (170).

As obsessed as Han Shaogong is with the roots of China's backwardness, it is no surprise that Liu Zaifu extrapolates cultural as well as political implications from Bing Zai's inane utterances. However, we would not be reading "Ba Ba Ba" properly if we took Bing Zai as an isolated syndromic manifestation of China's cultural malaise. Indeed, the stigma of curse that pervades the tale would not have been so pronounced if his abnormalities were seen as the exception rather than the norm. For, though his fellow villagers are neither mentally retarded nor physically deformed, they are nevertheless disadvantaged by their state of insularity. Unable to make any objective judgment due to their isolation, the people in Chicken Head Village hold dear to their lives the "ancient ways" (*gufeng*), which, in the context of the tale, have become synonymous with ignorance, superstition, and cruelty.

Ignorance and superstition provide a convenient explanation for Bing Zai's retardation. His mother, so the rumor goes, incurred a curse by accidentally crushing a jar-sized green-eyed spider while piling firewood in the kitchen. She burned its remains in the wilderness, and the stench is said to have lingered for three days. What could this spider have been except a vindictive "ogre" capable of casting spells on people?

When unseasonable weather is blamed for a crop failure, the villagers resort to the only "ancient way" they know of for relief: the offering of a human sacrifice to appease the gods. According to traditional practice, the sacrifice has to be a male with bushy hair. After the ritual is performed, he is to be fed to the dogs. Bing Zai is picked. But just when the ax is about to fall, a clap of thunder strikes the sky. He is spared, because the villagers take the thunderbolt to be a sign of Heaven's displeasure with the offering.

A geomancer is consulted. The verdict is that the crop failure was caused not so much by bad weather as by the drooping head of Chicken Head Peak, which towers over the paddyfields. How can any grain be salvaged under the chicken's enormous beak? The logical thing to do would be to chop off the chicken head. Unfortunately the "chicken" is common property: it is shared by the neighboring Chicken Tail Village. Blasting off the chicken head would immediately endanger their well-being. How can the "tail" survive if the "head" is removed?

Armed conflict between these two villages is thus unavoidable. Before the confrontation, Chicken Head villagers decide to have their odds foretold by slaughtering an ox: if it falls forward, they will be the victors. After watching the beheaded ox tumble forward, the whole village gathers around a huge pot in which the corpse of an "enemy" from Chicken Tail Village is stewed together with the meat of a pig. Everyone is directed to partake in this communion of hatred toward the common adversary by taking a morsel of the man-pig stew. Should anyone refuse, his jaw will be pierced by a bamboo drill.

Despite the auspicious prediction, Chicken Head Village loses the war. Someone then recalls a strange incident: when the ox fell forward, Bing Zai was heard to have muttered his "F—— your mother" incantation, his unique expression for negative feelings. It is thus reasoned: if "F—— your mother" is the negative *yin*, then "Ba Ba Ba" should be the positive *yang* in the art of Chinese divination.

Leaving the decision of whether to wreak vengeance on Chicken Tail Village to Bing Zai, they carry him to the ancestral temple. They prostrate themselves before him and address him respectfully as "Your Lordship," "Your Honor," and "Bing the Immortal." Every movement of the "immortal" is watched with mute reverence. But the "celestial being" only rolls his eyes. As he munches his food, his attention is caught by the chirping of birds. Elated, Bing Zai casts his lot: "Ba Ba."

The outcome of the war is that they lose again. After making formal apologies and reparations to Chicken Tail Village, Bing Zai's tribesmen prepare to embark on a long journey of migration to another never-never land. So that the young and able have enough provisions for the journey, the old men and women in the village, after putting all the infants to death, commit mass suicide in accordance with the "ancient ways," as directed by Tailor Zhong Man. Considered disabled all his life, Bing Zai is the first one to be fed the *queyu* brew, a potent herbal poison. All the huts and shacks are set on fire as the migrants begin their journey, humming the same song about the tribe's creation myth that introduced the story. In the end, Bing Zai suddenly emerges from the wasteland. Not only has he survived the poisonous concoction, but also the festering boil on his head has healed to a scab. The mythical songs of his kinsmen fascinate him, and he sends them off with the litany of "Ba Ba."

The repetition of the creation myth at the end of the story is ominous enough, but what appears to be even more alarmingly portentous is Bing Zai's miraculous escape from death. First he is "saved" by the gods; now he has proved that he is stronger than poison. How are we to make sense of this ending? Are we to consider that history, in the narrator's view, is cyclical? That deeds of ignorance, stupidity, superstition, and cruelty as enacted in Chicken Head Village are to repeat themselves after the migrants are settled on new soil? What about Bing Zai? Is his twice-miraculous survival meant to make a mockery of the Darwinian concept of "survival of the fittest"? Such a startling view of the intellectual descent of the Chinese as a race from the glory that was Zhuangzi to the idiocy that is Bing Zai is not lost on the veteran writer Yan Wenjing. In compliance with Han Shaogong's request for an opinion of his work, Yan responds in the form of an open letter masochistically titled "Wo shibushi shangle nianjide Bing Zai?" (Am I an Aging Bing Zai?):

> Your creation of Bing Zai has helped raise my consciousness, especially consciousness about myself. Your Bing Zai seems to be a blood relation of Ah Q in one way or another. Since they are native products of China, they are bound to share something in common. We need not do any research on this. Bing Zai is, of course, not Ah Q. This monster is more frightening. He seems to be easy to deal with, but in reality he is invincible. Even if thunder did not strike [on the day of his sacrifice] and his head had been offered to the gods, his ghost would still haunt the forest and the mountain.[29]

That Yan Wenjing should feel threatened by the presence of Bing Zai and wonder to himself if he is this "monster's" alter ego bespeaks the affective authenticity of Han Shaogong's creation. Yan is, of course, not Bing Zai, but since this man-child and his kinfolk are paraded in the tale as obdurate symbols of what has gone wrong with China, Yan suffers shame if not guilt by association. Chinese intellectuals must have reacted to the characterization of Ah Q in similar fashion, since he became a household word in 1921 for all the negative qualities of the Chinese character. They are, in Leo Ou-fan Lee's summation: "Cowardice, greediness, ignorance, spinelessness, a fence-sitting attitude, a penchant for bullying the weak and cower-

ing before the strong, and finally, an affinity for self-deluding rationalizations which can turn physical defeat into 'spiritual victory.'"[30]
Unlike Han's earlier "Echoes," which seems merely to reenact some
of Ah Q's idiocies, "Ba Ba Ba" carries Lu Xun's negative symbolism
to a new degree.

Contrary to the findings of contemporary rootseekers like Ah
Cheng, the roots unearthed by Han Shaogong from the deeper
recesses of the Chinese psyche have more to do with vice than with
virtue.[31] In view of the tragic experiences Han went through during
the Cultural Revolution, culminating in the suicide of his father,[32] it
is little wonder that the "roots" surfacing from his writing are invariably stamped with psychological trauma. Though camouflaged as a
universalist parable of violence and irrationality, "Ba Ba Ba," in
Han's admission, is particularistic in its reference to the cannibalism
committed by peasants in the Dao County of Hunan province during
the hectic years of the Cultural Revolution.

When haunting memories become a nightmare, they have to be
exorcised. In this light, "Nü Nü Nü" (1986), like "Ba Ba Ba," is an
act of exorcism. Aunt Shu, variously referred to in "Nü Nü Nü" as
Yao Bo or Yao Gu, is modeled on Han's own aunt *(guma)*, who
changed into a completely different personality after a stroke (Shi
136). In Han's dramatic representation, however, the change in her
personality is accompanied by transformations in physical form: she
first degenerates into a monkey and then a fish.

In all respects a more ambitious undertaking than "Ba Ba Ba," "Nü
Nü Nü" marks another turning point in Han's career. In 1987 he
told Michael Duke that though he had read Faulkner, he had not
yet read Gabriel García Márquez's *One Hundred Years of Solitude* when
he wrote "Ba Ba Ba," even though "García Márquez was [subse-
quently] a great inspiration" (Duke 41nll). This "subsequent inspiration" is observable in "Nü Nü Nü." Guilt-ridden for having sent his
aunt to the countryside against her will, where she dies mysteriously,
the narrator, who is her nephew, still feels her presence two years
later; he yells at every old woman of similar age because Aunt Shu
was hard of hearing.

Aunt Shu, a widow, acts as the narrator's mother-surrogate until her stroke, helping his indigent family make ends meet. A paragon of self-sacrificing women in Chinese peasant society, she is hard-working, uncomplaining, generous to others but so tightfisted to herself that she refuses to use a hearing aid simply because it needs batteries. She eats leftovers even when they are clearly spoiled. Once disabled and in bed, however, she has a dramatic change of appetite. Formerly she refused to eat pork for economic reasons, claiming that the meat reminded her of the heads of executed criminals hung on a pole as a warning to citizens by the local government. Now she not only demands meat and fish prepared to her specifications, but she also complains frequently about the cooking of her nephew's wife. When garlic is added to the fish at her request, she demands more salt, but when she has enough salt, she simply picks at the fish with her chopsticks and gives up.

Determined to make a nuisance of herself, she often knocks on the wooden desk by the bedside with her knuckles to attract atten-tion. Just as frequently, she soils her sheets and bedding. Before we examine her condition further, let's pause for a moment and turn to the question of how García Márquez and "magical realism" enter into her depiction. Angel Flores was the first to coin the term "mag-ical realism" in a 1954 paper delivered at the sixty-ninth Annual Meeting of the MLA: "Meticulous craftsmen all, one finds in [the Spanish-American fiction writers] the same preoccupation with style and also the same transformation of the common and the everyday into the awesome and the unreal . . . [Magical realism] is predomi-nantly an art of surprises."[33]

Students of Chinese literature need not be reminded by Han Shaogong, as he declared to Shi Shuqing, that the practice of trans-forming the common and the diurnal into the awesome and the fantastic is not exclusively the property of Spanish-American writers (Shi 133). The very mention of the generic terms *zhiguai* and *chuanqi* in traditional Chinese fiction brings to mind characters no less bizarre than Melquíades in *One Hundred Years of Solitude,* who is able to live life through a number of reincarnations, or Remedios the Beauty, whose ascent to Heaven is described matter-of-factly.

In all likelihood, what Han Shaogong has learned from the 1982 Nobel Prize winner is not so much the art of transforming the real into the unreal and vice versa, as it is the respectability of elevating the unreal to the category of verisimilitude in the name of magical realism. The prestige of the Nobel Prize for García Márquez renews Han Shaogong's faith in the fiction making of Cao Xueqin (c. 1724–1764), who spent his life savoring the paradox of "Truth becomes fiction when fiction's true;/ Real becomes not-real when the unreal's real."[34]

The license of magical realism enables Han to realize his most daring of metaphors on the human condition in "Nü Nü Nü." After Aunt Shu is sent to the countryside to live with her sworn sister, her unreasonable demands take a turn for the worse. For meat, she now wants rabbit; for seafood, she wants eels. The sworn sister and her two sons try their best to be accommodating, but in the end they are merely exhausted and disgusted.

To save his mother the labor of washing Aunt Shu's soiled sheets and clothes, the elder son ingeniously cuts a hole in her bed and places a basin underneath it. But she refuses to take advantage of this "convenience device" and returns to her old ways. Finally, all the sheets and bedding are taken from her. Instead, she is given a pair of thick trousers open at the crotch.

To prevent her hair from lice infestations, her head is shaved. Instead of a bowl, she is fed in a wooden trough. Han Shaogong's gruesome imagery of animalism and imprisonment finally reaches the grotesque when Aunt Shu is put in a cage where, after having lost the power of speech, she undergoes the first phase of her counterevolutionary process. Now she is subject to neither hunger nor cold. In the winter, she is seen crawling inside the cage without a thread on her. But miraculously her palms are warmer than most people's.

Her frame begins to shrink. With elbows that habitually bow outward, hardened skin, and flaring nostrils, she looks like a monkey. Her degeneration does not end here: in no time her arms and feet dwindle to the size of fins. Now she looks more like a fish. Her favorite dishes consist of raw meat and vegetables, and she even feeds on the grass and the soil by the cage.

How Aunt Shu meets her end is treated as a mystery by the narrator. She could have been unintentionally tortured to death by the mischievous neighborhood children who refer to her as the *huowu* (living thing). Or, as darkly hinted by the narrator, she could have been put out of her misery by her sister with a cleaver when she spotted a few cockroaches on the forehead of the "fish."

After the death of the monkey-fish comes the deluge. The funeral is held amid rumors of an approaching earthquake. The ensuing vision of doom transcribed by Han Shaogong in elliptical terms recalls the horrors of the Apocalypse. Armies of rats suddenly emerge from all sides, rushing to the nearby river. "Those that had first jumped into the water began to sink, and those coming after them stepped on their heads"[35] in their effort to make it to the other side of the river. What is even more suggestive in Han's apocalyptic view of Chinese history is encoded in a passage styled in stream-of-consciousness fashion:

> Where am I? One massive ejaculation from time immemorial, one piercing scream at childbirth that separated the boundaries of Heaven and Earth, had let the blood of the Chinese progenitors seep through the walls and the pitch-dark coal seams, seep through the ideograms evolved from conspiratorial entanglements and mutual hostilities and clamor, seep through the slashed throats of the revolutionaries in death cells and the clank of shackles. Where are you heading? A person dies, the earth quakes, the walls crumble, no one can save her just as no one can turn the infinite universe in your heart and my heart into an inventory sheet. ("Nü Nü Nü" 161)

Where is the first-person narrator heading? After the funeral, he returns to Changsha. "What am I going to see? What have I been waiting for?" he asks himself. In the end, he concludes that it is futile to search for any meaning in his existence. He seems to have come to terms with life and with himself: "Life can and should be spent like this: after the meal, do the dishes. After doing the dishes, make the phone call . . . This is the simplest as well as the most profound of reasoning" ("Nü Nü Nü" 166).

In my analysis of "Nü Nü Nü" I have concentrated on the metamorphosis of Aunt Shu. Like any text taut with metaphorical tensions, other characters would also make a fruitful subject of study.[36]

Aunt Shu's goddaughter Lao Hei, for example, fascinates us with her fin-de-siècle pulsations. A foil to her godmother, she is a promiscuous hedonist. So that she can forever be available to the next qualified man, so that she can "disco" forty-nine hours straight and sleep three days afterward, she has no qualms about aborting whoever's child is in her womb. Her life is raw material for an investigation of the extent to which post-Mao China has been overtaken by ennui and nihilism.

I have refrained from discussing Lao Hei for the same reason I did not elaborate on the roles of Tailor Zhong Man and his son Ren Bao in "Ba Ba Ba," respectively an ultraconservative and a pseudoprogressive. This is not to say that their parts in the narrative are less significant; it is because I wanted to give a cohesive reading of what I believe to be most relevant to Han Shaogong's concern: the fossilization of the Chinese as a race. While this notion is only coyly enacted in the deformity of Bing Zai, it is dramatically advanced in the paralytic nakedness of Aunt Shu. Physiologically speaking, it is unlikely that human beings would ever reverse the course of evolution and backtrack to the form of a monkey or a fish. What is more pertinent to our study, therefore, is not the putative metamorphosis of Aunt Shu as scientific fact, but the psychological change she manifests after the stroke.

We have seen how the "walled" mentality breeds ignorance, superstition, and cruelty in Chicken Head Village, culminating in the arrested growth of Bing Zai. Insularity is a kind of "protection" for a people who regard their country as the Middle Kingdom. In the words of Sun Longji, "[T]here are numerous walls within the Chinese world; the Great Wall itself merely protects the Chinese against Devils from without."[37] Cloistered within the "wall" of Chinese culture, a woman like Aunt Shu willy-nilly defines her selfhood by conforming to what her community expects of her. Her sense of propriety and family ties dictates that she be devoted to her brother, loving to her nephew, and frugal. This is no different from the barren women in her village, who feel obligated to lie naked on the peak and take in the south wind, which was purported to be efficacious in inducing pregnancy. Ironically enough, though Aunt Shu is identifiably a woman of present-day China, to the degree that her moral conduct and value judgment are determined by her immediate social environment she is no different from the female dramatis persona emerging from the pages of a *san-yan* story. Like Mrs. Liu in "Shiwuguan xiyan chengqiaohuo" (The Jest that Leads to Disaster), which I have discussed elsewhere,[38] Aunt Shu is incapable of making an independent decision, for her mind is conditioned by the customs and conventions in which she was raised.

Aunt Shu's stroke occurs while she is taking a bath. As her nephew rushes to her rescue in the steaming bathroom, he discovers his aunt's naked body so emaciated that "the nipples were like two drops of darkness haphazardly glued onto the bony chest" ("Nü Nü Nü" 121). The nephew's encounter with his aunt under these unusual circumstances effects such a change in his perception of her that it frightens him: "This was the first time I had seen Yao Bo's [Aunt Shu's] body, had seen her true self. This whitish shadow of a body seems strange to me. It scares me. I dare not get close enough to touch it" ("Nü Nü Nü" 121–122).

Psychologically, it can be argued that Aunt Shu's inhibitions are removed when her nakedness is exposed. An invalid, she might feel that she is no longer answerable to the claims of social civility to which she has been a slave for the better part of her life. When taboo fails to restrain, instinct rules. Viewed in this light, the turnabout of Aunt Shu's personality assumes a more ominous nature than her unreasonable demands for special food and attention alone would warrant. Her drastic personality transformation summons memories of the anarchy and bestiality that visited China during the Cultural Revolution. As Aldous Huxley rightly reminds us, "Civilization, in one of its aspects, may be defined as a systematic withholding from individuals of certain occasions for barbarous behavior."[39] Subterranean barbaric energies were released in China during the sixties as soon as individuals received the sanction from Chairman Mao that it was correct to rebel. This is what makes the transformation of Aunt Shu so frightening.

My reading of Aunt Shu's stroke as a metaphor for the paroxysm of the Cultural Revolution is not arrived at unadvisedly. In answer to Shi Shuqing's question about the genesis of "Nü Nü Nü," Han Shaogong remarks: "Under the oppression of feudalism, people are prone to confine and repress themselves. In due course, such repression will result in physical and psychological sickness. Once the symptoms erupt, the other side of human nature will be exposed, which might appear so disgusting that all that remains is an unpleasant memory . . . I have often said that the armed conflicts during the Cultural Revolution were a reaction to sexual repression. Manslaughter and factional strife are but a kind of release" (Shi 136–137).

In this discussion I have demonstrated Han Shaogong's skill as a *zhiguai* writer in magical realist's garb. Though the material he employs is no longer topical, the achieved effects in his reinvention of China's hazy past make for good reading as cautionary tales. We have also seen him transform Shen Congwen's pastoral landscapes into citadels of bestiality, and Lu Xun's mocking satire into evocations of degradation that bring to mind the calamities of the Cultural Revolution. As a writer, he can do no more to improve the lot of China than resign himself to the routine of "after the meal, do the dishes," which, contextually understood, is an admission of intellectual impotence. The incorporation of the bizarre and grotesque elements in "Nü Nü Nü" is presumably for "shock therapy." In this, Han Shaogong has done a wondrous job: he has led us to visualize, in a magical-realist way, the terrible consequences of the "stroke" that paralyzed the once energetic, industrious, and loving Aunt Shu.

MICHAEL S. DUKE

2 | Past, Present, and Future in Mo Yan's Fiction of the 1980s

Images of Chinese Peasants

In the first chapter of *The Fall of Imperial China*,[1] Frederic Wakeman, Jr., delineated three images of the Chinese peasantry as a social unit. Confucian physiocrats viewed the peasants as diligent yeomen who practiced agriculture, the "fundamental vocation," and were second in social status only to themselves, the "scholar officials" or "gentry" who governed the empire. "Frugal and hardworking, this idealized peasant toiled productively, paying his taxes gratefully in return for the paternalistic care and devotion" of his rulers. Such were the peasants at peace. Another view of the peasants held by traditional Chinese officials was that of "sullen beasts of burden, easily transformed into red-turbaned bandits or fanatic sectarians" who, in times of political and economic dislocation and famine, formed into vast armies that rampaged across the country "in despair and rage, smashing city walls and attacking local officials." These two contradictory images were both quite accurate, because the peasants then, as in this century, did provide the economic foundation of Chinese society and did rise in rebellion "when political corruption and economic scarcity coincided," as they often did and still do (5–6). Traditional historians never, however, narrated the details of individual peasant mentality. As Wakeman writes: "Illiterate and faceless, (the peasants) could be defined only by their superiors until modern times gave them their own political reality, and they learned to speak for themselves" (5).[2]

In this century, Wakeman points out, quoting Mao Zedong from the *New York Times*, Maoism elevated the masses to the role of the unique "motive forces in the making of world history" (5). Most contemporary historians would probably agree that the revolutionary Communist Party's appeal to the peasantry through its promise to solve their economic and social problems was one of the most important reasons for the Communist victory over the Nationalists in the Chinese Revolution and Civil War, which culminated in the founding of the People's Republic of China. Despite the fact that he had intimate knowledge of peasant psychology, however, Mao Zedong's depiction of the peasants as the makers of history was supremely "ideological" in the Althusserian sense of being pragmatic and put forth in order to mobilize certain "social subjects" to act "within the limits of a given social project." Given to them by Mao himself, their social project was to build a "new China" in accordance with his idiosyncratic and often changing blueprints. After 1949, this Maoist image of the peasantry became even positively utopian in the sense of a highly systematized idée fixe that was demanded and enforced as an article of faith (regardless of evidence to the contrary) by a highly organized and coercive political party.[3] The Maoist image of a good peasant, ever obedient to Mao's will and eager to accomplish his vision of socialism and communism, has proved in the years since 1979 to be nearly as unrealistic as the traditional ruling bureaucrats' idealizations that preceded it.

Although modern times may have presented the peasants with a political reality in which they were often urged quite literally to "speak for themselves,"[4] with the exception of a few writers of genuine peasant origin, the narrative image of the Chinese peasantry as a group continued throughout the Maoist era and continues to this day to be "defined only by their superiors." Historically situated between the two traditional elite images of the Chinese peasantry mentioned above and the full-blown Maoist view[5] was another definition by their superiors: that of the May Fourth writers of realistic exposé fiction.

Early May Fourth writers created the modern Chinese short story in the 1920s by combining various lyrical elements from traditional Chinese poetry and essay forms with individual psychological analysis and expression borrowed from the West. Their sometimes romantic and sometimes realistic short stories were predominantly concerned with urban phenomena and "became the artistic mouthpiece of the urban intellectual writer."[6] This lyrical and urban character of the modern Chinese short story did not, however, continue with the emergence of the modern Chinese novel in the 1930s. The modern Chinese novel became an increasingly rural-based panorama of social realism in which humanistic or ideologically engagé writers attempted to depict the desperate problems of poverty, ignorance, cruelty, and backwardness that cried out for solution at the time. This shift from individual to social concern and from urban to rural setting was one symptom of a striking urban-rural polarity emerging in this century *for the first time* in Chinese social history. In this context, the increasingly leftist writers depicted urban China, especially the eastern coastal cities led by Shanghai (Babylon of the East), as the scene of political and economic oppression and moral corruption. With the arrival of a full-scale anti-Japanese war of aggression in 1937, "modern Chinese literature entered into a predominantly rural phase"[7] from which it only partially emerged on the mainland in the 1980s.

May Fourth writers such as Lu Xun, Shen Congwen, Lao She, Mao Dun, Zhang Tianyi, Wu Zuxiang, Xiao Jun, Xiao Hong, Rou Shi, and many others, all shared to some extent both an antiurban bias and a sympathetic, even nostalgic, identification with rural China. With the exception of Lu Xun, whose overall view of the Chinese national character was extremely dark, they generally depicted the peasants as victims of an evil social system controlled by a corrupt rural gentry, urban-based absentee landlords, or national and foreign capitalist exploiters. It would be pointless to summarize all of their works here, but we ought to mention a few with which Mo Yan's works may be seen, without either implying or denying direct influence, to be carrying on a dialogue reflecting both continuities and discontinuities.

In a certain sense, the central tension in Lu Xun's creative life was that between his genuine intellectual and moral commitment to some traditional Chinese values and his total revulsion at what he felt to be the immorality of China's cultural tradition as a whole. In stories like "Hometown," "An Unimportant Affair," "New Year's Sacrifice," and "Upstairs in a Wineshop," Lu Xun confronts the sophisticated May Fourth intellectual (his first-person narrator) with the traditional virtues of rural China and finds him wanting. But, and this is most important, Lu Xun does not idealize the masses. Though they may be the font of such exemplary virtues as honesty, decency, and friendship, they are also the practitioners of all the vileness, cowardice, artful cunning, cruelty, and megalomania embodied in Ah Q, a devastating collective portrait of the Chinese national character with no ideologically motivated privileging of one social class over another.[8]

Shen Congwen and Lao She's works convey both a deeply felt nostalgia for the traditional virtues of (respectively) the West Hunan countryside and traditional Peking before it became a modern city and a melancholy awareness of the inevitability of their passing if China is ever to achieve modern wealth and power. The savage irony directed at the foreignness of the city in Shen's *Alice's Travels in China* contrasts sharply with the pastoral indulgence he lavishes on the Miao tribes of West Hunan: "As with beauty, [Long Zhu, seventeen-year-old son of a Miao chieftain] was gifted also with moral virtues, which far surpassed the share for ordinary men."[9] Shen's story "Xiao Xiao" probably represents the outer limit for depictions of rural China as a world where innocence and spontaneity can be rewarded with good humor and natural justice through an act of narrative closure that preserves the circle of meaning in a culture on the verge of destruction.[10] Although Lao She's Peking may be seen as an embodiment of the finest values of traditional (rural) China,[11] nevertheless his *City of Cats* represents an unrelenting indictment of urban China. Despite his nostalgia for traditional values, Lao She heaps unmitigated scorn on his rural protagonist thrust into an urban setting—Luotuo Xiangzi (Camel Happy Boy)—precisely because he has not learned the value of modern collective political organization. His natural peasant selfishness, combined with the corrupt environment of Peking in the late 1930s, leads him to end up a completely defeated individualist.[12]

Leftist writers like Mao Dun and Wu Zuxiang were even more critical of the political, economic, and moral evils emanating from the cities. They were equally solicitous of the plight of China's increasingly impoverished peasants, and they believed in a revolutionary program for their salvation. In the first chapter of Mao Dun's *Midnight*, an automobile ride through the Babylon of the East and a brief look at a Shanghai dance party are enough to literally kill off an aged representative of China's rural gentry. The predetermined message of this highly ideological novel is the inevitable downfall of the national capitalists and the necessity of a turn toward socialism and communism to save China from the twin evils of capitalism and imperialism. In "Spring Silkworms," the first story in a trilogy embodying the same theme in a rural setting, Mao Dun created a sympathetic and almost celebratory picture of peasant life and labor that is far more moving than anything in his urban fiction.[13] In "Young Master Gets His Tonic," Wu Zuxiang penned a powerful indictment of a rural landlord literally sucking the lifeblood of his peasants (the young man's tonic is the milk from a peasant woman's breasts), while "Fan Village" demonstrates the peasants' inevitable turn to banditry and rebellion as a result of their impoverishment. "Fan Village" also contains a penetrating exploration of a young peasant woman's hatred for her miserly mother. Her mother has been corrupted by a stint of urban employment in a well-to-do home, and she sides with her employer's class against the impoverished peasants turned bandits, including her own son-in-law. On the night the bandits break her husband out of jail, the daughter actually kills her mother in a scene that is both dramatically effective and symbolic of peasant release from their traditional bondage. The liberation of the peasantry through revolutionary violence is fully adumbrated here; it remains only to add the leadership of the Communist Party to arrive at one of the main themes of Chinese fiction from 1937 to 1977 and beyond.

The Rural Nightmare of Mo Yan's Short Fiction

Mo Yan's real name is Guan Moye. He was born in an impoverished village in Shandong province in 1956. His family was classified as "upper-middle peasants" and often suffered on that account. He left school and spent the Cultural Revolution years tending cattle, cutting hay, and working as a part-time laborer in a linseed oil factory. In March 1976 at the age of twenty, he entered the People's Liberation Army, the most prestigious way for a peasant boy to make good at the time. He began writing fiction in 1981. By 1982 he had advanced to the position of propaganda officer charged with teaching Marxism-Leninism to the troops. In 1984 he passed the entrance examination to the literature department of the People's Liberation Army Academy of Arts. After his works won both national and international recognition, he was admitted to Beijing's Lu Xun Academy of Literature, where he is currently (December 1990) a graduate student. He knows peasant life from the inside and he knows Party policy toward the peasants since the 1970s just as well. He regularly returns to Shandong to help with the harvests and to visit his family.

In a series of powerful works, including "Touming de hong luobo" (The Crystal Carrot), "Ku he" (Dry River), "Baigou qiuqianjia" (White Dog and the Swings), and "Huanle" (Happiness),[14] Mo Yan deliberately challenged the Maoist mythology of Zhao Shuli, Zhou Libo, Li Zhun, Hao Ran, and other post-1949 writers of rural fiction who followed the twists and turns of Party policy and attempted to conform to the "worker-peasant-soldier fiction" guidelines of Mao Zedong's "Yan'an Talks on Literature and Art." In these works, he consistently portrays the Chinese countryside as a nightmarish world, thus presenting a vision of rural China as a near total contrast to that found in those earlier works. Rather than depicting the Maoist peasants dutifully struggling to build socialism, a major theme of 1949-through-1977 fiction, Mo Yan's works hark back to the May Fourth writers' vision of the peasants as victims of an unequal social system over which they have no control.

Here we see the first major thematic continuity with the May Fourth tradition of exposé realism. But this continuity is balanced by an equally striking discontinuity: the dramatis personae of Mo Yan's fiction, reflecting, as I believe they do, real knowledge of his times (*pace* much contemporary Western literary criticism), have changed dramatically. The mass of peasants are still for the most part on the bottom of the social hierarchy, sharing an egalitarianism of backwardness, poverty, and ignorance; but, in the fashion of Orwell's

Animal Farm, some peasants are more equal than others. Some peasants are rural Communist Party cadres; they support and are supported by the county, provincial, and national Party apparatus. Together these two groups constitute a *tequan jieji* (lit. "a class with special powers") that has been oppressing the mass of the peasants ever since the Great Leap Forward.[15] During the Cultural Revolution, a period in which many of Mo Yan's short stories are set, their predations were practiced in extremis; but the burden of a vast amount of post-Mao literature has been to demonstrate the persistent power and influence of Cultural Revolution cadres in many parts of China. In a terrible historical irony, which could hardly have been anticipated by either humanistic or Marxist May Fourth writers, the party and the ideology they believed would liberate the peasants have only managed to subject them to another cruel master.[16]

A fitting motto for Mo Yan's profoundly anti-*xiangtu* literature (at least anti-*xiangtu* in the sense of the writers mentioned above) would be "I hate green," green being a bucolic emblem of rural China.[17] His Chinese countryside is a nightmarish world of ignorance, poverty, cruelty, bitterly hard work, suffering, sadness, misery, and broken dreams, the bleakness of which is only infrequently and temporarily relieved by very small doses of simple human kindness, friendship, and love.

In many of his finest short stories, Mo Yan's narrative tone is one of controlled anger, befitting an environment in which irrational violence may break out at any time and engulf his protagonists in tragic misfortune or death. The friendly young stonemason of "The Crystal Carrot" is beaten by the bitter young blacksmith in a fight in which his young lover, Chrysanthemum, has one of her beautiful dark eyes put out by a misdirected handful of gravel. In the dénouement, the young blacksmith goes back to his miserable drunken existence as an uncivilized, but ironically model, Cultural Revolution worker. The kindly and sensitive old master blacksmith, a lover of the wistfully melancholy folk music of rural China, and the loving young couple disappear. The little mute, Blacky, who has a dreamlike epiphany in which a completely transparent and crystalline carrot becomes a fragile symbol of hope in an otherwise bleak existence, is caught stealing sweet potatoes, stripped of his new coat, new shoes and pants, and sent running home naked to his alcoholic stepmother by none other than the Brigade Leader.

Another major continuity with May Fourth depictions of rural (or even urban) China is that whenever the peasants try to rise in the social hierarchy, the result is tragic failure. This is true even when their attempted rise toward the exalted level of the new rural elite is only hinted at through symbolic action. In "Dry River," the small boy Little Tiger climbs a tree to show a high cadre's daughter how brave he is. Just as he is wondering at the magnificence of her family's never-before-seen courtyard as glimpsed from the top of the tree, the branch snaps and he falls right down on her, killing her instantly. He commits suicide after being nearly beaten to death by his father and reviled by his mother and elder brother, whose chances for advancement have been ruined for life. And it is all because of their bad class background. Although great scorn is reserved for the high cadre and his wife, the narrator's repetition of lines describing the faces of "the common people *(lao baixing)* [as] barren as the desert" emphasizes his indictment of all Chinese people for their cruelty and docility. This narrative repetition and the theme it supports call to mind the crowd's cruel reactions to Xianglin Sao's sad story in Lu Xun's "New Year's Sacrifice." Just at the point when the narrator of "White Dog and the Swings" is pushing his girlfriend Nuan and her puppy so high in a swing that they can nearly see Heaven, the rope breaks and she has one eye put out in her fall into a bush. As a result of this blemish on an otherwise very beautiful face, she loses both a young PLA officer and the narrator as potential husbands. She ends up married to a fiercely jealous mute who gives her three mute children and treats her with great brutality. As the first-person narrator is rationalizing her fate to himself, in a passage again reminiscent of the narrator of Lu Xun's "New Year's Sacrifice," Mo Yan goes beyond Lu Xun's pessimism by offering the narrator a way to make it up to the woman. Mo Yan is one of the contemporary writers most concerned with the status of women in Chinese society, and it is characteristic of him that he has Nuan plead with the first-person narrator, in a manner he could not possibly refuse, to make love with her for the sake of their childhood friendship and give her at least one child who will be able to talk to her.[18] The unfortunate protagonist of "Happiness" fails five times to pass the college entrance examinations. His family nearly bankrupt themselves supporting his studies in the hope that if he becomes a member of the educated elite, their future prosperity will be assured. In his grief and shame, he sets off to commit suicide by swallowing pesticide. As he thinks back over his past in scene after scene of bitter stream-of-consciousness narrative, the only act of kindness and tenderness he can remember in his entire life occurred once in a secluded hideaway in the fields when an older woman friend opened her blouse and permitted him a fleeting glimpse of her breasts.

As indicated by this brief survey of some of his short stories, prior to the publication of *Tiantang suantai zhi ge* (Paradise County Garlic Song)[19] of 1988 Mo Yan's nightmare vision of the Chinese countryside did not actually center on the evils of traditional culture as embodied in popular rural practices but rather on the barbaric cruelty of rural elites—rural Communist Party cadres who have taken the place of the defeated and departed gentry of the past. In every case it is these local agents of government policy who are responsible for the tragic fates of his peasant protagonists. The only exception to this rule is his treatment of the war against the Japanese in *Hong gaoliang jiazu* (The Red Sorghum Clan) of 1987, which lies outside the scope of this essay.[20]

Paradise County, 1988

The fierceness of a lion, the timidity of a rabbit, the craftiness of a fox.
Lu Xun, "Diary of a Madman"

In *Tiantang suantai zhi ge,* his second full-length novel, Mo Yan once more creates a world of rural nightmare similar to that found in much of his short fiction written before *Red Sorghum*. This time, in a long work based on an actual peasant riot that took place in the summer of 1987,[21] the temporal locus of this rural nightmare is unmistakably the late 1980s. Set in the heyday of the reform era of 1978 to 1989, the novel explores the effects of the reforms in one rural county in northern China. In contrast to *Red Sorghum*'s nostalgia for rural values, which is decidedly muted here, in this novel Mo Yan combines all of the technical and thematic elements we have discussed so far to produce a mature work of art that is stylistically impressive, emotionally powerful, and intellectually engaging.

This is Mo Yan's most overtly ideological text. It supports reform, but not any particular political faction. The last chapter consists largely of a series of articles from the fictional *Masses Daily* (a transparent reference to the *People's Daily*) of July 30, 1987. They call for a continuation and deepening of the political and economic reforms that began in 1979—increasing democratization and more market economy—and an end to the squeeze on the peasants' livelihood practiced by corrupt local cadres who refuse to follow central government policies. This squeeze reminds one of nothing more than the often capricious taxation of the late Qing dynasty and the depredations of the warlord era. In spite of its obvious proreform ideological bias, this is no simple work of reportage fiction. It is one of the most imaginatively conceived and artistically accomplished narrative evocations of the complexity of peasant life ever written in twentieth-century Chinese fiction. More knowledge of the physical, material, emotional, and psychological lives of the Chinese peasants in the 1980s and the social, political, and cultural practices (and their agents) that envelop those lives is transmitted in this work of narrative imagination than may be found in a host of general social science studies of the subject. The reader comes away from this work with a heightened awareness and understanding of how the experience of the Chinese peasants—their love, hate, goodness, cruelty, decency, and indecency—feels to them as they live it. In this novel Mo Yan, more systematically perhaps than any other twentieth-century Chinese writer on the subject, gets inside the Chinese peasants and induces us to feel their feelings and to understand their lives.[22]

The novel begins with the arrest of two of the main male characters, Gao Yang and Gao Ma, for their participation in a riot. The riot breaks out because, after encouraging the peasants to plant large amounts of garlic *(suantai)*,[23] which they expect to sell at a good price, the local officials arbitrarily tax the peasants on their way to market, refuse to allow them to sell their surplus produce to out-of-town buyers, lower the price paid for the garlic, declare their storage facilities to be full, and refuse to buy any more. The peasants are all counting on selling the garlic to improve their generally impoverished conditions, conditions that the novel shows to have improved since 1979, but to be threatened by official squeeze and national inflation. Becoming even more enraged when the county Party secretary refuses to talk to them, the peasants trash and burn the county government offices. Gao Ma, who needs to sell his garlic in order to buy his bride from her hard-hearted father, is a willing participant in the riot; Gao Yang and his Aunt Fang are simply swept along in the crowd and participate in the riot with less than full knowledge of what they are doing.

In nineteen chapters the novel describes in detail the lives of the peasants who grow garlic in Paradise County a few weeks before and after the riot. At the same time it delineates their different past experiences and, to a lesser extent, their past and present suffering at the hands of local officials since 1949. The main characters include Gao Yang, the son of ex-landlords, in his forties; Gao Ma, the main protagonist, a younger demobilized soldier who struggles with the Fangs and the local government for the love of Fang Jinju (Golden Chrysanthemum), the Fangs' only daughter; the peasant family of Uncle Fang (Fang Sishu), Aunt Fang (Fang Sishen), their daughter Jinju and her two older brothers, Fang Yijun, the eldest, a physical cripple and a spiritual weakling, and Fang Yixiang, the second, an ill-tempered and cruel young man; people's government Representative Yang, who connives with three local families, one of which he is a brother-in-law to, in an illegal arranged marriage that amounts to bartering away three young women (including Fang Jinju) to three older men; various male and female police, jailors, and common criminals; judges and lawyers; and one passionate young army officer who tries to defend the peasants in court. The officer undoubtedly speaks for the implied author. All of the characters, except for the Fang men, are brought together in the trial scenes in which Chinese justice is shown to be pretty much the mockery it so often is. The final chapter, mentioned above, provides a dénouement in which the last thing we learn from the third-person narrator is that the rioters have been given unspecified punishments in order to prevent the spread of such anarchy as their actions represent, and the criminally guilty Party officials, having been disciplined by the usual Party methods, are given promotions in other places in rural China.

From this brief plot outline, we can see that the novel exhibits many thematic continuities with May Fourth fiction. Most saliently, it agrees with many May Fourth writers' visions by depicting the peasants as victims of an evil and unequal social system over which they have no control. That system is seen to be controlled by a corrupt rural elite now made up of peasant or ex-peasant cadres who continue to practice traditional rural corruption and cruelty despite their membership in a Communist Party officially dedicated to improving the peasants' lives. They either refuse to implement the central government's reform policies, which have been contributing to the enrichment of the peasants since 1979, or they step in at strategic points to squeeze the peasants out of the profits of their labor. In the changed historical situation, the implied author is still solicitous of the plight of China's impoverished but economically improving peasants, but unlike Mao Dun, Wu Zuxiang, and other May Fourth writers, he is more critical of the political, economic, and moral evils typical of the rural hinterland than of the cities. The cities (the capital, Beijing, in particular) are in the background only as the embodiment of central government policies distorted by local cadres against the interests of the peasants.

In congruity with the works of Lu Xun, though not with many other May Fourth writings, this work does not in any way idealize the rural masses. The characters in the novel demonstrate a very wide range of both good and bad "virtues."[24] Gao Yang is a model of honesty, filial piety, and friendship, and he also shows exemplary courage in defying the 1960s Party leadership in order to bury his mother. But he is as frightened of cadres, government officials, or police as any peasant in traditional times would have been. Bitter experience as a landlord's son has taught him to be self-effacing and to always do what he is told. Mo Yan's realism rises to the level of the grotesque in his depiction of Gao Yang when Gao is forced to drink his own urine during the 1960s and once again in jail in 1987. At the end of his interrogation, he is a beaten man. Reflecting that one month in prison would be enough to kill him, he makes a vow to Heaven that if he gets out, he will never again stick up for himself, even if other people shit on his head.[25]

Gao Ma and Jinju also demonstrate great courage, the ability to love, and a desire for happiness by running away from her family. Courage, love, and desire are not enough, however, and in the end they both react irrationally in the face of crisis and defeat. With her father killed, her mother arrested, and Gao Ma on the run from the police, the pregnant Jinju cannot bear to bring another child into this world. She tells the unborn child all of life's hardships and then hangs herself in Gao Ma's broken-down shack. After he is mistreated by the local representative of the people's government, nearly beaten to death by the Fang brothers, denied the profits of his year's labor, and thrown into jail by the police at home, where he has just cut down the hanged body of his beloved Jinju, Gao Ma has nothing left but hatred for the authorities. He has lost the will to live. When a sympathetic older procurator shows some interest in defending him, Gao Ma asks if his crime is "enough for execution?" The procurator continues: "It's not enough. I'd like you to go along with me, tell me all the details of your love affair with Fang Jinju. I believe that your unfortunate love experience was one of the main reasons for your criminal behavior . . . " "No!" Gao Ma replies. "I hate all of you corrupt officials! I wish I could flay all of you alive!" (255). He refuses to cooperate with the procurator, who is obviously working on a plausible defense.

The Fang family is struggling mightily to improve their material conditions, and they have had some moments of family warmth and companionship, but the men treat the women and each other with considerable cruelty. Uncle Fang may be regarded as a typical peasant patriarch. He thinks first of his eldest son's future and the future of his own surname. He must find a bride for his crippled son, so that his second son can then be taken care of. Thus he must barter his young daughter away to a much older man in exchange for an equally younger daughter who is being forced to marry his undesirable eldest son. He is a harsh taskmaster to his sons, and there is no love lost between them; the eldest son fears him, while the second son hates him. After his death, they ruthlessly divide his meager property, leaving almost nothing for their mother and sister. Most of the time Uncle Fang orders his wife and daughter around in the fields and at home like hired servants. His daughter is his family property, and he intends to dispose of her in a manner suiting his own felt interests. The question of her personal happiness never enters his mind, and he does not give a damn for the official marriage law. When she refuses to marry the man he has contracted her to, he beats her, tells her mother to shut up when she tries to interfere, and orders his sons to beat up the man his daughter wants to marry. After Jinju runs away with Gao Ma and is apprehended, Uncle Fang has her brothers strip her and hang her up by the hands so that he can whip her. He feels he has the right to beat her to death if she does not obey him. When she adamantly refuses to denounce her love for Gao Ma, saying he will have to kill her to keep her from running away again, he relents and agrees to sell her to Gao Ma for the extremely high sum of 10,000 *yuan*—several years' profit from the sale of garlic. As he puts it: "I'll help you out! Tell Gao Ma, tell him to bring me 10,000 *yuan!* When he hands over the money, I'll hand over the goods!" (149).

In keeping with the complexity of Mo Yan's narrative, the reader is not allowed simply to despise Uncle Fang for his backwardness and cruelty. He may be breaking the marriage law, but he is not consciously immoral or dishonest. And he gives his family physical protection and emotional warmth to the extent that his economic and cultural levels allow. Despite all of his rough treatment, when Jinju first runs off with Gao Ma, she cannot help feeling sorry for her parents and her older brother, whose infirmity will indeed prevent him from ever marrying. In jail Aunt Fang thinks fondly of her now dead husband when she remembers the good-humored way he collected lice from his padded jacket to sell to Mr. Wang of West Village, which the latter used to concoct Chinese medicine. When Jinju questions him about lice, he offers this proverb: "The poor have lice and the rich have scabies!" He has to collect 847 lice, and Jinju cannot help him because the lice would lose their efficacy as medicine if touched by a woman's hands.[26] Finally, Aunt Fang recalls, he tells a sadly humorous story about a city louse and a country louse complaining to each other. The country louse lives in peril because the peasants are always taking off their shabby padded coats and searching for lice, but the city louse lives in equal danger because city people are always changing their silks and satins to have them cleaned and ironed. The two lice end up committing suicide by throwing themselves into a well. These pictures of their "once beautiful family life" make Aunt Fang and the reader very sad (139–141). From these scenes we can see that, like Shen Congwen and Lao She, Mo Yan has a deep sympathy for some of the traditional rural virtues and sees in them the staying power, for better or worse, of China's rural ethos as a whole.

The characters who *are* irremediably corrupt and consciously dishonest are the rural cadres who control the peasants' lives. People's government representative Yang connives with three rural families to subvert the marriage law, and they perform free services (slave labor) for him, just as the peasants did for the landlords in imperial times. The first time the Fang brothers beat up Gao Ma, Gao Ma complains to Yang, but Yang, being in league with the Fangs, turns him away. Later Yang advises the Fangs that the next time they beat up somebody, they should not hit him on the head but on the ass and lower parts where the bruises will not show (64). When Yang's brother-in-law, Cao Jinzhu, curses the law that says he cannot beat his daughter if she disobeys him, Yang shows his real contempt for the peasants he is supposed to serve with the following reply:

The Communist Party may be afraid of almost anything, but it's not afraid of big talkers like you. Beating a person is against the law; your daughter is a person; beating your daughter is beating a person and beating your daughter is against the law. If you break the law we'll tie you up with a rope and take you in as usual. Haven't you seen it on T.V.? If a provincial governor breaks the law, they put the handcuffs right on him. Are you bigger than a provincial governor? A stinking garlic grower like you!

Yang's brother-in-law angrily replies:

If it weren't for us stinking garlic growers, all you big shots would have to live off the northwest wind. Isn't it our taxes that support all of you, keep you all eating meat, drinking wine, and dreaming up more laws to squeeze the oil out of the common people?

Yang's reply to that is even more revealing of this rural cadre's feeling of power and privilege as well as the implied author's contempt for him:

> You support us? Shit! I'm a national cadre; if I lie in the shade and watch the ants crawl up a tree, my wages are still paid, and not a penny less; if your garlic rots into pulp, I still collect my pay. (63)

The conclusion of the novel demonstrates that Yang, the rural people's representative, is ultimately correct in his judgment of the relative position of the national cadres and the peasant masses. Uncle Fang and his old cow are run over and killed by a drunken chauffeur driving the village government Party secretary, Wang Jiaxiu, back from a banquet. The secretary himself is the one who urges his chauffeur to drive on without going back to help the injured peasant. Aunt Fang, her sons, and Gao Ma take Uncle Fang's body to the seat of village government for restitution, but Secretary Wang refuses to see them. Instead people's Representative Yang persuades them not to press charges. His logic is impeccable. The most they can expect to receive from the government is a few hundred *yuan* for burial expenses. If Secretary Wang's driver is sent to jail, he will be out in a couple of months and right back at his old job. But they will have offended Secretary Wang, and that will make it tough on them for the rest of their lives. They will get a bad reputation, and the Fang brothers will never be able to find wives. It really isn't worth it. Under such a political system, the peasants simply cannot win. In the dénouement, Secretary Wang is actually put in charge of a law-and-order campaign aimed at preventing future popular disturbances. When Gao Ma insists on an earth burial rather than the usual cremation for Jinju and his unborn child,[27] they have to be buried without a coffin because the Daxinanling forest fire, a nightmare of bureaucratic corruption and bungling,[28] has resulted in a shortage of wood. Zhong Weimin and Ji Nancheng, the vice-secretary and the secretary of the Paradise County Party Committee, having been found chiefly responsible for the "Paradise

County Affair," are suspended from office for a short time. After they have "conscientiously studied" the Party line, they are both reinstated as Party vice-secretaries and as a vice-county magistrate and a county magistrate *(xianzhang)*, respectively. "This is only a rumor on the grapevine," says the third-person narrator, but "Oh, our grapevine rumors are almost always accurate" (298).

The real nightmare of the Chinese peasants' lives is most poignantly expressed in their reactions to being in jail. In spite of the terrors and indignities of jail life, especially for Gao Yang, both he and Aunt Fang think to themselves on more than one occasion that jail life is in some respects better than their life on the outside. Their thoughts are reminiscent of Ba Jin's famous short story "Gou" (Dog), in which a hungry and impoverished young Shanghai man prays that he might become a dog owned and pampered by a foreign mistress. The message one receives from their reflections, however, is not Ba Jin's blatant anti-imperialism. Listening in on their thoughts, narrated in a humorous (Gao Yang) or a nostalgic (Aunt Fang) vein, one is left with an overwhelming sense of sadness at the continuing impoverishment and oppression of the Chinese peasants in "the socialist era."[29] Gao Yang is put in a cell with an old man who committed incest with his daughter-in-law and then infanticide when a child was born, a middle-aged murderer who is the cell boss and forces him to drink his own urine to demonstrate his obedience, and a cowardly young thief. The filth and inhumanity of the cell are almost unimaginable, but Gao Yang is nevertheless favorably impressed with several things that happen to him. First of all he rides to jail in an automobile, the fastest he has ever gone in his life. Next he is given a physical examination and an injection by a "high-class woman" *(gaoji nüren)* in a white uniform who smells delicious to him. In seventh heaven when she touches him, he reflects that now he has not lived in vain. Then he is given a haircut by another "high-class woman," and it is almost too much for him. Finally, when he grows feverishly ill, he is served a bowl of noodles that is better than anything he usually has to eat. "Gao Yang, he ate the noodles and called out his own name, Gao Yang, you've run into some real luck: the kind of high-class woman you could only gaze at from a distance has rubbed your head; the kind of high-class noodles you've never even set eyes on before are now going into your stomach; Gao Yang, people cannot be content when they're suffering, but you ought to be content now" (181). Aunt Fang also finds the jail's black and fly-covered steamed *mantou*, made with wheat flour, better than the fried corn flour cakes she has at home. As she says, trying to console her younger cellmate, it is all a matter of fate and cannot be altered: "The two of us being locked in here was long ago planned by the Old Man of Heaven. It's not so bad here; there's a bed and a blanket and you don't need ration tickets to eat; only this window is a little too small, too suffocating" (136).

In the thematic realm, continuities outnumber discontinuities when we compare Mo Yan's fiction with that of the May Fourth era. It is rather in the realm of narrative technique and artistry that we discover the greatest discontinuity between Mo Yan's writing and that of the majority of May Fourth writers.

Compared with the works of most May Fourth writers, Mo Yan has already shown himself to be much more concerned with artistic style and structure, and with the artistic use of language. In less than a decade he has produced several works of greater technical sophistication, among which *Garlic Song* is his finest effort.[30] Without a detailed study it would be difficult to trace definite influences on his works. He was only eleven in 1967, when both May Fourth fiction and fiction of "the first seventeen years" (1950–1967) were branded as too reactionary by the Cultural Revolution literary bureaucracy controlled by Jiang Qing. Thus, although he certainly read Lu Xun's fiction and essays, and other forbidden works were available in the late seventies, we do not know what Chinese originals he read before the 1979 rehabilitation of both these two bodies of fiction. He began the formal study of literature in 1984, and by 1987 he had read with particular admiration a few miscellaneous works by Western novelists (and one Japanese) of the nineteenth and twentieth centuries, including Gustave Flaubert, James Joyce, William Faulkner (his avowed favorite), Ernest Hemingway, Yasunari Kawabata, M. A. Sholokov, Stephan Zweig, and, perhaps, Alain Robbe-Grillet. It has never been his intention to, as the conservative and controlled Chinese press puts it, "slavishly imitate" any of them. Like many of his contemporaries in the "post-Mao generation" of writers, Mo Yan has tried to combine traditional Chinese and modern Western literary techniques to bring about an imaginative transformation of his rich life experiences and thoughts, thus creating a genuinely modern Chinese narrative style expressive of both his individual voice and his vision.[31]

In *Garlic Song* he has successfully produced a novel of considerably more complex structure and involved plotting than most novels of the May Fourth era. This structural complexity also leads to a much more comprehensive and multifaceted picture of the complex social and individual realities of life in the Chinese countryside. The various realms of personal character, public morality, national-versus-local political and economic relationships, conflicts between self and society, and the confrontation and congruence of tradition and modernity are all penetratingly explored in this sophisticated yet moving narrative. In *Garlic Song*, much more successfully than in *Red Sorghum*, Mo Yan goes beyond the ordinary conventions of realist narrative *as they have been heretofore understood and practiced in China*, borrows techniques both from China's traditional fiction and the literary world of Western modernism, and produces an emotionally and intellectually attractive narrative. Making no pretense of being written for the "workers, peasants, and soldiers" *to read*,[32] this narrative requires a very alert "interactive reading" in order to naturalize and comprehend. Thus, although the ideological import or thematic meaning of his work is readily comprehensible, the reader is never bored in the retelling of "the old story" of rural oppression so often told in the May Fourth era.

In *Garlic Song* Mo Yan employs two clusters of artistic techniques in order to simultaneously (literally, one should say repeatedly and serially) destabilize (or disunify) and unify (or guide) the text and the reader's understanding and expectations. In Western terms, the work is distinctly "modern" rather than "postmodern" in that he has a definite story to tell and all of his techniques are employed in the service of telling it with the maximum possible artistic, emotional, and intellectual force.[33]

His primary destabilizing technique is the use of disunifying (or defamiliarizing) structural networking throughout the first nineteen chapters, the entire story of the "Paradise County Affair." In a dis-

tinctly nonlinear narrative, Mo Yan manipulates many time sequences as experienced from the point of view of each of the main
characters. If we think of each character as representing a different
color of thread, we may describe this narrative technique as a form
of intricate weaving.[34] As we read, our experience is analogous to
that of someone watching a weaver working on a complex pattern;
since he frequently changes colors and directions, it is difficult for
us to visualize the final pattern very long before it is completed. Each
partial pattern is so skillfully executed, however, that we never grow
tired of watching something we cannot completely comprehend
emerge before our eyes. In the end, all of the threads are employed
at the same time. That is, all of the main characters are brought
together in the final trial scene, a scene in which we are certain their
fates are sealed, but we are not told what those fates are to be.

In the process of telling each character's story in a number of
different time sequences, Mo Yan uses several of the Proustian techniques for dealing with time described by Gérard Genette in *Narrative Discourse*.[35] In a novel less than one-tenth the length of Proust's
multivolume oeuvre, there are enough *prolepses* (anticipations) and
analepses (retrospectives) for them to be regarded as a significant
technical element.[36] What do these narrative strategies accomplish?
First of all they add reader-motivating "instabilities."[37] That is, they
create a strong desire on the part of the reader to continue in the
company of this text to discover what kind of openness or closure
lies ahead, to discover how the lives of these characters are going to
interact and what kind of an overall picture is going to emerge in
the end.[38] Secondly they both call upon and assist the reader to
interact with the text, to hold in mind all of the characters' incomplete stories, and to naturalize the entire story after all of the characters have come together in the final trial scene. Narrated in this
way, Mo Yan's structural architectonics keep one reading, thinking,
and feeling to the end with intellectual and emotional engagement.

In the course of this nonlinear story or plot line, several other
modern techniques are used to create temporal disunities that turn
out to be part of an overall structure of meaning (thematic unity).
Third-person narratives of memory flashbacks and first-person
stream-of-consciousness narratives naturally occur out of normal

chronological order even within the already nonlinear narratives of particular characters' stories. Taken as a whole, they amount to a series of temporal juxtapositions of great thematic importance. They serve to link *the past*—the land reform period, the Cultural Revolution era, times of extreme poverty—with *the present* and to throw doubt on *the future* of the entire revolutionary social project. Gao Yang's delirious memory of his mother's burial and the cruel treatment he received at the hands of school authorities and rural cadres demonstrates that the cadres are just as bad now as they were then; that "class struggle" was cruel, dehumanizing, and (in Gao Yang's case) unjustified; and that peasants like Gao Yang are just as sheeplike as they ever were. Aunt Fang's reminiscences about picking lice, read in conjunction with her family's current struggles, highlight the fact that rural poverty is nearly as bad in 1987 as it was ten years ago. Their lot has improved, but it is still an extremely bitter life the Fang family leads.

Two very effective chronologically impossible devices—talking to the dead and to the as yet unborn—are also used to express inner states of despair, sadness, and defeat in two cases and minor victory in one instance. Jinju's arguments with her unborn child as it tries to tear through her body and out into human time represent her ultimate despair at life in rural China. Gao Ma's conversation with Jinju's corpse likewise represents both the fragility of their hopes for happiness and his feelings of despair and guilt at being unable to make those hopes come true. Gao Yang's dream visitation from his mother's ghost, although it ends in a nightmare of putrefaction, still gives him a chance to tell her of his rehabilitation, the birth of his children, and their current surplus of grain, which is a direct result of the recent economic reforms. The fact that this macabre conversation takes place in a filthy jail cell makes it an integral part of the thematic pattern of the novel as a whole.

The reader's understanding and expectations are guided by a cluster of traditional and modern unifying techniques. Of the traditional techniques, the most important one is borrowed from the premodern vernacular novel *(zhanghui xiaoshuo)*. Each of the novel's twenty chapters is preceded by a folksong said to be sung by Paradise County's famous blind singer, Zhang Kou. The use of a folksong prologue for each chapter makes explicit the meaning of the action to come (prolepsis) or the action just completed in a previous section (analepsis). Taken as a whole, the songs add up to a "Ballad of Paradise County" that points out "the moral of the story" in words any peasant could understand.[39] Another technique characteristic of traditional short stories and novels is the use of allegorical tales within tales to reinforce a particular thematic reading of the larger narrative. Uncle Fang's story about lice as recalled by Aunt Fang reinforces the theme of peasant poverty. The even longer story told to Gao Ma by the aged peasant Old Wang and narrated in sections alternating with Gao Ma's interrogation in chapter 17 supports Gao Ma's explicit statement that socialism is a farce when China is ruled by the kind of corrupt rural cadres he has had to deal with. The clear implication of Old Wang's story is that the revolutionary transformation from the imperial to the communist bureaucracies is a case of "changing the soup without changing the medicine" or "changing the bones without changing the teeth." The cadres still have the teeth, and their word is still law for any common peasant who wants to survive.

The most significant modernistic unifying technique is the use of powerfully evocative animal imagery and symbolism both to enhance the artistic texture and to contribute to the thematic depth of his narrative. Inasmuch as such imagery was used quite forcefully in Lu Xun's classic stories "Diary of a Madman" and "The True Story of Ah Q," Mo Yan's usage may be seen as a direct challenge to the ideas of China's most celebrated modern writer. At one point Lu Xun's madman whispers mysteriously to himself, "The fierceness of a lion, the timidity of a rabbit, the craftiness of a fox," and in the story this animal imagery is used to brand the entire Chinese cultural tradition as worse than bestial. The story implies that the Chinese people, all of them, are worse than animals because they practice cannibalism.[40] As Ah Q is being paraded to the execution ground, he looks at the faces of the jeering crowd and sees that their eyes are "more terrible even than the wolf's . . . (and they) seem to have merged into one." Once again, Lu Xun employs animal imagery to accuse the entire Chinese race of bestiality.[41] Lu Xun's imagery is of a piece with what Lin Yü-sheng calls his "cultural-intellectualistic" approach and his "totalistic iconoclasm."[42] The images express his totalistic condemnation of Chinese culture and the personality structure or character he believes it produces. As mentioned above, Lu Xun does not privilege any particular social stratum in Chinese society. Ah Q represents *the* Chinese character. All Chinese are equally inheritors of Chinese culture; all Chinese are equally guilty; all, including the madman himself, the first-person narrator, the implied author, and (the logic of his argument requires this last step) the flesh-and-blood author. This being the case, the madman's famous cry of "Save the children!" in spite of its grounding in Darwin via Spenser and Nietzsche, can be no more than a gesture of ironic futility. If, as Lu Xun argued in the May Fourth era and many critics of culture still argue today, we are all locked up in prison houses of language and culture, then there is no hope for any of us. Lu Xun's animal imagery only reinforces a totally pessimistic view of Chinese character.[43]

Animal imagery is pervasive in *Garlic Song*. At least twenty-two different animals are employed in eighty different instances as simile, metaphor, and symbol. The most commonly used animals are dog (sixteen times), horse (four times), cow (four times), wolf, tiger, rat, chickens, and cat (two times each). Virtually every character in the story, even the crowd as a unit, is at some point described with an animal image.

The man who resists the corrupt cadres and the cruelty of the old family system most strongly is Gao Ma. His name means "High Horse," and he is described as "like a big tall horse caught in a noose" as he runs from the police (12). At the same time he is also like a rat being chased by a cat (the police) (10) and like a "clever wild hare" limping away from their trap (12). He is "like a wounded dog" when rebuffed by the local government representative the day after his first beating by the Fang brothers (34). He goes to the local government to complain about the Fangs' violation of the law against arranged marriages, but a drunken Representative Yang waves him away "as if he were shooing away flies" (32). When he slips and falls later due to the blow to his head, he crawls in a ditch like a dog (35). Asleep at Jinju's side in a field, his dirty black hair looks like a dog's (79), and when he wakes with a start, his eyes have a frightened look "like those of a dog that has been driven into a corner" (80). While hiding out in the fields, he is described as waking up like a "stupid chicken" (83), drinking out of a pool like a "mule" (157), and dreaming of dogs biting at his heels (164). His last relationship to animals occurs when he kills his neighbor's parrots in a rage after finding Jinju's hanged body and then breaks down crying in front of a red pony (192–193). Caged up like an animal at the end of the story, he abandons his rationality in favor of an uncontrollable rage against all government cadres, even the procurator who is trying to help him.

Gao Yang is the second most important male character. His name is literally "High (= Big) Goat/Sheep," but it is also a homophone for "young lamb," a symbol of innocence or docility. In jail he too is described as a rat in the clutches of a cat (102). Although he is sometimes courageous, he is basically a follower, and his stint in jail, especially his visit to the cell of a man condemned to execution the next day, is enough to convince him never again to resist what the authorities do to him. He is also described as a dog. In his jail cell, the middle-aged bully reviles him as a "filthy tail-wagging ass-licking cur" just before he punches him in the chest, causing him to vomit up the special noodles he was given for his illness (186). This is a cruel epithet from the mouth of a thoroughly repugnant person, but in a sense it is an accurate description of Gao Yang's character. He is used to being kicked around by the rural cadres, people no less ruthless and cruel than this jailhouse bully, and he simply lacks the courage to stick up for his rights, which experience has taught him he does not have anyway. He buries his mother surreptitiously and refuses under torture to reveal where, but unlike Gao Ma or the young army officer, he is too afraid of the authorities to confront them directly. His participation in the riot was as a confused follower, but under interrogation, like Ah Q of old but for different reasons, he admits to what he did not intentionally do and signs a confession. Like the majority of China's peasants, he is satisfied with the gains available under the reforms and only hopes to go on enjoying whatever the higher-ups are willing to give him.

Fang Jinju (Golden Chrysanthemum)'s healthy twenty-two-year-old peasant beauty is seen by Gao Ma as "just like [that of] a young heifer" (15). When she runs away with him and after they make love (like animals) in a field, she tells Gao Ma she has given him everything: "Gao Ma, now I've given you everything. I'm just like a dog now; as soon as you call me, I'll just run along with you" (88). She collapses and cries out as her labor pains begin: "Child—you're biting me open—biting me open—I'm crawling on the ground just like a dog" (114). In the end she too abandons her rationality and commits suicide. The last creature she sees is also a red pony. Her mother, Aunt Fang, is described as an old bitch and an old cow in a terribly sad scene when the pregnant Jinju visits her while she is tied to a tree in front of the local government offices, waiting to be taken to jail. When Jinju wakes her from her exhausted sleep, "Gao Yang sees Aunt Fang stick out her white-spotted tongue and lick Jinju's forehead, like an old bitch licking a puppy, like an old cow licking a calf" (53). Uncle Fang and his cow are hit and killed at the same time by a high cadre's car, which Gao Yang sees as "a leaping black beast with huge staring eyes" (217). At home later when his sons remove his body from the cart, "the old man lies there on the ground like a dead dog" (222). Having lived a bestially hard life, and having been run over and killed like an animal on the road, even in death he looks like an animal. Actually in death he is worth less than an animal. His sons refuse their mother's tearful appeal to carry him into the house and lay him down on the *kang*. They leave him lying there face up in the yard while they set to work to clean and dress the cow as village Chairman Gao Jinjiao suggests. Although they will have to pay a ten-*yuan* tax to the village Party Committee for selling beef, at least the dead cow can bring in a little money. As for their father, they will have to *pay* to have him cremated. The last we see of Uncle Fang is when his wife is sitting beside his body, cleaning the maggots out of his nose and ears.

The red pony mentioned above seems, like the crystal carrot in the story by that name, to be a symbol of Gao Ma and Jinju's fragile hope for a life of love and happiness. It joins Gao Ma shortly after he is beaten and tossed into a field by the Fang brothers, and its presence comforts him (32). When Gao Ma recovers from his second and near fatal beating, the red pony appears and Jinju hears Gao Ma's heart beating to the rhythm of the pony's prancing hooves

(129). Remembering the red pony and the colors she saw while making love with Gao Ma helps a delirious Jinju bear the pain of the beating her father gives her (149). The red pony is helpless, however, to prevent Jinju's suicide, because in her despair she rejects it. As her labor pains increase, she tries to convince her unborn child that life is not worth being born into. Just then the pony runs over and looks at her, and when she cries, tears come into the pony's eyes. When the child says it sees the sun, smells flowers, and wants to touch the pony's head, Jinju strikes the pony and drives it away. "Child, there's no red pony; it's only a shadow!" she screams, and the child gives up and stops moving (151). The last time we see the red pony is when it looks on pityingly while Gao Ma cries for the dead Jinju not to leave him. The pony then runs off, gradually "swallowed up by the darkness" (193). With it goes all hope for these unfortunate peasant lovers.

This pervasive animal imagery supports a fundamentally different argument from that of Lu Xun's May Fourth usage. From it we can abstract three interrelated themes: the peasants' material and spiritual poverty often reduces them to a state lower than that of the animals;[44] this state of impoverishment is reinforced not by culturally determined character in the abstract but by specific political institutions of superiority and subordination in the countryside; and the peasants are victims of the political domination of corrupt rural cadres, which is analogous to that of stronger and fiercer animals over weaker ones. The police and the cadres are described as cats catching mice (10) and wild beasts ("the fierceness of a lion") pouncing upon innocent and unsuspecting cattle (217).

In the final analysis, however, the peasants in *Garlic Song* are not all cattle willing to be slaughtered or lambs waiting patiently to be fleeced by the authorities. And they are not latter-day Ah Qs. Ah Q's character defects have been summarized as follows: cowardice, greediness, ignorance, spinelessness, a fence-sitting attitude, a penchant for bullying the weak and cowering before the strong, a gift for self-deluding rationalizations that turn real defeats into spiritual victories, and lack of an interior self. He has a slave mentality completely lacking in the moral qualities of love and honesty.[45] He represents Lu Xun's totalistic revulsion at the moral failings of traditional Chinese culture. Though some of Mo Yan's peasants, most notably the rural cadres and a traditional rural family patriarch, may be seen to have some of Ah Q's character defects, most of them do not. Despite their defeat and despair, Jinju and Gao Ma are certainly not without love and honesty, and they have a very rich interior self. It is just this interior self that, as we have seen, Mo Yan takes great pains to reveal to the reader. Precisely because we are led to think and feel through their interior selves, their story moves us and provokes us to thought. By means of Gao Ma, Jinju, Gao Yang, Aunt Fang, and the unnamed peasant masses' struggles against traditional family and government oppression, we are made aware that it is not some abstract and holistic "culture" that keeps the peasants down, but rather specific political and economic institutional arrangements that ought to be changed in the interests of a better life. Culture as a whole not being the deterministic cause of modern China's every weakness, Mo Yan's work offers hope of gradual, dialectic changes—of reform rather than revolution—to facilitate improvement in every aspect of modern Chinese life.

The political outlook of the young army officer is a result of just such changes as they might have taken place in the decade since 1978. He is also a peasant. At least he is from a peasant family, and he returns to his native village to help his family out during busy periods. His appearance at the mass trial articulates the position of the peasants and the implied author of this proreform novel. I have no doubt that he speaks for the flesh-and-blood author as well. His speech to the court, set in the summer of 1987, is sadly evocative of grievances against the rural cadres—their economic corruption, local government violations of national laws, nepotism, and bureaucratism—that would lead to the democratic protest movement of the spring and summer of 1989. As he says, "the accused Gao Ma's shouting out 'Down with corrupt officials! Down with bureaucratism!' represents a progressive awareness on the part of the peasants, and really does not amount to the crime of counter-revolutionary incitement!" (283). The peasants' social awareness is increasing, they consciously favor the reforms of the past eight years, they want the reforms to continue, but the local cadres are too greedy and corrupt. Their squeeze operations threaten both the peasants' livelihood and the success of the national reform movement. In the context of the reforms then being carried out by the highest Party and government leadership under the direction of now deposed Party Secretary Zhao Ziyang, this novel pleads for the extension of those reforms to the grass roots in order to head off the kind of understandable but destructive peasant violence represented by the Paradise County garlic riot. It is not peasant violence, however understandable, that can save the Chinese countryside. It is more vigorous Party and government enforcement of the laws against corruption, more awareness on the part of the peasants, and increasing adherence to the reform movement by the rural cadres. The narrator's final ironic report of "grapevine rumors" is sadly predictive of what did in fact happen in the Chinese countryside over the course of the two years following the real "garlic riot" upon which this novel is based.

3 | Shen Congwen's Legacy in Chinese Literature of the 1980s

Shen Congwen (1902–1988) was once one of modern China's most creative and influential writers. His disciples included Xiao Qian, Tian Tao, Liu Zuqun, Cheng Yingliu (Liu Jin), Lin Pu, and Wang Zengqi; his sometime protégés, Bian Zhilin, Li Guangtian, and He Qifang. But his larger influence naturally was through his many works. With a touch of exaggeration, the West Hunanese Ling Yu credits Shen Congwen with China's first literary involvement in "rural subject matter," "lyric rural romanticism," and "cultural holism."[1]

By 1949 Shen Congwen and those who wrote like him, Wang Zengqi included, had ceased to write fiction. Shen's works were effectively banned in 1953. China's Communist writers could enjoy access to copies remaining in libraries and private collections, but they were not interested. Shen's students ceased to visit him, and his very name was stricken from the literary histories, except for a few that put in a bad word for him in passing.

Yet, in the 1980s, dozens of new Chinese writers were again being compared to Shen Congwen and linked to him by influence: Cai Cehai (Tujia), Gu Hua, Han Shaogong, He Liwei, Jiang Zidan, Ling Yu (Miao), Liu Jianping, Mo Yingfeng, Nie Xinsen, Peng Jianming, Shi Tairui, Shui Yunxian, Sun Jianzhong (Tujia), Tan Tan, Wei Yang, Wu Xuenao (Miao), Xiao Jianguo, Xiao

Yuxuan, Xie Pu, Xu Xiaohe, Yan Jiawen (Tujia), Ye Weilin, Ye Zhizhen, and Zhong Tiefu (Dai). And this lists only Hunanese, omitting writers whose alleged indebtedness to Shen seems dubious (like Can Xue) and minor West Hunanese local colorists who follow Shen too closely for their own good.[2]

What are we to make of this sudden turnaround? And do Shen Congwen's May Fourth works and those by 1980s writers shed any light on each other?

Cross-Cultural Problems in the Writing of Literary History

Four kinds of methodological difficulty emerge. First, the sterility of Chinese letters from 1949 to 1979 denied later Chinese writers continuous twentieth-century literary traditions to develop, and that in turn denies us "tradition" as a tool for interpreting literary history. The hiatus looms so large that we can be startled to see any continuities between May Fourth and the 1980s works, hence prone to exaggerate them. Or do we still tend to overlook continuities, having forgotten that the metatradition of imitating literary models transcends fickle trends in content, style, and ideology? Shen Congwen claimed to have influenced Sha Ting, who flourished under Mao; works by Yan Wenjing and even Liu Baiyu may have affinities with Shen's.[3]

A second problem is the irrelevance of much of the most highly charged criticism in the West. Despising traditional "source hunting," formalists, from the New Critics on, have disdained historical questions. An influential statement by Claudio Guillén reveals ambivalence even in that relatively sympathetic comparatist.[4] Guillén claimed, unexceptionably, that influence takes place psychologically, in the mind of an author, not literarily, between two texts. But he also called for a fail-safe theory of literary creation (that is, of psychology, and more, since psychology does not make value judgments on creativity as we mean it), while continuing to scorn *rapports de fait* (extratextual "direct confirming evidence"), though whether, say, B has read texts by A is a firmer statement about B than most that psychology can make. Deconstruction and reader-response approaches remove the author as creator from textual studies still further, although reception theorists do help us to understand indebted authors as readers of those who influenced them.[5] To be sure, Shen Congwen's works are read differently by Gu Hua, Wang Zengqi, and He Liwei. Yet the uniformities in how they read him are just as remarkable.

A third problem is the incompatibility of Chinese and Western assumptions about literature. When so many claim influence from Shen Congwen, even the "solid" world of *rapports de fait* must come under scrutiny, not just for significance but for validity. The high Chinese valuation of literary indebtedness is changing; in one overreaction, a story by Ye Weilin was criticized simply for resembling Turgenev's *A Sportsman's Tale*.[6] But in most Chinese circles it is still a matter of pride to be the disciple of a worthy master—like Lu Xun.

The divergence in scholarship runs deeper than that. Aside from the many articles that are cavalier with facts,[7] one finds in China a continued penchant for classifying authors into schools according to a few shared traits and tracing presumed influence accordingly. This essay eschews that approach, but in China it is so widespread as to affect creative writing itself. To use Stanley Fish's term, Chinese critics in this vein are an "interpretive community" of some authority.[8] And there are even more fundamental gulfs, beginning with vocabulary, that *are* potentially absorbable at least by relativist Western critics. Take, for instance, this interesting, although to me not yet fully usable, observation by Cai Cehai: "He Liwei has Shen Congwen's style, while Sun Jianzhong and Xiao Jianguo share his spirit."[9]

To give Chinese values their due, nail down *rapports de fait* without which our textual analyses might remain mere studies of literary parallelism, and enter into the psychology of the authors as far as we can, this essay takes a two-track approach, contextual and textual. Unfortunately, here one encounters the fourth and most serious handicap: most Chinese authors have not published revealing-enough diaries, letters, or manuscript marginalia for reconstruction of their mental universes as has been done for Coleridge, Melville, and, if I may say so, Shen Congwen.[10]

The social links to Shen are unequivocal. The authors cited as influenced by Shen Congwen are related, or have willed themselves to be related, to him through very familiar kinds of personal and regional bonds. The writers are almost a community, a *zuojia qun*, not on the basis of one abstract criterion of region or affiliation, but due to combinations of those traditional individual bonds that link A to B to C to D, and thus, potentially, A to D. Shen Congwen's literary resistance to politics is one of the central links. Society so overwhelmed literature during the Mao years that one must take seriously even such vague statements as "Shen Congwen influenced us by his personal example as much as by his works. He was independent [of the Party line]."[11] In an environment in which authors may truly ponder whether or not to think for themselves, an apotheosized loner like Shen Congwen can exert such an influence, a strong psychological influence of the sort Guillén would have us search for.

China's literary press likes to speak in regional terms, of a "Hunan Army" *(Xiang Jun)* that includes even Can Xue, whose abstract modernism lies at an opposite pole from the Hunanese local color that characterizes most other young Hunanese.[12] Can Xue has ties of friendship to some of the latter, and Hunanese do stick together; even Han Shaogong's *Hainan Documentary Literature* was edited in Changsha. Today, Tujia and Miao authors from West Hunan can bond with Changsha writers, if only from their perception of shared oppression by the eastern seaboard, the capital, and their ever-leftist provincial government. But not all Hunanese writers belong to the special fraternity that concerns us, whereas Jiangsu native Wang Zengqi does, even by acknowledgment of the Hunanese; Jiang Zidan chose him to write the preface for He Liwei's first story collection.[13]

The period 1979–1989 is already long enough to entail the kinds of methodological problems associated with distinguishing between influence from a single major author such as Shen Congwen and a tradition created by many authors.[14] In the words of Can Xue, "We [in my generation] were influenced less by Shen Congwen than by He Liwei."[15] That leaves open the possibility of indirect influence, from Shen Congwen via He Liwei. But Shen himself belonged to a tradition of sorts; he once attributed his "rural lyricism" to Fei Ming. Thus Wang Zengqi, choosing to overlook the more obvious affinity of He Liwei for Shen Congwen, pointed out that the younger Hunanese author's rural lyricism reminded him of Fei Ming's. (He

Liwei had never read Fei Ming, though he acknowledged similarity after the fact.)[16]

We ought not to cast our net too narrowly. When an author as seminal as Shen Congwen influences other writers, the result is not necessarily a parallelism of technique, subject matter, or effect. If Shen has perhaps influenced Sha Ting and Sun Li, and once upon a time influenced and been influenced by Ding Ling, how do we know that he had no impact on Wang Meng, Bai Hua, Jia Pingwa, or Ah Cheng (the last two cases have already been suggested),[17] or indeed Ba Jin, Lao She, and Wen Yiduo, earlier on? Focus on the most obvious affinities, literary or sociological, may lead downward toward lesser and perhaps less-original authors.

And how absolute was the hiatus of 1949–1979? Did old or new traditions in fact exist in those years, ones still viable today? Some speak of a post-Mao Peking School, descended from a 1930s Peking School under Shen Congwen, now "headed" by Wang Zengqi and Liu Xinwu (not a one of whom was born in Peking). The idea was mostly just a polemical concept even in the 1930s.

Are 1980s authors who write about rural subject matter, then, heir to a *xiangtu* (rural) tradition that waxed after 1949, possibly after being born under writers such as Lu Xun and Shen Congwen in the "old society"? Since oceans of Maoist works were, to begin with, set in the countryside, the post-1949 *xiangtu* tradition that Liu Shaotang and Sun Li lay claim to would have to contain a less politicized view of the countryside to profess any difference.

Whether such a *xiangtu* literature did exist after 1949, where it came from, and how influential it was, are interesting questions, but they are enmeshed in polemics. Wang Zengqi warns that in current usage, "*xiangtu* literature" is writing that looks to China's Maoist past. Comforted by the fact that the concept and the post-1949 works associated with it are seldom invoked by our Hunanese authors, who typically point to pre-1949 works as having led them back onto the path of creativity, I omit these questions.[18]

This essay deals with four 1980s authors whose reputations are national, not provincial. After assembling the meager available facts about how they interacted with Shen Congwen and his works, I shall examine a major work or two by each to see what inferences may be drawn. My study of Gu Hua is formalistic. For Wang Zengqi, psychological inferences seem possible. In the case of He Liwei, the focus is on style. For Han Shaogong, the link to Shen is through an intellectual construct they shared, a modern-day myth.

Gu Hua's Selective Imitation: Chapters and Verse

Gu Hua's origin and his works' relationship to it are sufficiently reminiscent of Shen Congwen's that some have confused the two writers as regionalists of the same region. It is in that ultimately rather superficial man-land relationship that Shen's chief "influence" rests.

Gu Hua (b. 1942) is from a foothill village in Jiahe County (region: southern Hunan), near the Guangdong and Guangxi borders. The minorities that have contributed to the local culture are Yao and Zhuang rather than West Hunan's Miao and Tujia, but they share with Shen's hill folk a greater sexual freedom for youngsters and widows, a tradition of antiphonal boy–girl singing across mountain slopes, lore preserved in the memories of singing masters and oral storytellers, colorful ethnic female dress, and special turns of speech. Many of these aspects make their way into Gu Hua's novels. He was particularly moved by the three-day-and-night wedding song festivals for which his region was famous, and what he heard from storytellers. Also like Shen Congwen, he was born into a declining landlord family, was sketchily self-educated, and got to know his corner of Hunan as a poverty-stricken exile from home. Shen Congwen became a wanderer in the army when his father abandoned and bankrupted his family; Gu Hua's journeys came from his father's bad class status and imprisonment, about 1960.[19]

Gu Hua is relatively quick to attribute his style to authors he has read, and lately he has claimed that his fiction was "learned under Shen Congwen."[20] He means his recent fiction, for he had been writing stories for twenty years in a standard socialist-realist mold not very reminiscent of Shen or most other writers of Shen's generation. Gu Hua's translator, Gladys Yang, indicates that he made a study of Shen Congwen and Zhao Shuli just prior to penning his major works *Furongzhen* (Hibiscus Town), *Futuling* (Pagoda Ridge), and "Paman qing teng de mu wu" (The Log Cabin Overgrown with Creepers), a story with a Yao heroine. Liu Shaotang, the journal publisher of *Hibiscus Town*, boasted that Hunan had "produced another Shen Congwen," a linkage that became disparaging in the mouths of others as early as 1982. Ironically, although Gu Hua's quite political fiction did cast deep doubt on core attributes of Chinese socialism, his critics considered it more damaging to allege that he had inherited Shen Congwen's commitment to art at the expense of ideology. Being influenced by Shen subsequently became a major charge against Gu Hua under the more understandable class theory that "Shen Congwen prettifies the old society, [leaving] Gu Hua to uglify the new."[21]

Gu Hua saw in Shen Congwen's works a "special artistic quality" and a "beauty of human nature" in his characters. At the Chinese Writers' Association training class he attended in the spring of 1980, as he began drafting *Hibiscus Town* and "The Log Cabin Overgrown with Creepers," Gu Hua asked, in vain, that Shen Congwen be invited as a teacher. A year later he paid the older writer his first visit. Shen Congwen had read *Hibiscus Town*, an honor he scarcely paid other contemporary writing, and had enjoyed it. He gave Gu Hua some fatherly advice, established a long-term friendship with him, and gently fielded his innocently hopeful query: "Mr. Shen, so many people have called me your disciple, 'Shen Congwen the second'; I'm really embarrassed to hear such talk, but what do you think?" (Shen responded that Gu Hua was more political, more didactic, and far more prone to use classical clichés [*chengyu*].[22] Shen Congwen's success in breaking out from an economically underdeveloped part of Hunan to become a major Chinese writer surely gave Gu Hua much personal career inspiration. But to judge influence, let us compare the two authors' master works: Gu Hua's *Hibiscus Town* and Shen Congwen's *Bian cheng* (Border Town).

Viewed from a distance, *Hibiscus Town* appears to have taken *Border Town* as a model for emulation in theme, setting, and "ethos." The novels share a restriction of the action to one small town, an economy of narration and dialogue, an ill-fated romance that carries the plot, and a final sentence that leaves the novel open-ended. But these features are skeletal. A close reading of the two novels' four opening chapters uncovers finer parallels in structure and set pieces that suggest imitation. And yet, when we pull back again to the midground, the politics in *Hibiscus Town* come into view in such a way as to create a world wholly different from that of the lyric and metaphysical *Border Town*. Gu Hua's first four chapters are the exception. And that proves just how superficial Shen's influence has been.

Hibiscus Town is what Chinese critics might call a *fengsu hua*, a "portrait of local folkways."[23] The mores in Hibiscus resemble those in Chadong, Shen's "border town," down to the stilt houses and seasonal customs, and both are border towns. Gu Hua has even stretched geography to locate his fictitious setting in a *sanbuguan*, or no-man's land between three provinces, like Chadong, which really is in such a place. Shen Congwen did not, however, name his novel *Chadong*, but *Border Town*. It lies symbolically across many brinks in the lives of its characters. But Gu Hua's title, too, is symbolic. According to a Five Dynasties allusion best known to Gu Hua's generation from a poem by Mao Zedong, "Furong" represents Hunan ("Furongguo," the ancient kingdom of hibiscus, or more probably lotus blossoms). The trope dates back to the *Li sao* (On Encountering Sorrow),[24] which heightens the identification of Hunan with ancient Chu, as Shen also was fond of doing.

As to ethos, Gu Hua, like Shen, flavors his novel with authentic local folksongs. His girls and boys in love serenade each other with antiphonal songs and romance each other between ferry crossings, being forward in action but innocent at heart. Despite strict mores, his characters are apt to have had a love affair or two outside of marriage, and Gu Hua's narrator does not censure them: "Who didn't sow a few wild oats before marriage?" (25). Older generations may have come to tragic ends (like Cuicui's parents), but there are no evil characters at the outset. As late as chapter 4, when the villain Wang Qiushe is introduced, we find him pitiable rather than frightening. Character is delineated with a few simple strokes, and motivation, as in Shen Congwen's *Border Town*, is indicated through simple speech and exterior gestures rather than interior monologues of the sort found in later chapters of *Hibiscus Town*. "Fate" motivates the plot. Like the heroine of "Guisheng," Sister Hibiscus is told by a fortune-teller that she is destined to cause the demise of her husband.

Such similarities might of themselves be called simply Gu Hua's homage to Shen Congwen. But in the early chapters of *Hibiscus Town* there is much more, a virtual study of *Border Town*. Gu Hua's description of Hibiscus Town at the outset appears to imitate Shen Congwen's of Chadong in style, set pieces, and even phrasing. Gu Hua opens most of his regional novels with such a formula, and this continues still in such recent works as *Zhen nü* (Chaste Women) and *Rulinyuan* (The Scholars' Garden, 1990).[25] His peculiarity is a penchant for locating his setting in time—with "allusions" to history, local products, and an account of the derivation of the place name, as in Shen Congwen's story "Xue" (Snow) and his travelogues. For Gu Hua, the special bow to historical origins supports subsequent themes about the stubbornness of Chinese "feudal" habit and the timeless decency it so often undoes (rather than serve an antiquarian interest, as in Wang Zengqi's works). Even Shen Congwen is formulaic, as may be seen in the relatively uniform scene settings of his *Border Town*, autobiography, and *Chang he* (Long River). I have argued elsewhere that Shen's panoramic view of Chadong is itself indebted to Gorky's description of a provincial Russian town in *Mother.*[26]

Border Town has two consecutive geographical openings. Chapter 1 leads us up a highway and a stream until we meet the central characters, a ferryman and his granddaughter Cuicui, at a crossing just a *li* upstream from the town. Chapter 2 starts over again, with a panoramic description of Chadong, then follows its streets back to the stream and the other major characters, wharfmaster Shunshun and his two sons, both of whom are destined to love the beautiful and innocent Cuicui. Chapter 3, describing the annual Dragon Boat races, is followed by a flashback chapter, recalling Cuicui's first trip to see them. Then the action begins, in present time.

Gu Hua's chapter titles in part 1 of *Hibiscus Town* suggest a succession of nonlinear, independently standing chapters, each its own ethnographic essay (chapter 1 is "Local Customs," chapter 5 is "A Feast for the Mind and *Wedding Songs*"), or an exposition about one or two of the major characters—for Gu Hua, more like Shen Congwen than most epic writers of the 1980s, fashions his plot using just a half-dozen named actors. (And Gu Hua, even more than Shen Congwen, takes his characters and plots from life, typically from tragic cases he has heard about.)[27] Gu Hua's structure is in reality far more linear than the thematic chapter titles suggest; in this it is like Shen Congwen's, except that it has one geographical starting point instead of two. A view of the town leads to an account of its history, to its streets and its stream, to the calendar of festivals and to the market, and finally to the beautiful and innocent heroine Sister Hibiscus' bean curd stand, to what goes on there, and how fairly she treats her customers, thanks to country custom. Gu Hua lets us listen in as she banters with her customers. The stall is the equivalent of Cuicui's ferry, where Shen Congwen presents a short disquisition on the ferryman's refusal to take money, again with sample snippets of rustic bantering. (The formula is repeated in *Long River*, at a tangerine orchard whose owner distributes the fruit to passersby for free.) Gu Hua's chapter 2, titularly about a female character, Li Guoxiang, provides a flashback of Li's past, but with a focus on her prior romances (much like Shen Congwen's flashback recounting of how Shunshun won his fortune), and this leads to the main subject, an overview, still panoramic, of the male characters in town, some of them eligible and some of them not. The third chapter starts anew with the river, à la Shen Congwen, telling of the events it has witnessed and the fate of the hibiscus trees lining its bank, then proceeds to the relationship between Sister Hibiscus and Comrade Li Mangeng, in flashback. With the onset of chapter 4, a negative character is introduced, and history begins at last to move.

Even certain sentences in *Hibiscus Town* are startlingly like Shen Congwen's. Gu Hua presents a virtual list of ten consecutive seasonal festivals: "On the third of the third lunar month they made cakes; on the eighth of the fourth month they steamed rice flour and meat; on the Double Fifth they prepared glutinous rice dumplings and wine with realgar and mugwort," and so on, until the twelfth month.[28] Only Shen Congwen could be so relentlessly complete in his ethnography, notably in *Long River*: "At the Time of Eating Food Cold and the Qingming Festival afterward they would go up to their ancestors' graves, gathering there for a picnic of boiled Hunan preserved pork. On the Dragon Boat Festival they wrapped glutinous rice dumplings and hung seasonal artemisia on the door . . . in the sixth month . . . in the seventh month" and so on, likewise to the end of the year.[29] Human life merges with the cycles of nature.

Gu Hua's style is not Shen Congwen's, although both authors write in the vernacular and mostly without dialect. Gu Hua uses a little classical syntax in the very first sentence of *Hibiscus Town*, but his sentences must generally be called simpler and more colloquial than Shen's idiosyncratic style. He does, however, borrow a few stylistic devices from Shen. Gu Hua periodically recaps previous action with a short and folksy summary: "In her private life, Li Guoxiang often found herself stranded, but politically she forged full-sail ahead" (27). Or he comments with a plain but pithy metaphor: "She very soon joined the Party and was promoted. But nothing is ever plain sailing." Adages are self-consciously quoted "from the folk": "'Do business with a smile, you'll make a pile.' Yuyin had learned this from her parents." Above all, the country characters converse with each other in jokes, riddles, and feigned insults—in the early chapters only.

Gu Hua's quotation of Shen is limited to the first four chapters. After the action starts, the novels of Gu Hua and Shen Congwen diverge so much that the borrowings at the start of *Hibiscus Town* reveal in the novel a great, unmarked seam; midway through part 1, Gu Hua's work is transformed from a timeless social panorama of a sleepy mountain town into a political novel: the telling (sometimes repetitious, in a way that Shen Congwen is not) of a historical tragedy. Content, style, and mood differ on either side of the divide. Shen Congwen's Chadong, by contrast, remains eternal and inviolable, despite two deaths and its heroine's loss of innocence, and this is reinforced by the uniformity in Shen Congwen's style.

The bulk of *Hibiscus Town* in fact resembles the epic tradition of social realism that has dominated the Chinese novel for the past sixty years. Gu Hua's politics are *anti*-Maoist, showing how political movements destroy his characters, but no longer does he, in Shen's tradition, reveal their dreams, their relationship to nature, or the outer gestures that give away their inner thoughts. Instead he dramatizes their arguments about class stand, and when they are alone, presents rhetorically charged interior monologues in which they puzzle out their own future or the reasons for the other characters' slights and reprisals. Like any pre-1980s novelist, Gu Hua telegraphs the direction of his plot by dividing his characters in advance into good souls and bad ones. He intervenes in the text, occasionally sermonizing about the story in the first person like a traditional storyteller: "Here I would like to point out that this spate of modern superstitions was a new variety of the benighted feudal ideas which had prevailed in China for thousands of years" (151). The country people become "typical characters," socially defined by the buffeting they take during campaigns. When Gu Hua departs from the social script, it is again to generalize and philosophize: "Time is a river, a river of life, flowing through men's memories" (202). The sentiments are fully in sympathy with Shen Congwen's, but the statement of them could not be more at odds with his style. Gu Hua has "learned" from his teacher, copied his rural lyricism more exactly than any other, but in the end taken a far different path—reverted, in form if not in content, to habits from before the thaw.

The indebted author can surpass his or her predecessor, even be the more original author. While some political critics do prefer Gu Hua's writing to Shen Congwen's,[30] most of us would consider that evaluation grotesque. Yet Gu Hua's fiction points to absences in Shen Congwen's work: not just of a sense of history (something Shen was only working up to in *Long River*), but of a strong plot line and a theme, a "point." Still, the fact that Shen Congwen could captivate readers of *Border Town* without dramatizing social conflicts, and hint at psychology and the cosmos with mere signs and gestures, illustrates the subtlety of his craft. It is not local color alone that sustains the work of either Shen Congwen or Gu Hua. Or did Gu Hua, in his pursuit of political themes, abandon even local color?

Wang Zengqi's Revival of Shen: "Misreading" the Teacher

Since Wang Zengqi also writes "pastoral" scenes, again using anecdotes from his childhood, it is easy to assume that he, too, recapitulates Shen Congwen's romantic relationship between "man and land"—only more deeply than Gu Hua, since Wang has the linguistic skills of an older generation and a broader memory of ideologies and sensibilities, and appears to duplicate Shen's own moral dichotomy of city artificiality versus rural spontaneity. In truth, Wang's relationship with Shen, though closer than Gu Hua's, is much more tortured, and his ideological agenda has more complicated origins.

Born in 1920, Wang began writing fiction in 1940 under the "old society," after a formal education of the sort not enjoyed by Shen Congwen or equaled by Gu Hua and the younger Hunanese. Virtually apprenticed to Shen as a creative writer at Southwest Associated University in the 1940s, he published a book of stories after the war, but abandoned the genre for thirty years in the New China, except for a few he penned during the 1961–1962 thaw. A journal editor subsequently sent down to labor as a rightist (1958–1961), Wang turned to Peking opera, an art form Shen had always detested, when Jiang Qing picked him as a librettist for her reformed operas during the Cultural Revolution.[31] He remains with the Peking Opera Troupe of Beijing even now. But in 1980 Wang was suddenly "reborn" as a writer in Shen Congwen's image.

It was in May 1980, when he was possibly in trouble from an implied connection with the Gang of Four and still denying having written fiction,[32] that Wang Zengqi produced "Yibing" (Special Talent), by rewriting an old 1948 manuscript that was returned to him. His first story wholly conceived during the thaw was "Shoujie" (Ordination), composed in August 1980.

Wang Zengqi completed his redraft of "Yibing" on May 20. Meantime, inspired by Shen's May preparation of his old works for republication, Wang had been poring over *Border Town,* noting down what made it great. The result, a sensitively drawn critical essay about the novel, was completed at dawn on May 22 and published in February 1981, thereby breaking Wang Zengqi's spell of silence about Shen Congwen. Later it occurred to Wang that even his adolescent heroine Yingzi in "Ordination" bore unconscious influence from Cuicui in *Border Town.* His return to personal essay writing was likewise preceded by a thoughtful study of Shen Congwen's nonfiction.[33]

Wang Zengqi's continual mention of his old teacher at meetings and in books such as *Wancui wentan* (Literary Talks from My Late Blooming), half of whose longer essays reverently mention "my teacher Shen Congwen,"[34] cast him in the role of major reviver of Shen Congwen's reputation. Shen's rehabilitation rehabilitated Wang Zengqi as well. Wang said that he was noting down Shen's lessons for the sake of the young. Thus he, too, became a teacher, a link in the chain of a tradition. As a creative writer he became the teacher, even the honorary head, of the young people's "search for roots" movement in the mid-1980s.[35]

Wang Zengqi's obsessive concern with his model brings to mind Harold Bloom's problematic of the "anxiety of influence."[36] But though Shen Congwen's creative path no doubt preoccupied Wang and led him to "swerve" from it as a matter of self-definition, that must have been overshadowed by far more gut-wrenching outright guilt and confusion about his authorial identity. For not only had he quit the literary path of Shen Congwen, he had also devoted himself to pet projects of the Gang of Four that overturned the entire May Fourth tradition. The main stress line visible in Wang Zengqi's essays about Shen is still political. He emphasizes that Shen was a patriotic writer who supported the Communist revolution, although this clashes with the apolitical spirit of the fiction of both Shen and Wang, exaggerates Shen's sympathies with the left, and reintroduces an old question about Shen's loyalty that need not have been dignified with a response. Wang harped on Shen's patriotism even in his 1988 memorial piece, when it was time to move on to the reasons for Shen's greatness.[37]

In fact Wang Zengqi remains defensive about himself, and by implication his teacher, when addressing what Chinese critics say is a major trait they have in common: writing of the old society without condemning it. "I don't want there to be too many of my sort of works," he once said.[38] Given the earlier rarity of literary nostalgia about the old society, Shen may have influenced Wang, and Wang may in turn have influenced others, to write in that vein. But here we must adopt what Hermerén calls an "action-dominated" rather than "object-dominated conception of art," and observe that writing nostalgically about the old society has a different import for Wang from the one it had for Shen's generation.[39] If Shen was nostalgic, Wang is "neonostalgic." And Shen Congwen did not paint a pretty picture of pre-1949 *society*. Moreover, Wang Zengqi considers himself

Confucian in outlook[40] (certainly he is not pro-Buddhist, as we shall see from "Ordination"). He extols the high or written culture much more than does Shen Congwen, who cherishes mainly arts, crafts, and oral traditions. "Rehabilitation" of China's old civilization describes not so much the modern fiction of Shen Congwen or Wang Zengqi as it does Wang Zengqi's interest in traditional painting, learning, and, above all, Peking opera, as well as the Confucian side of Wang Zengqi that enters his writing mostly in the essay form. But here too, he parts company with Shen Congwen. Shen disdained the short essay, partly *because* it was linked to the Confucian literati. Best, then, to examine Wang's "swerve" or "poetic misprision," as Bloom would call it, in fiction, the genre both men loved.

That Wang's major stories "Ordination" and "Da Nao jishi" (A Tale of Big Nur, February 1981) are set in the old society, unlike the works of other authors who flourished in 1980–1981, does overshadow the fact that Wang's native region in Gaoyou, Jiangsu, is as far away from Shen Congwen's home culturally and economically as it is geographically. (Wang says that its speech is a peripheral dialect of Mandarin, like West Hunan's.)[41] Wang's characters are, broadly speaking, "country folk," though far from starving; all the parties in "Ordination" are as well-off as Shen's "Sansan" and other millowners' daughters. Like Shen Congwen, Wang Zengqi has an eye out not for farming but for the guild mores of marginal crafts and occupations of the towns and suburbs. In "Big Nur," tinsmiths and porters represent pristine moral communities that are, by virtue of their residence on different sides of a lake spit (of the track, we would say), mutually distinctive and in a hierarchy, with the tinsmiths on top and the more vulnerable porters standing together defensively on behalf of their own. The latter, with their latent *ressentiment,* play the part of Guisheng in Shen Congwen's story by that name, with the tinsmiths filling in for the country shopkeeper's daughter. In both stories, a sublimely innocent star-crossed romance transgresses an age-old social barrier, and the threat to the liaison comes not from tension between the folk communities, but from the outside: from the landlord class and "fate" in Shen's story, and from the town in "A Tale of Big Nur." Wang's town runs roughshod over both folk communities. "Their lives, customs, and morals were quite unlike those of the town dwellers, who wore long gowns and studied Confucian philosophy."[42]

The triumph of "healthy," untrammeled country love over Confucian restrictions is a major theme in Shen Congwen's fiction. Wang as ethnographer writes of the lowly porters: "There was nothing strange about a girl giving birth to an illegitimate child at her mother's home. A married woman could have a lover. The only criterion for a woman to take delight in a man was her consent. Most girls or women asked their lovers for money to buy flowers, but some gave money to their lovers instead" (13–14). Compare this with *Border Town*, on the prostitutes of Chadong: "Border ways are so simple that even these girls remain honest . . . In the case of an old customer, the matter of payment is left up to him."[43]

The same theme dominates "Ordination." Mingzi, an innocent thirteen-year-old boy (about the age of Shen's heroine Cuicui) is ordained after four years of the monk's life. Then his artless little girlfriend, Yingzi, sweeps him off into a reed marsh in a boat, to "become his wife." As in Shen's "After Rain," no strictures from "civilization" can stop the consummation.

"Ordination" is especially reminiscent of *Border Town* in its pacing; even its ribald folksongs contain a direct quotation from Shen Congwen, his favorite "Zhen'gan Song No. 1," which Wang evidently discovered in "After Rain" and rephrased in his Anhui dialect.[44] The formal subject of each story is a rite of passage: Mingzi's ordination and Cuicui's awakening to sexuality. But the narrators frequently stop for flashbacks and for lengthy description: in "Ordination," of the Buddhist temple, its daily, annual, and occasional routines (as during funerals); the bounties of nature in orchards and vegetable gardens (as in "Guisheng"); the skills of local tradesmen; particular customs (when and how girls' hair is tied into a bun, how the locals tie a knot in their belts when wishing upon a shooting star); and local handicrafts, such as shoe embroidery (by Yingzi, as by the women of *Border Town*) and preparation of wedding paraphernalia (by Yingzi's mother, as by various characters in Shen's novel). In *Border Town*, it is the annual Dragon Boat Festival against which Cuicui's progression toward womanhood is set. In "Ordination," the rites and preparations of the monk's life provide the rhythm for a still greater rite of passage—Mingzi's belated discovery that he is a sexual being. In each case, the loss of innocence is symbolized by a painful image. In Cuicui's case, her future love object warns her of being bitten by a fish; in Mingzi's, his future "spouse" warns him that twelve holes will be burned into his scalp with incense sticks. The latter is part of the ordination ceremony, but the Buddhist rite is nearly simultaneous with, and in effect displaced by, the more important and lasting initiation into worldly dust.

Wang Zengqi remembers Shen Congwen telling him to "remain in touch with your characters": make them more than cardboard cutouts, adopt their point of view when writing dialogue and "objective" descriptions of scenery (avoid what Bakhtin calls "heteroglossia"), and identify with them, without embracing them too passionately.[45] Certainly Wang has made his characters and their human predicaments the center of his stories, even while using Shen's stylistic predilection for delineating character and physical traits indirectly (e.g., the beauty of the heroine of "Big Nur," by others' reactions to it).[46] In his optimism he has, like his teacher, seldom written about human evil or even about social impasses that could not be settled by some sort of grudging forgiveness such as that which resolves the crisis in "Xiaoxiao"; in "Big Nur," a meeting is called, the injured family is paid off, and the offending soldier is packed off to another town. As to point of view—though Wang Zengqi's writing is kept in check by an elegant harmony and economy, "Ordination" often enough adopts an Olympian "Confucian" tone (even a cocky one, David Pollard points out)[47] as it lingers over the origins and errors in place names, the motivations for becoming a monk (wealth and power—Wang Zengqi betrays great cynicism about religion), and the reasons why some did or did not win at gambling. Shen Congwen, Gu Hua, and Wang Zengqi have all generally adopted the omniscient narrator of traditional Chinese fiction. It is Shen Congwen who departs from tradition most fully, with his probing of his characters' daydreams, and Wang Zengqi who sticks closest to classical elegance, in action, physical description, and dialogue.

Wang Zengqi's sentences are not just unornamented but short and simple, quite unlike his teacher's at any stage of his career. Nor has he ever launched off on a long and rambling piece like *Long River*, or even *Border Town*. "Brevity" is Wang Zengqi's watchword, as if he had indeed swerved so as to learn from his teacher's "mistakes" as well as his lessons. Despite his defense (in argument) of a natural, discursive *(songsan)* plot, Wang Zengqi carefully plans his stories in advance, working from an outline, and usually achieves the well-made structure with beginning, middle, and end that Shen Congwen achieved only in a few stories of the 1930s—those that now form his "classic" oeuvre. Wang's famous story "Chen Xiaoshou" (Small-Hands Chen) even has an O. Henry–style sudden reversal at the end of its short plot, when a warlord expresses gratitude to a male gynecologist for saving his wife, then has him shot for his familiarity with her. Despite his tolerance of discursiveness, Wang has not only written that fiction should have a (unified) "theme" or "point," he has also explicated the "points" of a few of his own works and reflected his commitment to neat structure back onto Shen Congwen, who may indeed have embraced it in principle, but not consistently in practice.[48]

Here we begin to see Wang Zengqi's swerve from Shen Congwen: a swerve to the left. As Pollard points out, Wang's references to religion are "dismissive or downright hostile."[49] His militia are running dogs of the townspeople; in "Big Nur" it is their leader who spoils a romance between a tinsmith boy and a porter's daughter. Moreover, although the latent tragic tone of *Border Town* is evoked by Wang Zengqi, he undoes it with a happy ending. After the militiaman nearly beats the young tinsmith to death, his lover brings him back to health. The rhetoric closing "Big Nur" directly imitates that of *Border Town*, but then Wang answers his own question, almost as if parodying the earlier novel. Writes Shen Congwen: "He may never come back. Or he may come back tomorrow." Wang Zengqi: "Would Eleventh Boy recover? Possibly. Yes, of course he would!"

Wang Zengqi has grappled with his model and then swerved in the final sentence, evidently to "correct" the gloomy uncertainty in works like *Border Town* and "Guisheng." The outcome is, in a word, positive. Another lesson Wang Zengqi says he learned from Shen Congwen in the 1940s was "Don't ever be cynical." Wang claims that that advice rescued him from a deep and paralyzing pessimism he had acquired from reading in Western modernism.[50] What he neglects to say is that Shen in the 1940s was buttressing his waning interest in life with ecstatic readings in modernist texts.

So Wang Zengqi has driven Shen's tradition in a still more classical and "pastoral" direction: that of *Border Town* without the Freudianism. But he has swerved much further than that. The teacher from whom Wang learned in the 1940s was not the Shen Congwen of *Border Town*, but the Joycian Shen Congwen of "Gazing at Rainbows," the "difficult" Kunming author who favored flowery diction, open-ended essaylike structure, and a contemplative, pantheistic worship of "life."[51] Shen probably guided his students toward well-made structures at the start of their careers, but Wang Zengqi of all people knew the "modern" Shen, for in those days he was a modernist himself.

Wang Zengqi prefers not to dwell on his early experiments. He allows that he was influenced by stream-of-consciousness and existentialism, and that he tried to break down the formal barriers between fiction and the essay; in fact his first works were what Chinese of the 1980s might call "misty poems." "Fuchou" (Revenge, 1944) exemplifies how far he had once ventured from the Shen Congwen of *Border Town*.[52]

Without clarifying the scene, the voice, the time, or the occasion, aside from an epigram from Zhuangzi opposing revenge, Wang's tale relates a young man's daydream, and then a night dream, in free indirect, then direct, stream-of-consciousness style.[53] The opening sentence, lacking a predicate, establishes a synesthetic rather than a logical link to what follows: "A white candle, a half jar of wild honey. Now his eyes could not see the honey. The honey was in the jar and he was sitting on the couch. But he was filled with a sensation of the honey, strong, thick. There was no sour taste in his throat. His appetite was good. He'd hardly vomited in all his life. All one's life. How long that?" The free associations go still further afield. The boy imagines a bald-headed Buddhist monk having white hair, and from that his mother, and from that his little sister. But he has no sister. It can only be his last image of his mother, who has by now grown old at home. Twice the narrative voice breaks into the interior monologue like a Greek chorus (or the ghost of Zhuangzi) to address the traveling young man directly. Gradually one learns that he is on a quest, for the killer of his father. The boy is beginning to vacillate.

Within this fantastic world the young man finally finds himself inexplicably drawn into a dark cave. There he hears a man chiseling into the rock. He is a long-haired monk, with the boy's father's name tattooed on his hand. There is mutual recognition, and the boy forgives. He throws down his sword to help his erstwhile foe to cut a path through the rock.

Illogical progressions, frequent changes in narrative voice, and incomplete sentences render Wang Zengqi's style difficult. Several loose ends, like the honey and candle, suggest a coming reconciliation and breakout into the light, but only vaguely. Even Wang's psychology leads to philosophy, not character study. We cannot of course assume that his modernism comes from Shen Congwen, for Wang had done his own reading in authors as diverse as Woolf and Sartre. But one ideological aspect was nearly unique to the writings of Wang and Shen in the year 1944, when Free China was in danger of losing the war: pacifism. The Daoist (far more than Buddhist) conversion of the young man is evident in his quest to tunnel through to "emptiness" and in his joining of hands with the foe. Shen Congwen was attacked at Kunming simply for writing "literature unrelated to the war effort"; few realized that he was in fact a pacifist. Imagine how bold it was for twenty-three-year-old Wang Zengqi to espouse pacifism, even in fiction.

Yet the Shen Congwen whom Wang has revived is an image of the author as if he had ceased to develop—indeed, as he was before Wang met him. Wang Zengqi has "swerved" not just from his teacher, but from his former self. His atonement *to* Shen Congwen has ended up as atonement *for* him.

He Liwei's Recapitulation: Making Safe Havens

He Liwei acknowledges direct influence from the works of Shen Congwen, and he may also be indirectly indebted, through Wang Zengqi, who for his part cleared the way politically for nostalgic writing. He Liwei's much-acclaimed early stories do not reproduce, but recapitulate, the sensuousness of Shen's early style, when Shen drew upon dialect and local color.[54]

He Liwei, born in 1954 in Changsha, is of China's "rusticated youth" generation. Shen Congwen's writings were barely available during He Liwei's youth, even in Changsha. After serving as a laborer and teacher during the 1970s, He Liwei graduated from Hunan Teachers' College in 1978. He began publishing nationally only in 1983. By then not only the classic works but also the major portion of Shen Congwen's oeuvre were being sold, particularly in Hunan. Today He Liwei is a professional writer still living in Changsha.

The Hunanese countryside is the setting for most of He Liwei's stories, though some unfold in quiet, social backwaters of Changsha. A few are set in Shen Congwen's West Hunan, where He Liwei worked for a year, in 1985. The stories discussed below take place in unspecified rural areas of the province. West Hunanese characterize the dialect in He Liwei's stories as "Changsha dialect."

He Liwei attributes his affinity with Shen to a similar temperament: Shen is an author of many dreams, he says, and he wraps his portraits of West Hunanese lives in dreams (an opinion with which Shen agreed). He Liwei also sees Shen's writing as a quest for a safe haven from the perils of the age, adding that Shen's tribespeople offer such a retreat. This is not meant as criticism; "people *like* to dream," he says.[55]

And so in He Liwei's early works, words like *dreams, hopes,* and *stories* recur as if their intonement could itself impart mystery to the telling. "Taojinren" (Panning for Gold) is subtitled "A Legend Set Out of Time." The ensuing tale is punctuated by the phrases "Nowadays no one knows . . . what was it called? . . . where are they now? . . . mountains with unknown names . . . While there are people on this earth they will always have extraordinarily brilliant dreams. And who knows how many prospectors, enticed by the dream of gold, were led to their deaths? . . . It was . . . the end of one dream and the beginning of the next. The new dream was no more than of the gleaming flame of gold . . . Innumerable fireflies flew up, searching for lost tales with their lanterns."[56] He Liwei's most famous short story is titled "Xiao cheng wu gushi" (No Story in This Little Town).

The moat outside its protective wall, "like the days of the citizens within, had no stories to tell." "Dreams? Sometimes yes, sometimes no."[57] Unfortunately, the dream, legend, and out-of-time themes are repeated too monotonously—in the absence of genuinely fantastic subject matter and imagery—to impart a full sense of remoteness, either directly, in "Panning for Gold," or ironically, in "No Story in This Little Town."

It is his elegiac mood that most reminds He's readers of Shen Congwen. Their styles are far from identical; He Liwei creates a soothing simplicity with short sentences, colloquial grammar, and seemingly childlike repetitions, which nevertheless provide rhythm through parallelism. The repetition in the very title of "Haoqing haoqing de Shamu He" (How Clear How Clear the Fir Tree River) is developed to an extreme in "Baise niao" (The White Birds), whose second paragraph begins, "Raner *changchang* hetan shang, bu jiu ji youle *xiaoxiao* liang hei dian; you *manman* huangdong, *manman* fangda" (But along the long, long riverbank, there soon appeared two tiny, tiny specks; slowly, slowly they shifted from side to side, and slowly, slowly they grew larger). Thus He Liwei, like Shen Congwen, analyzes complicated things into their basic components. The white birds of the story remain just that, for the species is never identified.[58] But, for all the narrative simplicity in such passages as that just cited, He Liwei also follows Shen in favoring a rich and complex vocabulary to describe plants and waters, and he occasionally uses classical vocabulary within the colloquial syntax, such as Shen's favorite *yanran* (just as if), for economy of expression.

Eschewing *chengyu* and four-character phrases, He Liwei creates his own simple and startling metaphors. Stars and the sun "bathe" in the river. A daughter is as clear as grapes. Waves are like flowers, blossoming and then shedding their efflorescence. "On the tall mountains clasping the river bank on either side grew hardy trees, grew weird rocks, each clothed from head to foot in gowns of moss— standing, kneeling, in their verdure, as if listening to an ancient legend, their attitude very solemn, very respectful. It was intriguing."[59] Both authors favor anthropomorphic tropes. Often the romantic eye of the human viewer itself appears, during a direct appreciation ("It was intriguing"; cf. Shen Congwen's famous description of the banks of the You River in *Border Town,* chap. 2). And He Liwei often writes dialogue in local dialect, reminiscent not of the "classic" Shen Congwen, author of *Border Town,* but of the less-refined, early Shen Congwen. The two authors' dialects are not the same, but He Liwei's decision to write in dialect in the 1980s (when other "pastoral writers" such as Gu Hua and Wang Zengqi preferred an elegant *putonghua*) is as startling as Shen Congwen's commitment to his southern dialect in the 1920s. However, by the look of it, He Liwei is again recapitulating Shen's example by weeding out dialect in his later works.

Themes that to the Hunanese mind are "quintessential Shen Congwen" inspired He Liwei's early writing. "How Clear How Clear the Fir Tree River" features a limpid stream and a young country boy's first trip to see the Dragon Boat Festival. The story relates an unusual secondary custom seen also in *Border Town,* of loosing ducks into the river after the race as prizes for any rower or spectator who can catch one. He Liwei adds the interesting detail that the ducks are dosed with alcohol to slow them down. A further comparison with *Border Town* is in fact instructive in showing how abstracted Shen's account is from mainstream Hunanese tradition, for Shen Congwen, unlike He Liwei, does not mention Qu Yuan or the *zongzi* (glutinous rice dumplings) thrown into the river in his memory. Although the river named in the story is not easily located and probably fictitious, discouraging identification of the local culture, many tropes familiar from Shen Congwen's West Hunanese stories add color to this mood piece, such as silver earrings and antiphonal singing, as well as less regionally specific figures, including a country ferryman who makes a deep impression on the story's young protagonist, country folk's passion where festivals are concerned, fruits growing along the roadway, and rowers' chants.

"The White Birds," also filled with water imagery, treats Shen Congwen's favorite themes of childhood innocence and the country folk's superior sensitivity to nature. It moreover develops them together, like Shen Congwen in his "Xue" (Snow), by showing a city boy and his country cousin at play. Simple dramatization of the two boys speaking Xiang dialect is the major narrative mode. At first we know them only as a white boy and a dark boy, the latter "blackened down to his toes, charred by the sun everywhere but on his one remaining front tooth." "Aiyo," says the other, "I'm done in. By that killer sun!"—"Go ahead and rest then. City people aren't up to this," the dark one chides. He promises to catch snakes for his friend and show him all sorts of other marvels. As the boys gather purple purslane in their rustic baskets, the narrator comments, à la Shen Congwen, that only country folk know how to use the herb to flavor the hotness of their red chilies. They create a taste that is unknown to city people.[60]

"No Story in This Little Town" directly pits the mores of country folk against those of travelers from the city. The town has two bean-curd peddlers, an old lady and a hunchback, who have grudgingly learned to share the community's meager demand for their wares. One other thing draws the peddlers into a single moral commu-nity—the pretty young madwoman in town, who parades down the street bearing cape jasmine flowers, singing lewd songs, and loudly accosting every young man she meets for an imaginary love tryst out by the town moat. The two peddlers show their concern by offering her free bowls of their wares in turn, to help settle her down. The city strangers, however, are curious to see if such a pretty and vulner-able young woman might really be induced to meet them. And, in the sight of the locals, they make a spectacle of her by listening to her songs. So the peddlers "run out of food" when the city people drop by. The town has no stories for them.

Three other devices familiar from Shen Congwen appear in He Liwei's stories, which like Shen's are often praised as "prose poems," or accused of plotlessness, which is to say, of lacking action. First, He Liwei uses children's partial comprehension and adults' incom-pletely heard conversations to further pastoralize his already very socially uncomplicated environment. Second, smells and sounds cre-ate mood; in "No Story in This Little Town," an olfactory reference accentuates the main theme of city aggressiveness versus country stolidness with a bit of Daoist logic: "The faded and departed scent of cape jasmine filled every street and lane. But if you made an effort to smell it, it wasn't there" (34). Third, there is also a dialectic of opposites: motion within stillness and kindness within severity (as when the peddlers scold the madwoman while giving her bean curd), and the direct contrast of opposites in descriptions: "Many of the townspeople made their living from little stands. The hot and the cold, the hard and the soft, the sour and the spicy, they sold every style and every kind" (29).

He Liwei's style has recapitulated much of Shen Congwen's achievement, though his indebtedness is sufficiently technical and yet so integrated into original new wholes that one need not speak of imitation. Does He's fiction, then, offer escape from social "reality," as he interprets Shen Congwen's? Without imputing any social motives to He's writing, as is done to Shen's by the leftist critics, perhaps artistically it does. For He Liwei's stories are often lifted up out of any clear social context.

Wang Zengqi's fiction about Buddhist monks and stevedores working for private masters is pointedly about the "old society." He Liwei has never seen the old society; despite the haze of nostalgia, there is no reason to think that he is not writing of China during his own time. Yet social references are so few that he could be writing about any era. "Panning for Gold" is explicitly said to unfold outside of time; even that stipulation is insufficient to buttress its unworldly story of greedy prospectors who give up all their material possessions when a pure woman who has been gradually civilizing them is violated and then killed. He Liwei's vignettes of a Dragon Boat Festival and of peddlers mobilized against ignorant outsiders are equally timeless—the setting could be any time before 1957 or after 1979. "The White Birds" is the exception that proves the rule. Its two little boys, out for a swim, escape to the wildness of a "farther shore." Stripped totally naked, they hide among the reeds to watch a pair of white water birds enjoy their freedom. After the brief, possibly premonitory, trespass against this stillness by the city boy's plan to hit one of the birds with his slingshot, or cage it, the boys accede to its joy in liberty. Then a gong rings. At last it is apparent just why the white boy's grandmother has come down to the countryside. "'Aiyo, I forgot,' said the swarthy one, standing straight up like a rubber ball inflating, mud all over his belly. 'There's a struggle meeting'" (132).

The white birds of freedom take wing, and the safe haven momentarily created for the boys is destroyed. It was, it turns out, a short-lived haven, from politics. And so, perhaps, are He Liwei's other idylls.

Han Shaogong's Bifurcation: Regional Cultural Critique in Reverse

Han Shaogong follows in Shen Congwen's distinctive intellectual tradition of celebrating West Hunan as the "last stand" of the culture of the ancient kingdom of Chu. Yet Han's fiction is spiritually at odds with his theory. This bifurcation in his writing uncovers one in Shen's as well, for Shen's novels, too, praise Chu culture without being truly indebted to it. Perhaps the mutual bifurcation is because Shen Congwen wanted to damn Chinese tradition through the mirror of a good West Hunan, whereas Han Shaogong wants to damn the Chinese tradition through a bad West Hunan. In either case, the authors had to reinvent the regional culture for it to serve as a suitably flexible tool of cultural criticism.

Like He Liwei, Han Shaogong was born in Changsha (Han in 1953, He in 1954) and graduated from Hunan Teachers' College (Han in 1982, He in 1978). But Han Shaogong has a much stronger connection to West Hunan. It is even commonly stated—in error—that Han Shaogong's nine-year youth rustication took place in West Hunan. In fact his place of exile was rural Changle, on the Miluo River at the east end of the province. But this, too, was part of Chu in ancient times. Legend holds that Qu Yuan drowned himself in the Miluo River, and ancient Chu artifacts from a battlefield were dug up in the fields even as Han Shaogong worked on them in the 1970s.[61]

Apart from the broad link to Chu, Han Shaogong is connected to West Hunan through his parents, who are both West Hunanese, and a trip to West Hunan in 1985–1986 to live, work, and "search for roots." He has not expatiated on Shen Congwen's legacy, evidently because he feels both attracted to and repelled by it: "I very much like certain works by Shen Congwen; I like their Eastern-style imperturbability and quietude. His weakness is that he is too escapist.

The ideal would be to keep the strong things understated, while adding movement within the stillness."[62]

It was only in his new, attention-getting works of 1985 that Chinese critics saw in Han Shaogong signs of influence from Shen Congwen (as well as Kafka, García Márquez, and Kundera—Han also counts Zhuangzi and Qu Yuan as favorite authors). But even in 1983 Han had admonished young authors to study Lu Xun and Shen Congwen for lessons on how to show action and the passage of time indirectly. That he practiced this is apparent from a forced example in "Lan gaizi" (Blue Bottlecap), which marks the death of a prisoner with the words, "A pair of chopsticks in the shed went unused that day; a bunk remained empty." Otherwise, Han's style is too consistently dense—nearly half classical in its conciseness—to show much affinity with Shen Congwen's, except for heavy use of reduplicative adjectives and of words favored by Shen Congwen such as *zhaoli* (as a rule).[63]

Han Shaogong's most famous advice to his generation was that they search for native Chinese literary and cultural roots, lest new Chinese literature be condemned eternally to follow the latest trends in the West. To his own question, "Where has the splendid culture of Chu gone to?" he answered, in effect, "to West Hunan." What he sought was not just the language, motifs, symbols, and philosophy from ancient "high culture" preserved in the *Chu ci* (Songs of the South), but a legacy from the preliterate "low" cultural substratum of religion, mores, songs, legends, material culture, and "ethos" of ancient Chu, which many Hunanese presumed, as did Shen Congwen so many years before, to be preserved among West Hunan's tribal hill folk. From this he proceeded to a romantic reconceptualization of Chinese culture as a mélange of regional cultures descended from the ancient kingdoms of the Warring States era: romantic, but also socioculturally deterministic, with obeisances to Hippolyte Taine, who had moved the May Fourth generation of writers. However, whereas the May Fourth writers stressed society as the determinant of literature, Han Shaogong, reacting against Marxist formulations, looked to culture for a new literature.[64]

Han Shaogong considered the rational, modern, urban cultures of today to have come from "primitive" cultures that function instead on the basis of "instinctive" and "nonrational" thought—holistic cultures in which religion, philosophy, science, and art are "not yet fully differentiated." Yet he did not take the "instinctive" mode to be wholly superseded in modern life. "Literary thought" still today is "instinctive thought," he says. Not only do tribal peoples' cultures constitute a treasury of that which is sublime in the *Chu ci*, their instinctive apprehension of reality as such is the missing ancient element in China's modern literature.

Han Shaogong's pronouncements do not mention Shen Congwen, but those who accompanied him to West Hunan in 1985 included Shen's friends and spiritual godchildren Cai Cehai, a Tujia from Longshan, and Ling Yu, a Miao who is a biographer of Shen. Han must have read the accounts of bizarre witchcraft cults and other Chu inheritances in Shen's *Xiangxi* (West Hunan).

The idea of going to West Hunan to find cultural material for fiction certainly was not original with Han. The Hunan branch of the Chinese Writers' Association sent a group of young writers west for that purpose in 1985, including not just Han Shaogong, Cai Cehai, and Ling Yu, but Jiang Zidan, Tan Tan, Tan Zhiheng, Shi Tairui, Xiao Gong, and Zhang Xinqi. That followed a Hangzhou conference about roots in the winter of 1984 attended by young writers and critics; literary historians further trace the "roots" movement to statements by Li Tuo in March 1984, or even a speech by Wang Zengqi in early 1982. Ling Yu thinks the thrust toward West Hunan came from the revival of Shen Congwen and from Fan Wenlan's *Zhongguo tongshi* (Comprehensive History of China, 1978), which intimates that the ancient kingdom of Chu was culturally Miao. There was in the 1980s an upsurge of books about ancient Chu, most of them less speculative than Fan's.[65]

Despite the influence that Han's positive ideas about ancient regional culture had on other writers of his age, they seem to have played little role in his own creativity. Practice seldom directly follows theory. And perhaps Han never fully believed in his beautiful myth. Only a year later he embraced a broad concept of "Eastern culture" (distinct from "Western culture") that inflated his idea of instinctual and holistic regional culture into a national, or even transnational, concept of Orientalism such as might have appealed to Liang Shu-

ming.[66] I shall argue that Han Shaogong from the start, in depicting
the negative side of West Hunanese culture, made it into less of a
regional than a national construct: a symbol of China, and even
human nature. In both its negativity and its abandonment of the
myth of regional uniqueness, Han's idea of West Hunanese culture
became quite the opposite of Shen Congwen's myth. Yet most
"roots" writers have been attacked on the same grounds as Shen
Congwen: for valuing the past.

Han's most positive vision of a nonrational land appears in his story
"Guiqulai" (Return, 1985). The setting is evidently the mountains of
West Hunan, as one judges by the villagers' dialect, opium growing,
and women's earrings. The title, strangely, alludes not to the *Chu ci*
(whose "Summons of the Soul" resounds so often with the words
"Return [*guilai*] oh soul!" that Han's title resonates with the "Summons" even so), but to Tao Qian's *ci* poem "Return." Tao Qian does
himself call up the memory of Qu Yuan as dissident poet, and the
reader is apt to recall Tao's story of a fisherman stumbling upon a
Shangri-La of warm-hearted villagers. The Peach Blossom Spring is
traditionally linked to Taoyuan, in lower West Hunan.[67]

Three consecutive realities confront the reader of "Return." The
first-person narrator, a young man identifying himself as Huang
Zhixian, ascends to a mountain village he has never seen before, but
every detail of which is strangely familiar, as if by déjà vu. And the
villagers already know him, as one "Glasses Ma," a sent-down youth
who came among them as a teacher until he was removed to jail
down in the country eight years earlier—for committing a murder,
they all agree. So far the scene is reminiscent of *The Trial,* with
Huang Zhixian as Joseph K., a lone voice protesting his innocence
while an unreal but universal conspiracy forces on him an identity
that is alien and unfathomable—though also alarmingly convincing
in a subconscious way. As he vainly struggles to assert his separate
identity, the villagers shower on him warmth and hospitality of the
sort reserved for kinsmen. This ushers in the second reality. The
narrator finds himself talking to villagers with the privileged knowledge of an insider—as is only too apparent to the puzzled reader.
He speaks of a lover he left behind. She has died and turned into a

bird, a parrot that now admonishes him from a tree. It begins to appear that he is in fact Glasses Ma; the trauma of imprisonment must have given him amnesia. Yet, before this second reality can resolve the situation, the narrator somehow is able to leave the unleavable village, with the "parrot." Bedding down in an inn at the county town, he telephones an old friend who knows him as Huang Zhixian. But now he begins to doubt that identity, finally observing, "I am tired. I can never leave this immense being which is me." The journey up the mountain becomes an imaginary recurring dream that has invested him with an identity truer than his apparent one.

The story has philosophical depth, in the Western modernist tradition, but does it speak to Han Shaogong's cultural concerns? Broadly, the narrator "returns" to where he has and yet never has been, to cultural and familial roots. The natives love him, remonstrate with him, even justify his murder of one of their own, though he is an outsider from the city. The welcome "back" of his spiritually hungry and dreaming soul resonates with the quest of Qu Yuan's wandering soul in the *Chu ci*, as does the bird motif. The village is alive with the spirits of the dead, and the narrator has a conversation with Ma's departed grandfather. Otherwise, Han's exploration of reality as such overpowers questions of cultural context, urban or rural, past or present.

"Ba Ba Ba" (Da Da Da) develops an eerie sense of being in a West Hunanese never-never land with more attention to ethnography. The setting is the same: an isolated mountain village, "a tiny lonely island" above the clouds in a prefecture anciently called Qianzhong, where the thresholds in the homes are inexplicably high and thick, inside walls are oppressively blackened by soot from the cooking fire, and the furniture is rude blocks and benches. Knowledge—notably an ancient tribal creation myth—is passed on through "ancient songs." Only one character, Renbao, ever goes down the slope to learn of new things in town, and, having spied on women at the toilet, he is ridiculed by the villagers (this, and Han's scenes of a mental defective accosting villagers in the street, may be quotations from He Liwei). Superstitious taboos dominate the lives of the villagers. Ghosts and premonitions fill their dreams.[68]

The bizarre local rites come to revolve around the main protagonist, Bing Zai, a cretin who can say only two phrases, "Dada" and "Fuck Mama," a yin-yang pair that comes to symbolize the belief system of the locals. At one point they do take Bing Zai to be an oracle, seizing upon his random binary expletives as a substitute for their yin-yang fortune-telling sticks. But Bing Zai is an Ah Q of Chu, a crystallization of the idiocy and complacency of his people's way of life, and, like Lu Xun's character, an object who brings out the basic cruelty of the whole village. Young men slap him around just for the fun of it. When hard times come, he is selected as a human sacrifice to the harvest god, saved only by a clap of thunder that the villagers take to be divine displeasure at the cheapness of the offering. Han Shaogong maintains that "Da Da Da" deals with "the decline of a race, as seen through the prism of Chu culture."[69]

There is little plot, simply a parade of superstitions, climaxing in famine, bloody war between villagers over conflicting geomantic interests in appeasing a god, cannibalism of the enemy, and finally a stoic Jonestown-style administration of poison to the old, the weak, and the young, so that the strong may burn down the village and go in quest of a more propitious mountainside to slash and burn. That sacrifice perpetuates both the race and its permanent stupidity. Somehow the cretin survives the poison; at the end, village children are seen blithely imitating him, chanting "Da-da-da-da-da."

This story has especially puzzled Han Shaogong's readers, even if it lacks the metaphysical mystery of "Return." The weird setting and goings-on are related with graphic realism (there are repeated references to Bing Zai's snotty nose, his messing with chicken droppings, cruel attempts by village boys to make him eat cow dung, and so forth), and yet the era of this "magical-realistic" narrative is a riddle. That the folk still talk of bandits, corvée, and opium are tantalizing clues that the time is pre-Liberation—except that Han Shaogong might be just the one to admit that such phenomena still exist under the "new society." (The villagers of "Return," who have already had to "learn from Dazhai," plant opium—for medicinal purposes, it is added.) Han in fact drops a hint that "Da Da Da" takes place after 1930, or more probably 1949, by having Renbao inform the others that one no longer addresses the local government with a "petition," but with a "report." And there are public fields. The tribal warfare and human sacrifice rituals seem all the more absurd in this modern context.

Han Shaogong seconds Shen Congwen in giving as much attention to his characters' "dreams" as to their deeds. He has tried to capture the spirit of life among the montagnards, who, by all accounts, do perceive spirits lurking in every rock, tree, and breath of air. Shen Congwen was not so ambitious, even in, or particularly in, *Shenwu zhi ai* (The Shaman's Love); Han must be credited with having created a splendidly and unrelentingly alien and mysterious atmosphere, one in which common sense and the laws of nature no longer hold. Bizarre ideas of nature blend in with an already strange dialect, and the mystery is both heightened and accommodated through the device of never entering deeply into the minds of the characters—only letting one listen in on inevitably enigmatic speech and thought fragments. Bing Zai, who cannot think, provides appropriate "comment."

But that is to say that the irrationality is largely exterior, in the mind of the implied urban reader, not in the minds of the montagnards, as Han's manifesto had led us to hope. Moreover Han's defamiliarizing devices clash, one Chinese critic has pointed out, with his ordinary realistic technique.[70] The spectacular ordure and cruelty evoke "bourgeois" feelings of disgust and humane sympathy that undo the sense of mystery, while Han's descriptions of superstition objectify it to the point of revealing his hostility. Bing Zai's mother thus prays "before men made of wood or made of clay" (156). Han's omniscient narrator even steps into the role of "field researcher" by stopping to explain local dialect (161). Bing Zai's repeated nonsensical answers finally turn comic, as do the overabundant magic rites. It is said, for instance, that by custom one keeps the Road Fork Ghost at bay by urinating on and cursing him (159). And these practices are there for effect, not ethnographic authenticity. Although some of the beliefs are verifiable and indeed were discussed by Shen Congwen, such as the ancient *gu* poison cult, Han Shaogong admitted to Ling Yu that there was no West Hunanese precedent for the central rite of the story, human sacrifice. He borrowed it from another culture.[71]

The other paradox is that these very negative roots can hardly recover the *aesthetic* sensibilities of ancient Chu. Han Shaogong agrees that "both the rational and the nonrational" in "Da Da Da" have "become absurd." This shows, he says, that all the village's "ideas, old and new," are useless to "save the situation."[72] But absurdity is not to be equated with instinctual thinking. It evokes modern alienation instead of the ancients' nonrational aestheticism. Hence it provides no link to the brilliant local color of Chu that Han Shaogong saw in the *Chu ci,* or even to its shamanism. Han offers up a pepper mill, a spider spirit, and a water snake, but no exhilarating journeys, no lush, exotic fauna, no breathtaking metaphors, not even the bird spirit of "Return." His quest for primitive spiritual inspiration has been sidetracked by his old love of exposing the moronic and the ugly. Lately he has proclaimed "Da Da Da" to be a statement on the prehistoric idiocy of the entire human race—and a metaphor for the insanity of the Cultural Revolution.[73] Whether his vision is reinterpreted abstractly or topically, it is diverging ever further from concern with regional culture.

Yet this reminds us that Shen Congwen's culturally positive and appropriately god-filled, pantheistic images of West Hunan are likewise related to ancient Chu only tangentially. As in most works by contemporary writers, Shen's "mysticism" is more often linked to Zhuangzi than to Qu Yuan. Lu Xun immersed himself in Qu Yuan's imagery and sentiments more fully than either Shen Congwen or Han Shaogong. The cultural gap between present-day Hunan and ancient Chu may be too great; or perhaps Shen and Han have been too conditioned to see Qu Yuan's legacy in its politicized and Confucianized form. Neither has explored the legacy of Chu to its limits.[74]

Conclusion: Versions of the Pastoral in 1980s China

The four writers just analyzed, while not representing a cross section of 1980s Chinese creativity, cut a very wide swath through that decade. They are strong enough writers to have occasionally influenced each other. Each of them not only was enriched but in some sense "came to life" after discovering or rediscovering the legacy of Shen Congwen. Why they were so receptive to him is no mystery. Not only were they recovering from the "cultural desert" of the Cultural Revolution, but also the decades-old orthodoxy of "realism" showed no signs of diminution in the 1980s, and the alternative, a romantic or modernist subjectivism, seemed to many a passing fad of the young people. Shen Congwen's legacy was free from all entanglements with orthodoxy—except insofar as it had become a social force unto itself, a "cause" for the Hunanese. Perhaps the relatively low level of social engagement in Shen Congwen's legacy explains the lack of major women writers in his tradition, except for Jiang Zidan. Women have another agenda.

To be sure, the four contemporary authors' discovery of Shen Congwen was only one part of a renewed contact with vast, previously taboo literary traditions of both East and West, and it coincided with China's rediscovery of the self. Yet all four writers became pastoralists of sorts, and all gave unusual attention to style. Consider the timing. Gu Hua reemerged in 1981 a completely new writer, after studying the style of Shen Congwen and Zhao Shuli. Wang Zengqi appeared full-blown as a fiction writer in Shen Congwen's image after many years of silence; indeed he became a writer of pastoral fiction for the first time in his life, just after a meticulous study of *Border Town*. Later, when Shen Congwen was available to the public, He Liwei likewise arose from silence to become a stylist in Shen's image. Han Shaogong, too, completely changed his previous course as late as 1985, to concoct an ethnographically detailed world allegedly of West Hunan. The achievement of these writers is so broad that it redefines Shen Congwen's own. This, despite the fact that all of them seem to have read Shen somewhat narrowly. And this, without even mentioning the *West* Hunanese writers who were influenced by him, such as Cai Cehai, Sun Jianzhong, and Xiao Jianguo— or the honorary Hunanese writer Ye Weilin (born in Canton)—or the other young writers who were influenced more subtly.

All four writers are linked to Shen Congwen through their treatment of time and place, yet all have taken a distinctive road. Shen Congwen was at times nostalgic about the recent past, in the "old society." Gu Hua shared Shen's image of nearly that same society's bedrock ethos, even copied it, but, living in the "new society," he used his fiction for devastating social criticism. Wang Zengqi wrote nostalgically of the "old society" Shen Congwen made sound so beautiful, but he lives in the "new society," so his nostalgia becomes another kind of social criticism of the present, by inversion—a criticism made all the stronger by the fact that Wang's old society is even sweeter than Shen's, although with certain leftist modifications. It is remarkable, in New China, that He Liwei often simply ignores "the present," particularly its very politically defined reality, and so seems in some ways closest to Shen Congwen. Han Shaogong, ever conscious of history, makes one anxious to discover whether he is writing about the old, the new, or the ancient China, but never provides the answer. He leaves one feeling apprehensive about China in all eras.

The four authors' different ways of handling place are just as notable, considering their common attention to ethnographic description and their inspiration by an author with a firm regional commitment. Gu Hua's region is simply the setting for a universal statement about history and politics in China under communism. Wang Zengqi's region is closer to China's cultural "core"; he makes his region appear even less unique. Perhaps Wang could take over for Liu Xinwu and Lu Wenfu and write local-color accounts of life in Peking and Suzhou. He Liwei's fiction is full of the specificity of region, his style (including dialect) inextricably enmeshed with his subject matter. But he makes no statement about Hunan's place within China. Han Shaogong, on the other hand, makes West Hunan out to be a unique place (discounting his new theory of Orientalism), but it turns out to be quite a bad place, more like that of a U.S. southerner than of a Chinese regionalist. Like the other three, Han lacks a sectionalist political commitment of the sort that Shen's works conveyed on behalf of West Hunan.

The seeming lack of interest in regional politics on the part of the four contemporary authors is a legacy of Mao's China, which has ameliorated conflicts of place much more successfully than it has desynchronizations of development. Culturally, though, there is in all these writers a value commitment to the South—to its people and its scenery—at the expense of the North. That would surely please Shen Congwen. In He Liwei and Wang Zengqi there is furthermore a preference for the country as opposed to the city; but Han Shaogong and Gu Hua seem instead to fear primitive terrors in the countryside that the city has the power to tame.

All four contemporary authors are "poets in prose" defying boundaries between genres. Yet quite traditional questions of subject matter and theme appear still to be uppermost in their minds. And traditional conceptions of personal and regional ties, indeed of discipleship and faction, play a real, if not a determining, role in their creativity. That modern authors have developed only part of Shen Congwen's legacy suggests that, to become a tradition, the legacy must be developed further.

4 | Imaginary Nostalgia: Shen Congwen, Song Zelai, Mo Yan, and Li Yongping

Shen Congwen (1902–1988) has long been regarded as one of the most important "native soil" writers of modern Chinese literature.[1] For all their thematic and stylistic differences, Shen's native soil writings display a cluster of motifs and images that would be elaborated by writers in the next fifty years: the passage of time, the clash between old and new values, yearning for the lost days of innocence or childhood, (re)encounters with quaint, backward country figures, observations of customs, anxieties about impending change, and mixed feelings of homesickness and fear of going home—all part of the bittersweet experience called *nostalgia*.

Yet Shen Congwen is neither a romantic, yearning for a lost paradise, nor a utopian, allegorizing what the given political condition lacks. Romantic and utopian elements play an important part in Shen's writing, but he has a much more intricate vision of a homeland in mind. The "homeland" he reconstructs must not be regarded merely as a geographical wonderland but as a topographical locus, a textual coordinate that demands multiple readings to lay out its contours. His nostalgia refers not so much to a representational effort to enliven the irretrievable past as to a creation of an imaginary past on behalf of the present.

This "imaginary nostalgia" constitutes one of the most

sophisticated parts of Shen Congwen's native soil writings, and its lasting influence can be discerned in the native soil fiction of the eighties. This essay represents a preliminary attempt to define Shen Congwen's discourse of imaginary nostalgia. In the first part, I will try to lay out guidelines toward a poetics of imaginary nostalgia, with Shen's *Xiangxing sanji* (Random Sketches on a Trip to Hunan) as major example. In the second part, I will focus on selected works by three contemporary native soil writers: Song Zelai (b. 1952), one of the last members of the Taiwan native soil movement; Mo Yan (b. 1956), the mainland *xun'gen* ("search for roots") writer acclaimed for his fantastic family-cycles; and Li Yongping (b. 1947), an overseas Chinese (now settled in Taiwan) who has fascinated readers by presenting a native soil landscape as a *pastiche* of literary images, conventions, and clichés about one's "hometown." These writers may not write "like" Shen Congwen, yet the way they elaborate the aesthetic and conceptual motivations of imaginary nostalgia brings to light an aspect of Shen's fiction hitherto unnoticed by critics. My concern is not with rigid reception/influence studies. I am more interested in the mutual illumination between Shen Congwen and contemporary writers exploring the geographical/textual dialectic of nostalgia.

When a genealogy of native soil fiction of the past seven decades is mapped out, Lu Xun has to be treated as one of the initiators. While writing in many short stories and familiar essays about his hometown, Shaoxing, making it a literary locus rich in symbolism, Lu Xun was one of the earliest critics trying to circumscribe the theme and structure of native soil literature. In his introduction to an anthology of modern Chinese fiction, Lu Xun used the term *xiangtu xiaoshuo* (native soil fiction) to describe the kind of short stories written by authors like Wang Luyan and Xu Qinwen, and he expresses his opinions about the burgeoning trend of native soil literature:

> Although [native soil] writers live in a place other than their homeland *(qiaoyu)*, their writings are not about the place they currently live in. Therefore, what emerges is a feeling of nostalgia, rather than an exoticism that might either open up readers' minds or

expose them to the writer's experience . . . Before a writer sets out to write native soil literature, he finds himself already exiled from his home, driven by life to a strange place. What can he do but recall his father's garden, a garden which does not exist any more? It is more comfortable and self-consoling to recall things at home which do not exist any more than things which still exist yet are inaccessible.[2]

Lu Xun's comments are suggestive not only because he first notices a new literary trend that is taking shape in the early twenties, but also because he tries to describe the paradoxical position a native soil writer assumes. Native soil literature, as the term indicates, is nurtured on a writer's deep-rooted concern with his home region, but this concern can be acutely felt only after the author is uprooted from the soil he cherishes so much and, more ironically, has been denied any possibility of savoring or understanding its actuality.

But Lu Xun reveals his attachment to the ontological impulse beneath native soil fiction, an impulse he sets out to question when he contrasts nostalgia with exoticism. Lu Xun holds that nostalgia appears only in writings with regard to a loss of something one is already familiar with, whereas exoticism indicates an effect coming from perceiving something totally strange or foreign. This contrast is less clear-cut than it sounds; when all questions of imagination and textuality are introduced, there must be a recalculation of the boundaries of nostalgia.

Going one step beyond Lu Xun's observations, I would like to argue that native soil literature is literally and rhetorically a "rootless" literature, a kind of literature whose meaning hinges on the simultaneous (re)discovery and erasure of the treasured image of the homeland. Native soil writers come forth to write out what they fail to experience in reality. Their imagination plays just as much a role as their lived experience, and their "gesture" of remembering is no less important than the things remembered. Insofar as the lost past can be regained only through the act of writing, the "form" of remembrance may become itself the content of what is to be remembered. Shen Congwen is one of the few modern Chinese writers keenly aware of this paradox. At his best, he exposes the verisimilar norms native soil literature adheres to and plays with the dialects of realism it speaks. Having no illusion of exhausting these issues, I would like to circumscribe my discussion in certain ways before proceeding to Shen Congwen's *Random Sketches on a Trip to Hunan*.

To begin with, native soil writers may claim that they derive the local color of their works from objects and moments they are or were most familiar with, but in rendering these objects and moments, they are engaged in a task of defamiliarization, a task that allows them to assume an outsider's viewpoint and see things on a contrastive basis. Not unlike a tour guide who cashes in on his knowledge by emphasizing qualities of a locale that are exotic to its visitors, a native soil writer takes a double viewpoint of the image of his homeland. We may thus reach a different conclusion from Lu Xun's with regard to the nostalgia/exoticism dichotomy. Describing the homeland as a both familiar and foreign place, and taking objects seen and experienced as "ordinary" in their own land and "making them strange," writers of native soil fiction entertain a secret alliance with exoticism.

Accordingly, the framing of temporal and spatial schemes in native soil literature is more complicated than we usually think it is. Dealing with conventional themes like the contrast between the new and old, the loss of childhood or youth, and the effort to remember things past, native soil writers always have to refer to an inevitable passage of time. Time plays a crucial role in the discourse of native soil literature. Beyond the linear concept of temporality, native soil writers try hard to recapture lost time by reorienting the order of time. Through the ritual of memory, imagination, or writing, they twist, multiply, and even transform what has happened and what is happening. They tentatively bring together the past and the present, defining or undercutting the meaning of one at the expense of the other. They reconstruct the past in terms of the present; and they see in the present a residue of the past. Time is reorganized or "anachronized," so to speak, in native soil literature, in the service of the liberation or repression of writers' and readers' regressive nostalgia.

Just as the idea of anachronism works behind the temporal scheme of native soil fiction, so too the idea of displacement can be adopted to describe its spatial scheme. I have referred to Lu Xun's ironic observation that a writer's reminiscences of his native soil presuppose his own dislocation. Actually, displacement does not point merely to a writer's physical dislocation from his homeland; rather it indicates a relocation of his social status and intellectual/emotional capacity. A writer feels homesick not just because of his separation from his homeland but also because of his loss of the "aura" of the homeland he believes himself to have had. Moreover, in mythological and psychological terms, displacement points to a narrative device or psychic mechanism that makes possible the (re)definition of something either irretrievable or unspeakable, and to the eternally regressive state of such a narrative and psychological quest. Displacement, therefore, implies the condition in which a native soil writer is situated, the method he employs in search of a lost time and place, and the result he obtains in words. As long as the meaning of the lost time and place can be regained only in a mediated, hence displaced and incomplete, form, nostalgia is equatable to insatiable desire for more narrative and more memory.

The reassessment of the spatial-temporal scheme may lead us to the following two observations. First, as a literary convention, the image of native soil or homeland suggests not so much a geographically verifiable place, which bears exclusive significance to a writer born there or growing up there, as a topographical system of coordinates, which lends itself to anyone wanting to locate the "origins" of a text. Texts, like sites, are essential loci of nostalgia, bounded spaces in which the complexities of human nature and experience are concentrated. More than just his birthplace, Shen's West Hunan is a textual locus where his discourse "about" the homeland has germinated, and through which he transports his social/political ideas. In its textual transcription, West Hunan is as much a "homeland" for Shen Congwen as it is for his readers, wherever their actual homelands are.

Second, the above argument calls into question the realistic project underlying native soil literature. Native soil writers may start their literary journey with a sense of clear perspectives: overcoming the power of time by recalling figures, events, and values from the realm of oblivion, and making sense of the present by resorting to an original meaning that is identifiable with the vision of the homeland or native soil. What is at stake here is a firm belief in the transtemporal and transspatial power of literary representation. Both literally and symbolically, this quest is doomed to end with the recognition of gaps between the words and the world, memory and desire, history and originary being. Native soil literature does not just present stories of vainly seeking lost childhoods or inaccessible homelands. The genre itself enacts the split of representation, and the incongruity of what realist literature proposes to do and what it can do.

Instead of nostalgia, therefore, it is more interesting to talk about "imaginary nostalgia" as the fundamental theme of native soil literature—imaginary, in the sense that nostalgia is something that comes not as the effect but as the "absent cause" of native soil literature, and that nostalgia is as much a spontaneous overflow of personal feeling as a convention of writing, overdetermined by literary and nonliterary factors. Insofar as the "real" native soil and homeland can be recapitulated only in the form of continuous regression, native soil literature always appears as a "belated" form of writing, nurtured ironically on the "imagination" of loss that calls itself nostalgia. In this, I do not deny the individual experiences each native soil writer might have undergone. But I would question the psychological and ideological mandate by which we might have equated the whereabouts of native soil and homeland with the origin of time, history, and writing. Imaginary nostalgia, therefore, questions the ontological assumption often associated with the concept of nostalgia and refers us to the intratextual and intertextual dynamics that configure the yearning for home.

At the center of Shen Congwen's discourse about his home region is the conflicting image it projects into history. West Hunan is an area historically best known for its mountainous land, tribal riots, voodoo customs, banditry, and poverty—a barbarous country to people living in the "Middle Kingdom." But West Hunan also provides the landscape that allegedly inspired two great masterpieces of classical Chinese literature: Qu Yuan's *Chuci* (Songs of the South) and Tao Qian's "Taohuayuan ji" (Peach Blossom Spring).[3]

Shen Congwen is quite conscious that he is writing within the tradition of the *Songs of the South* and "Peach Blossom Spring."[4] But he writes about his homeland with more dialogical tensions. A native of West Hunan, he knows only too well that his homeland is not as immaculate as depicted in the ancient works; wars, riots, ignorance, and poverty are the reality that has existed all along. A latest practitioner of the great *Songs of the South* and "Peach Blossom Spring" tradition, he knows his impressions and inscriptions of his homeland, for good or for ill, cannot do away with the impacts of Qu Yuan and Tao Qian. His nostalgia for West Hunan stems not only from a biographical attachment to his birthplace but also from an imaginative tie to the literary place.

Beneath Shen Congwen's seemingly soft, smooth writing about West Hunan, one finds a radical melancholy. He writes to project a view of Chinese reality and of writing about reality, but he is aware that any attempt has invoked self-irony. If there is an ideal West Hunan that has fallen into the present and the "real," reconstituting it yields to an aesthetic of residuality and incompleteness: his homeland tour, actual or textual, must betray its imaginary roots.

Shen Congwen moved with his family out of their native region of Fenghuang in 1917, and he never went back till 1934. The homecoming experience brought Shen Congwen mixed feelings. He was stunned by the haunting beauty of the landscape once so familiar to him, but he was saddened by the obvious incompatibility between the old and new values manifested by people's lifestyles. While local legends and anecdotes still fascinated him, he could not help noticing how the legendary region of Peach Blossom Spring was undergoing a rapid deterioration, due to military, political, economic, and cultural invasions from the outside world.

The results of the homecoming trip were the novella *Biancheng* (Border Town, 1934) and the travelogue *Random Sketches on a Trip to Hunan* (1936). Much has been said about *Border Town*, but any reading of the novella would not be complete without a reference to *Random Sketches on a Trip to Hunan* (hereafter referred to as *Random Sketches*). With an accumulation of data—natural and human scenery, detailed biographical information—and an intention of revealing the true image of West Hunan behind the veil of myth and misunderstanding, *Random Sketches* showcases the ideally transparent writing of realism. But close reading reveals that the work contains a dramatic intertextual play, prolonging and parodying the literary tradition of homecoming within which Shen Congwen is writing.

To begin with, *Random Sketches* calls for a reading parallel to Tao Qian's "Peach Blossom Spring," the ultimate Chinese utopian text. Shen's homecoming trip is subtly counterpointed to the ancient fisherman's explorations along the river leading to Peach Blossom Spring, and Shen's cultural/geographical (re)discovery is supplemented by a hermeneutic of the literary myth. What results is Shen's ironic recognition of the disappearance of utopia, in personal nostalgia as in literary nostalgia; he endeavors to discover a new entry to it.

Random Sketches opens with Shen Congwen's reunion with an old friend on his 1934 homecoming trip, a man always wearing an otterskin hat. This friend enjoys a dubious local reputation for his scoundrellike personality, his charm among women, and, ironically, his penchant for curios and classical painting. For Shen, the friend "may as well be called a 'fisherman,' because he is wearing an otterskin hat worth forty-eight dollars, which helps him catch women's attention whenever he goes by."[5] The "Peach Blossom Spring" the friend with an otterskin hat is "good at" discovering is not amid remote mountains but amid the bodies of women, as the friend's vulgar joke reveals at the end of the chapter. Traveling with such a friend, a "fisherman" of the 1930s, to famous Taoyuan County, Shen cannot but feel amused when thinking of the way "high school students all over China diligently study Tao Yuanming's 'Peach Blossom Spring.'"[6]

Shen demythifies the ancient utopian story by vulgarizing the crucial lines of Tao Yuanming's original. In his eyes, the current Taoyuan is anything but a blessed land. It is a place dominated by opium smugglers, sailors, small warlords, corrupt bureaucrats, and prostitutes. Signs of military threat, power struggle, and social injustice can be seen everywhere. "The local residents have never thought they themselves might be descendants of the previous dynasty or gods; nor have they ever met any descendants of the previous dynasty or gods."[7] The name "Taoyuan" or Peach Blossom Spring rings a bell only to those visiting "literati" who come, often with a collection of Tao Yuanming's works, to pay homage to the alleged grove and compose cliché-ridden poems, and then complete their pilgrimages by spending a night with a prostitute at bargain prices.

Shen Congwen's mockery actually extends to himself. If his friend with an otterskin hat is to be identified with the fisherman of "Peach Blossom Spring," to whom is Shen Congwen comparable? One still recalls how "Peach Blossom Spring" ends: "the learned and virtuous hermit Liu Ziji heard the story and went off elated to find the place. But he had no success, and died after a long sickness. Since that time there have been no further seekers of the ford."[8] Yet is Shen Congwen really comparable to Liu Ziji? Shen must have felt the double edge of his parodies of modern "seekers of the ford," since no matter how ironical an attitude he would assume, he too was making a trip based on the mythical path as recounted by the ancient story. His travelogue is but a repeat of the aborted attempts to approximate "Peach Blossom Spring"—the "utopian" text.

The irony implied in *Random Sketches* takes on yet another dimension. Shen Congwen's homeland is located in West Hunan, and he was accordingly once a resident of "Peach Blossom Spring." Seventeen years after leaving his homeland, he is now making a journey back to where he grew up, only to find that things he used to appreciate are no longer there. He has become a native son denied a right to reenter the mystical utopia. Shen tries hard to draw our attention to the beauty of the landscape, the "divine quality" hidden in the rustic people. Still, his glorification of the Hunan countryside betrays a certain degree of alienation. As Leo Ou-fan Lee has pointed out, Shen Congwen's "immersion in his familiar landscape is not so complete as he may have wished, for after years of absence he has become something of an outsider."[9] He has become a passive onlooker, unable to exert a personal impact on his environment.

Instead of recapitulating a full, coherent image of the homeland region as it was or should be, what Shen Congwen best manages to present are but "random sketches," fragments of what he sees and hears. He can spot lingering traces of the golden past only in one scene or one person he happens to pass by. In the alleged geographical site of Peach Blossom Spring, he therefore launches a new quest, and his chance to relocate the mythical utopia is no better than that of Tao Qian's fisherman, Liu Ziji, or Tao Qian himself.

Besides the sounds and sights of the rural landscape of West Hunan, Shen Congwen finds it most enjoyable to portray people from the lower classes: a young boatman who against all odds is carrying on a love affair with a "married" prostitute, a "wild child" who failed Shen's plan of civilizing him in Shanghai and regained his vigor back in his homeland, a seventy-year-old boat-puller with a tough look and spirit that reminds Shen of Tolstoy, and a coal miner who organized rebellions against local warlord troops and died a heroic death. One can easily sense Shen's admiration for these characters and his efforts to endorse their virtues. But these people are by ordinary standards not habitants of Peach Blossom Spring. To appreciate their "sacred" quality, as Shen would have it, a writer or reader needs a special sensibility to see what we normally do not see, and feel what we normally do not feel. At a time when Peach Blossom Spring is lost, it is the surviving elements of the "noble savages," residual remembrances of the golden time, or lingering impressions of the landscape that we must learn to capture and decipher so as to reconstruct things past.

What figures here is an aesthetic of the residue or the fragment, an aesthetic crucial not only to *Random Sketches* but to native soil fiction in general.[10] The fragmentary image serves as a synecdoche, suggesting what the missing whole might have been as well as the impossibility of restoring it. Thus, as he turns to the individual scenes, characters, or moments for an intense reflection of his ideal homeland, Shen tends to exercise a special kind of connoisseurship that calls for an imaginary configuration of what is to be seen and felt. However trivial they may be, the fragments or traces can be turned into autonomous signs, vindicating not so much the outside world of which they are part as the landscape envisioned by the writer by and for himself. At this point, the fragment becomes nothing more than a prop through which the writer's imagination can occupy center stage.

Nevertheless, although triggering ruminations about the lost utopia, the random sketches after all remain parts of a whole that can no longer be pieced together. The harder Shen Congwen works to sort out the precious traces of the past from the lump of present affairs, the more strongly he feels the sadness of incompleteness. While each sketch may be interesting or beautiful in its own right, it serves all the more poignantly as an index of absences, absences of the golden time, innocence, order, and the plenitude of meaning. The two tendencies form a paradoxical logic that evokes and denies at the same time the yearning for Peach Blossom Spring, yet drives home the verisimilar rule that substantiates the discourse of native soil literature.

Going back to my parallel reading of *Random Sketches* and "Peach Blossom Spring," I would therefore suggest that, for all his rhetoric of parody, Shen Congwen prolongs Tao Qian's quest for the ideal utopia through words. As yet another dialogical response to "Peach Blossom Spring," *Random Sketches* remains appropriately open on both ends, attached to the ancient story that is itself a "postscript" or "afterword" of what has already happened, and to many more like-minded writings to come. Shen lays bare the historical condition that makes it impossible for Peach Blossom Spring to (re)appear in reality, but, in so doing, he advocates the priority of imagination and writing over actual perception and experience, and thus tacitly reconfirms Tao Qian's project of "writing down" his utopia sixteen hundred years before. What he does best in *Random Sketches*, accordingly, is the inscription of personal sensibilities and impressions in terms of the fragments of a supposedly lost world, and the fantastic substitution of what should be for what is.

As of the late seventies, Shen Congwen was deliberately ignored by scholars on the mainland, for lacking political awareness, and he remained at best only an underground celebrity among literature lovers in Taiwan, for having political awareness. But the eighties witnessed the "return" of Shen Congwen's impact. In view of the reemergence of Shen Congwen, my questions are: how the vision of native soil established by Shen Congwen half a century before has undergone various stages of transformation; how contemporary writers have employed the image of a homeland to convey different concepts; and more important, how in so doing, these writers have responded to, clarified, or even amended Shen Congwen's kind of imaginary nostalgia.

Instead of Huang Chunming, the champion of Taiwan's native soil movement in the seventies, whose warmhearted portrait of country figures and events may well be reminiscent of Shen Congwen's, I will discuss Song Zelai, the writer who wrote in the footsteps of Huang at the turn of the eighties, exhausting the discourse of Taiwan's native soil literature. Instead of Wang Zengqi, Shen Congwen's former student and best imitator in terms of style and philosophy, I will discuss Mo Yan, who revivified northeastern Shandong in a mythical language so different from Shen Congwen's yet in a rhetorical strategy so close to his. And I will complete my discussion by looking over stories by Li Yongping, an overseas Chinese writer now living in Taiwan, who created a composite "homeland," a world out of words, uprooting the realistic links of native soil writings.

Song Zelai was a latecomer to Taiwan's native soil literature movement that bloomed in the early seventies. When his series of short stories titled "Daniunan cun" (Daniunan Village) first won critical acclaim, it was already the spring of 1978. By that time, well-known native soil writers had either turned their attention to other subjects (like Wang Zhenhe), or temporarily quit writing (like Huang Chunming), or committed themselves to political activity (like Wang Tuo and Yang Qingchu). The vehement debate over the "essence" of a native soil movement, which involved literati from the extreme right to the extreme left and resulted in an extensive writers' war over ideological convictions, had ended the previous year. In spring 1978 Taiwan was yet to encounter such economic and political storms as the U.S. recognition of the PRC and the Gaoxiong mass riots.

Writing at this historical juncture, Song Zelai had to face up to dilemmas his predecessors had not been obliged to deal with. Seeing that veteran writers had already done so much and so well with native soil themes, could Song Zelai come up with anything new and provocative while maintaining the charm of an established discourse? Seeing that radical peers had turned Taiwan's native soil movement into a political campaign, should Song Zelai keep describing impoverished country life, decorated with quaint customs and good-natured rustic figures, or should he propagate activism at the expense of writing itself?

Song Zelai has never been able to solve fully these dilemmas. His failure to do so might have been what led to his later dramatic turn to Zen Buddhism then to radical cultural/political criticism. But because of these dilemmas, I would argue, Song Zelai expresses in his best stories a strange nostalgia, nostalgia not so much about the loss of simple village life in an increasingly Philistine society—a common theme shared by almost all native soil writers—as about the loss of a simple "style" and environment his predecessors were privileged to dwell in and write about.

Critics have often overpraised Song Zelai's early works like "Daniunan Village" and other short stories dealing with the same village and its habitants. But for all its topical elements and southern Taiwan local color, "Daniunan Village" is at its best a competent remake of fiction like Mao Dun's "Chuncan" (Spring Silkworms), presenting a picture of Taiwan's farm villages undergoing fundamental economic and ethical transformation. Song Zelai's greatest contribution to the tradition of Taiwan's native soil fiction lies in his collection of short stories titled *Penglai zhiyi* (Bizarre Stories about Formosa, 1988).[11] This collection is composed of thirty-three short stories, covering a time span from the Japanese occupation period to the breakup of Taiwanese-American diplomatic relations in 1979. Song Zelai claims that the stories are meant to serve as "a testimony to his society," wherein "the life of the lower class (in villages, small towns, and harbor cities) is so grotesque and miserable that middle- and upper-class intellectuals can hardly imagine it."[12] He also labels his stories "naturalist" works, in that they are mostly concerned with the unchangeable fate of those who are oppressed and downtrodden.

But one has to make an extra effort to understand Song Zelai's definition of naturalism. As shown by his fictional practice, Song is less fascinated with the pseudoscientific determinism based on heredity and environment—the trademark of naturalist narrative—than with the romantic mysticism paradoxically underlying much of Zola and Maupassant. Song is a naturalist, but he has unwittingly exaggerated the "nonnatural" aspects inherent in the works of his French predecessors. In the name of protesting against social injustice and the pathetic lot of lower-class Taiwanese, Song Zelai actually tells a series of "bizarre stories" *(zhiyi)*, as the title of his book suggests, whose charm consists in nothing more than the mythical coincidences of human interaction and the inscrutable mechanism of the Wheel of Fortune.

Let us examine two examples. "Chuanghen" (Scar) tells from a child's viewpoint of the reunion of a group of Taiwanese soldiers who had been drafted by the Japanese at the end of the Second World War. The old soldiers show off their scars to each other, each representing a sad family story, a heroic adventure, or a bitter romance. In Song Zelai's plan, the scars may well indicate the wounds the imperialist invaders have inflicted on native Taiwanese. But his child(like) narrator would rather treat them as stigmata of a demonic curse—something so horrifying that it cannot be explained away in any human terms. The story's climax comes when one of the old soldiers takes off his hat, revealing that half of his head is missing, a scene so grotesque that one wonders if Song Zelai merely intends to impress his readers with the cruelty of war and military colonialism.

The mixture of mysticism and naturalism can also be illustrated by stories like "Yao" (Medicine), in which a woman repeatedly takes (a limited amount of) poison to scare her husband from the habit of gambling. The husband and wife eventually enter into a game whose stakes are her life, a game whose thrills exceed mere gambling. Ironically, when the wife wants to play it safe in this suicidal game by taking something different, she dies. The story could have stopped here and made itself a neat "naturalist" account of the folly of a lower-class couple. It is, nevertheless, followed by a twist: the husband quits gambling and becomes a successful businessman, as if truly assisted by the dead. Maybe the wife was doomed to die, after all, to bring forth her husband's good luck. Song Zelai is experimenting with his characters' fate à la naturalism, only to prove that Fate is beyond scientific calculation.

Stylistically, *Bizarre Stories about Formosa* is characterized by Song Zelai's extensive use of framing devices. More often than not, Song's stories begin with the narrator/character's visit to a town or village, where he is first lured by a strange figure or event and then (over)hears a story about that figure or event. Given the stories' limited length and simple plot, the design of story-within-a-story looks clumsy and obsolete. The people and land in his framed accounts are like figures in a shadow theater, registering an age so remote that it evades definition. Compared with the native soil writers at the turn of the seventies, such as Huang Chunming or Wang Zhenhe, Song seems unable to present the past, bitter or sweet, personal or communal, in its full immediacy and intimacy.

The way Song Zelai narrates his story naturally reminds us of Shen Congwen, who is also inclined to present stories through a frame, as illustrated by stories like "Sange nanren he yige nüren" (Three Men and One Woman) and "Deng" (Lamp). But Song's pose as a passive auditor and incompetent transcriber pits itself against Shen Congwen's earnest but troubled narratorial voice, which engages us with him in exploring the mysterious past, however unpalatable its secrets may turn out to be. Shen has a basic skepticism about the function of storytelling in unraveling a haunted past, yet he persists so as to articulate the desire to piece together memory. Song Zelai has the opposite problem. He fully believes using the narrative medium is the way to link present with past, but the ambience of his stories only confirms that there is no viable means of visiting the past again, even if the past poses as something palpable and retrievable.

In "Jiaohongcun zhisu" (One Night at Jiaohong Village), for example, our first-person narrator makes a one-night stay at Jiaohong and encounters a young man with a hat. Explaining why he has chosen to stay in country, the young man refers to an old scandal in the village that involves an arranged marriage, adultery, hard labor, an illegitimate child, and so on. As the child in the scandal grew up, he came to realize his true identity and had since decided to stay in the village, with the hope that his real father would come back someday. Unsurprisingly, the young man who tells the story is the child in the story. At the end of the framed narrative, our narrator concludes his account by seeming to hear "somebody sighing: 'of all kinds of love, there is nothing more touching than the love for one's parents and land.'"

Song Zelai could easily argue that, as a naturalist writer, he has to maintain distance so as to let the story speak for itself. I would take issue with the effect of "distance" in the story. As the young man tells his story to our narrator, a distance can be felt between the story-teller and his audience, the past and the present; but it can especially be felt between Song Zelai and the discursive convention that first motivates his story. From village to village, town to town, his narrator is now ever on the move, *not* going home. The vision of hometown figures only through "other people's" (re)telling of their past. For all his deep feelings for the legendary island named Formosa, Song seems to have lost the (posture of) spontaneity his predecessors assumed; he can only draw a tentative picture. A past that must always be put into a "frame," an artistic enclosure, soon becomes detached from the flux of reality.

Written in the late seventies when the legitimacy of Taiwan's economic, political, and historical position was facing a tremendous challenge from within and without, Song Zelai's native soil fiction can no longer capitalize on the existing native soil discourse that, even when condemning social/political abuses, arouses our desire to go back to the shabby hometown under description. The days for Huang Chunming's kind, earthy prostitute or stubborn, old-fashioned farmer making their "presence" in words are over. Song Zelai's nostalgia has doubled the nostalgia of Huang's period: it is derived from a yearning not just for the old Taiwan before it fell into the menacing web of history, but also for the simple, immaculate form of storytelling that renders that Taiwan reachable in imagination. Song can neither go back to the old world where naiveté and simplicity shine nor conjure up a world in the discourse where he actually lives. When the supposedly direct, genuine native soil experience has become unavailable in the given cultural/literary context, what remains is but a story of stories about a legendary past, nostalgia over the original (imaginary) nostalgia. Weary and melancholy, Song Zelai's native soil stories cannot usher us into the good or bad old days as his predecessors' did; rather, they signal a deeply changed literary and cultural climate in Taiwan of Song's own time.

By all standards, the rise of "search for roots" fiction should be considered one of the most sophisticated trends of the past decade on the mainland. Returning to the customs and morals of local regions, this fiction first appeared as a modest reaction against the increasingly formulaic "literature of the wounded." At a time when the whole nation of the PRC was "looking forward," the "search for roots" writers unblushingly looked "backward," even "downward." This gave their fiction a nonconformist spirit, adding an avant-garde dimension to the movement.

Although Shen Congwen never plays a visible role in the "search for roots" movement, he is at the base of the genealogical tree of the young writers' native soil imaginations. Wang Zengqi, Shen's student in the forties, has written dozens of stories after 1981 with the intention of recapturing the old master's style;[13] Ah Cheng, forerunner of the "search for roots" movement, has expressed his indebtedness to Shen Congwen; Jia Pingwa has also admitted that he had Shen's *Random Sketches* in mind when he created *Shangzhou chulu* (Preliminary Accounts of Shangzhou);[14] to say nothing of writers of the Hunan school such as Han Shaogong, Gu Hua, and He Liwei, who inherited Shen's deep feeling for the same region. But when one thinks of the magnitude and complexity of Shen Congwen's imaginary nostalgia, it is the Shandong writer Mo Yan who comes immediately to mind.

By this comparison, I do not mean that Mo Yan writes in any visible way like Shen Congwen. What I want to argue is that Mo Yan succeeds more than any of his peers in turning familiar hometown scenes into a fantastic landscape, and in creating a unique axiological system for that new territory—merits first achieved by Shen Congwen. In Mo Yan's own words, his homeland, "the northeastern Gaomi [in Shandong province,] is undoubtedly the prettiest and the ugliest, the most unworldly and the most mundane, the holiest and the most vulgar, the most heroic and the rottenest, the most drunken and the most romantic place on earth."[15] Mo Yan's vision of northeastern Gaomi may have nothing to do with Shen Congwen's West Hunan, but both writers show in their narrative the same ability to radicalize their nostalgia. The procedure is as follows: First they invest their nostalgia either with utopian fantasy or with heroic grandeur; then they problematize it with realist references; and they end up by exposing its fundamental complicity with illusion. Mo Yan's distinct difference from Shen Congwen, paradoxically, brings to the fore a belief in personal vision and the power of storytelling that Shen would have endorsed.

Of Mo Yan's homeland writings, the best-known one is *Honggaoliang jiazu* (The Red Sorghum Family, 1987), a novel chronicling the sufferings, romances, and heroic deeds of peasants of northeastern Shandong from 1923 to 1976. In the voice of a first-person narrator, Mo Yan makes it clear from the beginning that the novel is about "his own" family, and its hero and heroine are his grandfather and grandmother. By recollecting how his grandparents first met, got married, and then became estranged; how they were involved in different "businesses" from brewery to banditry; how they devoted themselves to the guerrilla war against the Japanese at the cost of his grandmother's life; and how the family suffered a downfall in the next two generations, Mo Yan develops a family saga full of epic grandeur and pathos. In his portrayal, Red Sorghum country is no longer the poorest area of Shandong but the exotic land of adventures; the residents there are no longer bloodthirsty, rustic barbarians but men and women with strong emotions and chivalric souls.

Mo Yan also construes *The Red Sorghum Family* as a historical romance, a novel about how modern China has come about through the trials of the warlord period, the second Sino-Japanese War, the Communist takeover, and the great Cultural Revolution. Recent criticism has noticed Mo Yan's relation with classical vernacular heroic cycles *(yanyi)*.[16] The two narrative modes of family saga and historical romance blend and contradict each other. On the one hand, Mo Yan sees his family members on a larger-than-life scale, judging them not by what they do but by how they carry out their deeds. On the other hand, he "minimizes" them, so to speak, by hurling them into huge torrents of national disaster, showing how little individual effort means against immense historical forces. The image of his hometown vacillates, depending on whether it is presented as the center of personal memory or as a negligible corner of official history, to the point that the line separating memory from history finally becomes indiscernible.

All this play with multiple readings depends on Mo Yan's modulation of his narrative voice, the most interesting device of the novel.

The first-person narrator is supposed to be a young man writing in the post–Cultural Revolution period. Unlike Song Zelai's narrator, he is not a passive transcriber of the past but a superomniscient observer who travels though the tunnel of time and brings his grandparents and their fellow homeland dwellers back to life again. In his efforts to reestablish a family genealogy, he not only takes the liberty of entering his grandparents' and parents' consciousness, speaking and thinking on their behalf, but also tries to speculate like a detective on what they could have done and what they must have done. Where facts and memory are incomplete, fantasy fills in. Scenes ranging from Grandma's sensuous thoughts before she gave herself away to her beloved, to the family ritual of urinating in the newly brewed wine, to Grandpa's stream-of-consciousness before an ambush, to dogs in red and green fighting for corpses after a guerrilla war, are all discernibly made-up events presented as if they actually had happened.

With its exuberant language and fantastic plotting, Mo Yan's style is often associated with magical realism. But "magic" works only in association with the narrator's remembrance of things past. In contrast to the glorious days of his grandparents, the present "realism" in which Mo Yan and his narrator live is dreadfully boring and petty. The immense red sorghum fields that used to nourish heroes and heroines now feed inhabitants whose greatest dream is to leave their homeland forever. This leads us to notice another group of native soil stories Mo Yan wrote while he was creating *The Red Sorghum Family*. Only when we juxtapose these two types of native soil fiction can we understand the dialogical tension inherent in Mo Yan's nostalgia and the revision he has made with regard to native soil conventions. Here I will focus on a single case, "Baigou qiuqianjia" (A White Dog and a Swing, 1985).

Dealing with a young college graduate's sentimental return to his desolate, provincial home village, before he takes a new job somewhere else, and his reencounter with a childhood playmate who has since lost one of her eyes, been betrayed by a PLA officer, grown up to marry a mute, and given birth to three mute children, "A White Dog and a Swing" is strongly reminiscent of Lu Xun's "homecoming" stories like "Zhufu" (New Year Sacrifice), and "Guxiang" (My

Old Home). Yet Mo Yan does not content himself with recapitulating the nostalgic pathos and guilty conscience Lu Xun feels before the stupor and backwardness of country lives—motifs too well extrapolated by writers since Lu Xun and Shen Congwen. What Mo Yan does instead is lay bare the "dark side" of the native soil writings of the thirties—nostalgia mixed with self-derogatory social criticism and an ambivalent attitude toward the past—a dark side that subverts the past and reinforces the stasis of the present.

By creating this grotesque one-eyed woman, Mo Yan has tacitly satirized the archetypal sweetheart in our hometown fantasy, best represented by Shen Congwen's Cuicui in *Border Town*. The woman's and her family's physical deformities also serve to objectify their inferior social and psychological states. Thirty years after the Communist "liberation," the "wall" of incommunicability that once separated Lu Xun's cynical urban intellectuals from his Runtu and Xianglin's wife, or Shen Congwen's city gentlemen from his sailors and prostitutes, has simply become more tangible in post–Cultural Revolution China. But for Mo Yan, intellectuals like his conscience-ridden hero cannot take shelter from this cruel fact. Neither the self-serving rationalization of "New Year Sacrifice" nor the evasive idyllism of *Border Town* makes any sense in the new historical context. Intellectuals have to be brought down from their lofty self-pity and nostalgic ambivalence to confront the most unbearable challenges in strictly physical terms. Thus, as he is leaving his hometown after an unhappy stay, our narrator is unexpectedly stopped by the one-eyed woman, who begs him to make love to her so that she might bear a child capable of "speaking" someday.

We never know what happened next; but the scene has pointedly ridiculed the "homecoming" complex shared by most intellectual writers after Lu Xun and Shen Congwen. As if reacting to the outcry of Lu Xun's madman, "Save the children," the one-eyed woman now challenges our similarly conscience-ridden narrator to "carry out" that outcry in a way she understands. "Save the children," as she would have it, is not so much an intellectual mandate as a blunt biological imperative, which, indeed, might prove the most efficient way to guarantee her and her family's well-being. Mixing desire for articulation with fantasies of eugenic improvement, sexual transgression with social-political opportunism, Mo Yan's portraiture of the peasant woman's confrontation with an urban intellectual becomes a skeptical inversion of Lu Xun's and Shen Congwen's homesick humanitarianism.

If Zhou Yingxiong is right in saying that red sorghum and dogs, as two major symbols of *The Red Sorghum Family*, point to its characters' gushing life force and animal virility,[17] we find in "A White Dog and a Swing" a degradation of the same two symbols. Almost seventy years ago, in the midst of the red sorghum fields, "my grandpa" grabbed "my grandma" from another man's wedding sedan chair and had sex with her, thereby giving the family saga an outrageous beginning. But now, our native son of northeast Gaomi is simply trapped in the same red sorghum field, unable to deal with the one-eyed woman's sexual request. The wild, colorful dogs that ran over the red sorghum fields, witnessing their days of war and peace, are all gone, too. Only one white dog is seen in the story, lagging behind our narrator and moaning to remind him of the past.

Beneath the dazzling imagery and dramatic actions of Mo Yan's native stories, we thus find a struggle between two nostalgic impulses. On the one hand, he relies heavily on the magic power of memory and language to enliven a legend about his homeland and ancestors. On the other, he shows that memory and language can lead nostalgia into a fragile, closed world that crumbles whenever "reality" intervenes. It is easy to talk about Mo Yan's grandiose homeland vision in *The Red Sorghum Family*. But in relatively "plain" stories like "A White Dog and a Swing," one sees his defiance vis-à-vis the modern Chinese tradition of native soil literature, and his skeptical attitude toward his own "writing" of nostalgia.

Li Yongping's novel *Jiling chunchiu* (Jiling Chronicles, 1986) represents yet another contemporary writer's radical attempt to rewrite the discourse of native soil fiction. Born and brought up in Brunei, Li Yongping went to Taiwan for advanced high school education. After college, he pursued graduate work in the States and ended up receiving a Ph.D. degree in comparative literature. He is currently a professional writer living in Taiwan. Unlike what is commonly assumed, Li Yongping's early overseas experience did not cripple his sensitivity to Chinese language and literature. Of the three writers under discussion, Li is in fact the most austere stylist, whose narrative continuously surprises us with how concise and lively the Chinese language can be. On the other hand, his training in foreign literature must have had a direct impact on him, especially in terms of the design of his plotting and structure.

Jiling Chronicles is composed of twelve apparently discrete short stories, each of which carries some link to the others. Chronologically in disarray, these stories call for an extremely careful reading if one wants to put all the clues together. At the center of the novel are the rape and suicide of a chaste woman in a town called Jiling. The rapist is the archvillain of the town. In revenge, the woman's husband, a coffinmaker, kills the villain's wife and his mistress, who is a whore, yet he never catches the villain. Years later, rumors have it that the coffinmaker has run away from jail and come back for more revenge. The townsfolk, especially those who assisted in the rape, tremble. Around this simple plot line, Li Yongping introduces a group of secondary characters, whose own lives and reactions before and after the rape and murder constitute the highlight of most of the stories.

Li Yongping's creation of a fictional homeland whose inhabitants act out a cycle of moral/political drama is, of course, not completely innovative. Counterparts of Jiling, though nonexistent in previous Chinese native soil fiction, can be found in Western works, such as Anderson's Winesburg, Ohio; Faulkner's Yoknatapawpha County; and García Márquez's Macondo, to name only a few. The irony we find in Li's project is, nevertheless, that he was born overseas as a "rootless" Chinese—one deprived of the "authentic" living Chinese experience—and yet he intends to draw a landscape that shows emotional and experiential intimacy with the motherland. Not only this. He wants to make his homeland appear even more "home-landlike" than that of other native writers, a homeland that contains as many elements as a "standard" native soil narrative could require.

With its kaleidoscopic symbolism and labyrinthine structure, *Jiling Chronicles* represents a potential playground for literature professors who would enjoy trying out different methodologies. Critics have declared that *Jiling Chronicles* evokes a vivid image of "a small Chinese township" in the early Republican years, that it endows Jiling with a regional atmosphere that is both familiar and strange, and that it projects a decadent, eschatological vision of the town, making it the moral allegory of the Chinese wasteland.[18] The novel lacks any direct temporal and spatial references and is excessively concerned about minute details. Judging by the local institutions, daily topics, and costumes of Jiling, we may surmise that the novel takes place in the twenties, yet we can hardly locate the geographical position of Jiling, since the town's landscape and weather conditions, and the towns-folk's linguistic registers and cultural habits, suggest not only southern and northern China, but also Southeastern Asia! In other words, Jiling is a fictive place designed to disorient cultural and geographical nostalgia.

Li Yongping has the story take place (possibly) in the twenties, a time when political and economic transformations of rural Chinese communities were most acutely felt. In Jiling a railroad will soon be completed to bring more business activity; students are going away for higher education; legality has yet to take hold of local government. Warlord armies and foreign missionaries coexist, while brothels and Buddhist temples prosper. Everything is changing in Jiling, but nothing can be said for sure about the future of the town.

In Shen Congwen's and other native soil fiction writers' works, we frequently come across the image of a rural society at the juncture of political and economic change. More often than not, the writers indicate moral anxiety over the degradation of the ideal home as it ceases to withstand the infiltration of external forces. Shen Congwen's *Changhe* (Long River), for example, anticipates the loss of the serenity and naiveté of his hometown region on the eve of the second Sino-Japanese War. What distinguishes Li Yongping's novel is that it is lacking in this sense of crisis about the passage of time. It thereby evokes a rather different grade of nostalgia.

Li carefully invests his novel with a symbolic network. Our saintly woman is married to a coffinmaker, and they have had no children; her rape and death take place on the day of the Guanyin Buddha's birthday, while the townsmen celebrate this festival in the red-light district. Those who plot the rape survive immediate punishment, only to be condemned either to an eternity of guilt or to an unpredictable death. Meanwhile, Li highlights the unfortunate fates of three other women characters—prolonged sexual abstinence, downfall into an abyss of lust, and accidental death in a robbery—all of which reinforce the novel's rhetorical despair, "a Heaven without clemency" *(tiandi buren)*. The irony is that, while Li Yongping lavishes love and lust, crime and punishment, divine mercy and human irrationality, death and redemptions, on his novel, the writing does not exert the same power of moral urgency that one finds in Lu Xun's and Shen Congwen's fictions, nor does it force the reader to reflect on the temporal chasm between the past and the present, the old and the new. The "surfeit" of moral symbolism brings forth an effect of sardonic playfulness.

As mentioned above, *Jiling Chronicles* is rich in stereotypical figures, familiar scenarios, and conventional themes, all catering to our taste for "a" past period. Yet these ingredients are so shuffled together that we can no longer be sure where, when, and even how the story happened. Despite its few historical references, Jiling is a town without past and future. Always floating one step beyond our reach, it "exists" like a mirage. The question is, if Jiling is such a phantom place, where does the effect of nostalgia come from? How do we define such a nostalgia with regard to those native writers who write about their "real" homelands?

In my discussion of Song Zelai's and Mo Yan's fiction, I have tried to call attention to their conscious play with the concept of a homeland and their renovations of the conventions of native soil fiction. Especially in the case of Mo Yan, home has been turned into a vast stage where fantasy and reality conflict and converge in a flagrantly dramatic manner. But no matter how wild their imaginations, these two writers do convey a general impression of a real-life homeland: southern Taiwan or northeastern Shandong. Li Yongping questions the very soil of native soil fiction. With his phantom place called Jiling, he seems to suggest that home can be a construction out of literary images and that nostalgia may come less from our yearning for what we have lost than our desire for what we can never have had. Stripping the hometown of all temporal and spatial connections, he shows nostalgia's tie to imagination.

Here one may notice a hidden paradox in Li Yongping's novel. Because of his "rootless" background, he may be less qualified than a Mo Yan or a Song Zelai to recapitulate his authentic past in his native land, but he is freer to seek roots at will, to show how "imaginary nostalgia" can be.[19] As if reflecting his personal condition, his Jiling has no ontology; Jiling is already beyond reach at the beginning of the novel and may never have existed at all. An extravagant wordplay, the existence of Jiling denies the necessity that a homeland be firmly grounded in history and reality. If Jiling arises only as the emblem of a prefigured moral or political agenda, it may be less important, if not irrelevant, to talk about its moral degeneration, as most critics have done.

I would therefore suggest that *Jiling Chronicles* is an important native soil novel of the eighties not so much because it renders a moral vision we have been familiar with as because it represents a literary *tour de force,* showing what a writer can do once he has mastered the rules of the game. In contrast to Lu Xun's Luzhen, which symbolizes the total moral stagnation of a traditional Chinese community, we find in Jiling a decadent utopia, a fallen Peach Blossom Spring, which points less to its writer's moral reflections on the outside world than to his aesthetic self-extension. From Li Yongping's self-indulgent play with the conventions of nostalgia, we discern that biographical "rootlessness" is not an original sin he wants to overcome through native soil writing but a fortunate state he has taken advantage of.

Li Yongping's *Jiling Chronicles* thus brings us full circle to the point at which our discussion of Shen Congwen began. Though Shen Congwen first looked like a conventional realist, his discourse of imaginary nostalgia engenders all the seeds that gave rise to Mo Yan's, Song Zelai's, and Li Yongping's radical harvest of nativism. These writers take up where Shen Congwen left off half a century ago, demonstrating that nostalgia is something more than a yearning for the lost home or past. By writing about specific native places, one has to come to terms with the genealogy of nostalgia in (literary) history. Song Zelai vacillates between a longing for the lost native soil and a longing for the lost verisimilitude of native soil writing; Mo Yan brings time and history into question through a fantastic intermingling of personal and national past; and Li Yong-ping exposes the utterly imaginary grounds of nostalgia by creating a homeland out of other texts. Together their works open up new horizons of native soil fiction and bring to light the modernist aspect of Shen Congwen we have previously overlooked.

5 | Urban Exoticism in Modern and Contemporary Chinese Literature

The inclusion of exotic imagery in Chinese art and literature is not a new phenomenon. One could even assert that artistic exotica are as old as the genres—painting, sculpting, and literature—in which they occur. Ever since the formation of the *zhiguai* genre (brief prose entries discussing out-of-the-ordinary people and events) during the period of the Eastern Jin (317–420), the topic of the "Strange," the "Foreign," and the "Supernatural" has been a standard element of Chinese literature.

The evolution of an "exoticist" consciousness, however, that elevates the exotic image from its traditional function of narrative ornamentation to the pivot of artistic motivation is a relatively recent phenomenon. As a vital expression of the modern "Oriental" predicament of being caught between East and West, tradition and modernity, it played a pronounced role in the development of modern Chinese literature, and has continued to play this role on the contemporary literary scene after 1985. Very similar to eastward-looking European exoticism, it reflects the struggle for aesthetic reinvigoration by initially employing new content in order to elicit new forms of expression. But whereas Western "Orientalism" has attracted close attention, "Occidentalism" has barely appeared on the map of cross-cultural criticism. A crucial element of the celebrated era of modernity has thus been neglected.

The Modern Era

The unfolding of Western exoticism in modern Chinese literature is closely tied to two events: the spatial development of urban Western enclaves in China, and the creative input of foreign-trained Chinese students who had returned home. The following synopsis centers upon the Shanghai phenomenon and, more specifically, upon the French and international concessions, which not only exhibited Asia's most elaborate Western façade, but also became the environment where most returning Chinese students chose to live and work.

Based on similarities in their aesthetic convictions, which in turn were greatly influenced by the literary fashions dominating the foreign country in which they had studied, clusters of foreign-educated writers began to form in 1920s Shanghai. As has been pointed out by several pioneering scholars of the field, the advent of May Fourth literature—and in particular, the Shanghai literary scene—would not have happened without the input of Chinese writers returning from abroad.[1] The Chuangzao She (Creation Society), the illustrious avant-garde clique of young writers educated in Japan, and the Wenxue Yanjiu Hui (Society for Literary Research), publisher of the predominantly realist magazine *Xiaoshuo yuebao* (Short Story Monthly), which featured many works by returnees from Europe and Japan, are probably the most famous and most widely researched literary circles.

In this study I introduce a number of writers and groups that also played a major part in shaping the Shanghai literary scene but have been purged from the annals of literary history during the recurrent Chinese renunciations of "decadent" literature and "imitation foreign devil" authors. If mentioned at all, and here the standard approaches of Eastern and Western scholars differ little, artistic associations outside the orthodox inventory of May Fourth writers have been consigned to the realm of the footnote. They are viewed as "exotic" writers who deal with marginal—"exotic"—topics in their work. This is a highly distorted view, since at the time many of these forgotten names were very much at the center of literary culture. Similarly, the issue of "exoticism" has always constituted an important element of modern Chinese literary discourse.

*   *   *

An assortment of anecdotal *wenyan* texts attest to the fact that Shanghai had been the object of popular curiosity well before the May Fourth revolution. *Huyou zaji* (Miscellaneous Notes on Touring Shanghai, 1875), *Shanghai yichang jingzhi* (A Vista of Shanghai's Concessions, 1894), or *Shanghai zazhi* (Shanghai Pictorial, 1910) are lively accounts of the city's oddities, comprising a mélange of popular poetry, gossipy anecdotes, illustrations of the "bizarre," and guidebook-style information about trendy entertainment facilities.

Even large-scale literary productions of the premodern period had broached the topic. China's last acclaimed novel of the premodern age, Zeng Pu's *Niehai hua* (Flower in an Ocean of Sin, 1905), profusely illustrates the rise of Shanghai and introduces the city's peculiarity as a suitable subject for literary fiction. One of Zeng's biographers has pertinently synopsized the urbane atmosphere presented in the novel:

> In Shanghai the old meets the new, and the East meets the West. There is a constant bustle of activity; if it is not a flower exhibition in a public park, then it is a secret revolutionary meeting somewhere else. In the streets and public places, young men and women dressed in Western clothing are talking to foreigners in an alien tongue. Even dignified officials, wearing their long gowns and official caps, can be found dining in Western-style restaurants, eating with knives and forks, and drinking champagne and coffee. In their conversations, they talk about the government, politics, literature, and the arts of foreign countries. In the last decades of the Qing dynasty, Shanghai was transformed from a busy trading port into the cosmopolitan, commercial center of China.[2]

Peking, on the other hand, is portrayed as the stronghold of stubborn, reactionary forces, a foil to the dynamic potential embodied by the rapidly developing metropolis of Shanghai.

"In our day, Paris is the only city that is permanently in the state of a volcano,"[3] Zeng Pu's idol Victor Hugo had stated once, and Zeng seemed to think the same about Shanghai. Just as the venerated *maître* of the French literary scene had become a principal recorder of Parisian life, Zeng Pu may have aspired to become the first literary chronicler of Asia's Paris—Shanghai, perilous whirlpool and vibrating harbinger of the new.

However, the Chinese writer's approach to Shanghai did not bear merely frolicsome qualities. Although Shanghai's concessions contained exhilarating "exotic" aspects, they rarely ceased to be a reminder of colonial humiliation. When the May Fourth movement took place in 1919, combining antitraditional slogans with an anti-imperialist agenda, the creative treatment of Shanghai became even more controversial.

The following analysis of nationalist, romanticist, and modernist exoticism outlines how the various branches of urban exoticism developed in spite of—or rather, as an integral part of—the Chinese discourse on colonialism. It shows, moreover, that within this discourse nationalist and aestheticist positions not only overlap but are indeed two sides of the same coin.

Nationalist Exoticism: The City as Aesthetic Laboratory and the Reappraisal of Colonial Shanghai

"Many Chinese saw Shanghai as a cause for shame, a great city built on Chinese soil by Chinese hands, yet not really part of China."[4] Thus an American scholar of Shanghai history defines the wave of "new nationalism" that rose during the 1920s, and his view aptly reflects the general assessment of the political atmosphere at the time. However, there is another aspect to the reaction of the "new nationalists" to colonial Shanghai. In *Ce qui ne s'avoue pas* (1927), Georges Soulié de Morant describes a typical crowd of locals rubbing shoulders in the bars of Fuzhou Road, Shanghai's busiest entertainment district: "This crowd of people, escaped convicts, businessmen, political activists, bankers, students, and literati, clamors all day long about fighting off the oppression of foreign terror, and how one should have reappropriated the foreign concessions a long time ago—when actually they hope the foreigners will stay there forever."[5]

As consul of the French concession, Soulié was part of the "foreign terror" himself, of course, and one could certainly argue that his irony reflects a typical bias of the colonialist mindset. Yet let us see how Fu Yanchang, one of the most outspoken nationalist art critics of the time, voices his opinion during the same year:

> Only since the foreigners have come to Shanghai does this city have parks, clean streets, fancy department stores, skyscrapers, a concert season from October to May, museums, libraries, and other tokens of a national cultivation of the arts . . . It is a shame that there is too little of that in the heritage of our Chinese nation. Those dramas featuring men dressed up as women, the utterly depressing and passionless tunes called Classical Music, landscape paintings that have nothing to do with our people, mud huts propped up by long poles—none of these can be considered to be a national cultivation of the arts. We should all admit that the civilization with the finest national culture, way ahead of other nations, is Europe.[6]

Fu Yanchang had lived in Japan and the United States during the years 1917–1923. When he finally returned to Shanghai, he launched a persistent campaign for the "aesthetics of everyday life" by writing prolifically in *Yishu pinglun* (Art Critique), the daily *Minguo ribao's* literary supplement, and later in his own magazine, *Yishu jie* (Art World). In literary reminiscences of the time, we meet him chiefly in his role as the respected elder of a loosely associated group of Shanghai art critics who were eagerly searching for a new concept of "Chinese national art."

His quest for a reinvigorating formula for native aesthetics led Fu to the orthodox roots of Western civilization: Greek culture. He and his literary companions viewed the Westerner's colonial success as directly related to cultural heritage. It is, in their reckoning, the legacy of the strong-man image in Greek mythology that enabled the Westerner, in a gesture of aristocratic aggression, to take over China.

"I love the Greeks," exclaims Fu in all earnestness, "I love the English, the Dutch, the Japanese, the Mongols, and the Manchus— they are the aristocrats among all nations; they are capable of enjoying an artistic civilization . . . and they possess a national consciousness, a fact that enables them to seek out colonies that will make their life richer and more beautiful."[7] Fu's only misgiving about the imperialist system arises from the weakness of his own country, not from what he sees as the fundamentally "admirable" expansionist urge exhibited by the colonial powers.

In the eyes of Fu and his acquaintances, the canons of Greek mythology (in particular Homer's *Iliad* and *Odyssey*), the German *Nibelungenlied,* and the Icelandic sagas were to constitute the most essential guidebooks for the aesthetic invigoration of China. To them, these writings exuded the positive energy that they felt was lacking in their own literary heritage. Jia Baoyu, as protagonist of the celebrated Qing novel *Honglou meng* (The Dream of the Red Chamber, 1791), China's most prototypical literary hero, was scornfully labeled a dreamy wimp who looked preposterous when set next to the handsome warriors of the *Iliad;* and Lin Daiyu, his tubercular female match, Fu reckoned, could even less stand a comparison with the rosy-cheeked, healthy heroines depicted in Greek tales.

"If China wants a new and alive art," declared Zhu Yingpeng, the painter of the group, "we will definitely have to 'Hellenize' our ideas!"[8] Zhu frequently illustrated his manifestoes with paintings of stark-naked, victorious pirates who have Herculean bodies attached to their Chinese features. Likewise, his female portraits display the ideal of a full-bosomed Chinese-style Venus, or a vivacious Asian Salomé. In a sense, Zhu's creative and educational work aims at a Chinese revival of the ideal citizen image as propagated by the ancient Greeks: *kalos kai agathos,* the good, sophisticated, and, last but not least, physically cultivated citizen.

The fascination with the naked body marks Zhu's condemnation of the code of Confucian morality, which he holds responsible for China's weakness. Zhu Yingpeng is delighted to find the Greek gods uninhibited in their sexual and gustatory desires. To him, the portrayal of Zeus seeking worldly pleasures, and the annual Bacchanalia commemorating Dionysus' frenzy, are indicators of an artistic culture that has captured the essence of life—*yinshi nannü,* the urge for food and sex, the primal instincts that constitute the basis of human nature.

Zhu's heroes in real life are thus situated in the "Golden Ages" of Western civilization, in particular ancient Greece, ancient Rome, and Renaissance Europe—the classic times that in nineteenth-century historiography so sharply contrast with the "Dark Era" of the

Christian Middle Ages. He was especially intrigued by popular images of the Roman emperor Nero and the French king Louis XIV. Following their zealous deification in the salons and the literature of the European fin de siècle, he regarded them as representative artist-heroes who had succeeded in the age-old task of transforming life into a gigantic piece of art. The burning of Rome thus becomes Nero's most beautiful poem, and Louis XIV's monumental architecture is viewed as the materialization of his artistic genius.

Using the main slogan of the group, Zhu Yingpeng proclaims the concept of *Wei rensheng er yishu* (Art for life's sake), but he brandishes its exoticist connotation—make life a unified piece of art—as opposed to the sense of socialist activism that this formula came to connote at a later date.

In retrospect, the "aesthetic world" evoked in Zhu Yingpeng's paintings and writings appears altogether familiar to scholars of nineteenth-century literature. We are reminded of Nietzsche—that "last disciple and initiate of Dionysus"—and his *Birth of Tragedy* (1872). We hear distinct echoes of Wagner's choruses and of Hippolyte Taine's eulogies for the genius of the Renaissance. Flaubert's literary veneration of Nero, and the eccentric poet-count Robert de Montesquiou's salon outings in the attire of Louis XIV, come to mind. In short, the Shanghai group assembled the varied intellectual ingredients of fin-de-siècle classicism into a theoretical stew designed to bring new life to Chinese aesthetics.

Fu Yanchang's and Zhu Yingpeng's involvement with "orthodox Western aesthetics" led directly to a reappraisal of their own cultural heritage. Chinese civilization itself, after all, embraces a rich reservoir of popular narratives such as the *bianwen* (chantefables) discovered just then at Dunhuang. But rigid Confucian values, they argued, had banned this splendid and colorful material from the canonized fund of national treasures and thereby not only obstructed its appreciation but also prevented its transformation into "life."

Consequently the group produced another slogan designed to put the maxim "Art for life's sake" into action: *Dao minjian qu* (Let's go among the people). This folkloristic by-product of their high-brow cultural interests linked Fu's clique closely to philologists such as

Zheng Zhenduo and Gu Jiegang. Zheng was both a respected scholar of Chinese popular literature and the first Chinese translator of Homer's *Iliad*. Not surprisingly, he was a favorite dinner guest among Fu's circle.

Gu Jiegang, the procreator of a movement that endeavored to discriminate between Confucian myth and historical truth, appears to have had even closer ties to the group. His pioneering fieldwork included excursions to folk festivals, and key figures of Fu's group such as Zhu Yingpeng, Xu Weinan, and Zhang Ruogu occasionally accompanied him on these outings. "Let's go among the people"—a slogan that later also came to bear socialist connotations[9]—thus becomes transparent as another manifestation of the group's exotic proclivities. To them, the trip to a Hangzhou temple feast was an expedition from the familiar "cultivated" literati haven of Shanghai into the unknown "wild" realms of Chinese popular culture.

The group's ideal of an "artful society" was a China of "classically" built men and women with exquisite aesthetic taste; "Art for life's sake" entails transforming life—and in nationalist terms, society—into a piece of art, but it also means utilizing art as the most important medium to reach this goal.

At first glance the artistic ideology of Fu Yanchang and his acquaintances appears to be a hodgepodge of incompatible currents of Western aesthetics, lacking a unifying idea. However, a synopsis of *Yishu sanjia yan* (Three Personal Views on Art, 1927), a collection of articles by Fu Yanchang, Zhu Yingpeng, and Zhang Ruogu, titled after Tanizaki Junichirō's 1920 essay, "Geijutsu ikkagen" (A Personal View on Art), clearly discloses the central idea of the group's aesthetic cosmos: the city. On the first pages of the volume, Fu Yanchang asserts that the city is the most essential precondition for art in a modern age: "Modern art, out of necessity, makes the city its center. Even those artists who consider nature as their aesthetic yardstick cannot avoid living in the city. Monumental architecture, concerts, opera, art exhibitions, spacious parks, grandiose sculptures, etc., owe their existence to the city. That is why I claim that modern art cannot happen outside the scope of the city."[10]

The city provides the temples of "Civilization," museums, opera houses, and the like, where urban culture celebrates and reaffirms itself. Moreover, the *civitas,* the city-state community, constitutes an accessible body of people that can be reached by means of education. This classically derived urban philosophy did not in any way contradict the group's maxim, "Let's go among the people"—a locution that in post–May Fourth China was generally associated with rural images. "Our slogan 'Let's go among the people' has nothing to do with going to the countryside and working the fields," Fu clarifies elsewhere, "but rather asks you not to disdain urban life."[11]

For Fu Yanchang and his circle, of course, "City" becomes a synonym for Shanghai, the only urban center in China that offered the necessary appearance of "Civilization." Consequently their concept of city literature bears the marks of Shanghai's local characteristics. As Fu asserted in 1923, "My artistic ideals are with edifice literature, with city literature, with modern drama and opera—and to my own queer reckoning, those plays should be entirely written in Shanghainese, China's most beautiful local dialect."[12]

The ardent promoter of local color further urged writers from other Chinese locales to reproduce the dialects of their respective hometowns in print. The Cantonese Lu Mengshu, for instance, was encouraged to insert native idioms into his novel *Achuan jie* (My Sister Achuan).[13] The result would at once be "exotic" and "nationalistic."

In the context of nationalist exoticism, the Shanghai phenomenon thus did not primarily connote a cause for shame but became the prototypical setting where the formation of a Chinese-style *civitas* was to take place. In the writings of Fu's clique, the ideological thrust of the indignant slur "Shanghai is not a part of China" was reversed. He and many like-minded intellectuals considered the special status of Shanghai as a circumstance that would eventually benefit the aesthetic outlook of the whole nation. Shanghai, because it was so "exotic," so different from the rest of China, could become a cultural laboratory where, *in vitro,* the experimental restoration of Chinese civilization would be undertaken. The foreigners had provided the necessary facilities, Fu calculated, and now the Chinese inhabitants of Shanghai had to be instructed in how to employ them for their own aesthetic evolution. In this manner perhaps the earliest stage of

post–May Fourth exoticism was founded upon two pillars: nationalism and the City, that is, Shanghai.

The Chinese Salon World of the French Concession, 1925–1929

Once the *Yishu jie* campaign for "orthodox" Greek art education had
been launched, the familiar objective of producing a French atmosphere took center stage; for the purpose of Fu Yanchang's and Zhu
Yingpeng's aesthetic proposition was not to return physically to an
archaic age, but to reproduce its fundamental ideals in the context
of modern Chinese society. It was clearly the image of France that
dominated their impressions of a current aesthetic paradise in the
West. Only in France, and not in impoverished Greece or lethargic
Italy, the group believed, had the dynamic spirit of old been preserved and "updated" in the various currents of nineteenth-century
art and literature.

The French concession was definitely the favorite excursion
ground of young Chinese street wanderers. To them the area's main
boulevard—the Avenue Joffre, which is today's Huaihai Lu—represented a miniature Champs-Élysées. In the many cafés along the
Avenue Joffre the curious visitor was greeted in melodious French—
not by this prattling "colonial world jargon,"[14] as Zhang Ruogu called
the English language—and was able to immerse himself in a symphony of mellifluous images. Zhang Ruogu's report of a solitary visit
to the Café Tikochenko is a suitable example:

> As I was quietly sitting at the window of this street-corner café,
> surveying the young urban couples strolling down the boulevard, a
> pleasurable feeling of the highest intensity came over me. There
> was no trace of the usual vehicle hubbub or the noisy barter of the
> street vendors, and no foul odors insulted the nose. There was just
> the delicate whirring sound of the electrical fan, and the tremor of
> silverware inadvertently grazing a porcelain cup, that blended with
> a few strains of piano music from upstairs and gently penetrated
> my ears.[15]

Zhang clearly defines the intriguing sensual atmosphere that he had
longed to experience in the French concession. The sketch of the

Tikochenko visit, along with other outings to the Avenue Joffre, is included in one of his essay collections that bears the programmatic title *Yiguo qingdiao—Exotic Atmospheres,* or EXOTISME, as the term is translated in Zeng Pu's preface.[16]

Thus were born the first salons modeled after the Chinese vision of Parisian lifestyle. Fu Yanchang, Zhu Yingpeng, Zhang Ruogu, and some of their acquaintances undoubtedly have to be credited for their prominent role in introducing the ideals of the literary café and the French-style salon to Shanghai. However, neither of them had the funds to create a "genuine" salon modeled after the fancy meeting grounds of the literary aristocracy of Paris.

This task was simultaneously taken up by their well-to-do friends Zeng Pu and Shao Xunmei, who possessed the resources to realize their exotic aspirations in truly material dimensions. First of all, both Zeng and Shao commanded a much more detailed knowledge of France than the three "Shanghai princes." Shao Xunmei had been an art student in Paris himself, and Zeng Pu, though he had not been abroad before the founding of his literary club in 1927, was looking back on three decades of dedicated enthusiasm for French salon literature.

Zeng's tutor had been the flamboyant "General" Chen Jitong, who already during the 1890s had seen the French concession as a pendant to Paris. Under his guidance Zeng Pu dedicated the years 1898–1902 almost exclusively to the study of French literature. Soon, however, he obtained a government post in the province of Jiangsu and took leave of Shanghai. It took him more than twenty years to return, but he was still determined to realize his youthful dream of creating a French enclave in China. Together with his oldest son, Zeng Xubai, he founded the publishing house Zhenmeishan in 1927. Its ambitious name—"The True, Beautiful, and Good"—was directly modeled after the popular parole of the French romantics. The publishing venture, via its affiliated literary magazine and a series of monographs, was intended to introduce world literature to a Chinese audience, with special consideration for the canon of French literature. In Zeng Pu's eyes, of course, the vision of France alone contained the promise of an intriguing, aesthetically perfect Other.

Until then, Zeng had never ventured beyond the boundaries of his native China, and his idealized visions originated exclusively in books from or about France. Similar to the French exoticists of the Parisian fin de siècle, Zeng celebrated the Other through the institution, selectively understood, of the salon. Zeng Xubai remembers: "The primary goal of the Zhenmeishan endeavor was the institution of a Francophile center around which other Parisian-style salons would group themselves. And since Shanghai was not only the primary meeting place for East and West, but also the most important gathering place for lovers of art and literature, our plan should naturally be realized here."[17]

Already the environs of the carefully selected Zeng residence at 115 rue Massenet were able to evoke the mirage of a Parisian existence. Situated in the heart of the French concession, Zeng Pu could conjure up images of an aesthetically saturated French life:

> Massenet is the name of a modern French composer, and as soon as I step out on the street, his operas LE ROI DE LAHARE and WERTHER come to my mind. Late in the afternoon when I stroll over the tightly knit shadows of the tree-lined walk, the tragic scenarios of LE CID and HORACE unfold on my left, vis-à-vis the RUE DE CORNEILLE. And on my right, from the direction of the RUE DE MOLIÈRE, the cynical laughter of a TARTUFFE or a MISANTHROPE seems to enter my ears. Horizontally in front of me stretches the AVENUE DE LAFAYETTE . . . which evokes the scenery depicted in her LA PRINCESSE DE CLEVES and the historic sites described in MEMOIRES INTERESSANTES. The French Park is my [Jardin du] LUX-EMBOURG and the Avenue Joffre my CHAMPS-ÉLYSÉES. My steadfast determination to stay in this area is solely rooted in this eccentric EXOTISME of mine.[18]

The disciples of the "salon" used to meet in the sanctuary of the house, Zeng's study. The walls were lined with imposing numbers of foreign books, of which a handwritten index was circulated among its members. Zeng's second son, Yaozhong, had been a student of medicine in Berlin. When German postwar inflation had reached its most desperate state, he used an opportune moment to acquire a thousand-volume collection of French literature from a private source for very little money.

Zeng Pu loved the role of the Francophile scholar, but just as much he indulged in the image of the nonchalant host who is adored by a crowd of young artists. Here is another passage from the memoirs of his son:

There was hardly an evening when the lights of our guest room didn't glow until very late at night. My father was not only extraordinarily hospitable, but he also exuded an intoxicating fascination that caused every guest to be drawn deeply into the stream of his conversation . . . Whoever came, came, and whoever felt like leaving, left, always without the exchange of notable formalities. My father cherished this free and unconstrained atmosphere; only in this manner, he believed, would everything resemble a genuine French salon.[19]

Frequent guests at Zeng's house were not only Francophile literati and translators, such as Li Qingyai, Xu Weinan, Xu Xiacun, Zhang Ruogu, or Shao Xunmei, but also publishers, painters, and writers who belonged to the cream of the contemporary Shanghai literature scene—Lu Mengshu, for example, forgotten founder of *Yinxing* (Silver Stars), China's first movie magazine; or famous writers such as Yu Dafu, Xu Zhimo, and Tian Han; and last but not least, the pioneers of the nationalist brand of Western exoticism, Fu Yanchang and Zhu Yingpeng.

Conversations at Zeng Pu's salon covered a wide range of topics. Naturally, the participants were particularly fond of "exotic" subjects. Zeng's young disciple Zhang Ruogu remembers:

Everything was discussed here: Lin Shu's translation endeavors, Gu Hongming's English publications, Anatôle France's impressionist method of literary criticism, Brunetière's theory of opposition, anecdotes about George Sand, Pierre Lôti, and other French writers, our critical opinions on contemporary Chinese authors such as Zhang Ziping, Yu Dafu, or Lu Xun, and our views on a standardized world language with Latin letters.[20]

Most of the colleagues even assumed a Chinese quasi-identity based on their favorite French idol. Xu Xiacun, for instance, had translated Pierre Lôti's *Madame Chrysanthème*. Consequently Zhang Ruogu availed himself of Anatôle France's eulogy for Loti to make

Xu a "Shanghai Loti."[21] This gesture, of course, implied his own status as "Shanghai's Anatôle France." In 1928 Zhang had published an essay collection titled *Wenxue shenghuo* (My Literary Life), which clearly emulated France's *Vie littéraire*. Zeng Pu himself was best known for his work on the literary legacy of Victor Hugo and, as his biographer remarks, "possibly regarded himself as a Chinese incarnation of Hugo."[22] In combination, moreover, Zeng Pu and Zeng Xubai were perceived as a Shanghai version of "Alexandre Dumas père et fils,"[23] and Zhang Ruogu's youthful esteem for the old Zeng Pu was labeled a duplicate of Loti's veneration of his early mentor, Pouvilion.[24]

Slightly different conditions inspired the exoticist feats of Zeng Pu's second young friend, Shao Xunmei. Shao was known as the independently wealthy mogul of the Shanghai literary scene who could afford to travel extensively in France and other parts of Europe. His forefathers included several notable officials who at some point had procured connubial bonds with the family of the eminent statesman Li Hongzhang. His father, Shao Heng, had been one of the notorious "four playboys" of Beijing; in order to continue this extravagant lifestyle after his move to Shanghai, he purchased a variety of small mansions in every section of the port city.

Xunmei, as the eldest son of the clan *(da shaoye)*, had inherited not only the bulk of the family's assets but also his father's spendthrift ways. When he was seventeen years old, he first journeyed to England, where he managed to enter college at Cambridge University. Two years later he proceeded to Paris, where he became a student at the École des Beaux-Arts. In 1926 wedding arrangements called him finally back to Shanghai.

Soon therafter Shao Xunmei founded Jinwu Shudian (the Gold Chamber Bookstore), an avant-garde press that especially accentuated the material aspects of publishing. In the vein of the English *Yellow Book*, the bookstore's journal *Jinwu yuekan* (Gold Chamber Monthly) brandished a golden cover design. The press also produced deluxe book editions that were lavishly bound and sumptuously illustrated. For the specific purpose of enhancing the synesthetic quality of his publications, the notorious decadent even acquired an offset machine that was capable of producing his eye-catching trademark—golden book covers—and multicolored illus-trations. Even decades later Shao's fancy printing equipment was the only thing of its kind in China; after the Communist takeover, it was reportedly used to print the new government's first colored propa-ganda pamphlets.

One of the bookstore's self-indulgent projects (the average sales rate being less than two thousand copies per item) was the edition of "decadent" poetry composed by the proprietor himself. Shao's maiden work, *Hua yiban de zui'e* (The Flowerlike Evil, 1928), should be mentioned specially here, since—as a takeoff of Baudelaire's *Fleurs du mal*—it constitutes another Chinese example of identifica-tion through epithet with one of the Parisian masters.

Affiliated with Shao Xunmei's publishing venture was a Franco-phile salon that had very close links with the Zhenmeishan clique. So elaborate were the material dimensions of this place that even visitors acquainted with the exotic interior of Zeng Pu's salon were awed. Here is a fictionalized account by Zhang Ruogu, printed by Zhenmeishan in 1929:

> The young master's residence was one of Shanghai's superior man-sions. Entirely built in marble, surrounded by a large garden, and approached by eight pathways wide enough for advancing automo-biles, the estate looked like a manifestation of the Eight Diagrams with a tall Western building in the middle. The center of the house formed a hall that was magnificently decorated like an emperor's throne room . . . And there was the host's private study, where he entertained guests. Here, too, the interior decoration was excep-tionally opulent; the wall was adorned by an authentic bust of the poetess Sappho recently excavated in the volcanic city of Pompei—this item alone was worth more than 5,000 dollars. Furthermore, there was a manuscript by the English poet Swinburne that had been acquired for 20,000 pounds in London . . . In the center of the room stood a STEINWAY piano . . . and right next to it there was a pile of music scores that were all bound in jade-colored snake leather.[25]

Sometime during the early 1930s, the "young master," as his friends endearingly called him, added a living attraction to his ornate fin-de-siècle enclave by "acquiring" a foreign mistress, namely, the American reporter Emily Hahn. For her he purchased a snug mansion in the vicinity of the Avenue Joffre, where, according to the memory of Zhang Kebiao, "many friends gathered to look at the exotic beauty."[26]

In sum, Shao Xunmei was a glamorous figure on China's primary salon circuit—a self-styled Shanghainese des Esseintes, the exemplary protagonist of the European fin de siècle (À rebours, 1884) that Huysmans had fashioned after Robert de Montesquiou, who first introduced the kimono to Paris and published his capricious poetry on Japanese silk paper; or a Chinese Fortunio, who resided in his Western villa in Shanghai just as Théophile Gautier's prototype of the exotic hero dwelt in an Oriental glass palace created in the middle of Paris (L'Eldorado, 1837).

Just like his Western idols, Shao Xunmei celebrated the revitalizing powers of an imaginary Other with the help of exotic fetishes. He was a true exoticist; no great poet, but indubitably the most eccentric urban dandy alive in late-1920s Shanghai. In this function he was admired, endearingly mocked, and frequently topicalized in the writings of the Jinwu and Zhenmeishan authors.

It becomes evident that the traditional Chinese custom of literary "colleagues" gathering habitually at a specified location was interpreted by the Shanghai exoticists as a "French" feature within their own cultural heritage. As demonstrated in my introduction of the Yishu jie, Zhenmeishan, and Jinwu cliques, the gregarious "salon" aspect of their endeavors was extremely important. Although the three circles flaunted agendas that seem different or even contradictory at first glance, such as hellenism, national and physical education, nineteenth-century romanticism, or fin-de-siècle decadence, people and ideas flowed freely among them. At a more fundamental level, they all joined hands in the common pursuit of "Civilization"—an ideal that was at once artful and lifelike, eccentric and nationalistic, modern and traditional, Franco-Greek and Sino-Japanese, and, one may add, exotic and familiar. In this capacity the three groups

constituted the base of a tightly interlinked salon network that flourished during the late 1920s in Shanghai and set the standards for
other salons still to come.

Shanghai Rhapsodies: Modernist Exoticism, 1929–1933

Nearing the 1930s, we find the Francophile salon and café enthusi-
asts still playing a major part in Shanghai's literary scene. Their
concept of "exotic atmospheres," however, was undergoing radical
changes. Whereas during the early and mid twenties the chimerical
vision of Paris had been styled after nineteenth-century renditions
of the Quartier Latin, Montmartre, and Montparnasse, it was now
being adjusted to the aesthetic trends pervading contemporary Paris
and modern Tokyo, which had just risen from the rubble of the 1923
Kanto earthquake.

By the late twenties Shanghai had acquired many of the faddish
features of the international compound metropolis. The booming
port city's cosmopolitan character intensified as an increasing number of immigrants, especially White-Russians, continued to stream
toward it from all corners of Asia. More and more cars appeared on
the streets, the local stock market emerged as one of the leading
exchanges in the world, and the commercial amusement facilities
expanded remarkably. This is the Shanghai we all know; epitomized
by *Ziye* (Midnight, 1933), Mao Dun's standardized portrait of burgeoning late-twenties Shanghai—best-selling in its time, widely translated, and prolifically reprinted due to its endorsement by Communist ideologues—the representation of the city as a sinful maelstrom
of lecherous and money-oriented obsessions had become engraved
in the minds of Chinese and foreign readers alike.

However, this conventional, unambiguously negative image of
urban Chinese self-representation is much too one-sided. As I have
demonstrated in previous studies, there exists a rich reservoir of
literary vignettes topicalizing the bright cosmopolis, Shanghai in
1927–1933.[27] By way of viewing the mushrooming amusement industry of the city as an indication of the evolution of real-life aesthetics,
the familiar group of Shanghai writers, among others, now contin-

ued their exoticist pursuit of "Civilization" even in the nonclassic "pandemonium" of the cosmopolitan age.

Shao Xunmei's ballad about Shanghai 1928 is perhaps the most concise introduction to the group's updated version of exotic atmospheres:

> I stand on top of a seven-story building,
> Above, there is the inaccessible sky;
> Below, the cars, telephone wires, and the horse race track.
>
> The front door of a theatre, the back view of a prostitute;
> Ah, these are the soul of a metropolis:
> Ah, these are the soul of Shanghai.
>
> Here one need not fear the rain or the sun:
> Or the autumn and winter of death, or the spring of life:
> How can any fiery summer be warmer than the lips!
>
> Here are true illusions, false sentiments;
> Here there are unsleeping evenings, smiling lights;
> Come, then, here is your burial ground.[28]

In this manner several writers now began to experiment with short stories that feature the growing world of European shops, restaurants, and cafés as an expansion of the narrow salon enclave. Xu Weinan's "Dushi de nannü" (City Romances, 1929), Zhang Ruogu's "Duhui jiaoxiangqu" (Urban Symphonies, 1929), and Liu Naou's "Dushi fengjing xian" (Urban Landscapes, 1930) are only the most prominent examples of this newfangled boom of urban exoticism.

The most notable protagonist of this faddish genre is the Western façade of Shanghai. Just as Zhang Ruogu had suggested in his *Yiguo qingdiao*, the exotic niches of Shanghai were associated with specific "foreign countries" and reflected as such. The narrator is generally assigned the role of exoticizing the Familiar by constructing *yiguo*, the Shanghainese vision of a glittering, breath-taking, and at times "forbidden" Other.

Typically, the fictional explorers of the familiarly strange—or, if you wish, strangely familiar—urban jungle often become transparent as prominent members of the group. Tian Han's experimental novel *Shanghai* (1927), for instance, describes the exploits of a clique of artists, among whom the informed reader can easily identify Fu Yanchang, Zhang Ruogu, Yu Dafu, Yu's fiancée Wang Yingxia, and the author himself.

Zhang Ruogu's novelette "Duhui jiaoxiangqu" (Urban Symphony, 1929), moreover, very clearly attests to the fact that Shanghai's foreign enclaves were viewed as an augmentation of the decorated salon at home. The story sets out from the fancy Western-style mansion of a certain "Mr. Peng," which apparently serves as a base camp for the host and two friends. After rejuvenating themselves in an extravagant bathroom (equipped with an electric razor, COTY cologne, and 4711 after-shave), the trio delves into the commercial exotica of the city. The curious night-revelers peruse the Orientalist decor of the bar CAIRO NIGHTS, indulge in the ambience of the CAFÉ DE RENAISSANCE (where, as rumor has it, a Russian PRINCESSE waits on guests), pace along the neon façade of the NEW YORK CAFÉ, and finally submerge into the dimly lit atmosphere of the Japanese dance club TROCADÉRO. The "two friends" are probably modeled after Fu Yanchang, the group's senior philosopher of urban culture, and Zhu Yingpeng. "Mr. Peng," doubtlessly, is a representation of Shao Xunmei.

Around 1930, urban exoticism had evolved into a multifaceted trend on the fast-paced literary circuit of Shanghai. After the institution of a dense salon network, city literature culminated in the formation of modernist prose. Xu Xiacun, Liu Naou, Mu Shiying, Shi Zhicun, Dai Wangshu, Liu Waiou, Ye Lingfeng, Xu Chi, Gao Ming, Hei Ying, Lou Shiyi, and a host of other young writers now sought to incorporate the intensity of urban stimuli into their literary style.

Mellifluous "Urban Symphonies" were suddenly sped up to "Urban Rhapsodies" (*Lou shiyi*) or "Shanghai Foxtrots" (*Mu shiying*). The intoxication with jazz, speed, strong coffee, and the exotic allure of the modern girl defines the circular-image staccato of this sensory prose: howling saxophones—flashing neon lights—strong perfume—howling saxophones—engine noise—perfume—flashing neon lights—*qianglie* (intense)—*ciji* (stimulation).

From nineteenth-century French romanticism to twentieth-century jazz age in five short years: fashions changed rapidly in 1920s

Shanghai. Typically the modernist short story's most common protagonist is thus the male seeker of romance who has yet to come to
terms with the rapidly unfolding urban jungle outside. In Liu Naou's
Dushi fengjing xian the anachronistic heroes generally end up as the
helpless prey of an evolutionary novelty—the self-assured urban girl
who pulls them into the sinful maelstrom of dance, alcohol, movies,
and unceremonious sex in anonymous hotel rooms.

In Europe this new set of cosmopolitan aesthetics had found its most
popular expression in the works of the novelist Paul Morand, who
between 1921 and 1935 produced a whole series of high-speed,
elliptical city portraits. Morand's images of intercity dining cars,
smoothly vibrating automobiles, and unscrupulous femmes fatales
quickly became very popular in Japan and left concrete imprints on
amorphous categories like "the West" or "modernity." His sensory
style, mostly in the translations of Horiguchi Daigaku, exerted a
crucial influence on the writers of the Shinkankakuha, the Japanese
avant-garde school of the neosensualists.

By 1929 Chinese students in Japan had imported Morand's unorthodox style and imagery via Tokyo into Shanghai. Especially Liu
Naou, the modernist writer who had spent his entire youth in Japan,
actively translated and emulated the dashing Frenchman and his
Japanese imitators. And interestingly, in his preface to *Duhui
jiaoxiangqu,* Zhang Ruogu remarks that he had "recently been ab-
sorbing the works of Paul Morand."

The Contemporary Era

*Shanghai, in the thirties, was one of the great cities of the world. And its luxurious
hotels were renowned for the attentive, yet unobtrusive, service that they lavished on
their guests. Now the magic that made Shanghai China's foremost business city has
returned.*

From an advertisement of the Yangtze New World Hotel, June 1990

Occidentalism is a mood, an atmosphere. After the Communists
purged Shanghai of its "decadent" elements, the city lost most of its

"exotic" allure. Although the new leaders opted for leaving all hotels and bank buildings intact, the famous Bund silhouette no longer harbored the urban spirit and quickly lost its evocative powers.

In 1981, however, foreign guests at the Peace Hotel, that is, the former Cathay Hotel, were surprised to find a jazz band in the ground-floor coffee shop. After the Central Committee had endorsed a new policy on tourism, not only were travel restrictions eased, but also controlled doses of nostalgic "decadence" were made available to restricted foreign audiences. "The seeds of the modernist twenties are budding again!" proclaimed the Japanese literary magazine *Yasō*, and it promptly produced *Shanghai Stardust*, a live recording of the curious Peace Hotel jazz band accompanied by a collection of photographs from prewar Shanghai. Hongkong's foreign-language presses began to reprint old-time guidebooks and novels such as Vicky Baum's *Shanghai 37*. Thus, after sampling Chinese culture (Beijing, Xian) and scenery (Hangzhou, Guilin), a growing number of European, American, and Japanese tour groups now came to Shanghai with the specific purpose of rediscovering "their" city. With a facsimile map of the foreign concessions in hand, they happily identified Huaihai Lu as Avenue Joffre, Shanghai Mansions as the Metropole, and People's Park as the Horse Race Track.

Since the commencement of tourism to the People's Republic, Westerners have their China exoticism back, but what about the Chinese themselves? Undoubtedly, China has changed a lot since the heyday of Shanghai sixty years ago. In many ways, however, the institution of the Peace Hotel jazz band marked the beginning of a new artistic era that again made the city its center. This discussion points out some of the motifs that establish urban exoticism in the contemporary period as a close relative, if not a direct successor, of its modern counterpart.

With the institution of the "foreigners-only" hotel, Shanghai, again, had its forbidden, mysterious, exotic space: a place where blonde and blue-eyed people in colorful clothes drank Johnny Walker, Coca-Cola, and Nescafé, smoked Winstons and Marlboros, and danced to jazz. It took another four years, however, before these exotic paraphernalia and the rhythm from an inaccessible "Inside" reached the streets. With the establishment of private enterprises (*getihu*) in 1985, the city as an atmospheric entity began to return.

Practically overnight, urban exoticism was back in Chinese literary discourse. A flood of novels, short stories, and poems appeared that focused exclusively on the characteristics of urban life; new magazines were created and new literary movements formed. A novel brand of literary criticism emerged that pondered the twofold face of urban existence, its creative and destructive powers.

The literary specimens I have mentioned were mostly published in the magazines *Chengshi wenxue* (City Literature), *Shanghai wenxue* (Shanghai Literature, bearing the English subtitle *Literary Modernity Exploration*), and *Guangzhou wenyi* (Guangzhou Art and Literature)— the three literary forums that, in comparison with other mainland periodicals, display the richest variety of urban themes during the period 1985–1991. Very similar to some of the magazines shaping the literary atmosphere of the 1920s and 1930s, they present a generation of young writers assimilating the newfangled urban stimuli that rapidly crop up around them, a generation that adheres to "Western aesthetics" as an alternative to the code of traditional literary values.

Many of the issues and images, and much of the vocabulary employed by these new urbanists, are strongly reminiscent of the modernist literature dominating the 1930s. In order to highlight the major motifs of contemporary Chinese city literature and their affinity to early Shanghai Occidentalism, I would like to return to the basic classification employed in the first part of this study.

"Xianshengmen, nüshimen" (Ladies and Gentlemen)—a young, bow-tie bedecked student startled the audience at the 1984 competition of Fudan University's annual speech contest—"I am here to talk to you about civilization, because absolutely none of you here have the tiniest inkling of what civilization means. Civilization, that is: Beethoven . . ." At this point he was ushered away from the microphone by a bystanding watchman. Fu Yanchang would have been delighted to hear a belated echo of his thoughts sixty years after he first propagated them. For the anonymous student was about to invoke Fu's vision of a Meiji-style China: an aesthetically reinvigorated nation run by tuxedo-clad administrators who orchestrate the orderly flow of urban traffic and waltzing couples into the spotless entity of "Civilization."

Chances are that one year later the silenced contestant would have been able to finish his speech, for the gist of his speech—packaged into a milder, less self-annihilating version—had by then grown into one of the mainstreams of officially sanctioned literary culture. In particular, in 1985 the Hunan-based magazine *Chengshi wenxue* set out to propagate the image of an iridescent Chinese metropolis without a Western dark side. "Ditie" (Subway) and "Zhoumo wuhui" (Weekend Dance), two poems published in 1985, exemplify this revitalized brand of nationalist aestheticism:

> Mightily it moves forward
> Welcoming glorious times with its high-pitched song
> It is the sound and the rhyme of a new age
> Which reverberates beneath the ground.[29]

> Lovely hair waves swing it:
> Streamlined, enchanting postures;
> Deep-red ties dance it:
> The romance of modern civilization;
> Right here—everybody can see it:
> A multicolored spring
> A spiraling, soaring nation.[30]

Once again, the city was established as the principal symbol of a booming national culture; its high-rises and technical assets employed as literary guideposts to a bright and uncomplicated future. And within this revitalized cultural space, we find all the familiar insignia of "Civilization" that had been defined half a century earlier: protagonists spend most of their allotted story time waltzing and riding taxis, while accompanying illustrations and cover sketches portray them (young urban Chinese with Western features in Western suits) standing before pianos, violins, or busts of Venus.

At first, the issue of reinstating formerly "decadent" culprits as cultural paragons was broached carefully. "Zai xuanzhuan de renliu zhong" (Among Spiraling Dancers) portrays an urban couple on their first date. While strolling down main street, they pass by a public dance that, for the first time, has been organized by city authorities. Both of them are passionate "salon dancers" at home, but, afraid that their potential mate might reject them for their controversial avocation, they each find pretenses for going home, only to return secretly to attend the dance by themselves. Among the frolicking crowds, of course, they meet again and some embarrassment is caused, but once freed of old value restrictions, their dancing skills immediately gain them the status of envy-arousing model in the eyes of the other participants as well as of the readers'.[31]

In a similar vein, "Weinasu de kanjian" (A Short-Sleeve Jacket for Venus) is a story about several young factory workers who install plaster copies of the Venus de Milo in their newly-wed homes—as a tribute to the (Western) concept of love. The old issue of "civilization or barbarianism" resurfaces via the conservative factory president, who, appalled by "this perverted thing," orders the immediate removal of the nudes. By clothing the busts, the young couples finally render the old-fashioned point of view ridiculous, and Venus—resurrected icon of exoticist urban culture—gets an official sanction for use in Chinese living rooms.[32]

Both stories reflect the upsurge of a new tide of urban culture, the phenomenology of which editors allowed to be treated in a far less circumspect manner by 1986. Private *shalong* (salons) for Western-style entertainment such as dance, guitar, or foreign-language conversation had blossomed since the early eighties. Now they became officially endorsed entities, like the regular exhibitions and poetry readings at Shanghai's Bali Kafeiting (Paris Café) or at Fudan University's student-run café Dajia Shalong (Everybody's), and writers felt more and more encouraged to topicalize this rapidly unfolding urban space and its inherent "mysteries."

The year 1986 marked an explosion of modernist urban themes in contemporary Chinese literature. Just as it was during the crucial years 1929–1933, the city is portrayed as a fast, noisy, vibrating whirlpool that draws everybody under its spell: an entity that devours the romantic hero, his past and his individual traits. The city is alive and feeds on people. From a first-paragraph urban long-shot, the typical story zooms in on an individual and his or her own drama; but while the individual gets entangled in the multifaceted web of urban stimuli, the city continues to breathe, rumble, and expand beyond the last words of the tale.

Just like their modern counterparts, contemporary "city people" are without history. Since metropolitans constantly meet for the first time, every encounter presents a fresh opportunity to act out a new role, a new personality, a new contingency of life. "Life is a play, and everybody is searching for his own stage,"[33] elucidates one contemporary urbanist. Thus the critic Wu Liang's contemplations on the "new" urban type read like a review of Liu Naou's novels, a guide to a world of nonchalantly meeting and parting lovers or business partners.[34]

After 1985, fashions rule the city again. Popular songs, the latest clothing design, the most recent cocktail combination, and foreign brands of cigarettes all figure prominently in contemporary urban stories. "City people" are shown to be users and producers of rapidly changing fashions, and the angle of their portrayal ranges from matter-of-fact reportage to existentialist drama.

Like its modern counterpart, the contemporary exploration of the city tries to distill its most characteristic "mood," its purest "atmosphere." The city as a whole emits a powerful centripetal force that operates on both its denizens and the people from the surrounding countryside. Within its boundaries exists a narrow range of urban sites where this energy is even further intensified. Thus urban exoticist literature focuses almost exclusively on those spaces that promise a particular density of *qifen* (atmosphere), *yunwei* (charm), *qingdiao* (sentiment), or *yiguo qingdiao* (exoticism): fancy apartments, restaurants, coffee shops, bars, discos, swimming pools, and so on; that is, the mysterious "Innermost" of urban life. Here the self-sustaining, centripetal force of the city is generated and represented in its purest form.

Gao Erpin's 1988 novel, *Dushi de nüer* (City Daughters), is probably the single most comprehensive inventory of contemporary city spaces. The author depicts the daily lives of a group of Chinese "yuppies," for the most part the pampered offspring of influential politicians and military cadres. They like to dance the tango, ride in privately owned Nissans, and guzzle gallons of Coca-Cola at their female trendsetter's "salon," a contemporary counterpart of Shao Xunmei's illustrious Shanghai abode:

Fei Honghong's home was part of a Western-style apartment complex and occupied at least sixty square meters. The light-yellow floor panels were freshly waxed and shone so brightly that they reflected the visitor's image. Two large French windows gave the place an extraordinarily stylish appeal, their double-layered curtains made from white georgette and purple velvet quivering faintly in the air conditioner's pathway . . . Right between the windows loomed a comfortable double bed of enormous proportions, wrapped smoothly in cream-colored silk embellished by a green ruffle. A stunning mermaid, clearly of European origin, served as reading lamp on one of the two bedside tables, while a stark-naked Western beauty, carved from mahogany, adorned the other one. Opposite the bed stood a three-door wardrobe and a small but exquisite sofa circle—a cozy and thoroughly pleasing arrangement.[35]

Here lavish parties with Hongkong businessmen are thrown, starring Honghong (Miss "Ultra-fashionable") in the self-chosen role of nineteenth-century urban hostess. She loves to read novels about Parisian salon life by Stendhal and Balzac, and her eager attempts to embody "an aristocratic Parisian lady" include the spectacle of a fin-de-siècle dress—designed after Mathilde de la Mole's costume in a popular film version of *The Red and the Black*.

While this private salon presents an interesting parallel to the Shanghai salon scene of the 1920s, the physical space that receives the most attention in Gao Erpin's novel is Luofu Binguan, the provincial capital's first modernized luxury hotel. Here the many plot lines converge. All of the protagonists either work here (cook, waitress), have a room here (deputy chief of province, secretary of foreign trade company), or are regular, foreign-currency-owning customers (violinist, businesswoman) at the hotel's "Innermost," that is, a bar and a restaurant on the seventeenth floor. Virtually everything happens in the hotel: the idealized modern couple meets, political decisions on the ever-present economic reforms are made, and not least of all, our young urbanites eat, drink, gossip, dance, court each other, and have sex.

It is a realm set apart from the rest of the world, yet it comes to represent the world. Modern life is crammed into this outlandish city within the city, and its relentless centripetal force draws the rest of town, the province, the country, even the world at large, inside.

"Dishigao" (Disco), Luo Jianlin's fact-based novelette on Shenzhen that was published the previous year, brings the literary phenomenon of the allegorical skyscraper to a climax:

> Like a majestic shrine, there towers a modern building above the industrial district of the special zone. Its roof forms a pyramid, condensing the essence of China's progressive thrust. Here, the special zone's high density of technical know-how is consolidated. While attentively listening to the voice of the Central Committee, every move on the far shore of the Pacific is scrutinized, so that news on the world's economy always detonates right here in this building. When the young executives take their lunch at the third-floor restaurant, everybody exhibits a most sophisticated manner, nothing suggests the usual running and shoving and clang-clanging of metal bowls and spoons. Conversation is hushed . . . Once every month they attend a salon on the eighth floor, where, among air conditioners, hanging lamps, and jasmine tea, they discuss themes such as "The Special Zone and China's Youth," "The Special Zone and the Future," "The Latest Trend of China's Reforms," and so on.[36]

Finally, it is the dance parlor—or disco, to use the up-to-date term—that is portrayed as the definitive interior of the modern high-rise. Just as Liu Naou, Mu Shiying, and Hei Ying had rendered the jazz hall of Shanghai's hotel world the figurative heart of modern, urban, exotic life during the period 1929–1933, contemporary urbanists have taken up the disco motif as the most pertinent allegory of human existence in the years after 1986.

Disco, according to contemporary city writers, condenses urban consciousness to its essence: everything is rhythm *(jiezou),* spiraling movements *(xuanzhuan),* and rapidly changing colors—only this, no distracting conversations, which allows the romantic imagination to roam. In modernist literature, an unremitting city maelstrom is always devouring the individual rather than letting the individual rule his city.

"I am losing myself," panics the tough female protagonist of "Disco." Blasted by pounding drum beats and pulsing strobe lights, she is close to a nervous breakdown. The final paragraph, however, brings a cathartic breakthrough: "The world is a mystic realm of rapidly changing shades," she realizes, "and in the eyes of the other dancers I am just a splinter in a heap of life, a most trifling fragment." Relieved, she lets life take over: "Disco! Disco! Disco!" is the closing verdict of the narrative.[37]

Evidently, urban exoticist works of the modern and contemporary periods share many features. Initially the polarization of "urban atmosphere" as a moral and political entity is most noteworthy. The literature of both periods at first exhibits efforts to differentiate a "good" city with a "healthy" dose of Western exoticism (standard insignia: suits, violins, pianos, ballet, Beethoven, Strauss, Chopin) from a "bad" city with "debauched" aspects (neon lights, sex, advertising culture). The basic issues are the same: although disco has replaced jazz as the twilight culprit of modern culture, "romantic" exotica such as coffee and waltzing appear on the "civilized" end of the value roster in both periods. Zhang Ruogu's *Kafei zuotan* (Café Confabulations, 1929) and many of the earlier urbanist writings in *Guangzhou wenyi* exemplify the elitist veneration of "classic" values while rejecting a pop culture ruled by short-lived fashions. Although both agree on the benefits of "healthy Civilization" for an aesthetically reinvigorated China, the low end of the scale is now mostly discussed in political terms ("capitalist") as opposed to the predominantly moralist tone of the 1930s ("decadent").

Furthermore, urban exoticist literature, today as sixty years ago, is a typology of urban existences: the "good" type, or at least the detached-journalist type, is contrasted with the debauched creatures who eventually drown in the urban vortex. Yet, also prominent in the typology of both eras is the mystifying femme fatale, or *nü qiangren*, as contemporary Chinese writers like to call her. She is the twilight figure who evades clear-cut boundaries. Strong, self-confident, and far more adaptable than her male counterparts, she alone is capable of mastering the dangerous game of the urban labyrinth. Although this feature makes her enviable even in the most moralizing portrait, she almost always remains a cryptic and unscrupulous being. In practically every story in *Dushi fengjing xian*, Liu Naou's females devour their mates "like praying mantises," and their contemporary counterparts humble even the toughest man.

Huang Jinhong's 1986 story "Nanzihan, ah, nanzihan" (Strong Man, Oh, Strong Man), for instance, a celebrated maiden work of contemporary urban consciousness, is not only a portrayal of new-fangled city spaces and their *getihu* connoisseurs but also an intro-duction of the inner-city tigress and the discomfiture of her unpre-pared mate. Huang's self-confident hero, Liu Bin, feels a strong attraction for the tenacious Cheng Yingyao, head of a successful private enterprise, but their marriage soon develops into a compet-itive show of domineering instincts.[38] And when a few years later the topic of the worldly heroine has developed into a well-worn stereo-type, the femme fatale is represented in terms that are even more suitable for evoking images of her 1930s counterpart. In "Heise bijini" (Black Bikini), Liao Xiaomian's 1990 story on the predica-ments of urban courtship, the mystifying heroine is introduced standing by a swimming pool: "A first look at her was like spotting an advertisement billboard: blue sky, azure waves, beach chairs, a young girl lifting her hand to sip cola, black hair, black bikini, snow white body, and everything melting into some sort of abstractionist sketch—an intriguing sight beyond proper description."[39]

Parallel to modernist literature of the 1930s, the urban woman is turning into the most pertinent symbol of modern city life: bright, alluring, unpredictable, just like the expanding metropolis itself. "Urban color is becoming feminized," notes a contemporary Guangzhou critic, and he elucidates: "Advertisement billboards, neon lights—tender seduction everywhere."[40] Typically, the male protagonist of Liao's story ends up like most of Liu Naou's dis-comfited antiheroes. A newcomer to the city, he is easy prey for the enigmatic black bikini who smokes, drinks, acts, and discards him after sex. Women turn on and off as unpredictably as neon lights, elsewhere ponders a disconcerted first-person narrator in the Jinwu Kafeiwu (Gold Chamber Café). And as if to avenge his perplexed species, he attacks his sexual partners with "an intense, inexplicable desire for revenge," but finally arrives at the conclusion: "Man, after all, is the weaker of the sexes."[41]

But apart from motific similarities, it is mostly the compelling search for an all-encompassing urban consciousness that accounts for the corresponding configuration of urban exoticist literature of the modern and contemporary eras. During the 1930s, it was the avant-garde group centered around the magazine *Xiandai (Modernité)* that ventured to formulate an "objective" aesthetics of urban phenomena; an aesthetics devoted to the kaleidoscopic representation of the city, aspiring to overcome standard moralist boundaries. During the period 1985–1991, it is clearly the magazine *Guangzhou wenyi* that aspires to duplicate this approach: "For several years now our publication has endeavored to pioneer the field of city literature,"[42] exclaimed a proud editor in February 1990.

Just as Shanghai urbanists tried to distinguish themselves from the pastoral mainstream of modern Chinese literature, the *Guangzhou wenyi* contributors take a vehement stand against leading literary fashions in search of "native soil" *(xiangtu wenxue)* and "native roots" *(xungen wenxue)*. One step further, they define urbanism as a southern domain; an aesthetic entity incongruous with the atmosphere of northern Beijing, where the depiction of urban life rarely transgresses the tight topical cycle of traditional customs, soldiers and peasants, and the country bumpkin marveling at six-story buildings. Northern city portraits, they reckon, invariably bring the countryside to the city—marketplace literature *(shijing wenxue)* at best, incapable of reflecting true urban consciousness and the density of pure city atmosphere. Just as modernists like Liu Naou, Shi Zhicun, or Mu Shiying used to draw a clear line between their own art and the "rustic" city pieces by Lao She and others, contemporary southern writers have coined the label *shijing wenxue* to distinguish themselves from "marketplace authors" like Liu Xinwu.

By late 1990 the metaphor of the colorful South—once utilized by avant-garde Shanghai writers during the 1920s—is exclusively being claimed by Cantonese writers and their main literary outlet, *Guangzhou wenyi*. This development is partly due to the rapid recovery of the magazine's agenda after the Tiananmen incident in June 1989, when publications elsewhere remained trapped in the artistically restrictive aftershock of the event. Until then Shanghai, too, had been a lively epicenter of the contemporary urbanist cause. The old hotbed of experimental literature had again fostered a group of self-declared "urban poets" *(chengshi shiren)* whose leading representatives Sun Xiaogang, Li Binyong, Song Lin, and Zhang Xiaobo came forth with a pioneering collection of urban verse in 1987.[43] But in 1991 we see the Shanghai literary scene—always extremely sensitive to political tremors—still staggering from the blow dealt by the removal of most of its progressive editors.

Guangzhou wenyi, however, not only managed to reinstate its columns "Dushi zhi guang" (City Luster), "Dushi nihong" (City Neon), and "Moli shijie" (Mystic Realms) by early 1990 but even succeeded in expanding its urbanist agenda by establishing the monthly features "Dushi wenxue bitan" (Urban Literature Essay Corner) and "Guangzhou, 100 ge miankong" (100 Faces of Guangzhou). Since 1985, all of these experimental forums have produced and sustained a group of young writers from Guangzhou (Canton) and the nearby cities of Shenzhen and Zhuhai. Huang Jinhong's literary career, for instance, is a typical *Guangzhou wenyi* success story. The magazine published his first piece in 1978, and thirteen years later he is being celebrated as China's most accomplished master of contemporary city reportage.

"If you want to understand Chinese urban civilization and its typology of urban characters, you have to research Guangzhou first,"[44] one of the group's aesthetic ideologues exclaims confidently, and his colleagues are doing just this: exploring the many dance halls, movie theaters, coffee shops, and fashionable *getihu* (private enterprises) of the southern metropolis with the unbiased eye of the urban street wanderer. Guangzhou reportage, by evocatively using names of specific streets and shops, draws a literary map of the city in exactly the same manner as the exotica hunter Zhang Ruogu and his friends had mapped out modern Shanghai.

Literary exoticism in China, today as sixty years ago, thus receives its creative momentum not only from the youthful search for an international urban aesthetics but also from its deliberate use of local color. Huang Jinhong's struggling heroes speak a definite Cantonese, in exactly the same way in which Fu Yanchang had advocated the literary use of Shanghainese during the 1920s. In both periods the local color of "Southland" *(Nanguo)* contains the germs of protest, drawing a clear line between the coastal avant-garde and the "old" aesthetic system dominating the northern hinterlands. Just as modern Shanghai exoticists liked to view their city as an antipode to "quasi-dynastic" Peking, contemporary Cantonese writers frequently contrast Guangzhou's money-driven mass culture, its "taxis" and "telephones," with Beijing's cadre system and official paraphernalia such as the elitist "limousine."

When after forty years Guangzhou's People's Theater reclaimed its original name—Haizhu Theater—in 1989, Huang Jinhong saw the event as a symbol for the return of urban color, and maybe even as a direct bridge to the modernist legacy of the thirties.[45] But only time can tell whether contemporary writers will be able to propel Chinese urban literature beyond the experimental stage in which it has remained since the late 1930s.

II | Subjectivity and Gender

6 | Text, Intertext, and the Representation of the Writing Self in Lu Xun, Yu Dafu, and Wang Meng

"Everything requires careful consideration if one is to understand it," notes the madman in his diary. "Since I could not sleep anyway, I read intently half the night, and only then did I see words between the lines; throughout the book were written the two words—'Eat People.'"[1] In this 1918 Lu Xun story, it is by reading the gaps between the words *(zifeng)* of his history text, rather than the words themselves, that the central character arrives at the "truth" about the cannibalistic nature of Chinese history.

Lu Xun was, of course, launching a full-scale assault on traditional Chinese society in "A Madman's Diary" *(Kuangren riji),* the opening shot in what has been termed nothing less than a literary revolution; but in the process of producing China's first major "modern" work of fiction, he was also subverting the entire classical textual tradition. By presenting his story in the form of the diary entries of a designated madman, Lu Xun inserted into Chinese literature a new kind of problematic self, a self in a state of crisis over its own identity. The madman's sanity is at stake as he struggles to sort out his relation to the external world, but he must also learn how to reinterpret the traditional texts that had hitherto defined that world for him.

The mad first-person narrator through whom the story is told and the self revealed is not only a "reader" of historical texts and of society, he is also the "writer" of the diary. Just as his highly unconventional reading or perception of things helps to reveal his self to us, who are in turn readers of him, the unfolding of "his" diary is simultaneously an act of self-portrayal; he is a literary subject that comes into existence, as it were, through the writing process.

Reading, writing, the reinterpretations of prior texts, and the engendering of new, perhaps problematic, texts are important activities within "A Madman's Diary," for in the story such activities are the necessary means by which the individual character defines and constructs the self. These activities acquire a particular urgency precisely because the madman by definition feels alienated and lost, uncertain of where or who he is. If, as Leo Ou-fan Lee has suggested, the madman may be "regarded as an artistic version of Lu Xun's inner voice" or an alter ego,[2] such activities of reading and writing can also be seen as a foregrounding or a self-reflexive mirroring of the author's own attempts to create a story at a time when literature itself is undergoing an uncertain transformation.

While inspired by Western literary models—Gogol's story of the same name, among others[3]—Lu Xun's work achieves its most powerful ironic effects through his allusions and references to texts from the Chinese tradition. In that tradition, intertextuality[4]—the imitation, adaptation, revision, or quotation of prior texts in the construction of new texts—had long been a self-conscious and self-perpetuating exercise. It was a way to give one's own writing authority and meaning, even as the creative process often involved the transformation and transcending of previous literary material.[5] But as writers of the May Fourth era (i.e., from ca. 1918 to the early 1930s) strive to break with the past, intertextual activity will take on some radical twists; the madman's literary rebellion will continue to draw on texts from the tradition if only to reinterpret their meaning and undermine their authority. From now on, unfamiliar texts from foreign literary traditions will enter into the formation of new texts. In modern Chinese fictional works focusing on the search for a self apparently caught in a crisis brought on by cultural or political dislocations, multiple texts, as pieces or "tags" from multiple cultural systems, literary conventions, or ideological formulas, will interact or collide in complex ways within the story to complicate that search.

In this essay I propose to carry out a close reading of three stories that revolve around a common basic plot—the quest for the self, for an individual entity with a degree of coherence and intelligibility. If, as claimed by Yu Dafu in his often-quoted statement, "the greatest success of the May Fourth movement should be considered the discovery of the 'individual' *(geren),*"[6] then just who that individual is becomes a question of capital importance. The long line of individuals in modern Chinese literature headed by Lu Xun's madman includes an extreme example of the romantic, subjective self—the unnamed protagonist in Yu Dafu's own 1921 story, "Sinking" *(Chenlun),* who first appears in the story armed with a volume of Wordsworth's poems. Questions of reading and writing in this story, much of it involving texts from Western romantic literature, are deeply implicated in the central character's struggle to come to terms with himself as an individual alone in an alien land.

My third story will be Wang Meng's "Bolshevik Salute" *(Buli)* of 1979, written sixty years later, a story from another era, or rather from the "new era," as the contemporary post-Mao literary period, with considerable optimism, is being called. Writers are now looking again, according to Liu Zaifu and others, toward the "self" *(ji, ziwo)* and struggling for self-affirmation, self-liberation, and self-realization.[7] Written in an ostensibly Western-inspired modernist style that has been labeled "stream-of-consciousness" by some critics, the story portrays its protagonist, Zhong Yicheng, as seeking to identify an authentic self in terms of, or perhaps against, the imposed, authorizing texts of Party history and Party ideology.

In all these stories my primary interest is to see how the individual self is portrayed, fashioned, literally and verbally constructed, in the narrative text. Extending the linguist Emile Benveniste's statement, "It is in and through language that man constitutes himself as a *subject,*" many works of poststructuralist criticism have stressed the notion of the self as a textual production,[8] or by extension, since all texts are intertextual, as an intertextual production. In any case, each of the three stories draws conspicuously on other texts in the process of conceptualizing selves. But texts, as quoted, used, or revised, are important not just as structural elements or building material. All the stories consciously grapple with texts on other levels also. The central characters, as diarists (their diaries are quoted in all three stories), aspiring poets, or recorders of history, are presented as engaged in reading, writing, and interpreting, activities that are critical to plot development and that will fatefully affect their lives. What happens to texts, what the characters do with texts, what texts do to them, even as their fates unfold, become embedded instances of the relation between intertextuality and self-representation, instances that mirror *within* these highly self-reflexive stories the "behind-the-scenes" text-producing operations of their authors.

My intention is to sidestep the unresolvable question of the degree to which these fictional characters may be considered "true" reflections of their historical authors. Rather I choose to concentrate on the stories themselves, to examine each one as the locus, the site, or the theater, if you will, where a plurality of texts enter into dramatic dialogue with one another. But having borrowed from the poststructuralists' notions about text and intertext, I would like to avoid being similarly accused of "fleeing from history"[9] and emphasize that the specific intertextual dramas of each story are shaped by their taking place at particular fracture points in literary history. To put it another way, the stories are microcosms providing a focused view of the converging larger cultural, discursive, and ideological pressures of a given historical moment on the writing subject.

One way to describe the state of crisis in which the written/writing self finds itself is to see how in different ways each one is trying for a break from tradition. The madman diarist as first-person narrator is a radical departure from the oral storytelling model that was the dominant mode of narrative discourse in the past. Yu Dafu's attempt at a new kind of self-representation needs to be seen against certain traditional ideological conceptions of the autobiographical subject. And Wang Meng's story will raise unsettling questions about the relation of identity and self-perception to the established language of public discourse.

Whatever the analytical slant, running through all three stories is the theme of the self caught in the interaction between multiple literary forms and ideological codes, traditional and modern, Chinese and Western, as it struggles to emerge through textual representations. Our questions will be: Is there a resolution to the common plot? What is the end of the quest? Where, finally, does the self reaching for an identifiable, coherent, and intelligible entity come out?

Ironically (the word is inevitable whenever it comes to Lu Xun), one of the most radical (or unradical) features of China's first modern short story, as "A Madman's Diary" has frequently been called, is the preface in classical Chinese.[10] In traditional vernacular fiction, the preface—written in the classical language in contrast to the stories themselves, and presented usually as having been composed by someone who is not the author of the book—provides a solemn introduction to what follows by setting forth the purpose and circumstances of the stories' composition or compilation, and makes a case for their value and significance. On the surface, the "I" in Lu Xun's preface here would seem to be conforming to this formula: the text had been given to him, he states, by a former schoolmate, the brother of the madman, and after reading it he recognized (knew, *zhi*) that the diarist was suffering from some form of "persecution complex," and although the language was "confused and incoherent, and contained many wild statements," he had copied out a part to serve "as a subject for medical research." Such a preface immediately alerts the reader to look for an alternative reading of the story, a reading other than the unlikely one claimed for it in the preface.

Juxtaposed against the conventional, apparently reasonable first-person narrator in the preface is the "insane first-person narrator" who gives us the thirteen disconnected, incoherent fragments that make up the diary. Through this innovative narrator Lu Xun makes a decisive break with the Chinese tradition by substituting for the "simulated context"[11] of oral storytelling the "simulation" of a madman's diary.

Lu Xun has discussed how his reading of foreign novels and stories prepared him for his own writing, including the relation between his own story and Gogol's "Madman's Diary".[12] In spite of the great differences between the two—as indicative as anything else perhaps is the fact that the mental disintegration of Gogol's madman ends up in his crying for his mother, whereas Lu Xun's makes an anguished plea to save the children—there is little question of the Russian derivation of the story's form. Madmen are to be found in traditional Chinese literature, Confucius was challenged by one in the *Analects*,[13] and the diary is a literary genre of long standing.[14] Lu Xun's modernity lies in his particular combination of the two for the construction of a fictional narrative. All written fiction is "in the first instance the representation of another narrative text . . . it enacts not only the events but *the act of telling a story*."[15] When a diary, rather than an oral story, is the narrative text represented, the fictional work's contextual situation and its relationship with the implied audience will no longer be the same.

The process of subjectivization in late-Qing fiction has been much noted by scholars.[16] First-person narration, for example, makes its debut in Wu Woyao's *Strange Events Seen in the Past Twenty Years*, and even more remarkable is the fictional self-portrait in *The Travels of Lao Can*, a vehicle for communicating his personal view of the world. But both of these novels retain such traditional storyteller phrases as "to know what happened . . . wait till the next chapter," and with them the predication that the work is addressed directly to an audience "out there." It is this acknowledged audience that is apparently absent from "A Madman's Diary."

One of the outstanding features of the enduring traditional oral storytelling model was the built-in relationship between the narrator and the audience that was everywhere operative within the fictional world of the text; it was the way the story itself, as it were, reflected, contextualized, or *produced* the situation in which it was told. The storyteller was not an individualized personality, but embodied a "general social consciousness"; he presented himself, in David Der-wei Wang's words, as "one of us," speaking for the audience-community that was in turn acknowledged and valorized in the narrative performance.[17] Yet at the same time, while claiming to base his story on a consensus, on a view of the world that he shared with the audience, the storyteller did also, I would argue, set himself up as a figure of authority. "He," impersonal and anonymous as he was, and precisely because he was indeed that, would incorporate what was recognizably "our" human experience into a narrative, and in the process show that no matter how personal or mundane, how seemingly made up of the random or coincidental, the events would somehow exemplify the workings of a higher order in the world. It was his appeal to that higher order that gave coherence, meaning, and worth to what he had to say. The storyteller's narrative authority was powerfully reinforced by his energetic intertextual operations, by the historical analogies, the "evidence" *(zheng)* of quoted poems, the proverbs distilling communal wisdom, the allusions to prior writings, that were continually interwoven into the unfolding of the story's specific events. Even as later Chinese fiction showed an increasing self-consciousness and evinced an attitude of ironic detachment toward such rhetorical devices,[18] they were retained as the ready means whereby the novelist could affirm both his own authority and the implicit narrative contract with his readers.

Lu Xun was well acquainted with the tradition of vernacular fiction against which he had knowingly turned his back. Throughout his life he remained a scholar of traditional Chinese literature, making particularly significant contributions to the study of traditional fiction. Apart from compiling and collating anthologies of literary tales, work that began about six years before he wrote "A Madman's Diary" and continued long after, he also wrote the first comprehensive history of Chinese fiction, *Zhongguo xiaoshuo shilue* (A Brief History of Chinese Fiction).[19]

A story presented in the form of a personal diary presupposes a new problematic relationship between narrator and implied audience, particularly if the narrator is "insane." It drastically alters what Ross Chambers refers to as the "situational phenomena," including the human relationships, social agreements, and implicit pacts or contracts from which all narrative derives its "meaning" and "point."[20] What promises to be communicated by the incoherent ravings of a madman, and to whom?

Questions of meaning, failures in communication, gaps in understanding, and the ambiguities of perception are in fact the main issues within the story itself, and they are everywhere embedded in a text in which eyes and seeing are the major linking motifs. It is their eyes—those of the dog, the honorable Mr. Zhao, the people on the street, the crowd outside the gate, the children—that fill the madman with fear. "Get out of here, all of you! What is the point of looking at a madman!" his brother shouts to a group of onlookers.

The madman is the target of their looks because he has also looked at them. A confrontational drama of seeing, between subject and object, between the madman and the others around him, mutually reflecting their perceptions/misperceptions of each other, is unfolded in the story. By reading the expression in their eyes, which sends chills through him from head to foot, the madman discovers that they intend to eat him. They are determined to destroy him—fatten him up and eat him, drive him to suicide, declare him mad—because he has seen through them and recognizes who they actually are—people-eaters.

To *see* is to be entrapped in a dilemma from which there is no escape. On one level, the madman is "wrong," projecting his own "persecution complex" onto others, but on another level, he is "right," for he has truly perceived the cannibalism that characterizes Chinese society. Stuck in the confrontational stance vis-à-vis his spectator-audience, it is precisely his insight that makes understanding and communication with them impossible. His earnest message of reform, his exhortations to his brother, to the crowd, to "change, to change from the bottom of your hearts, you must know that in the future there will be no place for people-eaters in the world," are merely seen as further evidence of his insanity. Unlike the traditional storyteller/narrator, he is truly isolated from the community in his knowledge, his authority toward his audience undermined in the very process of attempting communication.

The alienated madman has also set himself in opposition to the textual tradition. When he first puzzles over what possible offense he might have committed to account for the hostile gazes around him, the only thing he can come up with is that twenty years ago he had trod on the old account books of Mr. Ancient *(Gujiu xiansheng)*—the records of the past. "It seems to me that I am not an evil person, but it's been hard to say ever since I stepped on the books of the Ancient family." He remembers that from ancient times human beings were often eaten, but he "was rather hazy about it." Looking it up in his history book, "scrawled all over each page are the words: 'Virtue and Morality.'" He is able to perceive the truth, not by accepting what is written in the texts, but by detecting *(kanchu)* what is unsaid; what is between the lines *(zifeng)* turns out to be the negation of what is explicitly stated: "throughout the book were written the two words—'Eat People.'" Again, as in his experience with people, now that he has deciphered/deconstructed the texts, he feels threatened by them: "All the words in the book . . . widely open strange eyes and glare at me."

In his continual shifting between the literal and the metaphorical lies the insanity, or perhaps the "wisdom," of the madman. He discovers literal incidents of "people-eating" in the story told by the resident of Wolf Cub Village, in the ancient story of Yiya's son, and in such bits of classical phrases as "eating exchanged children" *(yi zi er shi)* and "eating the flesh and sleeping on the hide" *(shi rou qin pi)* to support his holistic reading of Chinese history. But the most telling example of cannibalism in the name of virtue and morality is the overliteral (or is it metaphorical?) interpretation of "cutting a piece of one's thigh to cure one's parent" *(ge gu liao qin)*. It is at that point that his own probable complicity in cannibalism is literally "brought home"; he recognizes that he may have participated in the eating of his little sister's flesh, perhaps served up by his brother— his mentor in classical texts and composition—when she died. The despair at the end of the diary then is over himself: the realization that he is personally implicated in that cannibalistic tradition: "now I understand *(mingbai),* even though I did not know it at first; how can a man like myself with four thousand years of people-eating history *(luli)* face real people?"

The final entry, "Perhaps there are children who have not eaten people? Save the children . . ." would seem to be a plea, to save the children from being eaten, but also from eating the food of their parents, from continuing the cannibalistic system, to which the madman himself, as the preface informs us, later returns. He is described as having "recovered" and gone somewhere ready to assume an official post. The wishful question, the poignant plea trailing off into ellipsis, is not where the story ends; it actually ends where it began— in the preface. For the madman finally, in William Lyell's words, "rejoins the ranks of the *truly* mad."[21] Or has he, as the system would have it, been restored to sanity? Apart from the question of what constitutes madness and what sanity, there is the further question of who is the "real" madman, the self described "objectively" in the preface, or the one presented "subjectively" in the diary? Where does the madman actually end up?

In the process of telling his own story, the madman who had initially defined himself as in opposition to the others becomes more and more uncertain about that separation, and therefore of himself as an independent identity. These self-doubts are mirrored in his function as narrator; he is the center of consciousness in a narrative structure in which perception, meaning, and communication become increasingly ambiguous and problematic.

Although "careful consideration in order to understand" is a goal repeatedly stated by the diarist, his chronological recording of events (what a diary normally is) totally disorients him in time. In a series of undated "todays," incidents from myth, history, childhood, the last few days, dark times when night cannot be told from day, are jumbled together. It turns out that people and dialogue, as well as historical texts, have no clear, stable meaning but can be interpreted from opposite perspectives. Mr. He, the old man with glasses who comes to feel his pulse, could be a medical doctor come to cure him *or* an executioner in disguise; the mother may be scolding her child *or* threatening the madman, and so on. As a teller of his own story, the madman does not understand, and cannot be understood.

The one attempt to make sense of the diary's incoherent fragments is found in the opening traditional preface that presents it. It not only introduces the madman's story, it also gives us its first "authoritative" reading, the reading given by the elder brother/tutor who hands over the diary with a laugh, and the "author" of the preface who sees it as useful material for medical research. The world represented in the text of classical-language discourse is still apparently situated in "normal" space and time; the names of people may be withheld, but they come and go, move from past to present; things follow in a clear "natural" sequence. The preface is dated April 2, 1918 (seventh year, fourth month, second day), its actual date of composition, making its world seemingly contiguous with ours (the readers'). In such a world, the sickness of a madman is a temporary aberration that can be accommodated within the well-ordered scheme of things. While the preface gives the impression that only within the traditional classical-language discourse can a definitive reading of the diary be made, it suggests at the same time that such a reading cannot be a definitive one.

In a world where all authoritative knowledge is in question and the textual tradition is subject to deconstruction, any insights that are to be gained will themselves preclude the possibility of communication. The madman/diarist is a storyteller, a writer who is alienated from his audience, precisely because he has come upon important truths to tell them. Paradoxically the very first story that sets the new literature movement in motion is also filled with self-doubts about the nature and effectiveness of its own literary enterprise. The crisis of a self cut off from tradition is also a crisis of the self writing.

Yu Dafu's "Chenlun" (Sinking)[22] makes very different claims for the subjective self. Published in 1921, three years after "A Madman's Diary," it was for its time a "best-seller,"[23] and "immediately established [the author's] reputation as a writer of autobiographical compulsion unafraid to expose his weaknesses and fantasies."[24] Compared with Lu Xun, who was thirty-seven when he wrote "A Madman's Diary," the Yu Dafu of "Sinking" was a relatively youthful twenty-five; certainly the initial impression one gets from the story is that of an adolescent suffering through an identity crisis compounded by feelings of sexual inadequacy.

With the major exception of *Dream of the Red Chamber*, the subject of youth maturing into adulthood—a central theme in the Western novel from the end of the eighteenth century on—had not been an important theme in Chinese fiction. The focus on the preoccupations of youth was part of the May Fourth iconoclastic stance; thus the "audacious self-exposure" of Yu Dafu's first stories was likened by Guo Moruo to a "violent stormlike blitzkrieg on the hypocrisy of the scholar-official class *(shidafu)* that had been deeply hidden underneath a shell of thousands of years."[25] The shockingly candid portrait of the central character in "Sinking," whose sexual frustrations, compulsive masturbation, and ultimate suicide broke ground in terms of subject matter, was also seen as a political gesture of protest, since literature that disclosed "the inner life of an individual played a social role, it fulfilled a revolutionary task."[26] It was because the story had carried the disclosure of the inner life of a young person to such extreme lengths that it was greeted with hyperbolic praise as a powerful assault on the traditional family and social system.

According to Yu Dafu, the individual portrayed in his fiction was often himself. His attitude that "all literary works are autobiographies of their authors"[27] is manifest in the large number of works that incorporate facts from his own life. But rather than considering them truthful and realistic portraits of the historical author, we should see his various writings, as Leo Ou-fan Lee points out, as so many occasions for him to "construct visions of himself." In the following year, Yu Dafu will create another vision of himself through the short story "Caishi ji" (The Cliff of Colored Rock), a fictionalized biography of the poet Huang Zhongze (1749–1783),[28] but the vision constructed in the unnamed protagonist in "Sinking" is particularly instructive, because the textualization of its constituent elements makes them fairly easy to sort out.

Yu Dafu detaches his protagonist first of all from a social nexus, from the relation with others that had customarily been emphasized in Confucian teachings as a means of establishing the self. The unnamed central character is set loose to do his own thing and express his individuality as a young student in Japan, far removed from the constraints of his family or the old society. (Toward the end of the story he initiates a break with his older brother in Peking.) Merely referred to as "he" *(ta)* throughout the story, he first appears on the scene one bright September day, "strolling amidst the half-ripened rice fields or meandering on the highways" of the Japanese countryside, "on a great plain with not a single soul around." He is wandering, alone by himself, that is, but for a pocket edition of Wordsworth's poems he is carrying with him, and the first words he utters in the story are in English, "Oh, you serene gossamer! you beautiful gossamer!" words that, for "reasons unknown even to himself," bring tears (the first of many that will be shed copiously throughout the story) to his eyes.

Textual self-representation in "Sinking" will draw conspicuously upon works from Western romantic literature.[29] Quoted in their original English or German language, words and phrases like "Megalomania" and "Hypochondria" (as if only foreign terms could describe his particular psychological condition), book titles, authors, and whole stanzas of poetry are inserted into the story—obtrusive, unassimilated chunks standing in sharp contrast to the typography of their Chinese context. "He" chants aloud and translates two stanzas of Wordsworth's "The Solitary Highland Reaper [*sic*]" into Chinese, but dismisses his efforts as insipid and pointless. In depicting the reaper's loneliness and ambiguous melancholy song, the poem reflects his own self-pitying condition. "Sinking" may be seen as an experiment to use these chunks of Western literature, together with the supersensitive response they inspire in the protagonist, as the foundation on which to construct a new kind of autobiographical subject, a textual construction that appears to imply a radical rejection of some traditional language and ideologies.

Self-definition through linkage with a textual tradition was a critical point in the autobiography that Sima Qian appended to his *Shiji* (Records of the Historian). History itself, as Sima Qian first of all wrote it, was as much the assimilation of past texts into present texts as it was an investigation into what had happened in the past; more important, it was only his own participation in an ongoing textual tradition that validated his mission in life, indeed his very life itself. Speaking in the third person in the afterword, he explains that he chose not to commit suicide after his castration so as to carry on the historical work bequeathed him by his father, suggesting also that in "transmitting ancient matters and putting in order its hereditary traditions," he was following the example of Confucius.[30] Through the act of writing, defined as textual transmission, he would preserve his present life as an individual and also hope to attain future immortality.

Sima Qian's affirmation of the self by inserting it into an ongoing textual tradition was based on the self-conception of the scholar-official in accordance with orthodox Confucian ideology. The autobiographical writings of the system's dropouts, the Daoist recluses, which began to multiply in the third and fourth centuries, formed their own textual tradition and drew upon alternative ideological models. Written also in the third person, Tao Qian's "Biography of the Gentleman of the Five Willows" *(Wuliu xiansheng zhuan)*—unnamed, place of origin unknown—marked the beginning of a "paradoxical stereotype": autobiographies by "nameless selves," whose chief claim to attention was the effacing of the self.[31] While at first glance these life-stories might seem to be about idiosyncratic, free-wheeling individuals, their self-images, modeled after earlier Daoist ideals, carried their own *topoi* and formulas of rustic poverty, indifference to fame, love of wine, and so on.

For the narrative performance of "Sinking," Yu Dafu, in discarding both of these textual traditions and the ideological codes they carried, was trying out a different kind of cultural script.[32] Although he may have considered "Sinking," like all his literary works, as one of his autobiographies, and indeed it is filled with references to his personal life, he was also turning to a different set of literary conventions for figures of selfhood.[33] In utter isolation, with nothing but his volumes of Wordsworth and Heine, what the story's "he" *(ta)* had for self-affirmation was mainly his emotional precocity and his literary sensibility. And it is this same emotional precocity (unlike the perspicacity of Lu Xun's madman) that sets him apart, that places him "at absolute odds with his fellow men and inevitably the wall separating him from them had become higher and higher."

In this relative cultural and social vacuum, the character's subjective feelings become all-important. As Chen Pingyuan notes, the point about the opening line of the story—"Lately he had felt pitifully lonesome"—is not whether his circumstances were actually pitiful, but whether the character himself felt he was pitiful.[34] And he did indeed. The plot of "Sinking" is structured around the emotional states of its main character. It begins with his solitary walk and the chanting of "The Solitary Highland Reaper [*sic*]." He observes a flirtation between two female students in red skirts and three male students; feeling left out or simply snubbed, he confesses in his diary that what he wants above all is the love of a beautiful woman, "to possess the body and soul of an 'Yifu' [Eve] from the Garden of Eden." A section recalls the biographical facts that led him to this preparatory school in the outskirts of the Japanese town of N; thereafter the story's "action" is the escalation of his sexual experience: compulsive masturbation accompanied by feelings of guilt and anxiety, peeping at the landlord's daughter at her bath, overhearing a couple's lovemaking in the tall reeds, climaxed by a visit to a brothel.

Convinced the morning after of his own utter degradation, "suddenly he had the inexplicable urge to drown himself in the sea."

Throughout the narrative the focus is on the subjectivity of the character's response to events. "Although there exists a sharp conflict between the protagonist and the world around him, you do not see a concrete representation of the society that is ostracizing 'him,' or oppressing 'him'";[35] what you see is a character experiencing a world that may primarily be a projection of his own inferiority complex and sexual insecurities. He is imprisoned in a spiraling structure of voyeurism, masturbation, and paranoia, with self-destruction the only way out. The stroll in the open fields under the bright September sun that opens the story of "Sinking" will lead by the story's end to the moonlit ocean, the brink of suicide.

The story suggests that his attempts to write, to create poetry and fiction, and to translate that fiction into a simple foreign language, as well as the continued expansion of his fantasies all play a role in sowing the seeds of his melancholia. At the same time his ability to turn out a good poem on occasion relieves him of his extreme anxiety over whether his brain might have been damaged due to his sinful masturbation. While much of the story shows him deriving his inspiration for self-conception from Western romantic literature, he also harks back to the classical Chinese tradition as he strives for self-expression in a variety of modes. An excerpt from his diary reads like a spontaneous cry of despair over his personal condition in an alien land: "Why should I have come to Japan? . . . Already twenty-one! Dead as dried wood at twenty-one! Dead as cold ashes at twenty-one!" In marked contrast to this, a poem in the classical mode assimilates the theme of lament and homesickness into the language and conventions of the past. Highly formal and disciplined, shed of the specifically personal references of the hysterical, self-pitying diary, this poem is in the traditional eight-line, seven-character *lüshi* style. It is not located in the individual self's particular here and now.

The "I" is not emphasized in this classical poem; instead individual suffering is expressed through the analogous fates of mad or persecuted literary figures from the past, Ni Heng, Jia Yi, Han Xin, and Liang Hong. Yu Dafu, who has left over four hundred highly accomplished poems in the classical style, inserts here one of his own compositions.[36] It comes at a poignant moment near the end of the story, as the protagonist admits to the last human being he will talk to, the uncomprehending hostess of the brothel, "Yes, I am a poet. Go and bring me a brush and some paper, and I'll write a poem right away to show you." It is not clear that he actually manages to write it down, but he chants the poem loudly several times, while "in the next room those bastards were singing Japanese songs." This reaffirmation of the protagonist's identity with the classical literary tradition, in opposition, as it were, to the bawdy Japanese sounds on the other side of the wall, comes at the next-to-last minute of his life; it is the last gesture toward self-expression before self-annihilation.[37]

In spite of its obsessive focus on the subjective self, "Sinking" is not the single-minded or one-dimensional work it is often taken to be. The self as protagonist is presented as an unnamed "he," seen and reported on by a third-person narrator. Michael Egan reminds us that instead of seeing the character as the author's alter ego, we should note that the "objective technique serves . . . as an ironic counterpoint that undercuts the hero's sentimental view of himself."[38] Although closely following the protagonist as the center of consciousness, the narrator does suggest that there is a likely disjunction between his paranoid view of the world and the "objective" situation. The narration of the story alternates between quoted internal monologues, with the character talking to himself, and the third-person narrator's account of him as observed from the outside. These rapid shifts between dual points of view are not always handled with finesse, but they underscore the agitation of the main character's mental state. There is furthermore a split within the protagonist. He frequently addresses himself, at times in English, for example, "Oh coward, coward!" subjecting himself to reproach and ridicule, and creating an ironic gap between a self-pitying experiencing self and a more critical observing self.

Thus in this story several perspectives are set up on the self in a state of crisis. Issues of national humiliation and adolescent sexual hangups are implicated in the dilemmas over literary self-expression. The guilt over the desire for Japanese women, alluring foreign objects, derives in part from the fact that such desire is so utterly humiliating to the self. But the process of narration with its grab bag of modes from a range of textual traditions—diary, classical poem, verbalized internal thoughts, quotations from foreign literature—as well as the constant alternation between empathy and detachment, also reflects a discontinuous, fragmented self set on the path to self-destruction. In this first story Yu Dafu did not succeed in creating a totally finished work. Yet it is precisely its incoherence and lack of resolution that enable "Sinking" to dramatize in a powerful way the conflicting pressures exerted on the writing subject at a time when Chinese literature was wandering between the dying old literary tradition and the new one, "powerless to be born."[39]

When Wang Meng's "Bu li" (Bolshevik Salute)[40] appeared in 1979, Chinese literature had for some forty years largely given up on the subject of self-representation in writing. According to revolutionary ideology, the individual should subordinate the self to the collective goals of the masses. Mao Zedong's "Talks at the Yan'an Forum on Literature and Art" of 1942 represent the Communist Party's effort toward establishing a new authoritative textual tradition on the foundation of revolutionary ideology. Prescriptive and peremptory in tone, the purpose of the "Talks" was both to replace the discredited classical tradition of the past and put an end to the flounderings of the "May Fourth" literature that followed. Under Party guidance, when it came to expressions of the self, the conscientious Marxist writer had, as Robert Hegel puts it, two choices: "either to present himself as an exemplary character in his writing (one that is 'close to the ideal') or to erase any trace of individuality from his writings, replacing his particular consciousness with the desired ideology of the community."[41]

The deprecation of the self was a process that had already begun in the early 1930s with the increasing leftward turn of literature. Under the pressures of revolution and war, whatever crises intellectuals confronted as individuals or writers could not be taken with the same degree of seriousness; if they appeared as the subjects of fiction, it was often as targets of satire or criticism. Yet even decades later, when such themes as self-awareness and introspection are no longer "forbidden zones" (jinqu) under the relative liberalization of the post-Mao era, it is evident that the experiences about the individual self cannot really be explored without considering them in relation to the collective history, the succession of political events and campaigns, of the past thirty or forty years.

"Bolshevik Salute" begins by recounting what would seem like a minimal gesture toward textual self-representation. Minimal as it is, the time is 1957, and it turns out to be enough to hang the label of "rightist" on its author, Zhong Yicheng. In May of that year his piece "Little Winter Wheat Tells Its Own Tale" *(Dong xiaomai zishu),* "a small poem written for a very small children's book,"[42] is published. Its length makes it easy to quote it in full:

> When wild chrysanthemums wither,
> We start to come up;
> While ice and snow cover the ground,
> We are pregnant with a rich harvest. (223)

As the story explains:

> Poor Zhong Yicheng had fallen in love with poetry . . . He had read and memorized so much poetry, and tears flowing, staying up all night, weeping, laughing, chanting, shouting, murmuring, he had written so many, many poems, and for this "Little Winter Wheat Tells Its Own Tale" he had written so many, many lines. (223)

But due to the cutting of some "learned, prestigious, very near-sighted editor," only these four lines appeared, printed in "the lower right-hand corner to go with a country scene." This was the only poetry Zhong Yicheng had ever published. "Still it was glorious, it was happiness," "the four lines contained so much of his love, his dreams." (223–224)

"Poor Zhong Yicheng" has been seduced by the wonders of literature and language; it proves to be his undoing. The power of language, as the story will show, is treacherously double-edged. In the article "What His Own Tale Is Telling" *(ta zai zishu xie shenme),* a "rising new star in literary criticism" offers an analysis of the little poem "from the point of view of the total situation of political struggle." The poem is calling for the end of the Communist Party (the withering chrysanthemums); for the seizure of power by the capitalist cliques of rightists, Chiang Kai-shek, Song Meiling, and so on (we are coming up); it expresses the feeling of extreme gloom, hostility, and fear on the part of the dying reactionary classes against the powerful dictatorship of the proletariat (ice and snow cover the ground); and it actually is calling for open counterrevolutionary rebellion (we are pregnant with a rich harvest). An apparently simple, straightforward text can thus be interpreted to mean anything at all; a piece of literary composition, whatever its own intention or merits, merely provides an occasion for the all-determining work of the critic.

The effect of this political explication of the children's poem "explodes like a bomb"; it immediately changes everything in Zhong Yicheng's life. A young cadre at P——'s Party Central District Committee, he has himself been enthusiastically participating in the antirightist struggle as leader of the Investigative Study Team of his office. But from now on the attitude of the majority of people toward him is no longer the same. He wants to protest, but "the new star had already clutched at his throat." In his helpless, humiliated state he cries out to the inaccessible critic: "Why didn't you at least ask me what kind of person I was? How can you say I am *(ba wo shuochengle)* like this without trying to understand my political history and actual performance?" (225)

As compared with the main characters in "A Madman's Diary" and "Sinking," Zhong Yicheng can only be described as an aspiring but utterly thwarted writer. The effect of his puny literary output, however, is enormous, and fatal. This "small poem" with its self-presentation theme turns out ironically to be indeed the text that is seized upon to define him. Writing and, even more, the interpretation of writing are presented in "Bolshevik Salute" as activities that can determine one's life. The fact that Zhong Yicheng's one published work occupied only "the lower right-hand corner" of an illustration in a children's book may be a comment on the circumscribed space allowed for writing at that time. But in any case the writing self as constructed from the text is no longer a matter up to its producer but one up to its critics. Once Zhong Yicheng's writing permits him to be interpellated by the ideologized discourse, does it matter who he is as a concrete individual?[43]

While the stability of self-identity through times of political turmoil is a major theme in other Wang Meng stories such as "Butterfly" *(Hudie)* and "Piebald" *(Zase)*, "Bolshevik Salute" explores the issue specifically through the highly problematic relationship between individual identity on the one hand and the use and understanding of texts on the other.

The turning point in the fate of the protagonist, brought about by his poem and its explication in 1957, is the first episode in "Bolshevik Salute," but that is not where the history of events begins. When the novella *(zhongpian xiaoshuo)* appeared, its jumbling of chronological sequence and emphasis on psychological depiction were recognized as introducing a new kind of formal experimentation into Chinese fiction. Wang Meng became a focal point of controversy over what was considered his "modernist" "stream-of-consciousness" technique. Literary methods inevitably have political implications, and the problem was how to reconcile his apparent imitation of such "decadent bourgeois methods" with the usual requirement that literature be realistic and didactic.[44] But "stream-of-consciousness," insofar as it is a narrative technique that undertakes to portray the free flow of the character's mental processes in a seemingly free-associating, illogical, and random manner, is hardly the characteristic mode of "Bolshevik Salute." In fact the order of events—both internal and external—is artfully arranged and contrived, and very effectively brings into dramatic interplay the issues of language and self through time and history.

The novella is divided into twenty-six segments, their length ranging from one sentence to twelve pages, each headed by a time indicator, such as August 1957; June 1966; 1957–1979; November 23, 1959; or "year and date unclear." The earliest date is January 1949, the eve of liberation for the city of P——; the latest, January 1979, when the day of rehabilitation for Zhong Yicheng finally arrives. Rather than employing free association where the character might seem to respond to things as they come up, "Bolshevik Salute" can be described as using a technique analogous to the montage in film: it consists of a series of juxtaposed memories "dissolving" in and out of past and present, while the protagonist tries to make sense of his life as it is impinged upon by the events of revolutionary history.

The traditional form of omniscient, consecutive narration will not work in "Bolshevik Salute," because the sense of linear cause and effect, of linkage, of how one got from there to here is precisely what is absent from the story of Zhong Yicheng's life. On one unusually hot day, Lao Wei, the District Committee secretary, and Song Ming, the office chairman and thus Zhong Yicheng's immediate superior, who have both been reprimanded from above for their unsatisfactory performance in the antirightist campaign, call him in for a "talk." "Suddenly the temperature dropped to below absolute zero," for now he is a "rightist"; "a new phase of his life began, and any continuity there had ever been, was shattered" (228).

A narrative structure fragmented into segments of time provides a formal mirroring of the protagonist's frustrated attempts to see his life together as a whole. To bring past and present together, instead of establishing connections, merely underscores the violent disjunctions between them. One such moment occurs in June 1966, when Zhong Yicheng is savagely beaten with leather belts and metal chains by Red Guards, while they collectively recite from the "Quotations of Chairman Mao," the authoritative intertext that puts everyone under its absolute power. Zhong Yicheng passes out. In the instant before losing consciousness, he "saw what was forever fresh, forever alive, forever sacred and not far away at all" (230). "Dissolve" to January 1949, when the seventeen-year-old Zhong Yicheng, a high school student who had been doing underground work for the Party, carries out instructions to prepare for the liberation of P——. As he leads his group of fellow students triumphantly through the city, he is greeted by Ling Xue (later his wife) with "Bolshevik Salute," an abbreviated phrase much used on Party documents in the 1940s, which he is hearing for the first time in his life. "It was like a raging fire, a violent whirlwind, a greeting that was sacred, that filled one with joy! Bolshevik Salute! Bolshevik Salute!" (235).

"Dissolve" back to June 1966, and Zhong Yicheng's coming-to. He notes that these young people with red armbands are about seventeen, "like me in 1949! Seventeen, really an age for revolution! An age to wear armbands! . . . An age so fervid, so pure, so lovable!" As they beat him into unconsciousness again, he suddenly shouts "'Bolshevik Salute!' while the bloody corners of his mouth carry a suggestion of the smile in his heart." But the Red Guards do not under-

188 | Yi-tsi Mei Feuerwerker

stand him; they think he is quoting some Japanese phrase, a contact code perhaps; could he be a Japanese spy? In any case it looks like he is dead now, but that is all right, since, to quote an authorizing intertext, "there is no crime in revolution" (236). Past and present may be juxtaposed, but there is no continuity between them, there is only the shocking contrast between idealism and terror; the recall of the revolutionary language from those early days merely shows how utterly that language has lost its meaning.

During those heady days in the 1940s, to Zhong Yicheng and his comrades, joining the revolution meant reading new texts and learning a new language. They were young then, many of them children, but they had read progressive publications, Xinhua dispatches, works by Mao, and so on, and they were ready to sacrifice themselves to create a new world, a world to fit the new rhetoric. Zhong Yicheng had been only fifteen when he joined the Party. Three days after the struggle to liberate P—— is won, Zhong Yicheng receives a notice to go to a citywide meeting of Party members, the first one he has ever attended. He exchanges Bolshevik Salutes; eyes filled with hot tears, he hears "The Internationale" for the first time; he listens to the leaders as they report one after the other. Each speech is "clear, forthright, well reasoned, fully confident . . .

> the voice of the Party. Like a sponge Zhong Yicheng absorbed the wisdom and strength of the Party. He prostrated himself with enthusiasm and delight before this totally new content, this new faith, this utterly new language and totally new way of speaking. With each sentence he felt he had learned something new, had grown bigger, taller, and a bit more mature. (244)

Through the new language, the Party teaches him a new conception of himself. At eighteen as a regular member he attends a Party lesson *(dangke)* given by Lao Wei, the District Committee secretary. He hears that "to be truly Bolshevik, to assume the Party spirit completely and purely one must forget the self and throw oneself into the revolutionary struggle." One must "change one's thinking, overcome individualism, the wish to become an individual hero, liberalism, subjectivism" (248). "How true! How true!" Zhong Yicheng almost cries out as he eagerly soaks up the words.

Seventeen years later, in March 1967, the detailed notes taken on this occasion in the notebook he "had always treasured" are confiscated from his house during a bloody search and used in a struggle against Lao Wei, now himself a target as a "capitalist roader." The once-inspiring Party lesson has become "negative teaching material" *(fanmian jiaocai)*, which, "spewing out poison . . . waved the banner for Liu Shaoqi's black theories of cultivation, etc." (253). At any given moment some unpredictable force—a political campaign, mass hysteria—can take over, and the meaning of the language in a text will change—even into its opposite. What does this mean for the self molded by Party discourse?

That evening Comrade Song Ming, the office chairman, kills himself. His suicide signals the failure of one who had dedicated himself to the meticulous and conscientious work of studying Party texts and then evaluating individuals by the texts they themselves produced. Although Song Ming had instigated the antirightist campaign against him, Zhong Yicheng

> firmly believed Song Ming was not a bad person. Every day Song Ming read the books of Marx, Lenin, Chairman Mao, Central Committee documents, Party reports, Party publications, deep into the night. He was fond of using methods of inference and deduction to analyze each person's thinking; each sesame seed was analyzed into a watermelon . . . In 1957, with gusto he had logically, methodically, and with amazing ingenuity analyzed every single sentence Zhong Yicheng had said, every single line of poetry he had tried to write, and proved that Zhong Yicheng was a capitalist rightist from top to bottom. (254)

Devoted explicator as Song Ming is, his life, hitherto totally guided by "textual criticism," reaches an impasse when the interpretation of the texts is suddenly, inexplicably altered.

"Bolshevik Salute" is a story about Zhong Yicheng and individuals like him, and about a party, a revolutionary history, that is deeply entrapped in a world made up of language. In her perceptive discussion of the novella, Wendy Larson points out that "throughout *Bolshevik Salute* Wang Meng maintains a strong skepticism toward language as an indicator of 'true' reality,"[45] but perhaps one could go further to say that the story also suggests that language has replaced the "true reality" it might have been claiming to "indicate" or "represent."

As the story shows, the referents of language, what the various texts, interpreted and reinterpreted, are supposed to "be about," turn out to be irrelevant. More than any other self in our stories, Zhong Yicheng is to be constructed out of texts and intertextual quotations. In fact it hardly matters who the individual Zhong Yicheng—at different times defined as a "positive, zealous Party member," a "capitalist rightist," an "enemy of the Party," or a "counterrevolutionary revisionist"—might actually be. In 1959, a rightist still endlessly producing pieces of "self-criticism" (jiantao) to sort himself out, he risks his life and is severely burned one night when he puts out a fire in a storehouse. But because of his current status (shenfen), the authorities, instead of applauding his bravery, suspect him of arson or sabotage. His deeds cannot speak louder than the words—of others that are applied to him.

Since Zhong Yicheng is constantly exhorted to "remold and reform himself" (gaizao ziji), to "change his soul to another" (huan yige linghun), to "cast off his old self and be reborn" (tuotai huangu), he cannot maintain himself as a continuing individual identity. When Ling Xue, his wife to be, expresses her support of him in spite of the criticism of his "Little Winter Wheat Tells Its Own Tale," she asks: "Don't you yourself know what you are?" It is a question he truly cannot answer.

The self is defined and shaped by the Party through tags, labels, slogans, formulas, reports, documents, and by the dozens of constantly revised "self-criticisms" that one writes. As Zhong Yicheng acknowledges with gratitude, he would be nothing without the Party, since literally the Party defines him to himself, but at the same time, one could also say that the Party, through constant textual redefinitions and reconstructions, has made him into nothing. This is the language trap as revealed in "Bolshevik Salute": language whose reference to external "reality" is indeterminable, and that turns out to be a continually destabilizing, self-contradictory system.[46]

The self and its memories, the Party and its history, as Wang Meng strongly implies, do indeed exist—"real" people have lived and loved and fought and suffered—but they are not accessible through the language of the texts. The texts have taken over reality, but then keep referring in circular fashion throughout the story only to themselves, or rather to reinterpreted versions of themselves. While exposing this language trap, "Bolshevik Salute" is itself an enactment of the entrapment because it must remain within the language system on which it is premised.

In the last segment, January 1979, the day of Zhong Yicheng's rehabilitation finally arrives. Husband and wife receive a text, the "written conclusion" *(shumian jielun)* that exonerates and rehabilitates them and restores their Party membership. They jointly say in their hearts:

> Such a good country, such a good Party! . . . Although the term "Bolshevik Salute" has gradually disappeared from our letters and speech, although people generally do not use or have forgotten this term with its foreign language component, allow us to use it one more time: To Comrades Hua Guofeng, Ye Jianying, Deng Xiaoping, a Bolshevik Salute! Bolshevik Salute to the comrades of the Central Committee! Bolshevik Salute to . . . (307)

The circularity of the language system is hereby reaffirmed. Once again at the end, it seems difficult to reach beyond repeating what had already been repeated and yet revealed to be so problematic in the past, even in looking toward a brighter tomorrow. The lingering question is whether within an authoritative textual framework that relinquishes all claims to referentiality, the search for an authentic and continuing self is possible.

All texts may indeed be plural, yet the particular intertextual processes of these modern Chinese stories should also be seen as manifestations of the cultural dislocations and ideological uncertainties arising from their specific locations in history. Each story provides examples of multiple texts, from a range of literary genres, cultural systems, and ideological codes, entering into the textual construction of self. Some blending, some clashing, these texts raise rather than resolve questions about the coherence and intelligibility of this self. In all three stories the common plot, the quest for the self, leads to inconclusive endings. Lu Xun's pioneering story leaves indeterminate whether the madman is finally "restored" to "sanity"; his fate and "real" identity remain uncertain. Yu Dafu's unnamed protagonist exemplifies an attempt to make a radical break from traditional figures and formulas of selfhood, but the rhetorical reliance on Western sources and subjective feelings leads to paranoia and self-annihilation. Both of these early May Fourth stories dramatize the ambiguous status of the self while simultaneously invoking and subverting, in ironic or contradictory ways, the old literary tradition. Wang Meng's novella some sixty years later represents a frustrated effort to relocate and reconstitute the self within an apparently unsustainable textual system set up by the new revolutionary order.

The crises of the self and the dilemmas of writing in all three stories are ultimately linked in various ways to a loss of textual authority. While the departure from literary tradition concomitantly made possible some brilliant innovations in narrative techniques, it does not necessarily follow that formal experimentation in itself will open up wider possibilities of self-conception. Through Lu Xun's mad diarist and Yu Dafu's poet in exile, May Fourth literature did indeed explore new forms of perceptions or consciousness and venture into hitherto closed areas of subjective emotions, even at the risk of madness and suicide. Wang Meng's daring and modernistic narrative structure, on the other hand, reveals a much-reduced self, conceived in rather conventional terms, aware mainly of its loss of substantiality.

Self-reflexivity, the degree to which the self is presented as shaped by its own writing activities, decreases as we go through the three stories, as does the intensity with which they mirror the writing situation of their respective authors. If Lu Xun's story raises the most far-reaching questions about modern authorship, it is because the processes of self and text are presented as coincidental. The madman's questionable portrait in the preface notwithstanding, he cannot exist apart from his diary. While the fatal wandering of Yu Dafu's youthful poet is a depiction of the writer's crisis as he moves uncertainly between past and present, Wang Meng's story suggests a connection between the diminished self and the near impasse of literary production.

There are indications that contemporary Chinese literature is picking up where the breakthroughs of May Fourth left off, resuming since the mid-1980s those early explorations in subjectivity and narrative discourse. These have been taking place both by looking back to a newly reconceived tradition—the "search for roots" *(xungen)* movement attempting in some cases to reach farther back than the established texts to early myths—and under the influence of new Western literary imports. With a greatly expanded arena for the interplay of multiple texts, the continuing quest for the self is apparently reaching another critical juncture in Chinese history.

7 | Invention and Intervention:
The Making of a Female Tradition
in Modern Chinese Literature

Is there a female tradition in modern Chinese literature?

By asking this question, I intend to bring to critical attention a number of interesting claims put forth by women critics in post-Mao China, particularly the generation that came to maturity in the latter half of the 1980s. To many of them, *nüxing wenxue* (female literature) is more or less a fait accompli, something that preexists the critical effort to name it as such.[1] The job of a critic is thus to establish the collective identity of women writers, pinpoint their difference from male writers, rescue them from the lacunae of historical memory, and restore them to a rightful place in literary history. The whole enterprise is undertaken with a view to bringing the female tradition to light. (Incidentally, the same has also taken place in the West.) For instance, the critic Zhao Mei claims that women writers as a group are the first to bring about a radical break with the previous literature. "In grappling with the mysteries of existence and the nature of life and desire through the mediation of self-consciousness," says she, "women writers successfully broke down the dominant convention of broad social and political themes in fiction."[2] Another critic, Li Ziyun, attributes a good deal of avant-garde experiments in modern literature to the initiative of women. Describing the most-recent developments in Chinese literature, she boldly asserts: "We are witnessing a second upsurge in the literary output of female writers in mainland China. This is marked not only by the extraordinary number and quality of women's works but by the vanguard role some of those works have played in Chinese literature. I am referring to their disregard for existing literary conventions, their exploration of new horizons in terms of theme and experience, and their experimentation with form."[3]

In the meantime, the women's studies series edited by Li Xiaojiang includes a number of major historical projects devoted to recognizing a female literature that has developed over time, enjoys a homogeneous textual and intertextual tradition, and is capable of legislating its own critical vocabulary. *Emerging from the Horizon of History*, a book coauthored by Meng Yue and Dai Jinhua, represents one of the most ambitious efforts.[4] On the basis of a rigorous analysis of women's literary texts, this book suggests that modern literature has produced not only a good number of professional women writers but a female literature and a female literary tradition as well. The authors regard the May Fourth generation as the harbinger of that tradition: "Having rejected the status quo, May Fourth women writers were able to initiate their own tradition in the cracks and fissures of their culture."[5]

What strikes me as important here is less the truth value of various claims for a female literary tradition (which women critics have no vested interest in calling into question) than the peculiar historical circumstances that seem to compel those critics to identify, legitimate, and, perhaps, invent a homogeneous tradition on behalf of women writers from the May Fourth period down to the present.[6] To the extent that the female tradition did not come into its own until *after* women scholars began to make significant interventions in literary criticism and historiography (a field heretofore dominated by men) in the second half of the 1980s, their endeavor deserves our unmitigated attention. Indeed, what is a literary tradition, be it major, minor, male, or female, but a product of the collaborative efforts of writers and critics engaged in the specific historical issues of their own time? In undertaking this study, I neither assume nor contest the raison d'être of the so-called female tradition, but try to understand it as an important historical project that involves the agency of both women writers and women critics in post-Mao China.

Official Feminism and Chinese Women

The category of women, like that of class, has long been exploited by the hegemonic discourse of the state of China, one that posits the equality between men and women by depriving the latter of *their* difference (and not the other way around!). In the emancipatory discourse of the state, which always subsumes woman under the nationalist agenda, women's liberation means little more than equal opportunity to participate in public labor.[7] The image of the liberated daughter and the figure of the strong female Party leader celebrated in the literature of socialist realism are invented for the purpose of abolishing the patriarchal discriminatory construction of gender, but they end up denying difference to women.[8] During the Cultural Revolution, political correctness consisted largely in women wearing the same dark colors as men, keeping their hair short, and using no makeup. I am not suggesting that women ought to be feminine. The fact that the state did not require men to wear colorful clothes, grow long hair, or use makeup, which would have produced an equally iconoclastic effect, indicates that it was woman's symbolic difference that had been specifically targeted and suppressed on top of all other forms of political repression. Post-Mao Chinese women are therefore dealing with an order of reality vastly different from that which feminists in the West face within their own patriarchal society, where the female gender is exploited more on the grounds of her difference than the lack thereof. Being named as the "other" and marginalized, Western feminists can speak more or less from a politically enabling position against the centered capitalist ideology. By contrast, contemporary Chinese women find their political identity so completely inscribed within official discourse on gender and institutionalized by Fulian (the All-China Women's Federation) that they cannot even claim "feminism" for themselves. As Tani E. Barlow points out: "The importance of Fulian lay in its power to subordinate and dominate all inscriptions of womanhood in official discourse. It is not that Fulian actually represented the 'interests' of women, but rather that one could not until recently be 'represented' *as a woman* without the agency and mediation of Fulian."[9]

There are currently two translations of the word *feminism* in Chinese. The old *nüquan zhuyi* denotes militant demands for women's political rights reminiscent of the earlier women's suffrage movements in China and in the West. The new term *nüxing zhuyi*, emphasizing gender difference, has been in circulation for the past decade in Taiwan and only recently in China. The former is downright negative, and the latter sounds rather ambivalent. Contemporary women writers refuse to have their names associated with either term. When one scrutinizes their reluctance, one is furthermore struck by the fact that there is more at stake than the legitimacy of Western feminist discourse as applied to another culture. It appears that the very notion of *nü zuojia* (woman writer), a Chinese category, has been thrown into question by women writers such as Zhang Jie, Wang Anyi, and Zhang Kangkang. To them, once someone is designated (or stigmatized) as a woman writer, let alone as a feminist, she is trivialized by the mainstream (male) literature. Zhang Kangkang voices this fear in her article "We Need Two Worlds," using the analogy of the handicapped athlete to illustrate her point. In games held specially for the handicapped, people applaud the athletes because many of them think that "the handicapped cannot run in the first place." The same holds true for female writers, who are often classified as a category separate from mainstream male authors "as if it were a universally accepted truth that only men could be writers and as if they were born writers."[10] Women writers sharing the concerns of Zhang Kangkang feel that they must constantly fight against the condescension of their male colleagues and their own trivialization. The apparent contradiction between their objection to the term *woman writer* on the one hand and a strong female consciousness informing their works on the other must be understood in this light.[11]

To contemporary Chinese critics, it is not the term *woman writer* but *feminism* that must be kept at bay at all times. Most women scholars take care to stay away from the word even as they publish

sophisticated views on the politics of gender, views that would probably be deemed "feminist" by some Western feminists. This is what
critic Yu Qing does, for example, in her theorizing on the female
tradition in Chinese literature. In her view, women's marginal position need not trivialize them:

> In coming to maturity, female consciousness does not seek to sub-
> merge its gender in order to arrive at some abstractly conceived
> and genderless human condition. It aims to enter the overall
> human conception of the objective world from the special angle of
> the female subject and to view and participate in universal human
> activities from the particular viewpoint of the female gender that is
> uniquely constructed as such . . . the female gender is formulated
> in societal terms. And as long as the social factors constitutive of
> the female gender remain, gendered consciousness and gendered
> literature will not go away. The so-called ultimate (transcendental)
> consciousness and ultimate literature, therefore, do not and will
> not exist.[12]

Like most other scholars in women's studies, Yu rejects the word
feminism in her writing, although she has no scruples about quoting
the works of Western feminists in support of what she calls her
"female" position.[13] In order to grasp this complex situation, one
must take into account Chinese women's relationships with the state,
official feminism, and its representative, Fulian. As I mentioned
earlier, the latter takes a strong position on all gender issues, claiming to represent women and protect their rights but functioning in
reality very much like other hegemonic apparatuses used by the
Party, even though it is the least important of all state apparatuses.[14]
After all, the "ism" part of "feminism" seems to imply the same
masculine area of power and knowledge as "Marxism" and "communism."[15] Women's rejection of "feminism" therefore expresses a
strong desire to position themselves against state discourse on gender and its suppression of women's difference.[16] Consequently, terms
such as *nüxing yishi* (female consciousness) and *nüxing wenxue* (female literature) are invented by critics who wish to conceptualize a
female tradition that will recognize women as historical subjects
rather than objects of male patronage. The new crop of journals in

the eighties featuring women authors or female literature such as *Nü zuojia* (Female Writer) and *Nüzi wenxue* (Female Literature), the establishment of the first Women's Research Center in 1985 by Li Xiaojiang and her ambitious series on women's studies mentioned above, as well as the recent debates on female consciousness and female literature sponsored by critical journals such as *Wenyi pinglun* (Art and Literary Criticism), *Dangdai zuojia pinglun* (Studies on Contemporary Writers), *Dangdai wenyi sichao* (Current Trends in Art and Literature), and *Xiaoshuo pinglun* (Fiction Studies)[17]—all attest not only to a heightened awareness of women as historical agents but also to a significant breakaway from the totalizing discourse of official feminism.

Having invented the terms in which the debate on gender issues will be conducted, contemporary female critics proceed to reevaluate women's literature and identify a female tradition for which they claim nothing less than a vanguard role in modern Chinese literature. In so doing, they are actually reappropriating the historical category of women from state discourse for the purpose of empowering the female gender. When those critics talk about "female consciousness" and "the female literary tradition," they are not so much concerned with female identity as with female subject-position, or the question of who determines the meaning of female experience. The question "Who am I?" which is the title of a story by a contemporary writer named Zong Pu and which frequently appears in the works of Chinese women authors, indicates a desire to unfix the meanings that the state and traditional patriarchy have inscribed on the female body.[18]

The three women writers that I discuss here—Ding Ling, Zhang Jie, and Wang Anyi—figure prominently in contemporary literary criticism as architects of the female tradition. Ding Ling represents the legacy of the early twentieth century and is seen as prefiguring contemporary women's writing in a number of ways: the focus on female subjectivity; the critique of patriarchal ideology and institutions; and, most important, the problematization of writing and discourse through gender experience. When her "Diary of Miss Sophia" first appeared in the February issue of *The Short Story Magazine* in 1928, it was immediately perceived as a major event, as one critic recalled in 1930: "It was like a bomb exploding in the midst of a silent literary scene. Everyone was stunned by the author's extraordinary talent."[19] Other leading critics of the time such as Qian Qianwu and Mao Dun reviewed the story and called its author the first Chinese woman writer who "speaks out about the dilemmas of the liberated woman in China"[20] and whose understanding of the "modern girl" goes deeper than that of any of her contemporaries.[21] Some fifty years later, Zhang Jie's story "Love Must Not Be Forgotten" marked another turning point in Chinese literature following Mao's death, as is attested by the controversy it provoked. Chinese readers, accustomed as they were to socialist realism, were stunned by the subjective voice of the female narrator and the story's forbidden subject. A series of debates on love, gender, and the role of the writer began to appear in *Guangming Daily,* in the course of which a critic named Xiao Lin wrote: "As literary workers, shouldn't we be alert to and eradicate the corruptive influence of petty bourgeois ideas and sentiments? Shouldn't we stand in a higher position, command a broader vista, and think more deeply than the author of this story does?"[22] In rebuttal Dai Qing, a renowned writer and critic in the post-Mao period, defended Zhang Jie's story on the grounds of its moral complexity and bold exposé of social problems.[23] She argued for the legitimacy of the author's personal vision and welcomed her departure from the dominant literary orthodoxy.[24] Compared with Zhang Jie, the younger writer Wang Anyi is much less controversial. But her recent output has surprised readers with a wide range of experiments in eroticism, subjectivity, and socially transgressive themes. In the three stories known collectively as the "Three Themes on Love," she explores sexuality and female subjectivity as a means of testing the limits of reality and the boundaries of human consciousness.[25] "Brothers," a story published in March 1989, challenges the ideology of heterosexual love by pitting female bonding against the marital tie prescribed by the dominant culture. If Zhang Jie's novel *The Ark* centers on the sisterhood among divorced women, "Brothers" dramatizes the conflicting claims of marriage and the emotional attachment between women and, therefore, highlights the problematic of desire and choice. I hope that my reading of the three authors will help bring out the main features that most women critics in the eighties attribute to the female tradition.

Gender, Writing, and Authorship

Ding Ling's "Diary of Miss Sophia" contains an interesting allegory of reading in which the narrator, Sophia, casts the young man Weidi in the role of a reader by showing him her diary. Weidi fails to grasp the import of those entries and, believing that another man, Ling Jishi, has successfully become Sophia's lover, he complains: "You love him! . . . I am not good enough for you!"[26] The diary cannot explain Sophia to Weidi, because he insists on reading his own gendered discourse into Sophia's diary and finds in it a stereotyped triangular situation in which his rival gets the better of him. His reaction to the diary is, therefore, highly predictable according to conventional male-centered readings. Weidi "mis"-reads it despite clear evidence that Sophia is more interested in herself than in either man. In this allegorical encounter between female discourse and its male counterpart, writing and reading come across as profoundly gendered practices.

The narrator's writing and her choice of a male reader in this story introduce gender difference into the production of text and write the female gender into the authorial position. In her involvement with Ling Jishi, the narrator takes up a similar position: writing herself as a subject rather than as an object of desire. The description of her first encounter with Ling Jishi shows a devastating reversal of male literary conventions: "I raised my eyes. I looked at his soft, red, moist, deeply inset lips, and let out my breath slightly. How could I admit to anyone that I gazed at those provocative lips like a small hungry child eyeing sweets? I know very well that in this society I'm forbidden to take what I need to gratify my desires and frustrations, even when it clearly wouldn't hurt anybody" (49). It is the narrator's female gaze that turns the man into a sex object, reversing male discourse about desire. Not only does the narrator objectify the man's "lips" as if they were pieces of candy, but she ignores the phallus and feminizes male sexuality by associating it with lips (labia). She is empowered by writing that gives full play to her subversive desires and constitutes her as a subject. If the first scene mentioned helps establish gender difference in discourse, the reversed subject/object relation pinpoints the power struggle implied in the rewriting of gender.

Zhang Jie's "Love Must Not Be Forgotten" also emphasizes the relation of writing, gender, and authorship. Unlike Ding Ling's story, however, this narrative takes place between the narrator, Shanshan, and her late mother, Zhong Yu, whose writing and ghostly memory she strives to decipher; that is to say, instead of writing a diary herself, the daughter tries to interpret the incoherent words contained in a diarylike notebook the mother has left behind. The self-reflexive technique of taking a phrase from the mother's notebook and using it for the title of the story calls attention to the textuality of her narrative, so that it comes across as a writing about writing, reading, and critical interpretation. Read in this light, the expression "love must not be forgotten" becomes ambiguous, for in the context of the notebook it sums up the extraordinary love the mother feels for another married man. But when the same appears in the title of the daughter's narrative, it sounds curiously like a warning that the tragic lesson must be remembered so that it will not be repeated by herself and others. Through writing, the daughter conducts a dialogue with the mother about desire and suffering:

> At first I had thought that it contained only notes for future writing, because it didn't read like a novel, or like reading notes. Nor did it seem like letters or a diary. Only when I read it through from beginning to end did her cryptic comments join with my own scattered memories to suggest the vague outlines of something. After a great deal of reflection, it finally dawned on me that what I held in my hands was not lifeless, antiseptic writing; it was the searing expression of a heart afflicted with grief and love.[27]

The mother's love affair that the narrator reconstructs from the notebook also has much to do with literature and writing. A novelist herself, the mother has a life-long fondness for Chekhov. "Is she in love with Chekhov?" The daughter recalls the mother's extraordinary obsession with Chekhov's stories. "If Chekhov had been alive, such a thing might actually have happened"(109). As the narrator infers, part of the obsession comes from the fact that one of the two sets of Chekhov that the mother owns is a gift from her lover, a gift that, shortly before her death, she asks to have cremated with her. But, judging from her mother's almost religious devotion to romantic love, the narrator is not far wrong in suggesting that the mother is infatuated with Chekhov, for romantic love is the legacy of the literary tradition that Chekhov represents, a tradition that idealizes love and emphasizes internal drama and moral conflict. As if to reinforce her point, the narrator also situates the love tragedy in the intertextuality of Shakespeare's *Romeo and Juliet:* "Juliet compared her love to riches when she said: 'I cannot sum up half of my sum of wealth.' I suppose Mother couldn't have summed up half of her wealth, either" (116).

The literariness of the mother's love finds embodiment in one of her own novels in which she casts herself as a romantic heroine and her lover as a hero. Interestingly enough, her lover is a devoted reader of her novels. Literature and criticism thus become the field across which they indirectly "talk love" *(tan lian'ai)* to each other. During one of their rare encounters to which the young narrator is a witness, the man says: "I've read your latest novel. Frankly, it's not quite right in some places. I don't think you should be so hard on the heroine . . . you see, loving someone is not wrong in itself, and she hasn't really hurt anyone else. The hero might also have been in love. But for the sake of another person's happiness, they find that they must give up their love"(112). Submitting to the lover's discourse on self-sacrifice, the mother can only use her notebook as his substitute and pour into it her yearning and unfulfilled desire until the moment of her death.

The story would not be so interesting if it were simply the love story some critics have suggested it is.[28] It turns out that the insistent presence of the first-person narrator blurs the transparency of its language and problematizes the discourse on romantic tragedy. After all, the mother's story is told because the daughter herself faces the dilemma of deciding whether or not she should marry her friend Qiao Lin, whom she finds handsome but intellectually inadequate. She recalls her mother's advice: "Shanshan, if you can't decide what you want in a man, I think staying single is much better than marrying foolishly"(105). Behind that advice, of course, lies the wreckage of the mother's life: her own marriage has been a failure, and she ends up in love with a man with whom she cannot even shake hands. The daughter refuses to repeat the mother's marriage, but that is not all. She goes further and questions the latter's romantic approach to love: "I weep every time I see that notebook with 'Love must not be forgotten' written across its front. I weep bitterly again and again, as if I were the one who had suffered through that tragic love. The whole thing was either a great tragedy or *a massive joke*. Beautiful or poignant as it may have been, I have no intention of reenacting it!" (121, italics mine). The daughter's final choice is that of rebellion—rebellion against the discourse of the literary tradition (Chekhov and *Romeo and Juliet*) to which her mother has subscribed as novelist, heroine, and woman. By reconstructing the mother's life in writing, the narrator is able to rewrite the story of a woman's destiny so that independence rather than romantic attachment to a man will become her priority. When she declares toward the end that "living alone is not such a terrible thing" (122), her writing goes beyond the mother's wisdom and overcomes the tragic/ romantic discourse for which the latter has paid with her life. By asserting her difference and exercising independent authorship, the narrator achieves autonomy.

Insofar as the female subject is concerned, writing is always a matter of rewriting (the male text) and gaining authorial control. The same is true of Wang Anyi's story "Love in the Valley of Splendor," although, unlike the foregoing stories, it is told—playfully—in the third person. I say "playfully," because the narrator's subjectivity demands our attention, making us aware that she is making up a story about a young heroine whose life coincides exactly with hers in time and space. The story begins: "I want to tell a story, a story about a woman. The breeze of the early autumn feels so cool and clean, and the sunlight looks so transparent. All this fills my heart with tranquility; and in tranquility I imagine my story. As I think it over, it seems the story also takes place after an autumnal shower."[29] The narrator intervenes again and again to remind us of the fictionality of her work. For example, when the heroine stands in front of the office window looking out at a narrow lane, the narrator cuts in: "so I stand facing the narrow lane and continue to imagine my story"(7). The emphasis on fictionality might be interpreted as the author's reaction to the widely held view in China that fiction mirrors life itself. But this is not simply a case of modernistic subversion of realist conventions. The situation is greatly complicated by the narrator's gender. The recurrent imagery of the fallen leaves and the window, which provides the setting both for the fictional world and for the extradiegetic world of writing, pinpoints the female identity that the narrator shares with her heroine. Her closeness to the heroine in identity, gender and otherwise, is accentuated when she concludes the story thus: "She felt that nothing had really happened. It was true and absolutely true that nothing whatsoever had happened in actuality, except that the parasol outside the window had shed all of its leaves. And it's time that my story about a story that has never taken place came to a close" (43). In echoing the view that nothing has transpired in this story, the narrator more than coincides with the heroine. The truth is that the heroine exists as an extension of the narrator, who brings an alternative self into being through writing and imagination. Within the story proper, the heroine also tries to break out of the status quo by creating an alternative self during her trip to the Valley of Splendor in Lu Shan. This intricate relationship between the narrator, the heroine, and the latter's reconstructed self results in sophisticated writing about female subjectivity. If the narrator focalizes exclusively on the heroine's point of view, the fixed focalization does not mean the total effacement of the narrator behind the character as it normally does. The narrator does more here, for she claims that she knows more than the character: "I follow her on her way out . . . She felt tranquil in her heart at the moment. But something was going to happen to her. Yes, something was about to happen. I am the only one to know" (5). Of course, she is not an omniscient narrator in an ordinary sense, either. The authorial control derives solely from a sense of identification. The narrator knows what is going to happen to her heroine because the heroine is her written self. In short, she wills her story and her protagonist into being.

"Love in the Valley of Splendor" stands out from the rest of Wang Anyi's "Themes on Love," which focus on the human libido and its ubiquitous power. This story is not so much about indomitable sexual drives as about a woman's quest for self through the rewriting of the traditional story of adultery. The heroine yearns to break out of the old identity that her marriage has fixed upon her and to reconstruct a new self. When a total stranger, one who is about to become her lover, approaches her for the first time in Lu Shan, she takes him for granted: "He arrived as she had expected and she was not in the least surprised by it" (17). The language is highly reminiscent of the omniscient voice that the narrator used earlier, when she knew what was going to happen to her alternative self. The heroine anticipates her own story and takes authorial control over the situation. Her self-awareness and intelligence distinguish her from Flaubert's Emma Bovary and enable her to revise the old adultery plot: "She liked this new self, the self as presented to his [lover's] eyes. Her old self was so stale that she loathed it and wanted to cast it away. As a brand new, unfamiliar self, she was able to experience many brand new and unfamiliar feelings; or maybe the reverse was true: her brand new and unfamiliar feelings enabled her to discover and create a brand new, unfamiliar self. She was pleased to discover the boundless imaginative and creative powers this new self was capable of" (23). Echoing *Madame Bovary* (one of Wang's favorite novels) in an oblique way, the story rewrites the nineteenth-century French novel by situating the heroine in an authorial position. If Emma Bovary is a reader par excellence and deceives herself in terms of patriarchal discourse, our heroine and her creator, the narrator, reject the role of reader and engage in imaginatively reconstructing their female selfhood as "authors."

Constructing Female Subjectivity

Female subjectivity has occupied the center stage of women's literature since Ding Ling, although the latter eventually decided to circumvent the issue when her interest shifted from gender to class and relegated the former to a secondary and contingent priority.[30] Her first published story, "Meng Ke," contains a scene in which the young heroine presents herself before a film director, hoping to be hired: "She had to submit herself to a most unpleasant request: she raised her hands in silence and held back the short hair that covered her forehead and the sides, exposing her rounded forehead and delicate ears to the scrutinizing eyes of the man. She felt horrible and nearly broke down in tears. But the man was apparently pleased with what he saw."[31]

The revolt against such objectivization of the female body leads to the author's next work: "The Diary of Miss Sophia," which focuses on female subjectivity with a vengeance. The first entry of the diary records an interesting mirror scene: "Glancing from one side you've got a face a foot long; tilt your head slightly to the side and suddenly it gets so flat you startle yourself . . . It all infuriates me."[32] Examining her own image in the mirror seems to indicate narcissism. If so, the reflexive act of diary writing can also be seen as a mirroring of the self, for Sophia is at once the writer, the subject, and the reader of her text. In this story both the mirror and the diary come to us as powerful metaphors for Sophia's discourse about female selfhood. Ironically, the mirror's distortion of her image, which irritates her so much, seems to foreshadow the inadequacy of narcissism just as the diary fails to resolve the enigma of selfhood. Sophia's attitude toward writing and self reflects the female dilemma of wanting to reject male-centered discourse about gender and yet finding no alternative fully satisfying within a largely male-centered language. The text, therefore, is filled with contradictory expressions of self-love and self-loathing.

To the narrator endeavoring to rewrite herself into a different text, a text that will no longer portray her as someone's daughter, sister, lover, or friend but as an autonomous subject, the task is a difficult one. She has no idea of what the so-called subject is, for the "I" as an autonomous female subject has hardly existed in traditional Chinese discourse. Sophia asks herself repeatedly: "Can I tell what I really want?" (51) and tries to understand what she calls her "pitiful, ludicrous self" (79). Self-interrogation, ambivalence, and uncertainty fill the pages of the diary as the narrator struggles to "evolve an intelligible and authentic image of the self."[33] But that comforting image is nowhere to be found in this much-convoluted writing of self by the self. What her writing does succeed in doing, however, is subverting the closure, the authoritative tone, and the complacency of male-dominated writing. Her love need not be consummated to complete a romantic story. Her pains, desires, narcissism, perversity, and self-criticism form part of a work that struggles with itself and gives no final resolutions.

It is hardly surprising that half a century later Zhang Jie's novel *The Ark* still faced the question of female subjectivity. As it happens, the story also contains a mirror scene in which Liang Qian examines herself in a way that reminds us of Sophia: "Liang Qian stood up from her chair and saw herself reflected on the surface of the glass insulation in the studio. She was pale and shrunken, her hair disheveled. Weak and tired as she was, her eyes and brows wore a fierce look as if she were determined to quarrel with somebody and fight with him to death . . . She had barely reached forty and yet she already had the look of an elderly woman."[34] Facing herself, Liang faces a confused desire that renders her nonidentical with herself. She envies the twenty-one-year-old violinist in her crew, who is youthful looking with beautiful hair and bright eyes (for she seldom cries) and a wrinkle-free forehead (for she seldom uses her brains). She is torn by the conflicting desires to be a woman and to be a professional. She feels inadequate as a mother and yet cannot imagine living without a career. Her dilemma and her insecurity are shared by the other two women in the same apartment, which is jokingly referred to by the narrator as "the Widows' Club." Unlike Sophia, who is younger, these women must face the consequences of their divorce and separation as well as problems brought on by age and illness. Liu Quan is harassed by her boss at work and stigmatized by her colleagues; Cao Jinghua suffers from a spinal affliction that will probably lead to paralysis, and at work she is persecuted for publishing her political views. Liang Qian, a film director, is the only one who is not legally divorced from her husband, Bai Fushan (on the pretext of protecting her name, he has agreed to a separation but continues to utilize the prestige of Liang's family). The latter exploits and harasses her and schemes to prevent the release of her movie.

Focusing on the common plight of the three women, the narrator projects female subjectivity as a form of collective female consciousness, a consciousness that the symbolism of the title suggests. The ark is inspired by both Chinese and Western cultural traditions, for the word *Fang zhou* (the Ark) comes originally from the *History of the Latter Han* and only acquires its later biblical meaning via translation.[35] As critics have suggested,[36] the biblical symbolism of the ark implies the regeneration of mankind and the vision of an alternative world that would eventually replace the world these women inhabit, one in which "you are particularly unfortunate because you were born a woman."[37] The allusion to the *History of the Latter Han,* on the other hand, emphasizes the dynamic spirit of the women who defy tradition and brave hardships in their voyage to freedom. In fact, the symbolism is already prefigured in Zhang Jie's earlier story "Zumu lü" (Emerald), in which the metaphor of the sailboat conveys the triumph and the cost of being a self-reliant woman and contrasts with the comfortable but unreliable steamboat that symbolizes married life. If the ark projects a hope, a new world evoked by its Western etymology, it also provides the means (in the Chinese context) through which the new world can be reached. In short, it is a collective female consciousness that looks toward the future but is determined to wage its struggle here and now.

In view of the women's desire to protect their dignity as female subjects, it is not difficult to see why the sense of privacy and the fear of invasion figure so strongly in their response to the outside world. The apartment in which the women live is an embodiment of the ark of female consciousness that shelters them from a hostile world, but even here they are frequently threatened by invasions from Bai Fushan and inquisitive neighbors. On one occasion, Bai pokes his head into Liu Quan's bedroom before she can grab a blanket to cover herself up. He visits without the slightest consideration for the women's privacy. The following describes one of his surprise visits: "On an early morning like this, Liu Quan and Jinghua had just woken up from their nightmares. But before they could recover from the effects of their bad dreams, Bai intruded on them in such a rude manner and destroyed their mood. His invasion completely ruined their plans for a peaceful Sunday" (9). Bai thinks that his wife is hiding somewhere and insists on entering, but meets with firm resistance from Jinghua, who shuts the door in his face. Shortly after his departure there comes another knock at the door. The visitor turns out to be the head of the neighborhood committee, Jia Zhuren, who takes it upon herself to spy on them, assuming that divorced women always try to attract men. Overhearing Bai's knocking in the early morning, she has come to check things out. Again Jinghua guards the door and refuses to let her in:

"Has our cat by any chance gotten into your apartment?"

"No," Jinghua said clearly and firmly, "what's your cat got to do in our apartment?"

"Oh! Don't you know, Comrade Cao, that your tabby cat has turned on all six tomcats in our compound? Ha, Ha!" Jia giggled obscenely.

Jinghua laughed aloud: "Ha, ha, ha! I'm proud of my cat. She is fortunate enough to have so many admirers." (17–18)

The animal allegory used by the chairwoman exhibits the insidious language in which people in this society relate to sex and think about single women; it reduces woman to no more than a signifier of sexuality. Although Jia is herself a woman, the fact that she is the head of the neighborhood committee, which holds itself accountable to the All-China Women's Federation and spies for the authorities, pinpoints her as an upholder of the patriarchal order. Her invasion of the private world of the women, therefore, is a political conspiracy designed to deprive them of their dignity. But the fact that neither she nor Bai succeeds in getting into the apartment that morning implies that it is possible for the women to guard their privacy and subjectivity, provided that they have a room of their own and the support of a collective female consciousness.

In "Emerald," an earlier story by Zhang Jie, the protagonist, Zeng Ling'er, becomes a female subject not through identifying with other women but through enduring intense isolation and overcoming her romantic love. As a young girl, she is ready to sacrifice everything for the love of a man named Zuo Wei. During the Cultural Revolution she saves him several times, even confessing to his political "crimes." She is banished to the countryside, where she gives birth to his illegitimate child and suffers humiliation and ostracism. In the meantime, Zuo Wei has married another woman. However, the years of hardship and bereavement Zeng has to endure—her son drowns in a river—do not defeat her. Instead, she is transformed from a romantic young girl into the independent, resilient, and strong-willed woman that the title of the story, her birthstone, symbolizes. Transferred back to the institute where her ex-lover works, she discovers that she is no longer in love with him: "At this moment Zeng Ling'er felt that she had scaled another peak in her life. Yes, she would cooperate with Zuo Wei in his work, but this time out of neither love nor hate, nor any sense of pity for him. She simply wanted to make her contribution to society."[38]

If self-reliance and collective female consciousness are the responses that "Emerald" and *The Ark* make to the problematic of the female subject as first posed in Ding Ling's story, Wang Anyi takes a different approach in "Love in the Valley of Splendor." Since the story also contains a mirror scene, it is interesting to compare it with those in the other stories:

> She got back to her hotel room and shut herself up in the bathroom for a long time. She didn't know how long it was that she stood in front of the looking-glass, gazing at her own image. The image in the mirror was like another self gazing back at her as if that self had a lot to tell her but had decided to say nothing, because they were able to understand each other quite well without words. She turned her face a little to one side and studied its angles unconsciously. But all of a sudden, she felt alienated from the self in the mirror as if it had become a total stranger. She wanted to recapture the self, reexamine it, and be in touch with it again. But the self remained a blurred image and became so unfamiliar, so remote and yet also strangely familiar.[39]

The mirror scenes in "The Diary of Miss Sophia" and *The Ark* express a strong discontent with the self, as the women struggle with conflicting ideas about womanhood and subjectivity. In the passage above, however, the female subject appears not so much contradictory as indeterminate and elusive—something the heroine tries hard to grasp.

Lu Shan, where the mirror scene occurs and which, moreover, alludes to the classical motif of revelation in Chinese poetry, serves here as a metaphoric locus for the heroine's pursuit of self. The mountain, its face shrouded in clouds, symbolizes the unfathomable depths of self, which dissolve, transform, and consolidate along with the mist, fog, and white clouds.[40] This is a world of imagination, dream, and fantasy in which the self becomes fluid and capable of change and reconstruction. The heroine delights in the miraculous transformation of herself into someone whom she no longer recognizes: "That image was beautiful, so beautiful that she felt it utterly unfamiliar. For her own sake and for his [the lover's], she resolved to cherish the new self dearly. To damage it was to disappoint herself, him, his gaze, and his feelings" (21). The heroine's sense of self is so positive that the male gaze is not perceived as a threat to her subjectivity as in Ding Ling's early stories. Instead, the gaze, which is mutual, reinforces her desire to bring about a new sense of self and to "regain the gender she has lost" in marriage (27). Like subjectivity, gender is presented as something to be acquired and constructed through constant negotiation with other beings rather than as a fixed category of identity. The protagonist's marriage, which has fixed a sexual identity on her, succeeds only in alienating her from a fluid sense of gender, whereas her relative autonomy at the present moment enables her to rediscover it in relation to another man. She is proud of being different from man and of being reminded of the fact by the male gaze, for that difference is central to her self-consciousness as a woman. What is more important, it turns out that her love affair is more fiction than reality, in which the true object of desire is the heroine herself: "Her love for the self that grew out of her intimate relation with him surpassed by far her love for the man himself, although she did not fully realize it at the moment. She thought that she was in love with him and felt sad at the thought of departure. Many years were to go past before the truth would gradually dawn on her" (31).

Like Ding Ling and Zhang Jie, Wang Anyi situates female subjectivity in a process that challenges the received idea of womanhood. But in subverting patriarchal discourse, she also tries to involve the male gender in the constructive process, a fact that opens up the writing of gender to a wide range of possibilities—to gender relations that are predicated not on the desires of either man or woman alone but on the reworking of the subjectivity of male and female each in its own terms and in terms of each other.

Love, Marriage, and Female Bonding

Love and marriage have been almost synonymous with the female character in literature, but the responses of twentieth-century women authors to those perennial themes have shown significant departures from previous literary traditions. Their works tend to focus on the conflict between marriage and self-fulfillment, and between love and independence. Romantic love and marriage are often rejected as a result of woman's quest for selfhood, which explains why the majority of female protagonists we discuss here are single, divorced, or have troubled marriages.[41] In "The Diary of Miss Sophia," the narrator falls in love with the handsome Ling Jishi. But it is no ordinary case of romantic love. The equilibrium of the subject and object of desire proves fundamental in maintaining the relationship. In other words, the narrator's aggressive pursuit of Ling is also underscored by her secret fear that she will be reduced to becoming the object of his desire. So when Ling comes into her room to express his desire, Sophia recoils in fear and disgust: "The lust in his eyes scared me. I felt my self-respect revive finally as I listened to the disgusting pledges sworn out of the depths of Ling Jishi's depravity."[42] She revolts at the idea of becoming the object of the male gaze. As a result, her own desire is doomed by the need to overcome her lover's desire. This is how she describes their kiss: "That disgusting creature Ling Jishi kissed me! I endured it in silence! But what did my heart feel when the lips so warm and tender brushed my face? I couldn't allow myself to be like other women who faint into their lovers' arms! I screwed open my eyes wide and looked straight in his face. 'I've won!' I thought, 'I've won!' Because when he kissed me, I finally knew the taste of the thing that had so bewitched me. At the same moment I despised myself" (80–81). This is a revelation of the power relationship in sexual intimacy as perceived by a woman who writes, directs, plays, and observes the dangerous drama of sexual liaison. The usurpation of power by the male at the climactic moment seems to deny the possibility of heterosexual love in the patriarchal order without power struggle. Sophia wins the battle but loses the lover.

Another important reason for Sophia's revolt against Ling is his language as he takes it upon himself to teach her how to be a woman while reserving the role of a male chauvinist for himself: "Our most recent conversations have taught me a lot more about his really stupid ideas. All he wants is money. Money. A young wife to entertain his business associates in the living room, and several fat, fair-skinned, well-dressed little sons. What does love mean to him? Nothing more than spending money in a brothel, squandering it on a moment of pleasure" (65). Ling's dream of marriage, family, financial success, and even extramarital love is perceived as a typically male-centered capitalist dream. Sophia's lucid perception of the link between the capitalist system and patriarchal culture shows the firm ideological grounding of her feminism.[43] She refuses to be written back into patriarchal discourse either as a wife or as an extramarital lover. (She later learns that Ling Jishi has a wife in Singapore.) She suffers from the thought that she has offered herself to him for his amusement like a prostitute (66). These traditional female roles alienate Sophia from the man she adores. The lovers' encounter becomes a contest between two radically different ideologies that ends in the estrangement of the lovers and in Sophia's despair.

By contrast, her emotional attachment to another woman, Yunjie, does not require such antagonism. Her memory of Yunjie is always pleasant. Recalling their final moments together, she writes:

What a life I was living last year at this time! To trick Yunjie into babying me unreservedly, I'd pretend to be sick and refuse to get out of bed. I'd sit and whimper about the most trivial dissatisfactions to work on her tearful anxiety and get her to fondle me . . . It hurts even more to think about the nights I spent lying on the grass in French Park listening to Yunjie sing a song from *Peony Pavilion*. If she hadn't been tricked by God into loving that pale-faced man, she would never have died so fast and I wouldn't have wandered into Beijing alone, trying, sick as I was, to fend for myself, friendless and without family. (70)

The allusion to *Peony Pavilion* is important for undercutting fictions of romantic love.[44] In the light of her death after her husband's abuse of her, Yunjie's singing of love seems particularly ironical. Sophia's account of her life inserts what a traditional male-oriented text would leave out, that is, what would happen *after* the "euphoric closure" of united lovers. By evoking *Peony Pavilion,* Sophia in effect accuses traditional literature of enticing young people into romantic relations. Ding Ling's treatment of women's emotional bonding in this and other stories such as "Summer Vacation" does not, however, envision female bonding as a positive alternative to romantic love and marriage. With the arrival of contemporary writers like Zhang Jie and Wang Anyi, female bonding becomes an ideological choice just as important as subjectivity itself.[45]

The Ark ends with Liang Qian proposing: "Let's drink a toast to women," at which the women pledge a female bond. Each of them is disappointed in her husband and lacks faith in a male-dominated society. Cao Jinghua has been divorced by her husband because she does not share his dreams of raising a family and, without his permission, she goes through an abortion. Liu Quan's stingy husband exploits her sexually as if he has paid for her in cash. She dreads each night, but he always attacks her in the same manner: "You call yourself my wife, don't you?"[46] Liang Qian's husband, Bai Fushan, who treats marriage as a business transaction, is keen on making deals. When Cao Jinghua and Liu Quan overhear him plotting against his wife, Cao comments: "Here is what you call a husband . . . To hell with husbands. We must rely on ourselves" (113). The three women therefore seek mutual support in their own community: "The single women would often spend the night sitting together in the deep shade cast by the lamp and no one in the grimness of her mood thought of clearing the dinner table piled high with plates. While one recounted the unfair treatment she had received during the day, the others would smoke and listen in silence. Or they would smoke in silence and listen to her pounding the arms of the chair with her fists in anger" (49).

If the divorced women in *The Ark* manage to create an ark of their own—an ark of female consciousness—in order to contend with a hostile, male-dominated society, the three women in Wang Anyi's story, "Brothers," are not so successful and eventually drift apart. The story goes beyond the male/female antagonism and raises questions about desire, choice, female bonding, and women's relation to men and family.

Like the self-reflexive title of "Love Must Not Be Forgotten," "Dixiongmen" (Brothers) alludes to an art exhibition that the female protagonists talk of organizing but fail to realize. It also refers to the relationship among the women themselves, which ends in frustration like the art show. The opening lines of the story place the subversive relationship of the women in perspective: "At college, they [the women] were three brothers: Laoda, Lao'er, and Laosan. They called their husbands Laoda's, Lao'er's, and Laosan's, respectively. They were the only female students in the whole class and they surpassed their male classmates in everything they did."[47] In choosing the word *brothers* rather than *sisters,* the story calls attention to the lack of a conventional social and intellectual bond among women, particularly among married women. In the light of the time-honored cult of male bonding, the choice is highly symbolic. We are told that the "brothers," all art majors, are sloppier in their dress and behavior than the male students. They are anything but feminine. Like the three roommates in *The Ark,* they open their hearts to each other, describing their sexual involvements with men as self-destruction and their own bonding as salvation. But when the time for graduation comes, each is faced with a different choice. Laosan decides to adopt the traditional lifestyle in order to fulfill her obligations to her husband, and she takes a job in her hometown. Lao'er becomes an art teacher at a high school in Nanjing, and Laoda teaches at a normal school in Shanghai. After their graduation, the initial bond formed at school develops into a close emotional attachment between Laoda and Lao'er, who address each other afterward as Lao Li and Lao Wang.

In sharp contrast to Bai Fushan and most other men in *The Ark,* the husbands of both Lao Li and Lao Wang in this story are model husbands. They treat their wives with respect and understanding and perform the household duties with diligence. But Lao Wang is amazed at the way her husband divides life neatly into two orderly parts, career and family, each serving as the means and end of the other. When Lao Li visits her after many years of separation, she finds her freedom suddenly restored to her. For once she lives spontaneously: she need not get up, have meals, or go to sleep at the usual hours. From then on, the two women write long letters every few days and marvel at the fact that their attachment to each other is closer than to their own husbands:

> They noted cheerfully that their correspondence gave them the illusion that they had returned to the time of their girlhood. At that time each girl had a bosom girlfriend, with whom she could talk about practically anything she wanted to. The girls knew each other intimately and spent days and nights together, until the love affair of each drove a wedge between them. They began to betray each other, learning to tell lies, thinking about their boyfriends and guarding the secret from each other. The war of territory began. The women now felt that they had gone backward in time, that is, more than ten years ago before the discord of desire had invaded their female friendship. (20)

Lao Li and Lao Wang grow so attached to each other that, when the former gives birth to a son, the latter buys a longevity pendant for the child and is moved to tears at the thought that they finally have a child of their own. In her mind, the child has a mother and a godmother; the father is excluded from the picture. She offers to take care of the mother during her confinement. Lao Li's husband is grateful for her service but at the same time feels slightly resentful. Her presence seems to disrupt his normal relations with his wife and banish him from his own family. Lao Wang's husband is also puzzled by his wife's strange behavior. When the two families gather around the dinner table on the eve of the Spring Festival, he tries to understand what makes his wife so unlike her usual self when at home: "At first, he thought it was Lao Li's husband. But after a while he concluded it couldn't have been he, because underneath that man's politeness lay indifference to his wife. He then began to observe Lao Li. It was not long before he saw that it was Lao Li who indulged her whimsical behavior. Whenever his wife went to extremes, Lao Li would give her a loving, encouraging look" (26).

The climax of the relationship arrives with two juxtaposed events:

the two women's attempt to articulate their love for each other and the accidental fall of Lao Li's child. They are taking a walk in the park when Lao Wang suddenly asks Lao Li: "What would happen if we both fell desperately in love with one man?" Lao Li says she would let Lao Wang have the man. But Lao Wang presses her further: "What if we were so much in love that neither could surrender him to the other." "Then I'd kill him" (27), upon which Lao Wang's eyes fill with tears of gratitude. The two women talk about their emotional attachment in a roundabout manner, and their narrative cannot but be completed at the male's expense. To articulate love for the same sex is almost an impossibility, so that they must invent a fictional plot about triangular love in order to arrive at it. What makes the story so interesting is that there is something more than male discourse that stands in the women's way. The event that follows the conversation puts their love to the test, a test that finally estranges them. As the women are talking, Lao Li's son falls out of his carriage and hits his forehead on the curb. The mother is suddenly transformed into a different person. She forbids Lao Wang to go near the injured child, as if she were to blame for the accident. Lao Li's husband begins to hate her and orders her to leave. Ironically, it is not until love is damaged beyond repair that Lao Li is able to express it. As the two take leave of each other at the station, Lao Li says: "I love you. I truly love you!" and the story ends on a pessimistic note: "They had never said the word 'love' between themselves, a word that had become so contaminated by male/female copulation. But she said it now. Tears gushed from Lao Wang's eyes as she wept: 'Too late. It's too late!'" (30).

Motherhood need not have stood in the way of their love, because before the accident they had both tended the child with motherly care. Lao Li's overreaction to the accident reveals a mind torn by ambivalent feelings toward desire and motherhood. Feeling guilty for indulging her illicit desire, she opposes motherhood to female bonding so that the crisis of the self can be resolved through self-sacrifice and self-punishment. The fragility and rupture of the female bond testify to the difficulty a woman encounters in sorting out her desires in a society that privileges heterosexuality.

*   *   *

To return to the earlier question I raised at the outset, do the works of these writers suggest a female tradition in modern Chinese literature? Most critics of women's fiction agree that female writers tend to grapple with the problem of subjectivity in connection with gender and explore the relationship of the female subject to power, meaning, and the dominant ideology in which her gender is inscribed. Inasmuch as gender does make a difference in reading, writing, and other literary practices, as my analysis of the three authors has demonstrated, it is not difficult to conceptualize women writers as a separate category. However, one might still wonder what enables contemporary critics to jump from the category of woman writer—heretofore a subcategory in mainstream criticism—to that of female literature and female literary tradition. In other words, what happens when a radically different conceptual approach and historical imagination are brought to bear on the study of women's works? In this regard, it might be of particular interest to recall that women critics in the eighties and nineties almost unanimously evoke the early Ding Ling, that is, the author of "The Diary of Miss Sophia," as a pioneer in the female tradition while rejecting the later Ding Ling for being a chief collaborator in socialist realism. This seems to indicate that the idea of the female tradition is no less a potent form of historical intervention than it is an invention. Linking women's writing of the post-Mao era with that of the May Fourth generation across several decades, the female tradition opens up the possibility for women critics to envision a departure from the practice of male-centered literary criticism in the past decades, which they see as patronizing women writers but refusing to grant them a subject-position. What we are witnessing here, it seems to me, is a form of engagement and a profound moment of history making, as women critics seek to institute a different narrative that will enable them to contest the claims of the state, Fulian, and official feminism as the sole representatives of Chinese women. In that sense, the female literary tradition is surely in the making and, with more and more writers and critics joining in, it will probably take on a life of its own in the future. Nevertheless, I should not be taken as prophesying a bright future for female literature. While my fascination with this new literary tradition remains strong, the foregoing discussion is also intended as a reminder of the historical contingencies of our own academic practice: To what extent are we all implicated in the making of particular histories even at moments when those histories seem most neutral and transparent? What does the making of a female literary tradition in post-Mao China tell us about the general practice of historiography and literary scholarship? Finally, in what ways does such an understanding transform one's own knowledge about the object of study?

8 | Living in Sin: From May Fourth via the Antirightist Movement to the Present

Lu Xun, Fang Ji, and Gao Xiaosheng have each written stories about the "wages of living in sin." "Remorse" *(Shangshi),*[1] "The Visitor" *(Laifangzhe),*[2] and "Amorous Feelings in a Village" *(Cunzili de fengqing),*[3] respectively, are all tales of the cohabitation (or common law marriage) and eventual parting of a couple. These stories differ greatly in their narrative structure and political circumstances. Yet each text appropriates the motif of the oppressed condition of women, revealed through a socially unsanctioned cohabitation that inevitably fails, in order to present a more fundamental concern located in the male protagonist. This concern is basically one of complex intellectual and moral distress, and the social and sexual oppression of the women in the stories functions to expose and highlight this distress. In each of the stories the oppressed condition of women is important because it reveals something the text holds more important: the moral responsibility and potential hypocrisy of the mind defined as masculine. As a necessary corollary to this moral responsibility, the masculine mind is also the locus of moral conscience and the power to give moral meaning, or simply to assign meaning, to interpret.

What I want to show here is how these narratives work to affirm this greater consequence of the masculine mind as it relates to sexual oppression and as it grants or with-

holds the power of voice to women. Using different narrative structures, all three texts define a construct in masculine terms of the
relationship between morality and sexuality and of the possibility of
expression or interpretation. The purpose of this discussion of the
stories, then, is not to establish a specific literary antecedent function or influence of an earlier story for a later one but rather to
present the masculine conversation that develops when the stories
are brought together.

Nora Left Silent

Many have remarked that "Remorse" is Lu Xun's fictional expansion
of the question posed in his earlier essay "What Happens to Nora
after She Leaves Home."[4] In this essay, he pointed out that given real
social and economic circumstances, if women were to try to free
themselves of their humiliating dependence on husbands or fathers
and make it on their own in the world, they would either starve, end
up as prostitutes, or be forced to return home. Criticizing Ibsen, Lu
Xun remarked that when Ibsen wrote *The Doll's House,* he "was actually writing a poem; he was by no means responding for the benefit
of society to a problem that had arisen in that society."[5]

Logically, then, "Remorse" might be read as Lu Xun's response to
the social problems interfering with women's emancipation, yet
these are not the terms in which it has been discussed. In previous
interpretations of "Remorse," the issue of woman's oppression is
generally overlooked or referred to only briefly. This neglect has to
do largely with the manner of the story's presentation and the corresponding demands that this makes on one's reading of it. The
point of view of the story is entirely that of Juansheng, the male
protagonist. Leo Ou-fan Lee has written that "Remorse" is an example of Lu Xun's use of a simultaneously intensely subjective "I-narra-
tion" and an ironic objective distance.[6] By strict adherence to the
mental world of an involved male narrator, a narrator who is both
subject and teller of the story, Lu Xun creates possibilities of conscious and unconscious indirection and leaves open to question the
sincerity of the narrative voice.[7] This provides for a wide range of
interpretations, but also encourages neglect of certain areas of

significant indirection or silence in the text, particularly those regarding the female protagonist, Zijun. Comparatively little attention is given to the gender-specific social and economic realities that do ultimately force Zijun to return home and die mysteriously.

In Chinese critical circles the text is defined as a tragic love story, and the major interpretive issue is why the love failed. The answers put forth have ranged from socially imposed *shared* deprivations of hunger and cold, the lovers' *shared* ideology of bourgeois individualism,[8] or, more recently and quite to the contrary, their *shared* lack of firm, liberated individual consciousness. Although the issue of equality between men and women is raised in these arguments, this is done not to examine gender-specific oppression, but rather to mount a gender-neutral attack on the traditional marriage system and feudal family structure in general. Citing Engels' statement that modern love between the sexes "takes *mutual love* as its premise: *in this regard,* women have an equal status to men," Chinese critics hold that love, not sexual or gender oppression, is at issue.[9]

In American critical circles, Juansheng's feelings of regret or guilt regarding *his* failure in his relationship with Zijun dominate critical discussion. Consequently, to some Juansheng is a "typical May Fourth romantic intellectual" whose "excessively sentimental" language reveals his "silly emotionality."[10] Others emphasize Juansheng's intellectuality, his "intellectual prudery," against the *background* of Zijun's emotional sensitivity. The story expresses remorse for a missed chance at love, and in effect becomes Lu Xun's "love story."[11] These interpretations give only scant attention to Zijun's character or to the real social problems for women that Lu Xun had promised to bring to light.

The alternatives for Nora that Lu Xun's essay pointed out—starvation, prostitution, or return home—underlined his sense of the improbability, if not impossibility, of economic self-sufficiency for women in China of the 1920s. "Remorse" reiterates this quite forcefully in the rather depressing details of the couple's poverty once Juansheng has lost his clerical position, in its complete silence regarding the possibility of work for Zijun, and in her eventual return home and subsequent death. Related to this, it also presents, in rather subtle fashion, another oppressive social construct that women must battle against, one that is in many ways even further beyond their control because it relates to such a fundamental element of their being, their sexuality.

In "Remorse," Juansheng identifies suspicious public scrutiny and moral judgments for perceived sexual transgressions as part of feudal social attitudes, but is extraordinarily reticent and evasive about his own sexual interest in Zijun. He tells the reader eagerly enough about his intellectual discussions with Zijun on subjects like the despotism of the family system, the need to destroy old customs, equality between the sexes, Ibsen, Tagore, and Shelley. He responds joyfully but "abstractly"[12] to Zijun's declaration "I belong to myself,"[13] offering it to the reader as an indication that Chinese women are not as hopeless as pessimists would have one believe. However, is it simply evidence of the progressiveness of Chinese women that gives him joy in Zijun's declaration? In fact, isn't an important part of his pleasure that she has translated his subconsciously manipulative generalizations on emancipated women into the appropriate personal response, a response of sexual liberation at least in direct connection to him? Zijun's declaration is essentially her own indirect expression of willingness to go against convention specifically in terms of her relationship to Juansheng. It is this that gives Juansheng the encouragement actually to declare his love for her and propose that they live together, that is, become sexually involved.

Juansheng's sexual interest in Zijun is further revealed in his keen sensitivity to that element in the public gaze. He states that he is impressed by and proud of her ability to remain oblivious to the lecherous looks that she draws and that *he* observes as she walks ten paces ahead of him. Later, when they become bold enough to walk side by side, he, again not she, is "conscious of searching looks, sarcastic smiles or lewd and contemptuous glances." These set him shivering if his guard is down so that he has to "summon all [his] pride and defiance to [his] support."[14] Zijun, on the other hand, walks along "as if she had entered a realm without people."[15]

Placing "Regret" in the context of Lu Xun's other short stories, we see that Juansheng's state of mind here does not differ significantly from that of Siming in "Soap."[16] In that story, Siming's wife and friends draw obvious inferences regarding his excessive concern for the attractive young beggar girl whom he tries to present as an inspiring model of filial piety. He protests that his interest is pure and even noble, but his sensitivity and confusion when faced with others' suspicions of sexual attraction are sufficient to expose his less admissible, subconscious motivations. There seems ultimately little distinction between Siming's use of the veneer of pious Confucian concepts and Juansheng's similarly dissimulating use of popular modern ideas as vehicles to aid them in disguising the expression of their desires. Both stories reveal a complex interplay between ideological and psychological motivations.

A second matter having to do with sex and sexuality that goes unmentioned in discussions of "Remorse," again because the narrator is extraordinarily evasive about it, is the possibility of pregnancy as a consequence of this cohabitation. There are in fact a few tantalizing comments which suggest that Zijun does indeed become pregnant in the course of their life together. There is the matter of timing to begin with: the two live together for just less than a year. Twice the narrator mentions Zijun's figure: once, early on in their life together, he describes her as plumper, with rosier cheeks; and later, when their impoverished circumstances are leaving him hungry, he notes resentfully and with a significant ellipsis, "The strange thing was that she didn't look particularly thin . . ."[17] Her inability to leave even after the narrator has told her he does not love her, her father's eventual arrival to take her away, and her unexplained death (complications of abortion or childbirth?) might further imply that Zijun is drawn deeper into conventional domesticity and restricted from acting as an "emancipated woman" by pregnancy. The question arises, if she is pregnant, are we to understand that she is hiding this from him, that he is refusing to see it, or that this is not an entirely candid confessional narrative? His words "the strange thing" suggest that either he suspects the pregnancy but will not admit it, or he knows but cannot acknowledge his responsibility in this sexually related burden.

What of Zijun and her response to her circumstances? The reader can only observe her from the outside, and even this observation is filtered through Juansheng's mind. From what information he offers, it seems that she says little and that at first her silence is agreeable, convincing him that she is listening intelligently to him: "By that time I had told her all my views, all about myself, and what my failings were. I had hidden very little, and she understood me completely."[18] When he speaks to her about things, she nods understandingly.[19]

Later his observations and descriptions of her are less appreciative and eventually suggest that she is thinking little, if at all. Housekeeping preoccupies her, and she no longer has time for chatting, reading, or taking walks. She obsesses about food, is attentive to the four chicks and Pekingese they purchase, and feuds increasingly with their landlady over these chicks. With Juansheng's unemployment, his judgment of Zijun grows increasingly critical. She shows no comprehension of the difficulties in his mental labors of translation, and when Juansheng complains that she feeds the Pekingese better than him, she says she cannot stand having the landlady sneering at them for being too poor to keep a dog. Ultimately, much against Zijun's will, the chickens are eaten and Juansheng gets rid of the dog. At this point, he describes her as "obtuse" and remarks that she has lost her courage. Finally he states: "All the ideas and intelligent, fearless phrases she had learned were empty after all; yet she had no inkling of their emptiness. She had given up reading long ago, so did not understand that the first thing in life is to make a living . . . All she could do was cling to someone else's clothing, making it hard for even a fighter to struggle, and bringing ruin on both."[20] Juansheng has already gotten rid of his other economic dependents, the chickens and the dog, and now he feels his life would be easier without Zijun as well. For an instant, he wishes for her death.[21]

There is little in the text to challenge Juansheng's estimation of Zijun at this point, although her earlier shock at the news of his unemployment suggests that she knows, even without the benefit of book reading, that the "first thing in life is to make a living." Still, it apparently does not occur to her that there is any way she could make a living, and though he never says so directly, the narrator's description of her as clinging to someone else hints that he wishes she would (could) think of something along those lines.

What is it that inhibits Zijun from getting work? Even if she set aside jobs of less-savory reputation—working in teahouses, acting, or such—still, women were working in factories or teaching in girls' schools by this time. Speculating from the story, we can see at least three reasons why Zijun merely "clings." First, due to their cohabitation, she too would be likely to lose, even if she could obtain, any position. Second, if she were pregnant, it would be even more difficult for her to obtain and hold a job. Of equal or even more importance, though, from the first it apparently does not occur to her to look for a job.

This lack of interest in employment seems to be a matter of her class. Blindness and inhibitions that arise from class are intimated in Zijun's attitude toward the animals she raises: chickens could be considered a source of income, but according to Juansheng, she picked up her liking for animals from the landlady, the wife of an official, suggesting that these chicks are pets and symbols of status. Asui, the Pekingese, exposes further Zijun's class, not only in her affection for a plaything that will "beg or stand up on his hind legs," or her unwillingness to have the landlady sneer at them for not being able to afford the "heavy liability" of the dog's appetite,[22] but also revealingly when she cannot bring herself to take Asui to the market and sell the dog for "a few coppers."[23] Peasants, not well-bred young women, sell things for a few coppers.

The text thus presents Zijun as a rather superficially educated, unimaginative, petty bourgeois *xiaojie* (miss).[24] While she still represents women's economic and sexual oppression, nonetheless she also participates in its perpetuation through class-related habits and inhibitions. Her original statement of liberation is indeed empty. But what is the effect of revealing these negative aspects of Zijun? In order to appreciate their effect, it must be emphasized that Juansheng seems no more critically conscious of his own class failings and generally shares her attitudes. Early on, he speaks of the need for a servant to relieve Zijun of household tasks and for a larger home. Although he later complains of her unintelligent preoccupation with domestic drudgery, until he is fired, he is equally a drudge in his own employment. He, too, cannot bear to have acquaintances see him impoverished. In addition, although he is the one who insists on eating the chickens and getting rid of the dog, he is tremendously uneasy about these actions. He, no less than Zijun, cannot bring himself to sell the dog.

Zijun's facial expressions and gaze are central in creating the complex textual relationship between her and Juansheng. In fact, it is mainly through these that she speaks, if she can be said to speak at all. Juansheng seldom records her words, but he constantly interprets her face and eyes in his narrative, and always in terms of their implication for him.[25] Repeatedly he describes her eyes as childish or childlike (*zhiqi* and *haiziqi, haizi yibande*). At first he associates this with a happy curiosity aroused by his words and ideas. As their circumstances grow difficult and his ardor cools, however, the childishness seems to be more an expression of dependence that compels him to hide and lie about his feelings, until one morning when she looks "resentful" (*yuanqi*). He seizes this opportunity to announce that he no longer loves her, and immediately he describes her expression as becoming like that of "a hungry and thirsty child looking for her mother," as "a childishness in her eyes."[26] Later, after she has finally left with her father, he visualizes Zijun, her "childish eyes, looking at him imploringly."[27]

Zijun is granted innocence by this association of her gaze with that of a child. Correspondingly, as Juansheng "reads" that gaze for the reader, his sense of guilt emerges. On the surface, this might seem to offer moral privilege to Zijun, but in strictly formal terms it holds her in silence while Juansheng occupies the privileged position of the interpreting, moral, and self-reflective mind. Innocence is not moral superiority but rather a separation from and ignorance of the moral issue.

Despite Zijun's own shortcomings, then, the text fixes responsibility on Juansheng. Ultimately more important than her bourgeois ideology, which he shares, are his intellectual hypocrisy about his sexual desire, his evasion of possible responsibility as a father, and his self-deceiving, self-centered romantic notion that on his own he can and must "soar" by passively waiting for something to happen. With Zijun's off-stage death, what remains for critical appraisal at the end of the story is Juansheng, now "free" to go on living in self-absorbed guilt and agony. His one action and his "first step to a new life," the writing of his "love story," cannot be "for Zijun's sake as well as [his] own,"[28] nor to obtain the forgiveness it ostensibly seeks. Even his plea for such, along with this less than entirely honest rehearsal of his story for the reader's judgment, places him alone at the center, intensifying his self-absorption.

Juansheng provides the explanation of Zijun's function in the story through his expansive symbolic vision of her in the early stage of their romance. In her individual positive response to him, he envisions that "*Chinese women* were not as hopeless as the pessimists made out, and that we should see in the not too distant future the splendor of the dawn."[29] Here Juansheng translates an unspoken, private advantage for him in Zijun's repetition of his ideas on women's emancipation into a public, international advantage. Not only is this self-serving in that it gets Zijun into bed with him, it also transfers to her the burden of bringing about China's modernity. As far as we can tell from the text, this vision is not shared by Zijun. Her declaration of independence follows talk about her personal circumstances, her father and uncle. It is Juansheng who "fills the room with the sound of his voice"[30] on the ideas of family despotism, equality of the sexes, Ibsen, Tagore, and Shelley, who steps, as it were, into the national and international arena, and thereby identifies his life, his self, with the nation. For Juansheng, Zijun's "emancipation" symbolically demonstrates his/China's rightful claim to the status of "modernity." Similarly, her failure is emblematic for him of his/China's failure, not just that of her own or even of Chinese women, to be modern and emancipated.

Thus Juansheng finds himself implicated in Zijun's inability to step forward boldly into the future. She effectively exposes *his* class attitude and *his* uneasiness with sexuality and sexual desire. She reflects his own unacknowledged fear of unemployment, his passivity about struggling for social change, and reveals that "all the ideas and intelligent fearless phrases she had learned" from *him* "were empty after all; yet she [now read *he*] had no inkling of their emptiness." When he later tries to repeat these phrases, they sound hollow and mocking to him.[31] As he expresses it, he is left at the end, not wanting to remember "the [moral] forgetfulness that sent Zijun to her death," left "burying truth deep in the wound of [his] heart, and advancing silently with forgetfulness and falsehood as [his] guide."

To describe "Remorse," then, as a love story is not very accurate. Neither would it be true to say it leaves the reader with a clear vision of the social and economic realities that oppress women. At the individual level, Lu Xun does more to expose Juansheng's self-interest, his use and abuse of Zijun, than to describe his love for her. On

230 | Margaret H. Decker

a wider interpretive scheme, one that Juansheng initiates by his symbolic vision of Zijun, Juansheng in turn becomes symbolic of a more broadly conceived habit of hypocrisy, a habit shared in Lu Xun's works by self-acclaimed modernists or revolutionaries as much as by traditional Confucianists like Siming in "Soap." The text delimits this hypocrisy, this penchant for self-deception as masculine, by locating it in Juansheng, and the specifics of women's oppression quietly take a second place to this national character defect.

"Hearing" Nora

Fang Ji wrote "The Visitor" at the beginning of the antirightist movement. Despite obviously different political exigencies, much of the story suggests the influence of Lu Xun's story, particularly as that story was interpreted in the 1950s. Major critics of that time, like Feng Xuefeng, had located the tragic ending to "Remorse" in the ideological basis of the love, the bourgeois mentality of the characters.[32] Such an orthodox interpretation followed guidelines on the central issue of class stand as expressed in Mao Zedong's Yan'an talks on literature.[33] Much less subtly than was the case for Juansheng, the male character in "The Visitor" is severely, even incurably, hampered by his bourgeois intellectual mentality.

In formal terms as well, Fang Ji's story is similar to Lu Xun's. Most of "The Visitor" is told in the first person by Kang Minfu, the young man involved. However, the ambiguities that the first-person narrator created in "Remorse" were undoubtedly too risky at this later period, when so many authors were labeled as rightists and punished for presuming any right to criticize (apparently or actually) the Party. Consequently Kang's narrative in turn is framed by the first-person narration of a responsible Party cadre who listens to the young man's tale. Not only does this frame provide for the reader a guide to the proper (i.e., Party promoted and blessed) reaction to Kang's narrative, but it also permits Kang to make comments periodically to remind the reader of the "proper" listener response. Kang's telling of his tale is regularly punctuated with clues as to the proper listener reaction: "Don't laugh!" "Don't look at me like that." "I've tried to commit suicide twice—you consider that equivalent to a crime, don't you?" "You're shaking your head again," or "You're frowning at me again."

However, the manner of presentation of the text remains sufficiently subtle so that some readers underestimate the degree of this reproving attitude toward Kang and even find the story interesting primarily as a revelation of the ambivalent feelings of the cadre, or possibly the author.[34] Before we examine the presentation of the woman in the story, which in this case is buried twice under masculine narrations, it is important to clarify the negative attitude of the text toward Kang and the primary role of the cadre in revealing this. The judgment of Kang is shown immediately in the physical description the cadre offers: "His face, like the white shirt he wore, had lost its original appearance. It was filthy dirty and showed a bottomless pallor beneath a layer of oily sweat. In addition, perhaps due to the lighting of the room, a green, phosphorescentlike glow glimmered on his face."[35] Surely the reader is not being left in doubt here as to the hopeless, nearly satanic nature of Kang's fundamentally degenerate self. Correspondingly, at the end of the story the narrating cadre laughs in pleasure with a woman subordinate at learning that Kang fled in terror after a slap in the face from his former beloved. Such is a fate befitting this unredeemably weak and despicable type.

If the Party narrator reveals any ambivalence or self-doubts, it is only in the matter for which Kang takes him directly to task: Why hasn't the government been more thorough and decisive in dealing with social riffraff like the ex-procuress who is the young woman's adoptive mother? It is not, however, the ex-procuress who is the real riffraff, but rather bourgeois intellectuals like Kang. Of course, the entire antirightist movement was the government's response to that "problem." The cadre narrator makes this completely evident. While his first thoughts upon hearing the story are to wonder, "Did his plight deserve much sympathy? What did his story illustrate?"[36] these questions are immediately resolved when "Only a few days later, on the eighth of June, the *People's Daily* published a memorable editorial. The workers began to speak . . . As I learned more about the rightists, I began to see how similar to them my visitor was . . . I came to loathe him."[37] Whatever hesitation the cadre felt previously—hesitation that had to do with whether he should feel *more* generously toward Kang than he did—is now dissolved.

The woman in the story is not only never given the chance to speak directly, but is also never identified by name. Unlike Zijun, the woman in "The Visitor" has an occupation, one she has engaged in since pre-Liberation days and childhood: she is a drum singer. As prostitution was often coupled with performance careers in Zijun's day, such an occupation would have been far too unsavory for her, even if she had had the talent. By the time of "The Visitor," the drum singer's status had been raised as a folk art, a popular art, and therefore an art form "of the People." Nevertheless, in the eyes of Kang as well as of others still influenced by these earlier attitudes, it remains a questionable occupation. Kang first feels shame on the young woman's behalf when her performance draws catcalls from young men in the audience, and later he asks the cadre, "Are you familiar with the kind of life these people lead? Performers?"[38] At one point, Kang also overhears a member of the audience say, "Isn't she pretending to be hoity-toity! Time was when those stinking drum singers would go to bed with you, not to mention play cards."[39]

That the young woman is oppressed by popular perception of her easy sexuality, in direct conjunction with class issues, is thus made far more explicit here than it was in Lu Xun's work. Kang's participation in this oppression is also made clear in his narration. Much like Juansheng, the narrator is excessively sensitive to others viewing the young woman sexually but will not acknowledge his participation in this oppressive gaze. Again, this sensitivity alone implicates him, and the use of the listening cadre's reactions to his narrative provides even further opportunity for Kang to deny too insistently his sexual interest in the young woman. Having said that he was "moved and attracted" by her performance, he quickly adds, "Don't laugh at me! My arousal was entirely proper."[40] When he visits the woman and is confronted by her adoptive mother, he is horrified by the older woman's perception that something is going on between him and the drum singer. The mother even warns him later, "We're liberated now. It's not like it was before . . . We sell our artistry, not our bodies."[41] Mere glances caused Juansheng to shiver; this outrageous insinuation brings on a fit of trembling in Kang, and he tells his listener, "If *she* had not run up immediately and called out, 'Mother, Mother,' imploring her to say no more, I can't guarantee what might have happened next."⁴² The protest here of his virtuous nature is abruptly compromised when he tosses feverishly in bed that night and only two nights later has convinced the young woman to sleep with him. Subsequently he describes how he could not restrain himself from further meetings with her.

The issue of pregnancy remained ambiguous in "Remorse," but in "The Visitor" it explicitly becomes further evidence of the sexual oppression of the young woman, an oppression directly related to her social and economic independence. As the couple is neither married nor yet living together, the pregnancy is used by the foster mother as a tool of extortion. She threatens to force the young woman to have an abortion, and when Kang comes to the rescue, the mother allows him to take the singer away with him only after he agrees to send her fifty *yuan* a month. Still unmarried, the young woman goes with Kang to Beijing, away from her work unit. Once they are living together, Kang grows increasingly concerned about how she looks to his friends. Not only does he inhibit her behavior and attempt to buy "proper" clothes for her, he tells her she must give up her occupation as a performer.

Although the drum singer's thoughts are mediated through Kang's narrative, in this area as well the text ostensibly offers much less subconscious filtering from the narrator and more direct information than "Remorse" did. It is clear that the woman is not at all oblivious to the lustful attitude of her admirers; she has been surrounded by it from childhood. Her elder sister had been forced into prostitution and died of venereal disease, and even now her foster mother has a boyfriend who provides them with their breakfast each day. Her first encounter with Kang indicates that she is well practiced in handling unwanted attention. Thanking him for his concern about the catcalls, she politely but firmly sends him off: "But what's your business? We're backstage, so comrade, please don't let me keep you."⁴³ She also apparently chases off the catcalling type of young men her mother invites over to see her.

Why then does she fall prey to Kang? According to the text, it is precisely because he is different, he is from a different class. He is a college person, in the words of her foster mother, "a good man, educated and well-mannered."⁴⁴ The young woman tells him that "she used to think she deserved a better life, someone to care for her, show her warmth, and put an end to her constant anxiety. Since she had come to know [him], and seen [him] come such a long distance to see her, these hopes had rested with [him]."[45] Like the cadre who listens to this story, and by implication like all those who have been fooled by the wily rightists, she has been lulled by the "intellectuality" of his class, believing in the veneer of breeding that masks Kang's share in the sexually oppressive public gaze that has placed her in "constant anxiety." Kang's wish to have her quit her profession is an expression of his desire to cover her with this same hypocritical veneer and so disguise his baseness. Eventually she sees through him, realizes that he looks down on her profession and her class (her sex?), and leaves him.

As in "Remorse," the gaze of the woman in "The Visitor" is granted powerful significance. In "The Visitor," the singer's eyes are also referred to repeatedly; this time they are characterized as "clear" and "candid." At first, like Zijun's "childlike eyes," the clarity of the singer's vision implies innocence and trust, but later it asserts possession of a shrewd wisdom.

The woman's gaze or mind in both stories is presented as less susceptible and less inclined to (less capable of?) the hypocritical filtering that afflicts the impure masculine mind. With its childlike innocence and its honesty, it is like a mirror particularly useful for revealing that hypocrisy. Such a view of women's mind echoes that familiar equation found in *Dream of the Red Chamber:* women are water and men are mud. Lu Xun compromised Zijun's clarity (although retaining her childlike innocence) by situating her along with Juansheng as a bourgeois elite. By establishing a difference in Kang's and the singer's classes, Fang Ji evokes more insistently this traditional perception of feminine purity, further asserting the clarity of the drum singer's gaze. Kang tells the cadre that though she has left him, and driven him to attempt suicide twice, he is grateful to the singer: "because of her I have now come to know myself."[46]

The purity and power of the singer's gaze are supported by a voice that Kang relates is "crisp and clear, like the waters of a brook in autumn . . . I was overpowered the first time I saw her and heard her sing."[47] The extension of clarity to vocality in effect reassures the reader that one need not be suspicious of Kang's mediating narrative as one was encouraged to be of Juansheng's. Kang's voice does not have the power to interrupt or "muddy" the singer's voice. Her words are so pure as not to allow for distortion. The class connection is essential here because it is specifically due to her class that the singer's eyes and voice provide the solution to ambiguity and confusion. They are clear precisely because they are parallel to and participate in the speaking out of the workers that ultimately reveals the true nature of rightists to the cadre listening to the story.

Regardless of class, purity of voice, however, is evidently powerless if there is no appropriately trained ear to hear it. Kang demonstrates unquestionably that he lacks such an ear. Indeed, the singer's "constant state of anxiety" implies that at first no one had heard her clearly. It is only the June 8 editorial that actually *enables* the workers to speak out and *be heard,* and they in turn finally allow the singer's voice to be truly heard.

The centrality of this need to "hear" her correctly, that is, to *interpret* her correctly, is made evident as the frame of the story closes. Kang has left and the Party cadre is mulling over his story, wondering, "What does his story illustrate?" *(Ta de gushi, shuomingle shenme?).*[48] He quizzes a woman cadre, who is his subordinate, regarding the singer. It soon becomes obvious that the questions he puts to her are not merely to elicit information for his own benefit and enable him to interpret the story, but are also intended to guide and raise the interpretive ability of the woman answering him (and the reader by the way). In an aside to the reader, he comments that this woman cadre "was a good-hearted female comrade, who had suffered in matters of marriage and because of this was always desirous that all things in the world could be as she wished them."[49] The Party cadre responds with some amusement to her emotional description of Kang as someone who wants women for playthings, who is selfish, jealous, and vindictive. "Is that all?" he asks unable to keep back a smile. The woman quickly senses her mistake and adds, "Of course not, not just that. In addition this man is the epitome of a bourgeois, little master." Soon enough, though, her disgust for Kang and desire for everything to be as she wished it resurface, and she begins to complain, "If that man had only made a slightly better showing." The Party cadre cuts her off in annoyance at this subjective, wishful thinking and reflects to himself, "Completely a woman's point of view, can't regard an issue politically."[50]

What is the point of this discussion? Is this merely a repetition of the old claim that women are more "emotional," more "subjective," and that one must beware of emotions clouding analytic judgment? Since the June 8 editorial, the source of enlightenment, appears after this conversation, the text suggests that the vision of the Party cadre himself is also still in need of clarification. After the publication of the editorial and the subsequent speaking out of the workers, he remarks, "As the antirightist struggle grew increasingly deeper, [Kang's] face grew clearer in my eyes . . . and after seeing this kind of person more clearly, an absolute disgust emerged in my heart, *just like that which the woman performer felt toward him.*"[51]

The text explicitly presents here an effort to privilege the voice and feelings of the oppressed in accordance with Mao's Yan'an talks. Once the writer's standpoint is clear, he shares those *emotions* that arise from correct class feeling, which the oppressed feel "naturally." In effect, however, the effort to appropriate these feelings itself (and this is still in accordance with the implications of Mao's talks) is an indication of the subordinate position of these oppressed masses. The feminine representative of sexual and class oppression is most significant for her function in providing the raw data, the subjective element, that legitimates the analytic insight of the masculine mind. The masculine mind remains the authoritative source of interpretation, that which bestows meaning. The ultimate interpreting mind here is obviously the patriarchal mind of the Party. Evidence of the continued dependent position of the oppressed woman is revealed in that the drum singer is able to free herself at last of her foster mother's influence only through the Party-provided structures of formal accusation to the union and struggle sessions.

The frame of "The Visitor," thus, directs the reader to the proper matter of concern: how to interpret the story, or more specifically, how the cadre in the story, a male writer and consequently a professional interpreter, who claims subordinate membership in the authoritative Party, achieves and presents a correct reading of the oppressed. (One should note that later "misinterpretations," specifically Yao Wenyuan's attack on the story,[52] only serve to reinforce the central and very real significance of such a concern to writers.)

Nora's Departure

On the surface, Gao Xiaosheng's story offers many contrasts to the other two. There is no evidence of formal influence. "Amorous Feelings in a Village" does not make use of the first-person narrator and presents a much more complicated set of relationships in a different, rural setting. As a result, the interpretive construct of the role of bourgeois mentality in women's oppression is not at issue. However, in its particular use of the motif of a sexually oppressed woman, it participates in a very fundamental way in the masculine conversation established by the earlier two stories. "Amorous Feelings," like the other two stories, relates women's sexual oppression to men's intellectual and moral culpability. Since, however, there is no recourse to defining the problem as one arising from an ideology of bourgeois individualism, the greater burden of the masculine mind's interpretive task and moral distress is removed from the realm of class issues and expressed wholly in terms of gender. As in the earlier stories, this is effected in part by the narrative format, and in part by an apparent privileging of the woman's gaze and voice.

"Amorous Feelings in a Village" is presented in the third person by a satiric narrator who allows us access to the thoughts of several figures in the story and mixes with this a witty, often scathing, commentary. The "couple" who form the focus of the story do not live together. Li Aidi, the woman, is the common law wife of another man, Zhang Xiaogou. Zhang Yonghe, the central male protagonist and the seat of masculine mental agony, is married to someone else. In the course of the story, the reader discovers that as young teenagers before the Cultural Revolution, Yonghe and Aidi were drawn to each other, but her parents' rich-peasant background kept Yonghe from pursuing the relationship. Subsequently, this reversal of class stigma forced Aidi to go as a child bride into Xiaogou's household. Because of the illegality of such arrangements at the time, the couple never officially registered.

The occasion of the story is Li Aidi's elopement with a transport driver. In retrospect, the villagers realize this elopement was carefully planned. Childless people from town and city had come periodically to the village looking for children to adopt. Aidi has three children, the eldest a boy, fathered by Xiaogou, and a set of twins, one girl and one boy, presumably fathered by a lover. Since the family's economic circumstances are desperate, it is logical for Aidi to relinquish one of her children for adoption. She does, after an active and deliberate consideration of candidates, give up the boy twin. The prospective parent is a man who was driven to the village by his younger, unmarried brother, the transport driver. When Aidi later runs off to join the driver, general opinion on the matter is favorable at first. Her fellow villagers are all well aware of Xiaogou's shortcomings as a husband and father. Xiaogou is brutish and, to obtain the family's livelihood, has consistently depended either on Aidi's labor or on the neighbor's pity for her and the children. However, after he has gone twice, unsuccessfully, to plead with her to return, opinion shifts. An effort, in which Yonghe participates, is made to force her to return, and eventually she does so, but only temporarily. Aidi's purpose is not to stay but to collect the girl twin and persuade Xiaogou to stop pursuing her by promising to help him out economically when he needs it.

The situation of sexual oppression here is even more evident than in the other stories. As despicable and ineffective as Xiaogou is, the reader is informed that even he can "grab [Aidi] by the hair, press her to the floor, and have his way with her."[53] Furthermore, since her common law husband holds no respect in the community, and since Aidi is emotionally vulnerable, nothing protects her from the amorous advances of other men in the village. Her giving birth to the children of a lover provides fuel for village gossip and further marks her clearly as an easy target for sexual attentions.

Aidi's oppression is not resolved with her elopement. From the lengthy explanation of the shift in public opinion regarding her escape, the reader gathers this opinion is motivated by things other than sympathy for Xiaogou. Among the women, the text explains, there are jealousy, as people imagine the more luxurious life Aidi is enjoying, and dissatisfaction at being left to endure the pathetic sight of the abandoned children and husband. However, more powerfully and specific to the sexual aspect of Aidi's oppression, the men's feelings are "more complicated," a compassion tainted with hypocrisy and desire. While they previously regretted that Aidi was like "a fresh flower stuck in manure, they were secretly happy because plucking a fresh flower from manure is easy." Now, their compassion for her hard life is forgotten, and while they "clamored along with the others saying Aidi should return home, actually they were thinking of increasing the romantic interest in their own lives."[54]

The narrative focuses on three men who participate in a clandestine meeting with Xiaogou to get Aidi back. For various reasons, each is anxious to keep his participation in the meeting a secret. The motivation of the village head, who calls the meeting, is clearly the desire to continue his amorous relations with Aidi. He suspects that, should they be successful in forcing her to return, knowledge of his part in things would threaten that relationship. As for the village bookkeeper, though he apparently entertains no hope of obtaining pleasures Aidi might provide, as a subordinate cadre he seems to feel he cannot refuse to participate in this effort. Nevertheless, he is anxious that his part be kept secret because an earlier humiliating encounter between his brother and Aidi revealed the dangers of incurring Aidi's wrath. The third person is Yonghe, who has been asked to the meeting because he once mentioned that he had an army acquaintance in the public security office of the town where Aidi has gone.

As mentioned above, Yonghe and Aidi are the important "couple" of the story. Although Yonghe is married to someone else and has never been physically involved with Aidi, the most romantic and therefore most serious connection is between them; they were each other's first love. Although Yonghe was only a teenager and could hardly be held responsible for the political exigencies of the Cultural Revolution that forced them apart, now, after that revolution, he regrets his weakness and Aidi continues to have a hold on his imagination. Even after his marriage, he dreams of being with her, complicating his sense of guilt. Moreover, influenced by the general attitude toward her as easy prey, he attempts once to flirt with her. She meets this flirtation with a stern face, leaving Yonghe embarrassed by the failure of his amorous advance and ashamed that he has sullied the purity and innocence of his first love.

Because of his enduring, youthful attachment to Aidi, mixed as it is with romanticism, guilt, and desire, Yonghe is also not at all anxious to have it known he had any part in securing her return. Refusing to go and speak to the man in the public security office himself, he still cannot completely refuse the village head's request for help and so does finally write a letter of introduction for Xiaogou, carefully avoiding mention of Aidi and saying only that Xiaogou is a village relative with a personal matter to discuss.

Despite her history of sexual involvements, Li Aidi is presented as a heroine in the story, much along the lines of the drum singer, who struggled, albeit innocently, under a similarly questionable sexual reputation and rose above it in the end. Significantly, for Aidi there is no Party-supervised structure to aid her. The specific mechanisms that provide strategies for Aidi to escape her oppressive circumstances are precisely the two aspects of sexuality that oppress her and the other two women. It is her ability to produce children that makes possible a bond with the transport driver's family, and it is her physical attractiveness to men that secures his interest. She is not oblivious to her effect on men, as Zijun seemed to be, nor is she unhappy about it, as the drum singer was. Even as a young girl, the narrator remarks, "her hair was always neatly and cleanly groomed, so that it floated when the wind blew and shimmered when she shook her head. She was different from the other women in the village at that time; it was as if she already knew that hair is a woman's best ornament."[55]

From this presentation, quite unlike the description of the lustful gaze of the public in the other two stories, it is clear that Aidi's sexuality is not simply an unambiguous burden to her nor one that she is helpless to defend herself against. Aidi uses her sexuality both to improve her circumstances and to intimidate the men in the village. The most remarkable instance of this occurs in the humiliating encounter, referred to above, between her and the bookkeeper's brother, Li Tugen. Because Aidi's plot of land adjoins that of Tugen's, Tugen's wife accuses Aidi of a large theft of *qincai*, a celery-like vegetable, from their plot. Most of the reason for the accusation has to do with the wife's suspicion (apparently mistaken in this instance) that there is something going on between Aidi and her husband. The wife's cursing continues for days, getting filthier and filthier in the process, so that Aidi quickly figures out the real reason for the attack. Finally, Aidi can stand the haranguing no longer. She grabs a sickle and starts chopping all the remaining vegetables in Tugen's plot to shreds. Horrified, the wife goes to get her husband.

> Tugen came and was just about to give expression to a man's power and prestige, when Li Aidi went up to him and shouted, "Come here, come on over. Your wife's acting as the matchmaker for me. I'm willing all right, but first take out your prick and let's have a look!" As she shouted, she dashed forward, and grabbed right for Tugen's crotch. That sickle glittered and gleamed. Fearing she would cut off his prick, Tugen was so terrified his face went white and he started wailing for help. After this it was a full two years before he could hold up his head in the village.[56]

News of this incident helps Aidi intimidate the other men of the village. As the men are desirous of keeping their interest in or actual affairs with Aidi secret, she in effect comes to hold power over them. Knowing of this incident with Tugen, none of them wishes to draw her attention and ire onto himself and be exposed to such public humiliation.

Aidi's potential ability to intimidate or wreak havoc for the village men is further demonstrated when Yonghe is drawn into a fight with his wife regarding his motivations for helping to secure Aidi's return. It is Yonghe's "complicated" feelings that keep him from telling his wife exactly what went on at the meeting with the village head, the bookkeeper, and Xiaogou, and this holding back of information in turn arouses her suspicions, allowing for a "typical" husband-and-wife quarrel.

Yonghe's feelings of desire, shame, and guilt further allow Aidi to humiliate him specifically for his somewhat unwilling part in the effort to force her return to her miserable life in the village. As in the other two stories, Aidi's eyes, the woman's gaze, are given a special power to reveal the impurities of the masculine mind. When Yonghe runs into her after her return to the village, the narrator tells us, "He couldn't turn around and ignore her. He could only squat like a goalie and guess which direction the opponent would

kick from. Li Aidi, however, didn't kick. She merely looked at him
haughtily out of the corner of her eye, as if she wanted first to shoot
down this goalie with her gaze. And in the end, Zhang Yonghe
couldn't stand it."[57] He tries to plead his innocence in the matter of
her return, saying he was pestered into writing the letter by the
village head. Aidi shames him into immediate silence by demanding
to know what relationship the village head has with her. She then
tells him that his army acquaintance did not secure her return; in
fact, he merely asked her, *"Why is Zhang Yonghe involving himself in
this?"*[58] Yonghe does not shiver or tremble, as did Juansheng or
Kang, but muscles in his cheeks twitch upon hearing this. Aidi leaves
with the accusation that Yonghe is no better than the village head.

Aidi's power to intimidate both Yonghe and the other men in the
village, and the moral superiority granted her gaze, however, should
not be overestimated. This power is contingent upon men's sense of
guilt and their desire to disguise this guilt. Ultimately, the burden of
sexuality here is not on women. While it is true that Aidi's extramarital affairs provide gossip for the villagers and, along with her good
looks, encourage men to make advances, the reader is informed that
"Women are people too, and like men have needs."[59] Aidi must be
forgiven. By contrast, the reader is told that, for the men who are
involved, except for the one who fathered the twins but is conve-
niently dead, their involvement is not a matter of "true feelings"
(zhenqing).[60] Logically one might assume that if Aidi's sexual involvements are a result of "needs," they are not necessarily a matter of
"true feelings" either, but this seems of no moral consequence.

The burden of sexuality rests on men here, not as part of the
hypocrisy of a bourgeois ideology, but much more crudely because
the burden of greater power is theirs, whether that be the power of
the village head to press others into helping him secure Aidi's return, or the power that even the despicable Zhang Xiaogou has to
"have his way with her." Albeit rather unintentionally and certainly
unwillingly, it is men who grant Aidi what power she has. Their
sinfulness, their guilt as oppressors, compromises their power in
regard to her. In spite of her much more direct and lively presentation, Aidi functions in the text, similarly to Zijun or the drum singer,
as an essentially mute symbol of oppression that exposes or highlights her would-be lover's foibles and deceitfulness.

Like the drum singer, Aidi also functions to present a series of *uninterpreted* events for interpretation. The voice of the oppressed, *provided* there is a proper narrator or reader to interpret it, is privileged by that interpreter. Although there is nothing similar to the rigid structure used to ensure a proper reading of "The Visitor," there is a narrator who, since he stands outside the story, would seem to offer more guidance than Juansheng did in "Remorse."[61] In this instance it is a rather unruly, satiric narrator, "unruly" in the sense that he intrudes opinions in a free, sometimes confusing, consistently distracting manner. The narrator disrupts the flow of the narrative with an incongruous or witty use of language that draws attention from consideration of the story or the main characters to the imagined mind behind the writing and to speculations regarding what this story means to that mind or, as the obvious extension of this, how a reader is to interpret the text.

The most intrusive of these comments occurs at the very end of the story. After Aidi returns to the village, the village head attempts to rape her, and she gouges his cheek during the struggle. This event is followed by two rather startling paragraphs:

Chen Guoliang [the village head] didn't show his face after this. Naturally he had gone to treat the wound. Some people said that even after treating it, there would still be a scar. They feared this brand would be as unremovable as class. But people rich in knowledge shook their heads and said it didn't matter. Things weren't now as they had been in the past. Medical techniques had become very clever, so that even for someone who was born hideously ugly, there were methods of treatment to make him handsome. If there really were a scar left on his face, it would be extremely easy to get rid of. You only needed to dig it out and then cut off a piece of skin from the ass to patch it up.

One person who heard this sighed deeply as he nodded his head in approval and said he never imagined that when our ancestors invented wearing pants, it was in order to protect the skin on their asses for the purpose of sticking it on their faces.[62]

Comments on the marvels of plastic surgery, even if precipitated by the village head's wound, hardly further the narration of the story, particularly as it concerns Aidi or even the issue of male hypocrisy in regard to sexual attitudes toward women. The outrageous reasoning as to how plastic surgery explains why "our ancestors invented wearing pants" makes it clear that an image of broader interpretive or symbolic consequence is being offered here. The efforts of Zhang Yonghe, of the village head, or of any man to cover up any immoral behavior or thoughts become a matter of masculine heritage. The nature of this heritage is a shameless conspiracy of dishonesty that seeks to disguise moral transgressions, to pass off the skin of one's ass as the skin of one's cheek.

To belabor somewhat how far this passage tears the reader away from Aidi's difficulties, we may further recall here that in China, rubbing a finger across one's cheek is a gesture directed at someone to indicate that he or she has done or thought something shameful. It is not at all arbitrary that Aidi gouges the village head's cheek or that the wound requires plastic surgery, since the cheek is a metaphor for the repute and honor of a person. It stands quite literally in the story as the embodiment of the notion of "face." The metaphoric punning and association between the incident and the idea of "face" are immediate for readers familiar with modern Chinese literature and culture. "Love of face," or of the external façade of honorability, and the extents to which people go to establish or maintain this façade have long been attacked as a national infirmity in modern Chinese fiction, as an infirmity that encourages selfishness, hypocrisy, self-deception, forgetfulness, or apparently even plastic surgery.[63] As a result, this passage carries the reader immediately from concern with a peasant woman, or even Yonghe's sense of guilt in relation to her, to a problem conceived as being of larger national consequence.

Coming after this startling passage, the final few lines of the story are immediately demoted to the status of an epilogue, necessary only to satisfy the readers' desire to have loose ends tied up. It may be nice to know that Aidi settles all her business in the village—coming to an understanding with her common law husband, collecting her daughter, bidding farewell to the spirit of the twins' father—and then goes back to the transport driver. It does not, however, really seem to matter much, since it was, after all, pretty clear already that Aidi was going to manage. The essentially happy or "comic" ending arranged by her successful and final departure from the scene only intensifies the "tragic" one of Yonghe and the others who remain behind, trying to disguise their moral failings. Much as in "Remorse," what remains for our consideration is the masculine self-deceit and hypocrisy that have been uncovered and the impulse to cover them over again. As in the other two stories, the description of the woman protagonist's oppression functions to facilitate the male protagonist's (self-)criticism and confirm it as the more primary issue.

Although Lu Xun accused Ibsen of merely "writing a poem" when he wrote *A Doll's House,* I am not suggesting a similar verdict for these three stories. The authors are clearly attempting to do what Lu Xun held Ibsen had failed to do, that is, to respond "for the benefit of society to a problem that had arisen in that society." Their concern, as we have seen, is expressed in broad, ultimately national terms. However, the configuration and expression of the problem are not what the stories' inclusion of the figure of an oppressed woman might lead one to expect. The problem is not how women are oppressed, or even that they are oppressed, but rather how men and a nation are confronted by the moral obligation to interpret, to judge, and to expose (self-)deception and hypocrisy.

On the surface, there is nothing to restrict this human circumstance to men as an issue.[64] Yet as these stories express it fictionally, in concrete images, it is gendered. Sexual desire, as a fundamental and compelling source of personal and social moral dilemma, is identified and situated in the male mind, the ground of power and authority. Women are the victims in this encounter, and they remain childlike, innocent, and morally exempt.

The ostensible compassion or sense of guilt regarding women does virtually nothing to resolve gender-related oppression. Indeed, this form of oppression begins to seem too useful, as a tool for masculine self-incrimination and expression of authority, to sacrifice. Zijun dies, leaving Juansheng with the burden of his guilt but without the burden of resolving her social or economic circumstances as a woman. Although the singer is rescued from Kang Minfu through the Party's authoritative interpretation of class (not by either Kang or the Party cadre who hears about her situation from him), this rescue is in terms of class and not gender. She is saved from Kang only when he is defined as a "rightist." Li Aidi, quite tellingly, uses the same mechanisms of gender oppression that victimize her to "rescue" herself. This rescue consists of entering another man's household, a man who will presumably fulfill the socially expected roles of husband and father better than Xiaogou did. Thus, although these three stories seem to embrace the concern expressed by Lu Xun of how women might free themselves of their humiliating dependence on men and make it on their own in the world, they evidently conclude that this is not really the problem. It would seem that, as Juansheng feared, forgetfulness and falsehood are acting as guides here and diverting attention from the gender issue raised.

III | Narrative Voice and Cinematic Vision

9 | Lu Xun's Facetious Muse: The Creative Imperative in Modern Chinese Fiction

The May Fourth and the immediate post-Mao periods in Chinese literature shared an iconoclastic mission. Fiction was used, in the first case, to hasten the dismantling of Confucian social morality, and in the second, to subvert the Maoist "revolutionary romanticism" of the Cultural Revolution. These oppositional themes were aptly and forcefully conveyed in varieties of realism: in the critical realism of the May Fourth period and in the "new realist" or "scar" literature of the late seventies. In each case the critical message conveyed in such fiction triumphed more rapidly than the authors themselves could have imagined, forcing an early recognition of the essential negativity of their message. Writers, unsurprisingly, faced the resultant intellectual and psychological void with some anxiety. In both periods, some writers turned to mythology—and specifically to ancient myths of origin—in an attempt to restore their creative energies. In the May Fourth period, concern with the problem of creativity underlay most notably the appellation of the Creation Society, but it was not the property of a single group. As I will argue here, contemporary discussion of this problem was the inspiration behind Lu Xun's invention of the fractured-legend form he employed in his collection *Old Tales Retold*. The same anxiety, and the same impulse to express it through mythological references, is apparent in the varied fiction of China in the 1980s. I will here consider briefly the concluding scenes of three recent works of fiction, all of which allude to traditional Chinese myths of origin, and then examine Lu Xun's treatment of the theme in his *Old Tales Retold*. Lu Xun's collection provides us, I will argue, with a significant context in which to judge both the promise and the perils attending the introduction of mythopoetic tropes into contemporary fiction.

Zhang Xinxin's 1982 story "The Dreams of Our Generation" is, in the author's words, an attempt to "probe the psychological changes in an ordinary young working woman."[1] The story was the target of much criticism during the 1983 "anti–spiritual pollution" campaign, but the author's formal experimentation (involving primarily the generous use of interior monologue) and the story's thematic affirmation of the value of fantasy in human life seem tame when read in the context of the fictional experimentation of the late 1980s. The story remains, however, a compelling depiction of the search for feminine identity.[2] In the story the protagonist, who is trapped in an unfulfilling marriage, finds creative satisfaction only in her relationship with her son, a relationship that is nourished largely through the fairy tales and legends she tells or reads to him. She is not above using her stories as a "leash": in the opening scene she spins an inconclusive tale to keep her curious son from wandering off in the market. When the frustrated boy loses his temper and demands to hear the end of the story, a kindly stranger reassures him: "What happens next, my little friend, is for you to imagine."[3] The allure of stories, as the protagonist well understands, is their power to evoke the tenuous, unfinished world of one's private dreams. In the story's concluding scene, the mother reads her son the legend of Kua Fu, who left home to find the sun and persuade it to shine on his village. In the legend, Kua Fu dies of thirst while waiting for the sun to emerge from its hole; his staff is then transformed into a peach tree. As the mother reads, she wearies of the tale:

> Who had taken this ancient legend—which she remembered as a very brief and heroic tale from the *Classic of Mountains and Seas*— and written it up as a long and vivid fairy tale? The story described in great detail how Kua Fu traversed mountain after mountain,

forded stream after stream . . . it seemed she would never reach the inevitable conclusion. But maybe the ending had been changed as well. It was so long. As she read, she grew more and more tired . . .

My dream was not so splendid, but to me, it was also a momentous, protracted dream. While it was with me, it had neither substance nor weight, but was like an invisible shadow following me in silence. When it was taken from me, I was overcome by a sudden feeling of emptiness and for the first time perceived the space my dream had occupied.[4]

Never learning the original conclusion to the story, the son later tells his mother that the moon has been following him, a caprice that evidently represents his revision of the Kua Fu legend. As the man in the market had recommended, he has reimagined the tale's ending, weaving the elements of the legend into his personal dreamworld. In the boy's hopeful version, nature responds to human will rather than resists it. At the conclusion of "Dreams of Our Generation," the mother returns to the unsatisfying tasks of her married life. Her dream, however, has an afterlife independent of the dreamer; through its assimilation into the Kua Fu legend, it will continue to exert its influence into the next generation.

This view of folklore as a repository of deep-seated transgenerational yearnings is, of course, an item of faith among writers associated with the *xungen* or "search for roots" movement, of whom the representative figure is perhaps Han Shaogong. Han's 1986 novella "Woman Woman Woman" places the creation myth of Pangu at the very center of the spiritual epiphany that the narrator experiences late in the novella. This epiphany occurs in the narrator's ancestral home, where he has returned to witness the death and funeral of his aunt, a character who has been transformed during the course of the story from an unassuming old woman into, first, a demanding termagant, and finally—through the devices of "magical realism"—into a monstrous fish. All along, the narrator has guiltily wondered what purpose the fallow life of his aunt has served. But in fact she has, through her illness and death, functioned as a kind of personal shaman, drawing the narrator back to the mythical terrain of his village and preparing him for the spiritual revelation described in the penultimate chapter of the novella. In this hallucinatory scene, the narrator describes waking very early and walking the dark, deserted streets of the village. Suddenly the ground is crawling with rats, and the earth begins to move in waves, as if it "wanted to reenact the myth of the Great Flood."[5] He then hears the villagers singing, retelling the creation story of Pangu. Their song induces a vision that lies at the border of the expressible:

> Once the mountain ridges were Pangu's bones,
> Once the cliffs were his body,
> His two eyes became the sun and moon,
> His teeth became gold and silver,
> His hair became the grasses and the trees,
> And then birds and beasts emerged from the forests . . .

An old bard begins singing and everyone joins in. The ground is quaking, the cliffs collapsing. The Book of Heaven is unfurled, a bow is drawn, a bloody cow's head dangles overhead beneath a tribal banner. Where are you going? Legends, like bitter bracken, spread throughout the world, waking each era from its pitch-black dreams, in the desert, in deep forests, in palaces mottled with moonlight and rust. Just where am I? Long ago there was a single great spurt of semen, a single world-defining cry of child-birth, and crimson blood seeped through the base of the walls into the dark coal-stratum, seeped into ideographs born of hoarse murmuring and knotted with intrigue, seeped into the slit throats of convicted revolutionaries and into the clanking of their chains. Where are you going? The flood waters rise to heaven, a person dies, the earth quakes, walls crumble. No one can save her, just as no one can reduce the infinite universe in your heart or mine to a page in a ledger.[6]

In this scene the narrator breaks through the barriers of his everyday consciousness and taps into primal creative energies, what Han Shaogong in his influential essay "The Roots of Literature" calls the "magma" of the cultural substratum.[7] The villagers, we are given to understand, live in daily communion with these energies, but the narrator and the other urbanites depicted in the story have become thoroughly alienated from them. The primal forces released at creation, the text asserts, are disseminated in two ways, physically through blood-ties and spiritually through the transmission of myth. The narrator's glimpse at the raw forces of nature—which are also the source of true culture—is profoundly disturbing, but it allows him to return to his daily life with a new understanding of the value of the quotidian: "Eating dinner, then washing the dishes; washing the dishes, then making a phone call . . . In this lies the simplest and most profound principle."[8]

If Han strives for a kind of spiritual transcendence in "Woman Woman Woman," Liu Heng, one of several emerging novelists whose work has been dubbed "new realist," remains determinedly materialist in his 1988 novella "Fuxi Fuxi"; in the process he gives new meaning to the term "searching for roots." Instead of celebrating oceanic immersion in the female creative principle, Liu Heng chooses to explore critically the origins of social institutions in the male principle (and quite literally, in the phallus). Although the novella is on its surface a naturalistic account of a family tragedy beginning in the 1940s, the story invites the reader to explore associations between the narrated events and the legend of Fuxi, the mythical patriarch who is said to have instituted marriage by mating with his sister Nü Wa; the text also alludes, if less directly, to the story of Oedipus, with its analogous incest trope. Much of "Fuxi Fuxi" occurs against the backdrop of the land redistribution and communalization of the early years of the People's Republic; in what is clearly an indictment of the Party's social engineering, these policies completely fail to alleviate social disharmony. The tragic events recounted in "Fuxi Fuxi" stem not from the class divisions that the Party has labored to eradicate, but from the patriarchal sexual relations that continue to characterize the new order as profoundly as they did the old. Specifically, they emanate from an impotent man's inexpugnable desire for progeny. In the opening scene a middle-aged widower named Yang Jinshan sells most of his property to purchase a beautiful second wife, Judou. When she, like his first wife, fails to conceive, he takes to beating her. She soon falls in love with the landlord's orphaned nephew, Tianqing, and bears his son, whom she must present to the world as Jinshan's child. After Jinshan is paralyzed in a fall, the lovers exact a horrifying revenge on Jinshan by flaunting their relationship in front of him. Still, the long-term consequences of these events on the nephew are yet more terrible: After Jinshan's death Tianqing and Judou are forced to live apart, and years later their son, who has long called Tianqing "brother," refuses to acknowledge his true paternity when Tianqing reveals it to him. Distraught, Tianqing drowns himself in a cistern. The villagers who discover his naked body are fascinated by the sight of his genitals "floating with a romantic and solemn air" on the surface of the water.[9] The impressive size of what the village children call Tianqing's *ber-ber* (root-root) passes into local folklore. In an ironic coda to the story, the narrator recounts how young village lads some years later continue to use Tianqing as the standard when comparing their genitals:

> The children . . . had never seen the living Tianqing, nor even the dead Tianqing, but they had heard a timeless tale whose import sometimes disturbed their youthful dreams, stimulating or saddening them. Bachelor Yang Tianqing, who had suffered greatly and lived a life of loneliness, was now installed as an immortal figure in the history of Hongshuiyu.[10]

Tianqing has, in fact, been assimilated in the minds of the villagers to the "male spirit" (Fuxi himself?) whom they sometimes petition in their prayers. This outcome carries considerable tragic irony, as Tianqing is an evident victim of the patriarchal social structure such legends sustain. That social structure (enforced in the story by the abusive, impotent Jinshan) stands condemned above all for its failure to accommodate the natural permutations of human desire. On one level, "Fuxi Fuxi" is a call for sexual freedom, and it is as such that the story has primarily been received in China. The critic Yu Zheng, for example, has suggested that "Fuxi Fuxi" is an attempt to restore to the myth of Fuxi and Nü Wa the affirmative sexual puissance of the original myth, which has been sanitized in the process of euhemerization.[11] But in the stark naturalism of his account, Liu Heng sometimes presses beyond the boundaries of social critique to a kind of biological determinism; his lovers seem possessed in equal measures of drives for erotic fulfillment and for self-destruction. The root of Tianqing's passion is also the root of his extinction.

Each of these stories adopts a different view of the relation between the individual case (or narrated exemplum) and the cultural masterplot alluded to in the myth. In "Dreams of Our Generation" the masterplot is endlessly revisable, an open-ended expression of human yearning across generations. In "Woman Woman Woman" the legacy of myth and folklore carries identifying spiritual information, without which both teller and audience must forever remain unknown to themselves. In the far less benign picture of "Fuxi Fuxi," the cultural masterplot, through the destructive social institutions it undergirds, endlessly creates personal tragedies such as Tianqing's and endlessly reabsorbs them. In all three stories, strategically placed allusions to myths of origin allow the author to address individual anxiety over creativity (or potency in the case of "Fuxi Fuxi") in the context of another significant issue, that of genealogy, or the transmission of cultural identity between generations. Creativity is, for all three of these authors, a matter at once individual and universal, private and public.

Taken together, these stories raise broad questions about the relation of tradition to personal identity and about the place of individual creative effort in the more general struggle for national cultural rejuvenation. These are issues that have a long history in modern Chinese cultural and literary debates. They were asked with particular urgency in the May Fourth period, when reformers of all stripes insistently asked themselves: How could the Chinese, both as individuals and as a nation, overcome the malaise that followed loss of faith in their tradition and instill in its place an animating spirit equal to the challenges of the modern world? How could new life be bred from the "ditch of hopelessly dead water" that China had become, in Wen Yiduo's famous metaphor? In formulating a response to this question, writers of the May Fourth period found themselves, very much like contemporary Chinese writers, forced to construct a new literature out of disjointed cultural fragments—out of, on the one hand, those aspects of their own heritage that escaped the autocratic or enervating influences of orthodox Confucianism and Taoism, and out of, on the other, elements of Western culture that seemed free of overtly colonialist intentions. The result was a kind of literary *bricolage,* exemplified in Guo Moruo's 1921 poem "The Goddesses," which celebrated the goddess Nü Wa as one of many incarnations of the creative principle from world literature and mythology.

Lu Xun clearly conceived "Repairing Heaven," the opening story of *Old Tales Retold* and itself a reworking of the Nü Wa myth, as a meditation on the problem of creativity that so interested his contemporaries—if not, in fact, as a specific response to Guo Moruo's poem. Creation Society critics quickly recognized the relevance of Lu Xun's story to their own concerns: Cheng Fangwu, in his review of Lu Xun's short-story collection *The Outcry* (in which the story first appeared under the title "The Broken Mount"), singled it out as its author's "first masterpiece," evidence that Lu Xun had finally shaken off the shackles of realism and entered "the palace of pure literature."[12] This praise appalled Lu Xun, who disapproved of the Creationists' "art for art's sake" aesthetic. He later cited Cheng's comment as his reason for deleting the story from editions of *The Outcry* published after 1930.[13] But despite Lu Xun's later disputes with the Creation Society, he initially shared many of the beliefs with which the society became identified. This commonality of interests is particularly evident in the essays that Lu Xun wrote while studying in Japan from 1902 to 1909, in which he developed a theory of evolution that laid particular emphasis on individual consciousness as a determining force in historical change. Like other thinkers of the period, he deplored the apparent torpor of Chinese civilization and admired the capacity of the West to absorb and encourage change; Lu Xun, however, uniquely associated this aptitude for change with the creative powers of the individual "genius," who in striving for self-actualization led his entire nation in the direction of progress and light.[14] In literary terms, Lu Xun's evolutionism translated into a fascination with such Western writers as Goethe, Byron, and Nietzsche, in whose works he perceived a heroic quest for new forms of self-expression. Creation Society members were later attracted to the same authors, for many of the same reasons.

Lu Xun's views on creativity did not remain static, however, and by the late 1910s he had largely abandoned his interest in Western neoidealism. While he never betrayed his belief in artistic creation as self-expression, he increasingly tempered that belief with the recognition that all creative acts imply a particular relationship between the artist and his social environment. By 1924 he was mocking those who, like himself at an earlier time, pinned their hopes for China's cultural revival on the advent of a genius: "Geniuses are not self-generated prodigies, suddenly appearing out of the wilds; they arise when a people has developed the capacity to nourish genius."[15] While continuing to acknowledge the importance of individual creative efforts, Lu Xun accords a new priority to social context as the soil from which all individuals must take nourishment. Lu Xun's change of heart on this subject reflects the general trend toward collectivism among intellectuals in post–May Fourth China. His repudiation of individualism, however, was motivated not simply by political expediency, but by a mature recognition of the social construction of the human personality. This is apparent from the following "odd fancy" that he wrote in 1927:

> When a person is lonely, he can write; the minute he is free of loneliness, he is no longer able to write, for he is already without love.
> Writing is always rooted in love.
> Yang Zhu bequeathed no book.
> Although we say writing is the expression of one's innermost heart, we always hope for readers.
> Writing is a social activity, but sometimes it is enough to have only one reader: a good friend, a lover.[16]

Here Lu Xun describes creativity as originating in a feeling of separation from others ("loneliness") that is in its essence a longing for connection ("love"). Writing is at one and the same time a private matter of self-expression and an activity permeated, both in its derivation and in its consequences, with social significance. Notably, however, the social import of a work of literature need not always be of a highly public (or political) variety.

Lu Xun's views on creativity are explored directly in "Repairing Heaven," and, I will argue, subtly inform the technique Lu Xun employed in this and the other seven stories gathered in *Old Tales*

Retold. As Lu Xun's boldest experiment in narrative form, this book has puzzled many readers. Not only must its ideal reader recognize a wide range of historical and contemporary allusions; he or she also must contend with a rhetorical stance that can seem highly equivocal one moment and dauntingly overdetermined the next. Lu Xun's brilliant, self-mocking preface to the volume, which most critics take as the *point d'appui* of their interpretations, has in some ways compounded the critical difficulties. Most notoriously, Lu Xun charges that his own works are marred by "facetiousness." He writes that the story "Repairing Heaven," for example, was undertaken with the serious intention of "using Freudian theories to explain the origin of creation—the creation of men as well as of literature." Before the work was finished, however, he paused and browsed through a newspaper, where he found an article by a moralistic critic rebuking a young poet for writing love songs. Infuriated, Lu Xun could not resist introducing a new character into his story—a little man in antique dress who appears between the legs of the goddess and chastises her for her nakedness in a turgid classical idiom. Lu Xun observes: "That was how I lapsed from seriousness to facetiousness. Facetiousness is the worst enemy of writing; I was most displeased with myself."[17]

This charge of facetiousness, though clearly itself tongue-in-cheek, has governed much of the discussion of *Old Tales Retold* since its publication. Especially in the mid-fifties, as Lu Xun's reputation was being consolidated in China, critics competed to provide the definitive apologia for the collection, in the process explaining (or explaining away) Lu Xun's facetiousness. Critics fashioned their defense in one of two ways, depending on whether they most valued the historical or the contemporary ingredients in the stories. On one side the critic Wu Ying, for example, praised the stories as masterpieces of historical fiction. Lu Xun resorted to facetiousness, he wrote, only intermittently, when moved to righteous anger over current affairs; writing during the repressive regime of the Guomindang, Lu Xun had no choice but to express his political conscience in this indirect fashion, disguising his indignation with humor.[18] On the other side of this debate, the critic Li Sangwu vehemently argued that the stories are not historical fiction at all, but a form of topical political satire. Lu Xun's adoption of some of the techniques of historical fiction, he wrote, is a "smoke-screen," camouflaging his true aim, which is to comment on the "dark realities" of his time; the stories are best understood as parables, through which Lu Xun obliquely exposes and admonishes disreputable elements of the contemporary political and cultural scenes. The facetious elements in Lu Xun's stories serve as markers of political allegory, prompting the reader to search beyond the literal level of the text for the concealed "true" message. They are thus integral to Lu Xun's method.[19]

Both of these interpretations of *Old Tales Retold* force the collection into the mold of an officially recognized genre: historical fiction or satire. Yet passages in Lu Xun's own writings suggest that he would not have been happy with either classification. Lu Xun repeatedly called the source materials for his stories "myths" or "legends," and distinguished his works from fiction that "smacks of the schoolroom"—that is, serious historical fiction "based on extensive research with sound evidence."[20] Lu Xun also repeatedly discouraged overly narrow readings of his stories as topical political allegory: he expressed exasperation with readers who insisted on searching his fiction for veiled references to figures on the contemporary scene. Despite some evidence to the contrary,[21] he insisted that his fictional characters were never based on single real-life models, but were created by blending features of several models.

Lu Xun's formal experimentation in *Old Tales Retold* is finally more radical than his critics have recognized. The quality of facetiousness, which is more often playful than tendentious, results specifically from his liberal use of anachrony, a literary device with a rather poor reputation. Some writers (notably, George Bernard Shaw in his Roman plays and contemporary "magical realists" such as Alejo Carpentier) have employed anachronism self-consciously, but its occurrence in literary works is more frequently thought to mark a lapse in technique.[22] In a fundamental sense, however, all works that address historical subjects show evidence of anachrony; if nothing else, the use of contemporary language to describe a bygone world always carries the potential of generating an anachronistic dissonance between style and subject. Writers of historical fiction of the sort that, as Lu Xun puts it, "smacks of the schoolroom" devote much of their energies to minimizing this dissonance, to naturalizing the historical environment about which they write. In *Old Tales Retold* Lu Xun, on the contrary, relishes the dissonances that result when a modern author attempts to resuscitate the ancients. Sometimes Lu Xun simply identifies a clash of stylistic registers, as in the story "Opposing Aggression," where the philosopher Mo Zi asks the king in the fulsome, agglutinative style familiar to any reader of classical Chinese: "There is a man who scorns his own covered carriage but covets his neighbor's rickety cart, scorns his own brocade robes but covets his neighbor's short felt jacket, scorns his own rice and meat but covets his neighbor's dish of husks and chaff. What would you call such a man?" and the king bluntly answers, "A kleptomaniac."[23] At other times Lu Xun's facetiousness manifests itself in incongruous references to twentieth-century institutions or social phenomena, such as the "constable" in "Raising the Dead," who carts Zhuangzi off to "the bureau," or the pirates in "Gathering Vetch," who reassure their captives that they are civilized thiefs, not like those "Shanghai bandits who would go around stripping their victims."[24] Often anachrony is introduced to parody the May Fourth cultural stew we observed in "The Goddesses," as in the gathering of pedants in "Curbing the Floods," where Lu Xun has his characters speak in a mix of pidgin English and archaic Chinese, in the same breath alluding to Shakespeare, "Vitamin W," and the Emperor Shen Nong's *Bencao*.[25] Throughout *Old Tales Retold* Lu Xun uses anachrony to shock the reader into recognizing both the deep penetration of the past into the present and the modern world's perpetual reinterpretation of the past in the light of its own concerns. In striking contrast to most historical fiction, Lu Xun's tales are designed to denaturalize the complex amalgam of history, myth, and traditional ideology on which Lu Xun draws for his subject matter, in the process challenging the continued authority of these forces in the contemporary world.

The other formal aspect of *Old Tales Retold* that has eluded analysis is Lu Xun's complex use of symbolism and allegory. Symbolism is particularly evident in the three stories from the collection that were written in the 1920s ("Repairing Heaven," "Escape to the Moon," and "Forging the Swords"), during the same general time period that Lu Xun was composing the highly symbolic prose poems collected in *Wild Grasses* and translating into Chinese Kuriyagawa Hakuson's book *Kumon no shōchō* (Symbols of Agony). Lu Xun was particularly taken with Kuriyagawa's theory of creativity, which in turn owed much to Freud and Henri Bergson. According to Kuriyagawa, all creative acts are born out of a struggle between two primal adversaries: the force of life (or *élan vital*) and the forces of repression. The story "Repairing Heaven" is itself a symbolist exploration of this struggle, with Nü Wa embodying the *élan vital*. A familiar figure from Chinese mythology is thus made to represent a foreign rather than native concept of creativity. Even as Lu Xun draws on traditional images or figures, he does so in ways that run counter to culturally established interpretations. Not wishing to bestow further prestige on a tradition he condemned as "cannibalistic," Lu Xun seems intent on reinventing traditional images as he borrows them.

Allegory, evident throughout *Old Tales Retold*, replaces symbolism as the dominant rhetorical trope in the five stories Lu Xun wrote in the mid-thirties. But Lu Xun's use of allegory is highly irregular, and is undoubtedly the most controversial aspect of his technique. He never settles into the stable correspondence between signans and signatum that is assumed in most definitions of the trope (according to which "the events of the narrative obviously and continuously refer to another simultaneous structure of events and ideas").[26] Lu Xun's allegorizing is alternately highly specific (referring to a private field of reference, or to particular current events) and highly general (referring to a fairly rarefied realm of philosophical abstraction); sometimes the narrative seems to allude concurrently to several fields of reference.

As might be expected, political allegory is the aspect of *Old Tales Retold* that has received the most attention from scholars in the People's Republic. The story "Curbing the Flood" offers the most sustained example of such allegory: although ostensibly the tale of the mythical flood-controller Yu, it is laced with quite specific allusions to current events. Through these allusions Lu Xun ridicules China's ineffectual response to the Japanese encroachment. On the whole, however, political allegory is subordinated in the text to a more broad-based cultural allegory. Indeed, the five stories written

262 | Marston Anderson

in the mid-thirties together offer a broad review of traditional ideologies and their continuing influence in twentieth-century China. Lu Xun is primarily interested in the concept of "principled withdrawal" in Confucianism and Taoism, two systems of thought he believed, following Zhang Taiyan, to be organically related. He also, however, gives prominent treatment to what might be called a noninstitutionalized popular tradition (represented by the flood-controller Yu and the philosopher Mo Zi) that emphasizes pragmatism and egalitarianism. Lu Xun's intention is not to provide plausible historical portraits of these thinkers nor to explore their philosophical systems (of which he provides little more than cartoon sketches) with any intellectual rigor. He is interested instead in examining the reified social consequences of their ideas, in demonstrating how these ideas have impeded or advanced the welfare of China and its people. By telling the philosophers' life stories—that is, by reembodying familiar ideologies in the personal narratives of their creators—he subjects their teachings to a materialist critique, measuring philosophical assurances both against the claims of the individual body and against the demands of the collective body of the Chinese people, clamoring to be fed, clothed, and sheltered. Unsurprisingly, it is the pragmatic popular tradition that fares best in the light of this scrutiny.

There is yet another level of allegory in *Old Tales Retold,* though it has received little attention from critics. In several of the stories, certainly in the three stories written in the twenties and arguably in some of the later stories,[27] Lu Xun allegorized psychological issues of great personal concern to him at the time he wrote. In each early story Lu Xun unambiguously identifies himself with one of the culture-heroes he depicts—specifically with Nü Wa in "Repairing Heaven," with the archer Hou Yi in "Escape to the Moon," and with the "dark stranger" Yanzhi'aozhe in "Forging the Swords." In the character of Nü Wa, Lu Xun gave expression, as I will argue below, to his private search for creative inspiration. In his depiction of Hou Yi as an aging public figure subjected to the perfidious attacks of former allies, Lu Xun explored humorously the repercussions of his personal fame. Perhaps most poignantly, in the character of the implacable Yanzhi'aozhe, who incites the young and irresolute Mei Jian Zhi to an act of political martyrdom, Lu Xun investigated the nature and consequences of the revolutionary violence in which he and his students were involved. This variety of allegory makes what at first glance appear to be rather impersonal retellings of familiar tales into intimate expressions of Lu Xun's private anxieties. Despite this intimacy, Lu Xun's self-identification with these culture-heroes rarely appears self-serving, as his portraits always conspicuously call our attention to their clay feet.

The many varieties of allegory in *Old Tales Retold* are disarming because they are not discrete, but keep overlapping and interrupting each other. Any given textual signifier may refer to a private affair, to a political event, to a cultural or philosophical construct, or it may refer to all of these levels at once. Of course, in giving such a free rein to the allegorizing imagination, Lu Xun risked undermining the text's rhetorical stability, and the success or failure of this technique may need to be judged in the case of each story independently. But at its best Lu Xun's method is surprisingly effective: the discontinuities of his rhetoric allow Lu Xun to confound the conventional distinctions between public and private, between the philosophical and the political, and in this way to reveal unexpected continuities in the real world.

Through these layerings of symbolic and allegorical levels, for example, "Repairing Heaven" offers a meditation on creativity that is at once private, social, and cosmic. This polysemy has a curious effect on Lu Xun's characterization of his protagonist: Nü Wa, intransigent to the simple schematic interpretation of one-level allegory, takes on something of the opacity of a character in realist fiction. Indeed, opacity characterizes not only Nü Wa's symbolic value in the text, but her very consciousness of being. In the opening scene of the story, the goddess wakes in a "pink-white universe" from which she seems imperfectly differentiated. She is aware only, we are told, "of something missing as well as of a surfeit of some kind"—an emotional state we recognize as that mingling of loneliness and love which Lu Xun thought subtended all creative acts.[28] Listlessly and aimlessly she begins to form "small creatures much like herself" in the mud. Her own handiwork surprises her: "Though she had made the first man herself, she couldn't help wondering if he hadn't been lying there hidden in the mud all along."[29] Throughout this scene

Nü Wa seems the agent of a creative impulse not fully her own: rather than summoning the *élan vital*, she is temporarily possessed by it. The urge to create is a somatic rather than intellectual force; it inhabits the very body of the goddess and remains not fully fathomable to her rational mind. Her primal creativity, the passage suggests, is finally indistinguishable from her sexuality—and Lu Xun's description of the goddess, stretching her pink flesh, her body spattered with foam from the waves, is perhaps the most erotic passage he ever wrote.

But Lu Xun's view of creativity goes beyond a simple organicism. The second major act Nü Wa undertakes in the story, the "repair" of Heaven, epitomizes a maturer stage of creative endeavor, one made tragically necessary by the behavior of the creatures she has spawned. Almost as soon as she creates them, they grow estranged from her, start babbling in a language she cannot understand, and turn to making war on each other. Their bellicosity, in the version of the myth Lu Xun uses, precipitates the collapse of Heaven, making necessary the act of restoration that is Nü Wa's last heroic gesture.[30] Human society must itself be identified as the locus of the "forces of repression" opposing Nü Wa, and the society her creatures forge is subjected to the full fury of Lu Xun's satiric imagination. In Lu Xun's portrayal, human intercourse in all its variety is nothing but the disguised expression of human vanity: religion takes its source in fear of death (the futile search for an "elixir" to save lives that even the supplicants recognize are "worthless"); politics arises from the need to rationalize hegemonic ambitions (the losers in the global war blame Heaven for failing to protect the just, while the winners decry the "evil in human hearts" that prompted their opponents to resist their aggressions), and social morality is at heart a repudiation of nature—of the very source of life itself. In each case evil impulses triumph by exploiting the potential for hypocrisy inherent in language. Human society, as Lu Xun depicts it, grows malignantly from the first disturbing characteristic Nü Wa observes in her creations: their linguistic facility.

Nü Wa is baffled by her creatures and their language, but she is capable of pitying them. A new moral intentionality born of her sympathy informs her decision to repair Heaven. And with this assumption of moral responsibility, Nü Wa emerges for the first time into a full awareness of herself. Ironically, however, this discovery of self coincides with an act of self-sacrifice that is tragically unappreciated by the creatures for whom it is undertaken. In this version of *götterdämmerung*, the goddess sacrifices her immortality for nought: her creatures honor her memory only in fragmentary superstitions and rituals that misrepresent the true nature of her act.

The story of Nü Wa is thus, on one level, transformed in Lu Xun's hands into an allegory of society's alienation from the generative sources of nature. On another, however, Lu Xun intends his work to recount the "creation of literature" as well as of humankind. In Nü Wa the reader is invited to discover a portrait of the author—if not Lu Xun specifically, then a more general portrait of the May Fourth author-hero, assuming the enormous burdens of cultural rejuvenation in a period of national crisis, reviled by cultural conservatives at the same time as he is petitioned for miracles by a hopeful but naive public. Nü Wa's two acts, the one spontaneous but amoral, the other compassionate yet suicidal, epitomize the two contending axioms of Lu Xun's view of creativity: on the one hand, the assumption that true creation must be the spontaneous outflow of the subject's emotional life, and on the other, the belief that creative products must be held responsible to a strict assessment of their social consequences. These two axioms coexist uneasily in the text (as they do in Lu Xun's thought generally), but in the tension between them lies the interest and complexity of the story. Beyond this, the estrangement the story describes between creator and creation suggests Lu Xun's painful recognition of the wayward path a work of literature may follow once it has left the hands of its author. In this respect, at least, "Repairing Heaven" evokes what Thomas Greene calls "pathetic (or tragic) anachronism," the awareness that "all of us and all the things we wear and make and build and write, our rituals and styles and folkways, are condemned to anachronism insofar as we and they endure into an estranging future."[31]

Finally, I would like to look briefly at the concluding story in *Old Tales Retold,* "Raising the Dead," a retelling of Zhuangzi's dream in which he converses with a skull on the relative value of life and death. Lu Xun's account is a spare dramatic sketch in which

Zhuangzi instructs Fate to resurrect the owner of the skull. To Zhuangzi's surprise, the revivified man is not interested in having a philosophical discussion with him, but insistently demands clothing and food and laments his lack of family and friends in this new age. Zhuangzi's abstruse responses, characteristically paradoxical and self-refuting, sound increasingly hollow in the face of the man's straightforward expression of his material needs. In a sense, the story is another version of the paradigmatic encounter in Lu Xun's stories between the intellectual and the peasant in which the intellectual's vaunted sense of social duty is exposed as fraudulent during the course of a one-on-one encounter across class lines. But in "Raising the Dead" the personal obligation is magnified, as Zhuangzi is in a literal sense responsible for the second life of the man. Zhuangzi fails the test of this encounter; when the man becomes agitated, Zhuangzi summons a constable and, leaving the man in the hands of the law, goes off to talk philosophy with the king. Not only is Zhuangzi's philosophy exposed as unresponsive to the somatic needs of the common man, but his final act reveals his unacknowledged complicity with the machinery of social discipline that upholds the state.

From the perspective of the cultural critique in *Old Tales Retold*, Zhuangzi receives the most scathing treatment of all the volume's culture-heroes. But Zhuangzi is engaged here in an enterprise (reviving the dead) that presents an inescapable analogy with the act Lu Xun himself performs in his retelling of these "old tales." What, after all, is the resurrected skull but a corporealized anachronism? Guo Moruo, in a lengthy article published in 1940, once made the case for Lu Xun's deep indebtedness to Zhuangzi, citing numerous allusions in Lu Xun's writings and observing certain similarities in the quality of the two authors' imaginations.[32] I would go further and suggest that the very devices that make *Old Tales Retold* so stimulating—the audacious impersonation of culture-heroes, the anachronies, and the reckless allegorizing—have their formal origins in the text of the *Zhuangzi:* the treatment of Confucius in the *Zhuangzi* is certainly no more reverent nor more accurate (in a historical sense) than Lu Xun's treatment of his culture-heroes. Even as Lu Xun disavows Zhuangzi's philosophy, he has apparently drawn considerable inspiration from Zhuangzi's liberating model of creativity. Not, however, without certain reservations. When Fate accuses Zhuangzi of being "neither completely in earnest nor completely in jest,"[33] he seems to be leveling against the philosopher the familiar charge of "facetiousness." Ever self-reflexive, Lu Xun has planted in this final story an echo of the misgiving he expressed in his preface.

In the new context of postmodernism, Lu Xun's "fall into facetiousness" may no longer need a defense. His facetiousness seems, instead, the inevitable consequence of certain historical and aesthetic exigencies. Lu Xun first turned to traditional legends and tales to expand his expressive potential, hoping through them to treat themes not amenable to the kind of representational fiction in which he had already demonstrated such skill. It was never his intention, though, to use the myths as a fount of cultural or artistic authority. Lu Xun never lost his apprehension of the "cannibalistic" nature of traditional culture, and he needed to find a formal means to inhibit any tendency for his writing to encourage too reverent an attitude toward the traditional sources. Lu Xun's use of anachrony and allegory serves precisely this function in the stories; through them Lu Xun punctures the aura of inviolability that surrounds the legendary heroes whose stories he adapts. In this way, Lu Xun repossesses these fragments of the tradition for his own creative purposes, and earns a new sense of weightlessness in relation to the past. The stories in *Old Tales Retold* are grounded in a real agony, but the anguish they express results less from Lu Xun's grappling with an overburdening tradition (as had been the case in some of his more "realistic" stories) than from his pained struggle to reconcile the deeper impulses of his creativity with his scrupulous sense of moral and political responsibility. As he puts it in his preface, he resorts to facetiousness precisely because "he has less respect for the ancients than for his contemporaries."

Mythopoetic tropes appeal to contemporary Chinese writers, as demonstrated by the examples of Zhang Xinxin, Han Shaogong, and Liu Heng, for many of the same reasons they attracted Lu Xun. Like Lu Xun, contemporary writers have found in early Chinese mythology exemplary narrative investigations into the mysteries of human creativity and genealogy. Myths have further provided natural points of reference for authors concerned with problems of cultural identification. And perhaps most compellingly, the use of mythology has allowed contemporary authors to reclaim for literature a sense of the "numinous"—of aesthetic or spiritual elevation—long missing from Chinese literature; through mythology modern authors are able to evoke ultimate questions in a largely nontendentious fashion.[34] The dangers of mythopoesis that Lu Xun recognized, however, continue to haunt the contemporary writer as well. Primary among these is the temptation of a kind of cultural essentialism that grants myth such prestige that it comes to overshadow the contemporary phenomena it was originally called upon to elucidate. By encouraging an ahistorical view of the world in which all postmythical occurrences are interpreted as the rehearsal of a fixed repertory of master narratives, mythopoesis may actually serve to inhibit, rather than stimulate, creativity.

The stories in *Old Tales Retold*, whose eccentric form seems to derive from Lu Xun's intense awareness of both the promises and the dangers of mythopoesis, may yet carry important lessons for a new generation of Chinese writers—writers who have again become preoccupied with the problem of creativity in a sometimes disorienting new global culture; writers who feel the need to reassess the relation of tradition to national identity, but who hope to avoid the traps of nostalgia and cultural essentialism; writers who wish to expand the potential of their literature to express intense new subjectivities, but without reneging completely on the social mission modern Chinese literature has assumed since its invention in the May Fourth period. These new writers may yet find a way to apply the whimsical creativity of the young Nü Wa to the earnest task of restoring Chinese culture.

10 | Lives in Profile: On the Authorial Voice in Modern and Contemporary Chinese Literature

A variety of snares lie in the way of attempting to relate works of modern Chinese literature from different periods to one another. For one thing, the literary history of modern China is marked by ideological and political interventions that have been at once crude, intricate, subtle, and absolute; making useful distinctions about this literature is complicated by the web of ideas and injunctions that results from this overdetermined mix. For another, the critics and authors (often the same people) of modern Chinese literature have since the beginning been given to frequent announcements of abrupt new departures for the whole enterprise. The search for connections over time thus must also account for the large number of claims by participants in the discourse itself about the nature or even the possibility of such connections.

Underlying this seeming chaos, however, is a unity as easy to identify as it is difficult to define: fundamentally, modern Chinese writing is a literature of resistance. This resistance has taken many forms and has at times even been repressed by governmental pressure for decades, but it has always reemerged at the slightest ideological opening. On the surface, the object of this resistance has been social injustice, however defined; in this sense even the literature produced under Maoist tutelage in the 1940s and 1950s would fit within the general rubric. If defined, then, as writing that takes as its fundamental assumption the need to combat social and political inequity, the literature of the May Fourth period and that produced after 1977 can be seen as parts of an enduring totality.

Just under this apparently unchanging, if exceedingly unplacid, surface, however, lie darker and more desperate currents that are much harder to characterize. But these underlying patterns are also more powerful and confer upon modern Chinese literature a much stronger continuity than can be adduced from the examination of any theme found closer to the surface. One of these currents is anxiety concerning whether the literature will be heard and, if heard, its message understood. Lu Xun established the tone of this anxiety in his famous parable of the iron house, which, even beneath its scrupulous misgivings as to whether one should mobilize public attention or not, rests on the fear that the vast majority of any potential audience is "asleep" and therefore insensible to any message.

But literature in modern China seems gripped by an even deeper and more paralyzing fear—the gnawing sense that it would be close to impossible to create a literature uncontaminated by the influence of tradition. To come to grips with this problem, one must begin by taking May Fourth writers at their word when they said they were intent upon creating something new. However, one need not accept that this would be a simple matter of transcribing a reality that all their predecessors had somehow failed to perceive. If the new generation of writers after 1917 was determined not to regenerate the conventional patterns of meaning emblematic of the old order, the problems turned out to be more difficult than they could have anticipated. C. T. Hsia's astute perception about modern Chinese literature's "obsession with China"[1] has long provided us with a way of understanding the nature of the burden this literature has assigned to itself. If, however, we reinterpret his observation to be less a marker of nationalistic sentimentality and more a deep-seated perplexity about how to overcome powerful sets of norms inherited from the past, the resulting analysis will perhaps cut closer to its creators' most deeply felt concerns. That writers perceived literary norms to be inextricably linked with social and ideological norms rendered that perplexity all the more acute.

Since the very pervasiveness of this sense of the tradition's burden renders it a topic of innumerable ramifications, this essay must focus on a narrow attribute of the general case, with the hope that the close examination will have broader significance. What I propose to analyze is the issue of univocality within modern Chinese fiction. The term *univocality* derives from M. M. Bakhtin's notion of monologic discourse and refers to an intention to "seek in the stylistic phenomenon [of writing] a direct and unmediated expression of authorial individuality."[2] The greater part of Bakhtin's project involves distinguishing the monologic discourse from "heteroglossia." Heteroglossia signified for the Russian critic that desirable plurality of written voices that gives the novel its characteristic openness and, more to the point, both its self-critical function vis-à-vis fixed notions of how language operates and its critical function in general social discourse.

Univocality as defined here will refer to an impassive authorial voice determined not to dilute its control over a given text and all other voices, both actual and potential, within it. This voice carefully arranges ideas and opinion within its texts so that a particular notion or group of notions emerges from the rhetoric of each story marked as unambiguously correct. In such texts this enunciating position is so powerful as to render moot any analysis of whether it should be assigned to "implied author," narrator, or major character.[3] In practice, this dominant voice can be embedded either in a dramatized or undramatized narrator or in a major character within the text. In fact, the particular location within the narrative where this voice is lodged seems to make little difference. In its most characteristic form it is embodied in an omnipresent authorial voice that powerfully manipulates the narrative at some distance from it. This subject-position conditions every utterance and action within the text to follow a particular discursive line in regard to how the various elements in the text work themselves out.[4] The definitive feature of this dominating voice is how intent it seems on flattening out or bending to its will any alternate voices that it sets up in its own text.[5]

This essay attempts to demonstrate that univocality or, to put it more provocatively, authoritarian narration has a been central feature of modern Chinese literature. Invoking univocality in this fashion would seem to create a view of modern Chinese narratives hob-

bled by an authoritarian mode of discourse very much at odds with
Bakhtin's theories about the specific genius of the novelistic form.
To a certain extent, this is just what I try to establish. However, I do
not assume univocality to be a simple universal that works invariably
in modern Chinese fiction as Bakhtin's theory would anticipate.
Quite the contrary, in its more complex forms the authoritarian
narrative voice is a site of contestation where the most complex of
the negotiations between the legacy of the tradition and the desire
to escape it are carried out.

This hypothesis is built upon the following assumptions: Modern
writers perceived the burden of the past as being of almost stifling
proportions. Their sense of tradition's monolithic weight served to
push their writing toward a monological confrontation with it, as
they saw the concentration of rhetorical power in one voice as the
only effective means of gaining leverage against tradition's tenacious
influence. This put constraints on the possibility of creating a multi-
plicity of voices in modern narrative, but paradoxically brought with
it an acute awareness of the hazards of relying on a single powerful
voice, even if the writers considered it an authentic one of their own
devising. Many of the most important stories in the modern canon
thus included a critique of the authority of the dominant narrative
voice even as they relied on it to create new literary and intellectual
space. This essay describes some of the forces pushing toward univocality as well as the auto-critique that developed when these seemingly omnipotent narrators were being created.

That this narrative voice characterizes most fiction produced in
China after Mao Zedong's literary line was promulgated in 1942 at
Yan'an[6] will come as no surprise. I would argue, however, that this
powerful subject-position characterizes much narrative produced before that event. The vast ego of the narrative persona of Yu Dafu, for
instance, fits the description perfectly, even at those moments when
he appears to be holding it up for critical scrutiny. His 1923 story
"Chun feng chenzuide wanshang" (An Intoxicating Evening of
Spring Breeze) is a good example. Whereas the narratorial persona
seems through the middle of the story to be assaying a sympathetic
and nuanced portrait of the factory girl with whom he shares his
lodgings, the story ends with that sympathy transformed into a foil

to channel compassion toward his own, far less desperate situation.[7] Another, less obvious example can be found in the finely crafted stories of Wu Zuxiang from the early 1930s. "Tianxia taiping" (Let There Be Peace), for instance, an account of the precipitous decline of a rural shop attendant and his family, follows an utterly relentless trajectory. This track is so fixed as to preempt openings for any source of agency in the story other than the dour hand of the author and his firmly held ideas about the inevitability of rural decline.

While the tendency for one voice to dominate all others in a narrative is something critics have long been aware of, it has generally been subsumed under the rubric of an ideological imperative toward didactic literature.[8] The net effect of the domination of a single enunciating position within narratives has been to instill a didactic content into literature. To look at univocality strictly as a function of political dictation, however, obscures a much profounder issue, namely, the extent to which authoritarian narratives and authoritarian politics might stem from the same discursive roots rather than being simple products of each other.

Another disadvantage of such a focus is that it directs attention to the content of the political line and methods of Party enforcement rather than to the complicated rhetorical features of the stories themselves. Looking at this characteristic voice and its literary effects will not only allow more analytical rigor, it will also enable us to examine features that transcend the specifics of a particular political line. To cite but one example: concentrating on the nature of the narrative voice allows critics to recognize the underlying similarities in the hortatory enunciating postures of the video series *He shang* (River Elegy) and the government propaganda programs the series was designed to contradict.[9]

Finally, the stories chosen for scrutiny here are those in which the awareness and self-critique of this dominating narrative voice come through most strongly. In one type of story the voice itself becomes the subject of a meta-fiction that serves to expose the weaknesses or problems inherent in trying to make too strong an assertion of subjectivity. An example is Lu Xun's epochal "Kuangren riji" (A Madman's Diary), conventionally regarded as marking the beginning of modern Chinese literature. In this text the problems the "madman" encounters in fabricating his narrative become emblematic of the dilemmas later writers will face in creating their own fictions. Another type of story contains within it the signs of struggle between the impulse toward authoritarian narration and the emergence of other strong voices. Examples are the pieces in Zhang Xinxin and Sang Ye's *Beijing ren* (translated variously as *Chinese Profiles* or *Chinese Lives*). My argument is that the texts dating from 1983 to 1985 are interesting precisely to the extent they manifest the contention between a strong authorial voice and the voices of the people the authors represent in their writing.

I begin by examining the notion of authorial subjectivity in the critical writings of Shen Yanbing (better known by the pen name Mao Dun) that date from the crucial period 1920–1922. It was during this time that the Society for Literary Research (Wenxue Yanjiu Hui) was developing a program for the reform of Chinese literature centering on the critical examination of Western literary forms and ideas. The society took no formal position on which Western form should have privilege of place. That most of the writers affiliated with it adopted a general orientation in favor of "realism" or "naturalism" (terms that were rarely distinguished in any useful way), however, served to associate the society and realism firmly in the public mind. Mao Dun, as the new editor of *Fiction Monthly (Xiaoshuo yuebao)*, a prominent literary journal that became the official organ of the society at the end of 1920, thus speaks with considerable ex officio influence.

Like other young literary radicals of the time, Mao Dun gives a mostly negative evaluation of the Chinese literary heritage. Assuming, like most of his peers, a universal evolutionary process for literature, he finds Chinese literature trapped somewhere between classicism and romanticism—epochs that the West is assumed to have left behind long ago.[10] Once he begins to catalogue the specific qualities he finds objectionable in the indigenous tradition, however, he abruptly departs from this mechanical evolutionary scheme. He enters instead into a Chinese literary discourse that apparently cannot be so easily merged into a universal pattern. In finding fault with Chinese literature, both premodern and contemporary, Mao Dun identifies two ideas at the root of the problem, one the highly didactic notion of "literature as the conveyor of the way" *(wen yi zai dao)* and the other the apparently antipodal idea of "literature as casual amusement." While he readily sees that these two ideas are diametrically opposed, he finds—paradoxically—that they both lead in the same direction, namely, toward the disinclination of Chinese writers to "investigate and write about real life."[11] His analysis locates, in other words, a similarity of rhetorical effect that subsists in spite of authorial intentions that seem at odds with each other on the surface.

Mao Dun cannot, however, develop this argument much further. In seeking a root cause for this lack of interest in investigating real life, he can only say that writers "in a word, [share] an incapacity for objective description," something that comes from their "only knowing how to fabricate [things] subjectively" (391–392).[12] In the case of those writers attempting to "propagate the way," this subjectivity manifests itself as a solipsistic endeavor simply to speak for the idea that the writer has decided is worthy of his efforts. Those authors writing only for their own amusement, on the other hand, simply take inspiration from their own minds, not seeing any need to provide the kind of background richness that would bring life to their writings (392–393). In other words, Mao Dun finds *all* Chinese writing, didactic or frivolous, inherited from the past as well as being created around him, to be afflicted by the same characteristic flaw: an authorial consciousness that persistently fails to look beyond its own subjective interests, a voice that seems to define itself through the exclusion of other possible voices. To Mao Dun such an authorial disposition must always fail to do justice to the full possibilities of literature:

> Literature has never, in fact, absolutely forbidden the expression of an author's personal feelings. It is simply that these feelings cannot belong only to the occasional [efforts] of a single self and a single period. [Literature] that belongs only to the occasional [efforts] of a single self and a single period can, in fact, be good and beautiful, but it can only be the literature of the author himself, it cannot be a literature of an epoch and even less that of a nation. Historically,

most of our literature has this flaw. In sum, then, our writers from ancient times on only knew of the teachings bequeathed by the ancient worthies and did not know that there were feelings common to the human race; they knew only the subjective and did not know the objective. Their literature, therefore, was isolated from the human race and from [a sense of] epoch. It did not know the human race.[13]

This critique is at once comprehensive and pointed, but the impression remains after reading all Mao Dun has to say on the issue that he either cannot or will not define the question beyond broad generality. In the end, his statements amount to little more than a set of moral scruples undertaken with little effort to provide an empirical analysis that would anchor his insight in actual rhetorical practice. For our purposes, what is notable about Mao Dun's remarks is their assumption that the origins of what he regards as the solipsistic narratorial voice lie firmly in traditional practice. It is far beyond the scope of this essay to explore this question, other than to note a possible congruence between strong authorial subjectivity and ideas concerning the primacy of self-cultivation within post–Song dynasty neo-Confucian discourse. Whether Mao Dun is merely projecting a contemporary concern of his into the past or has in fact identified an important feature of premodern Chinese literary discourse, suffice it to say that concern over the shortcomings of a too strong authorial voice surfaced—with a good deal of conviction—at the very outset of modern Chinese criticism.

If Mao Dun's critique is kept in mind during a careful reading of Lu Xun's 1917 "A Madman's Diary," his point takes on a more incisive cast. It provides, in fact, a powerful guideline to interpreting that story as a key meta-narrative in the subsequent development of modern Chinese fiction. "A Madman's Diary" turns out to be both a manifestation of this imprisonment within the confines of a single voice as well as a critical examination of the potential of that voice. The voice of the "madman" as he writes himself into existence imparts a profound sense of the boundaries of authorial voice in general in that place and time. And the differences between Shen's characterization of the subjectivity of traditional writers and the way in which it is problematized in "Diary" sharply illuminate how that subjectivity became a key factor in the development of a literature that consciously set itself at odds with the past.

The story consists of a short introduction written in classical Chinese by a friend of the eponymous madman followed by thirteen sections of a diary.[14] The diary chronicles the madman's lurid discoveries about the society in which he lives. Within the scope of the diary, the madman develops his analysis of the truth of the world around him in complete isolation from the people that surround him. In fact, it is in their very resistance to his attempts to impose his understanding on them that he finds the inspiration to press on with his speculation about how the world works. This process leads him, in turn, into ever greater isolation. He first feels alienated from Mr. Gujiu and the ravenous crowd, then from his own brother and from the various people his brother brings home to consult about the illness, and finally—when it occurs to him that he has participated in the cannibalistic consumption of a sister who died in early childhood—even from the external trappings of his own self.

At the point in the narrative when he starts to have fundamental doubts about himself, however, the madman's speculation abruptly ceases. Something in his train of thought apparently snaps with this arrival at an utterly nihilistic rejection of all that he surveys. The narrative stops quite suddenly soon after, leaving only his famous—and feeble—plea to "save the children." What happens next we know only retrospectively. In the framing introduction recounted by an external narrator who has been given the diary to read by the madman's brother, we are told that the afflicted soul has been cured in the time between the writing and the reading of the diary. He has gone on to participate in ordinary social life, specifically by "going elsewhere" to await an official posting.

The madman does not present himself in the same fashion throughout the diary. In the first three sections he reveals himself to be overwhelmed by the barrage of perceptions that ultimately convince him of his alienation from society. But after section four, the madman seems to find solid ground to stand on and proceeds to develop an empirical basis on which to build a new order of perception. Having come to the conclusion that the people around him, including his brother, are cannibals, he sets down a "history" of this insight, followed by arguments to persuade others to give up cannibalism. He gains confidence from this new outlook: he is able to drive off a young intellectual sent to reason with him, and to develop an argument based on an evolutionary scheme as to why people should abandon the pursuit of human flesh. He is even able to see himself through his dark, paranoid delusions by recognizing that calling for others to transform themselves will ensure at least the possibility that the world will change.

In the final three sections of the story, however, this hard-won standpoint suddenly collapses under the weight of the madman's gradual realization that he had been initiated into the company of cannibals himself, albeit without his ever having been aware of it. And this initiation had come in the most horrible way imaginable: through the consumption of the flesh of his younger sister, who had died when she was five years old. At this point the diary quickly draws to a close after its author's final words about saving the children. In the end, then, the author's carefully constructed sense of his position vis-à-vis the external world turns out to be a delusion. Not only has his position been built out of a solipsistic failure to make real contact with any entity outside himself, but the self-consciousness at the madman's core is based on a failure even to examine its own roots sufficiently to allow it to stand on its own terms. This flawed subjectivity ends in collapse, significantly enough back in the "real" world, this time with no indication of the capacity for independent critique that had set the diary in motion in the first place.

The narrator's ultimate failure to communicate with anything other than his own feverish mind would seem to render him the precise embodiment of just that subjective isolation Mao Dun had set forth as a key issue but had failed to analyze in any real detail. The way in which the madman engages his environment, however, demonstrates the fully paradoxical nature of how Mao Dun's notion concerning authorial solipsism must work in a posttraditional age. At the heart of Mao Dun's critique lies his belief that traditional writers made no effort to investigate the attributes of reality. But the madman opens his diary with the confession that he has literally been in the dark for the past thirty years. Since he admits at the very outset that his perceptions have been blocked for so long, he in effect denies himself a priori any comfortable preexisting assumptions; he will be required to "investigate and write about real life" as a condition of the terms by which he writes the diary into existence. As a result, the madman exerts himself to the utmost to gather from observation the principles by which he exists in the world.

Each of the madman's efforts to understand the world, however, serves only to drive him more deeply into himself. The paradox of the madman's intellectual progress, then, while it mirrors the problem Mao Dun identifies in traditional Chinese writing, at the same time puts it in a much starker light. For the madman does try as sincerely as he can to engage the world empirically. But since each painfully gained insight only cuts him off from contact with the world outside himself, the categories of "investigation" and "real life" become problematic in themselves. For if the content of his "investigations" cannot be passed on to others, what do they end up being other than a kind of subjective fixation on his own mental process? In addition, the extraordinary contrast between the madman's aggressive conviction of the validity of his own perceptions throughout the diary and the cool presentation within the short framing section of the fact that he had subsequently abandoned them should, on its face, suggest that the very structure of the story must also contribute to the deconstruction of the process of conjecture that leads the madman to his conclusions.

As a meta-fiction, the "Diary" thus offers a bleak prognosis for the literature that will follow. The world would seem to offer no strong readings of itself other than those gained by retreat into the self. Mao Dun's apparent inability to give a more specific description of the damaging subjectivity he finds at the heart of Chinese letters is mirrored in the madman's inability to find an analysis of his own role in society that will allow him to take purposeful action. The sections of the story in which the madman builds his programs of reform are precisely those in which he is the most thoroughly isolated. Perhaps not so incidentally, this is also the portion that is the most thoroughly didactic, lending credence to Mao Dun's notion that "literature as the conveyor of the way" has its roots in a profoundly subjective mood of perception. The classic double-bind in which the madman is trapped, however, is far more severe than anything that Mao Dun had imagined: he is blocked on the one hand by his inability to find any external referent to attach his explanation to and on the other by his final discovery that even his internally generated story will not hold up.

In facing up to this pessimistic vision of the possibilities of narration, it is well to keep in mind Bakhtin's theory that an auto-critique of literary discourse is perhaps the feature of the novel that most sharply distinguishes it as a genre.[15] David Carroll summarizes the import of this idea as follows:

> Internally stratified within themselves and refracting the intentions of the speaking subject as well as the referent, the languages of the novel are representational only in that they demonstrate why *representation as such* is impossible, why novelistic representation is always an open, unresolvable conflict of representations. No representation, no narrative, and no theory can encompass and resolve such a fundamental conflict without denying its own dialogic foundations and becoming authoritarian and dogmatic.[16]

If "A Madman's Diary" is at its most profound a meta-discourse on the impossibilities of representation, then perhaps the ultimate irony of the tale is that almost no one ever reads it this way. There has been in China a virtually universal tendency for readers to take the madman's insights as symbolically true of the situation facing a China struggling to modernize, with everything he says about the society around him taken as metaphorical truth. The subjective delusions of the diary's author are taken to be the objective revelation of everyone's secret social unease. What has given this reading its durability, however, is its vision of how the traditional order of meaning functions. The "system" is seen ironically, as a ubiquitous presence that smothers all initiatives precisely because virtually everyone goes along with it without ever understanding how or why it works as it does. Any resistance to it must therefore appear to be merely willful or even "mad" to those unthinkingly caught up in its ordinary operations.

From all Lu Xun said throughout his voluminous writings regarding his attitudes toward the Chinese tradition, it is fairly clear he shared the iconoclastic perspective on tradition that finds its most extreme expression in some of the diary entries. He has, therefore, invested great rhetorical power and moral conviction in his depiction of the afflicted man's struggles toward understanding and in the accounts of the quality of the character's perceptions. The substance of the madman's critique of the evils of Chinese society and the ineluctable hypocrisy of those who seek to deny his insights powerfully affirm his fundamental revelations concerning Chinese life. The power of these convictions—clearly the property of the authorial voice as much as they are of the "madman"—has been such as to overwhelm the intricate structure that would warn the reader to mistrust the voice of too-insistent subjects.

Lu Xun has thus set up a highly problematic choice for the reader. One can read the text without taking account of the frame story, thus seeing the madman as a powerful guide with an ultimate grasp of the nature of reality. It follows from this reading that behind the madman in the text lies an author who is as confident of his own enunciating position as the narrator himself. Or one can take the frame story and the madman's weak exit from his own text as emblematic of the hollowness lying just behind a strong authorial voice. The problem with the first sort of reading is the more obvious. It negates the novel's capacity for auto-critique in exchange for affirming the genre's ability to advance urgently felt convictions. The problem with the second, or more critical, type of reading, however, has apparently been more compelling in modern China: If the story is primarily auto-critique, how can it justify itself in a society beset on all sides by social ills so urgent that all intellectual activity should be directed to their solution? That the consequence of an overreliance on strong subjects was eventually to become in itself one of China's principal social problems was an irony that perhaps only Lu Xun at his most gloomy could appreciate.

Lu Xun has thus created an immensely enigmatic text here, one that in the end has had the historical effect of reinforcing the power of the individual voice more than cautioning readers against its excesses. The urgent need Lu Xun clearly felt to bring about the realignment of perception induces him to tip the rhetorical scales in favor of asserting the powers of the writing subject. This aspect of the story celebrates the lonely voice of the writer, both of the madman and of the authorial persona, Lu Xun, standing just behind him, as the only possible agent of resistance to the tyranny of a monolithic tradition. With the Chinese world in shambles in the early part of this century, perhaps the only thing to fall back on is a Confucian memory—as profound as it is covert—of the responsibilities of the perceiving mind. There is a definite, if sentimental, wish embedded in the desperation of "Diary" to find in this mind something that can be built upon.

The basic structure of the story, however, persists in repeatedly cutting the ground out from under the narrator's feet and ends with his complete capitulation to the forces representing the status quo. This structural specificity remains as a corrective to the sentimental side of "Diary" and an ultimate reminder of the dangers of the solipsism Shen Yanbing was to allude to a few years later. The vision of authors as hostage to the limitations of their own subjective delusions was to abide as an alternative guide to measuring the boundaries surrounding narrators in the stories written after "Diary." It is only, in fact, if we see an imbalance between the voice of the author (as someone who conceives of his character as having a fundamental perceptual flaw) and that of the madman that the story takes on the complex play of voices that Bakhtin saw as the defining characteristic of the novel form.

An alternative construction of a central character is illustrated in Wang Anyi's 1984 "Lao Kang Came Back" *(Lao Kang huilai)*. Wang's story dramatizes the problems involved in depicting characters deemed too weak to qualify as worthy vessels for the omniscient voice or, more simply, a voice beyond the range of the vast powers of agency so commonly seen in modern Chinese literature. The question concerning narrative structure that emerges from this story is one of how a character must be conceived in order to have his or her voice register with any significance.

Lao Kang, one of the large number of intellectuals victimized by the antirightist movement in 1957–1958, has returned to Shanghai from internal exile in the distant hinterland only after 1977. The very thing that has inspired the narrator to become interested in Lao Kang's story also renders it almost impossible to write: on the eve of his return home, Lao Kang suffered a cerebral hemorrhage that has left him deaf, dumb, and severely limited intellectually and physically. Having heard about this, the narrator—a man of about fifty who had once been Lao Kang's schoolmate—determines to find out what has happened to his old friend. He eventually locates Lao Kang and learns he has become an invalid, requiring continual care to perform even the most minimal functions of everyday life.

The only hint that Lao Kang is able to give that he is still a conscious being is the constant repetition of the act of miming the writing of the character *mi* (rice) with his right hand. He produces no external signs of autonomous existence other than this, presenting himself to the narrator as a complete blank, unable either to transmit or to receive any information other than this unremittingly ambiguous act of mock self-expression. As a consequence, there is literally nothing the narrator can write about Lao Kang's thoughts and feelings in his present state or about Lao Kang's memories of the events that transpired in his life between his banishment and his return. This lost period coincides with the period of domination of Chinese political life by an extreme left intent upon bringing the intellectuals to heel with whatever degree of harshness it considered necessary.

That virtually every potential Chinese reader knows this enables one to hazard a secure guess about what the author intends to signify with this void at the center of her story. The fact that the character *mi* (rice) is almost identical in sound and shape with the character *mi* (confusion or enigma) also provides a clear indication that Wang Anyi is both lamenting the waste of human life and talent that resulted from the extreme policies of this period and posing a question—which is by the very nature of its formulation unanswerable—as to why it all happened. Thematically, then, the story demonstrates itself to be one of a large set of stories describing both the unknowable causes and the tragic consequences of the leftist policies the Communist Party pursued between 1957 and 1977.

Success at directing the rhetorical structure of the story so strongly toward establishing its meaning (or what Roland Barthes would call its hermeneutic code),[17] however, has been achieved at the cost of virtually effacing all other elements of Lao Kang's character. Both the actions he could contribute to the story and any semiotic complexity that could be attached to his person have been largely preempted by the narrative strategy the author has chosen. But even within the demands of this structure, Lao Kang has been depicted as a particularly blank entity. While Lao Kang's impassiveness is hardly remarkable, given the nature of his illness, there is a void about his history that, while less total than that of his stroke-induced catatonia, is even more striking. For the narrator mentions several times that in the memory of the other characters, Lao Kang seems to have made little more impression than he does in his much-reduced present state. Of all the classmates who had thought about going to see Lao Kang upon hearing of his return, for instance, only the narrator ever bestirs himself to do so. The reader's ultimate impression of Lao Kang is that his diminished presence now is in fact an appropriate emblem of the imprint his earlier life had left upon those who knew him then.[18]

The narrator, however, while concerned enough to pursue the enigma of Lao Kang as far as he does, provides the most important clue as to why Lao Kang cut such a weak figure. The narrator notes dismissively—and significantly—that Lao Kang suffered no more than many others and less than some and that the actions for which he was punished back in the 1950s "seemed to lack a certain air of tragic heroism." Hence "he never left much of an impression."[19] Given that the nature of Lao Kang's collision with and punishment by the arbitrary powers of the state had been much less remarkable than what had befallen many of his peers, neither the narrator nor, apparently, the other classmates could find much reason to devote time to thinking about the banished man. Even Lao Kang's own brother displays a chilling nonchalance over Lao Kang's fate. In other words, Lao Kang's insufficiency as an emblem in a larger narrative of the ongoing battle between the intellectuals and the state causes him to lose the power to signify even within his own family. On this level, the narrative is thus a critique of the inability of Lao Kang's family and friends to allow the narrated other enough density ever to have a real voice of his own.

The indifference of the other characters toward Lao Kang at least superficially recalls the treatment accorded the twice-widowed Xianglin Sao in Lu Xun's "Zhufu" (The New Year's Sacrifice), in which the woman who is the object of the narrator's sharply limited concern is at once manipulated and ignored by everyone she encounters in the story.[20] In Lu Xun's story, it is the widow's lowly social position that causes her to become the passive victim of the intentions of others toward her as she makes her way through life. For all her inability to act as an agent within the story, however, in serving as the butt of the injustices of the rigid and uncaring structure of the traditional Chinese patriarchal social order, Xianglin Sao can at least lay claim to that "certain air of tragic heroism" that is so conspicuously withheld from Lao Kang. Despite the narrator's coldness to her and his inability to respond when he reencounters her after a number of years, he is still obsessed enough about what has happened to her in the interim that he finds the information and devotes most of his narrative to passing it along to the reader. It is, in fact, the complex feelings engendered in the narrator by the news of her untimely death that causes "the fragments that [he] had earlier seen and heard of her life to form themselves into a piece."[21] For the narrator of "Sacrifice," in other words, it is Xianglin Sao's assumption of tragic stature that causes him to generate the narrative of her life. In the case of Lao Kang, however, even his pathetic condition after his return cannot bring either the narrator or Lao Kang's brother to investigate the events that transpired during the twenty years of his exile.

From the standpoint of the meta-narrative that comments on the possibilities for writing, then, Lao Kang cannot create a story around himself because he lacks the subjective self-focus needed to place himself at the center of things. The fact that the state effaced all his powers of agency does not make this less true. After all, the society surrounding the "madman" had been just as intent upon silencing him, and it was only his monomania that kept space open for him to write—for a time—with a vision of himself as the only legitimate voice within that society. If put in longer perspective, moreover, the narrator's and Lao Kang's brother's inability to supply Lao Kang with a story stems from the afflicted man's failure to cut a grander profile in his student days. He has left nothing to remember him by. As part of modern Chinese literature's auto-critique, "Lao Kang Came Back" poses the question of how and whether one can create a realized character who is not at the same time both dominant and self-important. If it is only such characters who can hold their own against the all-embracing claims of society and state, then the danger becomes that such uniformly extraordinary people must sacrifice self-irony in their struggle to affirm themselves. And without such irony they will with difficulty avoid falling into a prescribed trajectory that is, in the end, derived from a state-generated narrative of the inevitability of human progress. That this issue is also so close to the narrative problem in "A Madman's Diary" is testimony to the endurance of the issue for modern Chinese literature as a whole.

Upon encountering such stories, the Western reader probably perceives that their real point must be a thematization of the awareness of the gap between the representation of an event and the event itself. Seen in this light, the "madman's" struggle to create meaning for himself and the narratives both of Xianglin Sao and especially of Lao Kang draw our attention to the ultimate futility of trying to reconstruct linguistically events that cannot be present to us. Contemporary Western theories of reading concur that this gap is something always already inscribed in the very act of writing itself as well as being something that inevitably springs to the forefront in any attempt to re-present what is necessarily absent to us.[22]

Upon careful examination, however, such an interpretation does not seem to explain adequately how these particular stories work. Their focus appears, rather, to be almost exclusively on the failure of the narrators represented within them to perceive what it is assumed to be their responsibility to perceive.[23] The "madman" cannot in the end hold fast to his insights because of the blockage engendered by his own involvement, and the resolute clarity on the question of the meaning of what happened both to Lao Kang and to Xianglin Sao places the force of the narrative *mi* or enigma on the failure of the respective narrators to pursue matters much further than they have done. Such a pursuit, it is implied, if wholeheartedly undertaken, would resolve itself in a pragmatic comprehension that would contribute significantly to the amelioration of the terrible fates meted out to the protagonists. Perceptivity on the part of the central voice in the story is linked not only to an understanding of the world but to the pragmatic transformation of that world as well. Given this notion of the centrality of perception, one can easily understand the temptation to grant such extensive privileges to a single, responsible voice. That the enhanced subjectivity that ensued was subject to critique by authors who cover as large a span of time as do Shen Yanbing, Lu Xun, and Wang Anyi is indicative of its continuing significance.

In the brilliant group of first-person stories Lu Xun wrote after "Diary," the narrative voice is held up to relentless scrutiny.[24] In these stories, Lu Xun seems to be dogged by a suspicion that any firm subjectivity would eventually restore the long-standing link between individual perception and traditional conventions of behavior. For if the old conventions had proved poor guides to the new world of modern China, they still had a distressing durability at the level of customary use. The small group of writers that regarded any apotheosis of this powerful notion of the self as a dire omen in the effort to bring real reform to China perceived that sooner or later these customs would insinuate themselves into the aggrandized individual voice. But Lu Xun eventually became so obsessed with the possibilities of excess in the personal voice that he finally could not avoid the common pattern of being unable to move beyond a fixation upon the implications of his own voice.

The author's own voice, in other words, may be profoundly subversive of its own claim on privilege. In its wariness that other voices may be metonymically attached to a whole set of traditional conventions just, as it were, waiting in the wings to come on, however, it also may become too concerned about maintaining its control to avoid situating any real authority in the voices of the other characters it creates. Paradoxically, however, the author must still try to sort the myriad of phenomena into sensible patterns. The upshot has been the creation of Xianglin Sao and others like her, characters that attract authorial attention only because they signify the social critique that was part of an implied project to reconstruct a new order of meaning. Even for Lu Xun, then, externals could have no weight of their own without serving as milestones pointing to a determinate critique of the old order. But in feeling constrained to see things this way, Lu Xun cannot bring himself to invest in Xianglin Sao and others like her any voice of their own. She is acted upon only and given no chance to show how she would respond to this treatment. She in effect differs from the mute Lao Kang only in her emblematic treatment as active victim of a vicious system. For his part, Lao Kang—a character written into existence some sixty years after Xianglin Sao—is consigned to the status of cipher precisely because of his lack of emblematic qualities.

Thus, the narrative voice of Lu Xun and those who followed in its wake faces perpetual imprisonment—curiously reminiscent of Lao Kang's—within a paranoid self that was ever-mystified by the question of where it should turn to construct a new perceptual field.[25] That Lu Xun again and again felt obliged to settle for the creation of mute and passive social emblems is in itself an emblem of the aporetic nature of his project. In its turn, the constant iteration of failure on the part of a series of dominating voices within modern Chinese narrative to make any real effort to embody the particular qualities of the characters that surround them is but another manifestation of the writers' inability to move beyond their sequestered selves.

How, then, to break out of this fixation on the omnipotence of the tradition, with its tendency to lead to authoritarian dictation as to what the proper response should be? Clearly, the increasingly left-wing path political discourse took in the years after Lu Xun wrote his stories tended to heighten the dogmatic urgency to find the right answer. Each setback in politics after 1925 came to be viewed as yet another sign of the rootedness of traditional evils and thus strengthened the hand of those authors who would use their own enunciating position to warn ever more shrilly of the dangers of not adhering to their remedies for overcoming the cruel legacy of the past. As Liu Xiaobo has courageously pointed out, even the period of liberalization after 1979 witnessed an effloresence of a self-aggrandizing personal voice in literature that was far more domineering than anything seen in the literature of the May Fourth period.[26]

Making new departures perhaps requires radical moves by readers as well as by writers. The wide appeal of Ah Cheng's work, for instance, may lie not so much in any mystical resuscitation of national roots he may be engaged in or, for that matter, in the particular care he devotes to language. A more plausible explanation may lie in the fact that in significant portions of *Qi wang* (The Chess King) and *Haizi wang* (The King of Children), the narrators do not seem to care very much whether we respond to their texts in what readers have come to expect to be the approved fashion. The impressive number of devices arrayed throughout the stories to confound conventional expectations provides the best manifestation of this.[27] The sheer relief at being presented with texts that are serious without hectoring their readers to accept ideological direction from them may account for much of their popularity. This is a style so rare in post-1942 Chinese literature that Chinese critics have been at a loss to account for it in any useful fashion.

Perhaps the most drastic departure from conventional narration comes in the extensive group of oral histories collected in *Beijing ren*. These texts, begun, appropriately enough, when Zhang Xinxin was under a cloud during the "anti–spiritual pollution" movement of 1983–1984, were a response to political pressures to reform her writing into less unconventional paths.[28] Her response was to join the reporter Sang Ye in a series of interviews with Chinese citizens in 1984–1985. The resulting "transcripts" were initially published in New York, in the now defunct *Huaqiao ribao*, in 1984–1985 and eventually grew to a total of 108. Excerpts were first published in China—to considerable acclaim—simultaneously in five major literary journals in January 1985, followed by a Shanghai edition of 100 pieces published in August 1986. Two English translations, one from Beijing and the other from London and New York, followed soon thereafter.[29]

While there has been a good deal of contention within China as to the literary status of this collection, for the purposes at hand it will be sufficient to note that they are all without question narratives. A question does arise, however, when one tries to assess their formal characteristics. The narrator of each segment is clearly the person being interviewed, yet there is just as clearly a voice behind the narrator asking the questions that elicit the story being told. This voice behind the scenes almost precisely fits the standard definition of the concept of implied author.[30] But for these narratives to separate as distinctly as they do the voices of the characters they portray from the implied author that stands behind them would seem to challenge some of the narrative practices in posttraditional China that were outlined above. This is not to say that Zhang and Sang have effaced a dominant narrative voice in their work. As I shall attempt to demonstrate, it is there just as strong as ever, but the very form in which their effort to record the voice of the other is cast changes the nature of that voice significantly. This transformation is marked within the text through the process by which the interviewers represent themselves. By deliberately leaving out the questions or comments that it has uttered, the authorial voice of the interviewers allows itself to be discerned only through the responses that are recorded.

Thus, like listening to one side of an animated telephone conversation, the shape the authorial voice is giving to the conversation can be picked up in the words of the audible interlocutor as he or she responds to directions that cannot be heard by the audience. This spectral embodiment of the voice giving directions from behind the scenes exposes both the habitual posture and the expected privileges of that voice in a uniquely revealing way. As self-effacing as its deliberate withholding of itself from overt interposition in the text seems on the surface, the unheard voice draws attention to its own assumptions about itself in the very resistance to its direction evident in the responses themselves. And the imbalance between the fact that the voices of the others represented in the text occupy virtually the whole extent of the narrative and the fact that they must often still put forth a major effort to gain a full hearing demonstrates in the strongest way possible the enduring power of the authorial voice. In the end, the resulting contention of voices allows neither side to gain the upper hand and brings a degree of dialogism to modern Chinese literature that has rarely been heard in it before.

The second segment in the collection, "Xingguangxia de qilu" (Diverging Paths under Starlight), is part of an initial group of four stories titled "Overture." In addition to providing an illuminating contrast with "Madman's Diary," the construction of the piece illustrates the extent to which these texts are the sites of clashing voices as well as the extent to which the authorial voice assumes a power to shape other voices in its own image. The authors tip their hands concerning their attitude toward the character they are about to profile in the introduction to the piece, where they say in their own voice: "He said we could or, more than that, that we should reveal his name. But we would rather say that there is such a young man somewhere on the North China plain."[31] When given the floor to have his own say, the young man announces defensively that he has seen many such interviewers and that they have all told him "not to harbor ideas beyond my station" and then abruptly taken their leaves.

The young man reveals soon enough the reason for all this elaborate distancing. He has, he says, through his own studies devised a new theory of the origins of the universe that overturns all established cosmological theories. The notion that he has emerged with a world-shaking idea causes him to develop classic paranoid symptoms (or, more likely, the other way around): for fear of having his idea stolen by someone with more credentials and thus with more credibility, he will not reveal his discovery to anyone other than a group of prestigious astronomers. He adds, however, that since such astronomers have a vested interest in the present scheme of things, they will not grant him a hearing. He has nothing to do, then, other than persuade himself that it is the very singularity of his discovery that guarantees its importance: "all the inventions and discoveries in the world have been the fruits of the thinking of one person at one particular time" (11/42).

The resemblance between this young man and Lu Xun's madman suggests itself at this point, and it is a clinical resemblance: they are reinforced in their sense of the validity of their own insights by the resistance they encounter from others. In Lu Xun's story this resistance is provided by a series of encounters with his surroundings that the story's central figure records in his diary, whereas in "Starlight" the resistance is provided by the young man's abstract account of how he has been received in the past. But in "Starlight," there is another significant source of resistance, namely, the unrecorded questions of the two authors. Their constant goading of their subject is recorded exclusively in what are clearly negative responses to challenges they present him with: "No, even if you don't agree, I'll still say this is true." "That's right. I do think that on this question everyone else is wrong and only I'm right" (*8–9*/40). "Fail? No way" (*11*/43). Finally, the passage that ends the text: "I can only prove that you don't get it. I believe that there is nothing difficult in the world; all it takes is the willingness to make the attempt. Many successful people have undergone the same frustrations that I have. No, why am I different from them?" (*12*/44).

While it is understandable that the authors should feel their own frustration with such a person—one who can say with an apparently straight face that in the unlikely event that his theory should not pan out, he has another one concerning "the relationship between ex-tragalactic beings and the Bermuda Triangle"—the abrupt way the interview is reported to end still comes as a shock. The sense that emerges is that this voice is one that the authors do not want to admit into polite discourse, and, their efforts to convince him of his errors having been unavailing, they finally give him the lie directly. They deny him the recognition he seeks and thereby, like the people who surround the madman, only encourage his most extreme tendencies. In terms of the foregoing analysis, they confront his solipsism with a powerful subject-position of their own. Given the structure of their narrative, however, the young man never has to retreat from his position in rhetorical defeat. Much as they try to frame his narrative as disadvantageously as possible, they still do not deny him his opportunity to speak, and he is, quite literally, given the last word. This collision of two powerful subjects allows both of them space to exist.

The authors censorial tendencies are not always confined to such strange voices as this one. The by now celebrated narrative of the "ten-thousandaire" in segment fourteen is a case in which both the clash of voices and the rhetorical disposition of the implied author are even more pronounced. The principal speaker in this piece is a young peasant woman who is interviewed while she is eating with her husband at one of Tianjin's more expensive restaurants. Almost from the beginning of the interview the gap between the couple's social position ("Your eyesight's not bad at all. The two of us are both peasants" [*83*/130]) and the extravagant amounts of money they are able to flaunt is placed in the foreground of the text ("Doesn't bother us, we've got money, bills all over the place" [*83*/131]). The overall effect is eerily like what one would imagine would happen were Liu Laolao suddenly to come into possession of the Jia family's great wealth in *Dream of the Red Chamber.* The young woman is, moreover, irrepressible and determined to let everyone know about their new wealth in the most voluble way possible. Her behavior thus flouts all known Chinese social codes, from the Confucian to the Communist, and her husband continually interrupts her monologue to point out to her how out-of-line she is.

Beyond this, it is thoroughly evident from the manner in which the young woman's discourse is framed that the implied author frowns upon her as well. The author is able, however, initially to disguise this distaste by using the husband's words as a kind of chorus of disapproval whenever the woman says something that cannot go unchallenged. Eventually the author seems to lose patience and cannot prevent herself from intervening in the narrator's description of herself:

> These clothes of mine are from Hong Kong. I asked somebody to buy them for me in Shenzhen. Seventy dollars. Now that's some place! Everybody there's a "ten-thousandaire!" (Her husband said: "As if she'd been there herself, what crap." We also said to her: "Those clothes have no class, they aren't even up to middle-of-the-line, and the style doesn't suit you. If you wanted to spend that kind of money, you'd be better off buying local goods; for seventy dollars you could even buy wool.") (*88*/136)

This sudden and fairly vicious reminder of the sumptuary privileges that the educated classes have traditionally reserved for themselves retrospectively reveals the extent to which authorial animus has been working all along against allowing the assertion of this peasant woman's personality.

After this interjection, however, the stage is turned back over to the young woman, and she ends her story a few lines later on a utopian note: "We've been ten-thousandaires for three years running now, so going to Shenzhen is nothing; it wouldn't even be a big deal for us to go to America . . . Passport or no passport, we're poor and lower middle peasants; we've got thousands and thousands of dollars and we can go any old place we please" (*89*/137). However shaped it is, then, the voice of a person whose view of the world differs from that of the implied author forces its way through in the end. The skeptical, rational, and generally pessimistic voice of the author does its best to make the other voice look ridiculous, but the terms of the deal by which the dialogue was initiated are kept, however grudgingly, and the other voice finds its way out.

I do not mean to imply that the voice of the implied author in *Beijing ren* is not a generous one overall, simply that its innate generosity is affected by the same narrative conventions and prejudices that have characterized modern Chinese literature since its inception. In most of the segments, the authorial voice has no trouble accepting the other voices it encounters and finds ways to render highly sympathetic versions of them. Under no circumstances, however, should this openness be construed as somehow demonstrating a lack of authorial shaping or that the narratives themselves are simply the natural expression of the popular voice. But as the law is tested by its hard cases, so must the ultimate capacity of narrators be tested by the extent to which they will be fair to those with whom they have no native empathy. By that standard, the voice of the implied author demonstrates itself still to be constrained by its own notions of how things should work. The structure that has been adopted, however, guarantees that the voice will be subject to a discipline, the discipline of negative capability. Perhaps the ultimate effect of this considerable liberation of the voice of the other in *Beijing ren* (unlike those works of realism that try to make the fictional seem more real) is to allow perceptions of the real to seem more fictional, to reject the conventional definitions of the parameters of what real life is, and to liberate the particular from the context that has so long hemmed it in.

11 | Melodramatic Representation
and the "May Fourth" Tradition
of Chinese Cinema

The recovery of the Chinese film industry from the rav-
ages of the Cultural Revolution was nothing short of
breathtaking. The obvious quality of works by veteran
filmmakers like Xie Jin and irreverent newcomers like
Chen Kaige has forced Western scholars to take their first
serious look at Chinese cinema. Unlike the field of contemporary Chinese literature, however, the newly emerging field of Chinese film studies is severely handicapped
by the absence of a large scholarly literature that covers
all the decades of the twentieth century. As a result, the
new research on Chinese cinema is narrowly focused.
China specialists are inclined to locate recent Chinese
films in the decidedly contemporary context of political
and economic life in the post-Mao era, whereas film scholars (trained in American and European studies) tend to
analyze Chinese films in terms of feminism, modernism,
postmodernism, and other paradigms that were developed primarily for the purpose of criticizing the culture
of the contemporary industrial world.[1] But practically no
one looks at the accomplishments of post-Mao filmmaking in relation to the Chinese film traditions of the pre-
socialist Republican era. Scholars of contemporary literature want to explore the relationship between post-Mao
fiction and its May Fourth literary antecedents, but those
who work on contemporary Chinese cinema rarely ask

such questions. As a consequence, much of the new scholarship on Chinese filmmaking leaves the unintended, but misleading, impression that there is no meaningful connection between present-day and early-twentieth-century cinema and that serious Chinese filmmaking began around 1980.

The point of this essay is to suggest that one of the most important developments in post-Mao cinema is linked, in terms of both form and content, to the rich legacy of Republican era filmmaking. When scholars of literature refer to the legacy of Republican times, they are usually thinking of the May Fourth tradition of writing. But was there a corresponding May Fourth tradition of filmmaking that represented the best of Republican era cinema? The answer to this surprisingly complex and politically sensitive question is yes and no.

It is clear that when the New Culture and May Fourth movements were fundamentally reshaping the world of letters in the teens and twenties, they had almost no direct impact on filmmaking circles. In this narrow but crucial sense, we can say without hesitation that there was no May Fourth tradition of filmmaking. Most May Fourth literary intellectuals simply refused to take the film medium seriously. In spite of their professed interest in bringing about a democratization of culture, a modern culture for the masses, they expressed nothing but contempt for the cinema and made no effort whatsoever in the teens and early twenties to "bring" the May Fourth movement to the film studios of Shanghai. Most regarded filmmaking as a vulgar commercial activity that had nothing to do with art.[2] Film pioneers, for their part, showed little interest in May Fourth currents. During the social and political upheaval of the teens and early twenties, the film studios concentrated on producing popular entertainment, which included musicals, light comedies, episodes from traditional fiction and opera, martial arts adventures, detective stories, and morality tales.[3]

This does not mean that filmmakers never treated contemporary subjects. Such works as *Romance of the Fruit Peddler* (*Laogong aiqing,* 1922, d. Zhang Shichuan) and *A String of Pearls* (*Yi chuan zhenzhu,* 1925, d. Li Ziyuan) reveal a society in the throes of a disruptive, modern transformation; but, as a rule, the emphasis was on the need to shore up rather than subvert traditional values. Early Chinese filmmakers felt most comfortable when they were dealing with the themes that were the mainstays of traditional and contemporary popular culture.

The notion that one cannot speak of a May Fourth tradition of Chinese filmmaking in the teens and early twenties refers only to the issue of the basic intellectual and political content of May Fourth thought. To qualify as a May Fourth work a film would have to embrace one or more of the following political positions: nationalist opposition to imperialist aggression, support for the political democratization of Chinese life, and rejection of traditional Confucian morality and values. Generally speaking, Chinese films of the teens and early twenties did none of these things.

It is ironic, therefore, that in terms of form, early Chinese cinema was more thoroughly modern than May Fourth fiction. Making the transition from classical to vernacular literature was agonizing for modern writers. Filmmakers, however, did not have to make any emotionally wrenching transitions simply because there was no Chinese tradition of filmmaking to reject. They were commercial entertainers who accepted, without apology, the basics of the Hollywood approach to filmmaking because it made business sense. This does not mean that there was nothing Chinese about early Chinese films, that they were little more than crude copies of American originals. It simply means that Chinese filmmakers were making effective commercial use of an astonishingly popular cultural medium that everyone knew was foreign in origin.

It would be wrong, however, to suggest that mainstream May Fourth social and political thought made no impact whatsoever on the Chinese film industry in the twenties. Writings on film history published in China after 1949 leave the mistaken impression that May Fourth thought did not reach the film world until the early thirties. The veteran director Sun Yu (1900–1990) once recalled that upon returning from the United States in 1927, "Eight long years had already passed since the birth of the May Fourth Movement, but none of its revolutionary spirit had penetrated the film world, controlled as it was by commercial entrepreneurs."[4] Actually, by 1925–1927 a small number of recognized May Fourth intellectuals, including Hong Shen (1894–1955), Ouyang Yuqian (1889–1962), and Tian

Han (1898–1968), were writing screenplays and directing films. A small number of the films made in the mid-twenties advocated women's rights, criticized warlord rule, and described the hardships endured by factory workers. By this time there were also a number of Chinese film adaptations of foreign literature by Dumas, Maupassant, Ibsen, Molière, Wilde, and others. Moreover, state-of-the-art foreign films by such recognized masters as D. W. Griffith and Charles Chaplin were well known in China by the early twenties.[5] But none of this added up to a May Fourth–type revolution in the film world.

It was not until the early thirties, long after the original May Fourth movement had ended, that significant strains of basic May Fourth thought began to be reflected in highly simplified and popularized ways in Chinese silent films. We cannot speak of the direct participation of Chinese filmmakers in the original May Fourth movement, but basic ideas we associate with the May Fourth movement did, after all, begin to play a role in the partial reshaping of the film industry in the early thirties.

The formation of the Lianhua Film Company in 1930 by Luo Mingyou (1900–1967) was an important transitional event in the political history of the Chinese film industry.[6] Luo recruited a number of talented and relatively well educated young filmmakers, including Sun Yu, Cai Chusheng (1906–1968), Shi Dongshan (1902–1955), Zhu Shilin (1899–1967), and Bu Wancang (1903–1974), who were interested in making movies that treated social problems in an explicit way.[7] In part, Lianhua was looking for new ways to compete in the marketplace with the flood of American film exports. Between 1896 and 1937 over five thousand foreign films, most of them American, were marketed in China.[8] Young Chinese filmmakers were now eager to discuss modern social issues in their work, but progress was frustratingly slow in 1930 and 1931.

Japan's occupation of Manchuria in September 1931 and its attack on Shanghai in late January 1932 changed everything. These frightening events were as central to the early political transformation of the film industry as the announcement of the humiliating terms of the Treaty of Versailles had been to the burgeoning new literature movement after 1919. Virtually overnight it became easier for Sun

Yu, Cai Chusheng, and the newcomer Wu Yonggang (1907–1982) to inject modern politics into Lianhua films. In fact, circumstances had changed so much by early 1932 that the well-known Mingxing Film Company went so far as to encourage such May Fourth leftist intellectuals as Qian Xingcun (1900–1977), Xia Yan (b. 1900), Zheng Boqi (b. 1895), Yang Hansheng (b. 1902), Tian Han, and Hong Shen, some of whom were Communists, to submit screenplays. Most of these writers were Marxist romantics who had studied in Japan in the mid-twenties and founded the radical Sun Society in Shanghai in 1928 to advance the cause of proletarian literature.[9] For obvious political reasons, Chinese Marxist commentators have grossly exaggerated the significance of the activities of this small group of Party members.[10]

The presence in the film world of non-Communists and Communists sympathetic to May Fourth political traditions did not result in a May Fourth–type transformation of the Chinese film industry.[11] Neither the cultural and political environment of the thirties nor the nature of the film medium itself would permit such a development. True, anti-imperialist patriotism, a hallmark of May Fourth political thought, became an increasingly important element in Chinese films. But the May Fourth themes of radical antitraditionalism and social democracy were much more difficult, if not impossible, to introduce at this time. The problem was not simply a matter of Guomindang censorship.[12] For one thing, May Fourth liberalism and socialism were on the defensive in urban China in the early thirties. The new Guomindang government was building a base of social support in the urban sector and was advocating a type of nationalism that stressed respect for the Confucian cultural tradition. Some May Fourth intellectuals, including people who were affiliated with the Communist Party, were having second thoughts about the validity of the iconoclastic May Fourth analysis of Chinese society.

Furthermore, no matter how much they genuinely subscribed to the complex May Fourth intellectual tradition, those who are now credited with "bringing" the May Fourth movement to the Chinese film industry in 1932 were confronted by a new commercial medium that placed little value on complexity and subtlety. They faced the challenge of having to please a vast new audience whose tastes were already well established. Making movies for the market was not at all like writing fiction for bookish intellectuals.

Melodrama and the "May Fourth" Tradition of Filmmaking

In order to understand vital aspects of the relationship between post-Mao Chinese filmmaking and the Republican cinematic tradition, it is necessary to challenge the myth that the Communist Party brought the May Fourth movement to the film studios of Shanghai in 1932. This interpretation implies that the Party had a coherent policy toward filmmaking that was systematically implemented by its operatives in the film world. Before 1932, it is often said, Chinese films were "feudal," "mercenary," and "reactionary"; after 1932, thanks to Xia Yan and the Party, "progressive" films that "reflected" social reality were finally being made in significant numbers.[13] As Sun Yu put it in 1979, "The film industry of the thirties, under the guidance of the Communist Party, managed to uphold and further the revolutionary spirit and ideology of the May Fourth Movement."[14]

The reality was quite different. Reformist political content began to appear in Chinese movies in the mid-twenties and early thirties, before Xia Yan entered the film world. Individual Communists and leftists wrote screenplays and gave advice beginning in mid-1932, but the Party had no coherent policy toward filmmaking. Nothing at all like a multidimensional and rigorous May Fourth intellectual revolution unfolded at this time. The modern political content found in Chinese films before and after Xia Yan's arrival was a popularized and simplified version of such basic May Fourth ideas as anticapitalism, antiwarlordism, and anti-imperialism (some of which were consistent with official positions adopted by the Guomindang in the early thirties). But the new themes were mixed in with political content that was old, familiar, and quite inconsistent with May Fourth thought. For instance, there is little evidence of sophisticated May Fourth radical antitraditionalism in the films of the thirties. It is true that the censors did not encourage such content, but it is also the case that there was practically no popular audience for such messages and that the Guomindang's intellectual opposition, liber-

als and Communists alike, had backed away from the radical iconoclasm that one associates with the original May Fourth movement.

The film industry, one is tempted to say, ended up making a
bigger impact on the former May Fourth intellectuals in its ranks
than the intellectuals made on the film industry. Even if one gives
such directors and screenwriters as Sun Yu, Cai Chusheng, Wu
Yonggang, Shen Xiling, and Xia Yan the benefit of the doubt by
assuming that they intended to introduce unadulterated May Fourth
thought into Chinese films after 1930, it is hard to escape the conclusion that they became the prisoners of the film medium. In
particular, they became captives of melodrama, a multifaceted genre
that dominated American and Chinese filmmaking in the teens and
twenties.[15] To this day, Xia Yan insists that he and the others who had
May Fourth political pedigrees were fostering social realism in Chinese filmmaking. In fact, like the moguls of the early twenties, they
accepted without question the dominance of the melodramatic
genre and thereby doomed to failure any chance they had to introduce complex May Fourth ideas.

Melodrama, as Peter Brooks and others have suggested, is characterized by rhetorical excess, extravagant representation, and intensity of moral claim.[16] It is an aesthetic mode of "heightened dramatization" that refers to pure and polar concepts of darkness and
light, salvation and damnation. The melodramatic genre was developed first in the French theater in the immediate aftermath of the
revolution, at a time when a significant postrevolutionary democratization of culture was taking place. Although melodrama is a distinctively modern form, its initial political thrust was conservative.
The audience for melodrama included people from all social classes
who were frightened and confused by the modern transformation of
society. This new and powerful mode of representation had a major
impact on European fiction in the mid- and late nineteenth century
and has been kept alive by filmmakers and television producers in
the twentieth century.

The purpose of melodrama is not to deal with the monotony of
daily life. Rather, it seeks to put an insecure and troubled mass
audience in touch with the essential conflict between good and evil
that is being played out just below the surface of daily life. In the

melodramatic imagination, the world is essentially "a place of torment, where creatures of prey perpetually thrust their claws into the
quivering flesh of the doomed, defenseless children of light."[17] The
social mission of melodrama is to explain to the audience the nature
of the fundamental moral confrontations that define an unfamiliar
and threatening modern world. The petty conflicts of daily family
life may seem trivial, the audience is constantly warned, but they are
actually a manifestation of profound life-and-death struggles that
confront the human community. The melodramatic mode is hostile
to realism and naturalism because these modes of representation do
not allow the narrative to "break through" to the plane on which
moral polarities are visibly at war. The melodramatic artist must
"pressure the details of reality to make them yield the terms" of the
underlying and genuinely significant drama. Melodrama thus employs an inflated rhetoric that "can infuse the banal and the ordinary
with the excitement of grandiose conflict."[18]

The political significance of the melodramatic mode lies in its
insistence that ordinary people recognize and confront evil. But the
message must be nonmediated and irreducible if it is going to
arouse the passions of the audience; the underlying "truth" about
life must be kept simple. Consequently, melodramatists must rely
upon such devices as moral polarization, excessive emotionalism,
exaggerated expression, unusual human suffering, and extreme sus-
pense.

It is surely no coincidence that melodrama, a popular cultural
response to the anxieties and moral confusion caused by the revolution in France, became so entrenched in China just before and after
the 1911 Revolution. Although Perry Link does not use melodrama
as an analytical category, something closely resembling melodrama
was clearly central to the imagination of the "mandarin duck and
butterfly" writers who were popular in urban China in late Qing and
early Republican times.[19] These talented writers were well aware of
the appeals of serialized newspaper fiction in late-nineteenth-
century Europe. The fledgling Chinese film industry learned about
the seductiveness of melodramatic representation from Hollywood
and allowed the genre to dominate Chinese film production in the
teens and twenties.

Snobbish and high-brow New Culture and May Fourth literary intellectuals, interested as they were in systems of thought that were quite complex, naturally despised urban popular culture, including butterfly fiction and early Chinese commercial films. They missed the point by failing to see that melodramatic representation was, in its own way, addressing the crisis of twentieth-century Chinese culture and society. As Brooks points out, melodrama is popular in places where "the traditional imperatives of truth and ethics have been violently thrown into question, yet where the promulgation of truth and ethics, their insaturation as a way of life, is of immediate, daily, political concern." "Melodrama," he reminds us, "starts from and expresses the anxiety brought by a frightening new world in which the traditional patterns of moral order no longer provide the necessary social glue."[20]

Melodramatic representation was appealing to low-brow, nonintellectual consumers of urban popular culture in the troubled early Republican period because it provided clear answers to nagging questions. As Brooks demonstrates, melodramatic good and evil are highly personalized and can be named as persons are named. "The ritual of melodrama," he suggests, "involves the confrontation of clearly identified antagonists and the expulsion of one of them."[21] There is no ambiguous moral middle ground. Melodramatic representation generally excludes the middle condition and gives little priority to subtlety or nuance. Melodrama is about the persecution of innocence; it teaches a morally confused audience how to recognize the difference between goodness and evil.

Leftist Film Melodramas of the Thirties: The Case of Sun Yu

When Xia Yan and other leftists sought to inject May Fourth notions about patriotism, Marxism, and progressive social change into Chinese films in the thirties, the genre of melodrama was already deeply rooted in the industry. Their complaint about the film industry had nothing to do with the melodramatic form; it never occurred to them that there might be other ways to make films. They simply wanted to infuse larger doses of May Fourth political content into the popular melodramatic form. They accepted the genre without reservation, and were perceptive in rejecting the idea that popular and commercial cultural forms, by definition, were incapable of conveying forward-looking political messages. Melodrama was appealing to them because it used clear language to identify and combat evil. They understood that a disadvantage of the genre was that it could be put to almost any political use, conservative or revolutionary. The melodramas of the twenties (butterfly fiction and commercial films alike) often had conservative social implications; Xia Yan wanted to force the genre to serve revolutionary political ends. He liked the fact that melodrama was an inherently manipulative form of art. But what he and the other leftists did not comprehend was that there would be no place for the complexities and subtleties, and most of the crucial "middle ground," of May Fourth socialist thought in melodramatic representation.

When Chinese Marxists speak of the "May Fourth" tradition of filmmaking, they are not talking about anything that would strike Western scholars as a diverse, multidimensional, May Fourth–type intellectual revolution. The "May Fourth" tradition to which they refer is something much narrower. It amounts to a heroic, indeed, melodramatic, legend that was tailored after 1949 to meet the political needs of the new socialist state, which, among other things, required the expropriation and manipulation of popular memories of the May Fourth movement. When they speak of the introduction of "May Fourth thought" in the film world in the thirties, they mean the introduction of Marxism, which, to be sure, is a part, but only a part, of the original May Fourth tide. It refers to the now celebrated activities of such Communists and leftists as Xia Yan, Zheng Boqi, Qian Xingcun, Tian Han, Wang Chenwu (1908–1938), Shi Linghe, and Situ Huimin (1910–1987) in the 1932–1937 period and to the films made by such "converted" veteran directors as Cai Chusheng, Sun Yu, and Wu Yonggang and newcomers like Shen Xiling (1904–1940) and Ying Yunwei (b. 1904).[22] The myth of Xia Yan and the "May Fourth" Communist Film Group was trampled upon during the Cultural Revolution, but was revived with a vengeance by Xia and his backers in the late 1970s.[23] Pre– and post–Cultural Revolution Chinese writings consistently advance the cult of Xia Yan and other leftists by suppressing information about other developments and by failing to acknowledge the close connection between the "May

Fourth" films of the thirties and the popular melodramas of the twenties.[24]

It is extremely difficult to challenge the conventional interpretation because the Chinese authorities control almost all the archival resources and, until recently, have been inclined to allow access only to those films that appear to support the official view. But access to the films produced by the "progressive" camp after 1932 does at least provide us with an opportunity to evaluate the claim that they constitute a "May Fourth" tradition of filmmaking. What is most striking about these films is not their popularized "May Fourth" content (although it is clear that new social and political themes emerged in the thirties), but their melodramatic packaging. Sun Yu's *Dawn* (*Tianming*, 1933), Wu Yonggang's *Goddess* (*Shennü*, 1934), Ying Yunwei's *Plunder of Peach and Pear* (*Tao li jie*, 1934), Shen Xiling's *The Boatman's Daughter* (*Chuanjia nü*, 1935), Cai Chusheng's *Lost Lambs* (*Mitu de gaoyang*, 1936), and Yuan Muzhi's *Street Angel* (*Malu tianshi*, 1937) are among the scores of "May Fourth" or left-wing films of the 1932–1937 period that so clearly belong to the broad category of melodrama. Melodrama was not the only genre that existed in the thirties, but it was by far the most dominant. And it was a genre especially well suited to the task of popularizing and dramatizing basic Marxist ideas.

It is sufficient, for our purposes, to take a close look at one of these works, Sun Yu's leftist tear-jerker *Small Toys* (*Xiao wanyi*, 1933), a film that was praised by Xia Yan as soon as it appeared.[25] *Small Toys* contains precisely the type of rhetorical excess, grossly exaggerated representations, and extreme moral bipolarity that one finds in Chinese film melodramas of the twenties and, for that matter, in the classic American film melodramas made by D. W. Griffith that were so well known in China.[26] Sun Yu's work, like the work of almost all "May Fourth" filmmakers in the thirties, constituted a mode of excess that had little in common with the original May Fourth respect for diversity, complexity, and subtlety of social analysis.

Set in the early twenties, *Small Toys* tells the sad story of a virtuous and beautiful village woman who makes charming children's toys to support her family. Pastoral life is idyllic, and the woman is utterly devoted to her kind and unassuming husband. Suddenly, however, the handicraft industry and the tranquillity of family life are shattered by an imperialist economic invasion of China. To make matters worse, the woman's husband dies and her baby son is stolen and sold to a wealthy urbanite. When fighting between rival warlords breaks out, she flees with her innocent and lovely daughter to Shanghai, where they live in a simple shanty.

Ten years later (1932) the mother and teenage daughter still try to eke out a living making wholesome and quaint folk toys, but their existence is threatened now by Chinese industrialists who are mass producing such frightening but popular war toys as planes, cannons, and ships. Once again disaster strikes when the Japanese attack Shanghai. The woman's patriotic daughter volunteers to work in a first-aid unit and is killed in the fighting.

The pathetic woman wanders about aimlessly in the faceless and uncaring metropolis, trying in vain to sell her old-fashioned toys. On

The idyllic family life of a wholesome, but vulnerable, rural woman *(center)* is suddenly shattered by diabolical forces of evil in *Small Toys* (*Xiao wanyi*, d. Sun Yu, 1933, Lianhua Film Studio, Shanghai). Photo: Film Archive of China.

New Year's Day, a sacred time of family unity, she peddles a toy to a handsome rich boy. Of course, it is her long-lost son, but the woman fails to recognize him. A string of firecrackers explodes nearby. The half-crazed woman begins shouting: "The enemy is coming to kill us! Hurry up! We all must fight back! Save your country, save your families, save yourselves! Wake up, stop dreaming! Save China!" Some bystanders think she is insane, but others are beginning to listen.

On the one hand, we see in this classic leftist silent film virtually all of the elements of melodramatic representation that are present in the works of Bu Wancang and other leading melodramatists of the twenties.[27] The plain and innocent rural woman, a suffering victim of evil who represents Chinese purity, is played by the re-nowned starlet Ruan Lingyu, whose impressive mastery of the exaggerated style of melodramatic acting won her the adoration of the Chinese film audience in the twenties.[28] Shanghai, the wicked and corrupting modern metropolis, is correspondingly associated with murky and alien forces that prey on the virtuous. The confrontation, in short, involves clearly identifiable bipolar forces. Indeed, this tale conforms to mid-nineteenth-century French family melodramas that view the modern city as the "symbol of corruption lying in wait for peasant innocence."[29]

But in *Small Toys* we can also see the ways in which a streamlined and popularized Marxist political and economic analysis has been superimposed on the familiar and dominant melodramatic framework. For example, the struggle between good and evil is linked to class conflict. An important secondary plot in *Small Toys* involves the impossibility of a permanent love relationship between the folksy woman (who represents the innocent simplicity of preindustrial China) and a wealthy village lad who aspires to be a technologically sophisticated capitalist. Later in the film, the young man resurfaces as the owner of a modern toy factory that undermines the traditional handicraft industry, but can do nothing to defend China against the real military strength of Japan. Apart from the loving bond that ties mother to child, the only healthy relationships the woman has in the city are with poor working-class people in the neighborhood who, like her, have fled the ravaged countryside. The evil metropolis is identified with the bourgeoisie much more clearly than it was in melodramas of the twenties, while foreign economic and military threats are now explicitly labeled as "imperialist." *Small Toys* is a lesson in elementary Marxism whose ability to reach the public depends on the rhetorical excesses of the melodramatic format.

Part of the reason that melodrama has been so successful in China is that it invariably focuses on family life. The assumption is that everything one needs to know about the bedrock moral confrontations that are shaping the new and unfamiliar modern world can be revealed in a dramatically heightened and sensationalized presentation of ordinary family life. Nothing is more central to Chinese life than the family. The crisis of nineteenth- and early-twentieth-century China was experienced by common people, in large part, as a family crisis. In the classic film melodramas of the twenties, family crisis is precipitated by the erosion of traditional conceptions of morality, but we are not told why time-honored norms have broken down or what might restore them. In *Small Toys* the accusing finger is pointed directly at the ravenous economic and political appetites of domestic and foreign class enemies, who are presented as dehumanized "others." Salvation—that is, the "new" family—will spring from the class solidarity of the persecuted and cruelly victimized poor.[30]

Sadism, Masochism, and "May Fourth" Melodramas in the Forties: The Case of Tang Xiaodan

The "May Fourth"–leftist film project came to an abrupt halt in 1937 when the war with Japan erupted. Most of the film personalities discussed here fled the occupation and engaged in other artistic and literary work in the interior. The people involved in making leftist melodramas were not able to regroup and recruit new talent until 1946, when they began at once to make films that revived the critical traditions of the thirties. This time Xia Yan did not play a leading role. Consequently the films of the late forties have not received the accolades that are reserved exclusively for the thirties. In many respects, however, the films of the late forties, complete with detailed sound dialogues, are more interesting and complex than the mostly silent "May Fourth" films of the thirties and probaby did more to subvert the legitimacy and authority of the Nationalist state. Nevertheless, the genre adopted most often by postwar directors who had critical impulses was the leftist family melodrama pioneered by Sun Yu and others in the early thirties.

A typical example of the "May Fourth" films of the forties is a work by Tang Xiaodan (b. 1910), *Heavenly Spring Dream* (*Tiantang chun meng*, 1947), one of the first postwar efforts of the state-owned No. 2 China Film Studio in Shanghai. A native of Fujian, Tang Xiaodan learned how to make film melodramas after his arrival in Shanghai in 1929 at the tender age of nineteen. In the early thirties he established close personal relations with Shen Xiling, a key leftist melodramatist, who, in turn, introduced Tang to Tian Han, Yang Hansheng, Situ Huimin, and other leading Communist film personalities.[31]

Heavenly Spring Dream tells the excruciatingly painful story of the engineer Ding Jianhua (whose name means "builder of China"), a virtuous and patriotic man who participated and sacrificed in the military resistance to Japanese imperialism. On the day the war ends, Ding is in Sichuan. His faithful and devoted wife proudly announces that she is pregnant. The ecstatic couple rush back to Shanghai to start a new family, build a dream house, reunite with Ding's widowed mother, and help reconstruct a victorious China. Upon their return to Shanghai they are invited to stay in the home of a seemingly good-hearted contractor Ding knew before the war. But, we soon learn, appearances can be deceiving. During the occupation the contractor collaborated with the Japanese and became wealthy. After the war he bribed officials and obtained a falsified government document stating that he had been a patriotic "underground" operative during the war.

Naturally, multiple disasters strike before any of Ding's "spring dreams" can be realized. The postwar economy is in chaos, so he is unable to find a job "rebuilding China." Since he has no money, he becomes increasingly dependent on the unsavory collaborator. Since Ding's wife is pregnant and his mother is sick, he agrees to sell the blueprint of his dream house to the collaborator, who is in need of suitable lodgings for his seductive mistress.

Ding can neither pay his wife's hospital bills nor support the son she bears. The rich traitor agrees to pay all costs, on the condition that Ding give up his newborn son. The traitor and his vicious wife have no children. (In Chinese melodramas, evil people are often denied children of their own.) But the arrangement collapses when Ding's wife finds out about the plan and accuses the traitor's wife of abusing the infant. The Dings are then thrown out on the street to fend for themselves.

As they stagger along the highway, their dreams and hopes smashed to smithereens, the rich traitor pulls up in a shiny American car and talks in hushed tones with Ding, who once again, against the frantic protestations of his wife, surrenders his infant son. Further down the road the suffering couple happen upon the home the traitor has built for his mistress with Ding's blueprints. Inside the house the traitor, the mistress, and the mistress's mother are blissfully playing with Ding's baby boy.

This sensational and exaggerated representation of the struggle

A decent and honest man, Ding Jianhua *(center)*, is emasculated by sadistic agents of darkness in *Heavenly Spring Dream* (*Tiantang chun meng*, d. Tang Xiaodan, 1947, No. 2 China Film Studio, Shanghai). Photo: Shi Yu.

between darkness and light in postwar China is remarkably similar, in terms of both form and content, to the Marxist melodramas produced by Sun Yu, Cai Chusheng, and others in the thirties. The moral poles of vice and virtue stand out in stark, unmediated relief. Purity and innocence are represented by honest, hard-working people who love China. Greedy and lustful villainy is represented by the class enemy, bourgeois city slickers who are in league with foreign imperialism.

Heavenly Spring Dream opened on March 12, 1947, at two important Shanghai theaters, Huanghou and Guanghua. Its melodramatic essence is conveyed beautifully in emotionally charged advertising that appeared in local newspapers: "A great tragedy!" *(da beiju)*, "Victory turns into tears!" *(shengli liu yanlei)*, "Veterans are starving!" *(fuyuan e du pi)*, "Crazed anger, incredible bitterness!" *(qi de fafeng, ku dao jidian)*, "Anyone who wants to cry will have a good one here!" *(yao ku dajia ku yi chang)*, "The poor are at the mercy of the rich, bones and flesh are ripped asunder!" *(qiong bu di fu, gu rou bei duo)*, "Good can't compete with evil, gentlemen meet their doom!" *(hao buru huai, junzi lunluo)*.[32] In both the thirties and the forties it was precisely this type of heightened and intensified rhetoric and highly polarized moral clarity that ordinary people expected to find in feature films. In public declarations in 1947 the director Tang Xiaodan used the same melodramatic language to describe the main themes of *Heavenly Spring Dream:* "Honest and conscientious government employees could barely survive, while crooked, traitorous former collaborators were instantly formed into 'underground workers.'"[33]

In films like *Small Toys* and *Heavenly Spring Dream,* the suffering of weak and upstanding people is always painfully intense and excessive. Virtuous and traditionalistic women (or feminized male surrogates like Ding Jianhua) must be insulted and humiliated, innocent children must die needless deaths, and the elderly must perish. Good people must be plagued by death and destitution. The point, of course, is that the forces of evil are sadistic. In melodrama, it is not enough to say that the agents of darkness inflict pain; they must be portrayed as demons who actually derive pleasure from tormenting their victims. But the dialectic of melodramatic representation also involves masochism. For the mode of excess to work on the audience, it is not enough to show that the representatives of virtue and goodness are weak and defenseless; they must be like Ding Jianhua, that is, people who endure staggering amounts of pain without registering a protest. Indeed, the terrible pain they endure in silence is, in a perverse way, welcomed by the persecuted, because it provides righteous victims with an unambiguous identity and thus gives meaning to their lives.

It is easy to understand why leftists were attracted to melodrama before and after the war. They wanted to find a way to make this popular genre serve revolutionary rather than conservative politics. They introduced basic Marxist notions of class struggle, capitalism, and imperialism to sharpen the vague images of good and evil that abounded in classic melodramas. But, as Robert Lang demonstrates in his fine study of American film melodrama, the genre demands drastic simplification and stereotyping. The entrenched operations of melodrama "turn on repetition and ritual." "As a temporal medium, the narrative requirements of which compressed real time," Lang observes, "films learned how to signify as much as possible by means of condensation, displacement, and new codes peculiar to the medium and the form."[34] Leftists may have thought they were bringing the May Fourth tradition of Marxism to the Chinese cinema, but in many "May Fourth" films of the thirties and forties—movies that are still commonly referred to as works of "social realism"—Marxist ideas were swallowed up by the melodramatic genre and reduced to stereotypes and caricatures.[35]

Marxism, for instance, has a great deal to say about what motivates capitalists and imperialists. One might even say that it is crucial for any self-respecting Marxist to possess a sophisticated and nuanced understanding of what motivates the bourgeoisie. But the mode of excess has great difficulty explaining what motivates evil that is so utterly extreme and sadistic, or, for that matter, virtue that is so masochistic. There are no logical ways to account for a villain that is so profoundly diabolical. But as Brooks points out, "evil in the world of melodrama does not need justification."[36] It is enough to know that it exists and must be combatted. The audience does not need to know much and, melodramatists often assume, does not want to know much about the details of its origins. The purpose of melodrama is to arouse passions. Original May Fourth Marxism had to be distorted beyond recognition if it was going to be useful to melodramatists.

Xie Jin and "May Fourth" Melodrama in the Eighties

The official biography of Xie Jin (b. 1923), without a doubt the most important Chinese filmmaker of the post-1949 period in terms of audience appeal, confidently states that he is "a realist artist."[37] Actually, his work has very little to do with realism. Xie Jin is one of the most renowned melodramatists in Chinese film history, a man whose films are clearly linked to the "May Fourth" tradition of the thirties and forties. Although he is normally discussed within the framework of filmmaking in the socialist People's Republic, Xie received his basic training in stagecraft and filmmaking in the Republican forties. During the war he studied drama in a Nationalist school and did production work with Hong Shen, Chen Liting (b. 1910), and other leftists in Chongqing. After the war his former teacher Wu Renzhi, who began making film melodramas in the early forties, got Xie a job as an assistant director at the Datong Film Company in Shanghai. At Datong Xie worked closely with such veterans as Tian Han, Zheng Xiaoqiu (b. 1910), and Hong Shen.

Xie Jin made a number of important films in the fifties and sixties, following his conversion to Marxism, but the purpose of this essay is not to offer a detailed discussion of the fate of the melodramatic mode in the pre–Cultural Revolution and Cultural Revolution years. It would be misleading, however, to suggest that the advent of the socialist realist and Stalinist modes in China in 1949 spelled the end of melodramatic representation. Nothing could be further from the truth.

But in the thirty years between 1949 and 1979 melodrama clearly did not play the same critical role, in terms of politics and society, that it had played in the 1932–1937 and 1946–1949 periods and therefore does not belong to the "May Fourth" film tradition discussed here. "May Fourth" melodramas specialized in the criticism of contemporary society. Their criticisms may have had little in common with realism, but they were criticisms that subverted state authority nonetheless. The most memorable film melodramas of the fifties and sixties, by contrast, including Xie Jin's *Red Detachment of Women* (*Hongse niangzi jun,* 1960) and *Stage Sisters* (*Wutai jiemei,* 1964), did not focus on the new socialist society.[38] In thematic terms, film melodramas of the early socialist era were bogged down in the portrayal of the old Republican period. It was a propagandistic victor's cinema. Now that the Nationalists had been soundly defeated on the battlefield, the state-owned cinema industry could deal with the Republican era any way it wanted. The purpose of melodrama was now to legitimize the new rule of the Communist Party by portraying Republican times as hell on earth.

Film melodramas of the thirties and forties are more interesting because they confronted forces of evil that were very much alive and kicking. These melodramas had an explicit contemporary relevance, whereas new socialist treatments of the wicked Republican era felt more like guided museum tours. One of the strong appeals of such classic melodramas as *Small Toys* and *Heavenly Spring Dream* was that, while they identified and confronted villainy, and in terms that were consistent with an elementary Marxist viewpoint, it was not compulsory that virtue and justice win out by the end of the picture. In the melodramas Xie Jin made upon his graduation in the early fifties from the Political Research Institute of North China Revolutionary University, by contrast, the structure is always the same. First, the forces of evil (Guomindang, landlords, traitors, Japanese) sadistically torment virtuous people (masochistic poor peasants, women, children, and old people). The Communist Party then routs the enemies of humankind and delivers their innocent victims to the promised land of socialism.

The point is that Chinese filmmakers in the fifties and sixties broke with the "May Fourth" tradition of the thirties and forties by failing to make family melodramas that criticized contemporary social conditions and thus subverted state authority. Chinese filmmakers and the Chinese film audience slowly but surely began to lose touch with the "May Fourth" cinematic tradition. Classic leftist melodramas of the thirties and forties were rarely shown. Socialist society itself could not be subjected to the direct and highly exaggerated critical reviews typical of the melodramatic genre. To the extent that new film melodramas discussed problems in socialist society, the problems had to be blamed on remnant evils (class enemies, bourgeois ideology, imperialism) associated with the Republican era.[39] Prohibited from looking for evil within the socialist system itself, self-respecting melodramatists were unable to play their proper role. I do not mean to suggest that filmmakers failed completely to produce works that pointed to the weaknesses of the socialist system. But, interestingly, most of the critical films that were made, such as Lu Ban's *Before the New Director Arrives* (*Xin juzhang daolai zhi qian*, 1956) and Xie Jin's own *Big Li, Young Li, and Old Li* (*Da Li, Xiao Li, he Lao Li,* 1962), were satirical comedies, not melodramas.

It was not until Chinese society passed through the ordeal of the Cultural Revolution that the stage was set for the revival of melodramatic representation in Chinese films. The distinguished critic Shao Mujun is certainly right when he insists that the films made by Xie Jin after 1979 are "a contemporary expression" of the "tradition of Chinese progressive films which began to take shape in the 1930s, and became more and more mature in the 1940s." Shao refrains from using the term *melodrama,* preferring instead to perpetuate the idea of Xie Jin as a "realist." But even Shao, an arch-defender of the "Xie Jin style," resorts to the vocabulary of melodrama when he says that Xie Jin presses "close to reality by praising the good and denouncing the evil." "In the films made in the first three decades of New China," Shao observes, "this fine tradition vanished."[40]

Western observers, myself included, have shown the greatest amount of critical interest in the so-called Fifth Generation films of Chen Kaige, Tian Zhuangzhuang, Huang Jianxin, and others who, in their treatments of Republican and socialist China, thoroughly reject the melodramatic approach. By the mid-eighties many of these young deconstructionist filmmakers were openly (and naively) proclaiming that the Xie Jin era was over. There is no question that the most creative artists to emerge on the Chinese film scene in the post-Mao period were the 1982 graduates of the Beijing Film Institute. Still, from the perspective of the early nineties, it must be acknowledged that in many respects the most significant trend of the eighties was the amazing revival of "May Fourth" melodramas. This conclusion is based, in part, on the behavior of the film audience, whose numbers rose from ten billion to eighteen billion between 1982 and 1988.[41] Melodrama, more than any other genre, positioned itself to meet the psychological needs of an emotionally drained and politically battered urban film audience. Xie Jin was the leader of the revival.

Xie Jin made so many award-winning family melodramas in the 1980s that one hardly knows where to begin. *The Legend of Tianyun Mountain* (*Tianyun shan chuanqi*, 1980), *The Herdsman* (*Mumaren*, 1982), and *Garlands at the Foot of the Mountain* (*Gaoshan xia de huahuan*, 1984) are all excellent examples of critical melodramas that resonate with the nearly forgotten Republican era "May Fourth" tradition.[42] But Xie Jin's crowning achievement, released at a time when he was under enormous pressure from conservative political forces within the Communist Party and from young filmmakers and critics who were contemptuous of the Xie Jin mode, was *Hibiscus Town* (*Furongzhen*, 1987). Far from being a symbol of the end of the Xie Jin era, *Hibiscus Town* was selected by film professionals in January 1988 for first-place honors in four categories, including best picture, at the seventh annual Jinji Film Award ceremony and was also chosen by film fans for first place in four categories, including best picture, in the tenth annual Hundred Flowers film competition sponsored by *Popular Cinema* magazine. In the first ten Hundred Flower competitions, Xie Jin films were voted best picture of the year five times by ordinary filmgoers.[43]

The novel by Gu Hua, upon which Xie Jin's film is based, is not an especially distinguished work of fiction. But in Xie Jin's condensed and dramatically heightened telling, the story moved millions of people and, like all his films of the eighties, provided an opportunity for mass catharsis that no single work of fiction could provide. Melodramas of the Republican era, including "May Fourth" films, helped ordinary people deal with wrenching anxieties produced by the collapse of the traditional Chinese moral universe. Xie Jin's melodramas of the eighties were also produced in a context of profound cultural crisis, but this time it was the new socialist culture and morality that had taken root in the 1950s that were in crisis.[44]

Hibiscus Town opens in 1963 on the eve of the vindictive and destructive socialist education movement. The representative of the first polar extreme, goodness and virtue, is "hard-working" and "honest" Hu Yuyin, who also happens to be the "most beautiful woman" in town. Like the enterprising heroine of *Small Toys,* this symbol of virtue is vulnerable and innocent. The Chinese word *yu,* which appears in her name, means jade, a symbol of purity. Her privately run outdoor bean-curd stall is the most popular and lively place in Furongzhen. The picturesque setting of colorful people, cobblestone streets, and quaint houses seems idyllic.

It soon becomes apparent that something is dreadfully wrong with this pleasant scene. For one thing, Hu's marriage is passionless. Her husband is a good and simple person, but like Ding Jianhua in *Heavenly Spring Dream,* he is an ineffectual and timid shadow of a man. They have a sterile and childless marriage of convenience in the socialist promised land. Her true love, a lost love, is the easygoing but virtuous local Party secretary. The couple were engaged at one point, but he was advised by heartless and calculating Party elders to break it off, lest he ruin his chances for a political career by marrying a peddler who has shaky class credentials. He then enters into a loveless marriage with a mean-spirited, grasping harpy.

There are other indications that the socialist system of class labeling is in serious disarray. On the one hand, a small and pathetic group of people, who have been branded "bad elements" by the Party, look rather harmless. On the other hand, a disheveled young man named Wang Qiushe, who begs for free meals at Hu's stall, is identified as a former poor peasant activist in the local Party-led land reform movement. Wang is a parasite who dreads hard work. Rather than sweat to earn an honest living, Wang sold to Hu Yuyin an old house that had been given to him by the Party.

Suddenly, a Party work team, headed by a cunning and vicious woman named Li Guoxiang, the primary representative of the second polar extreme, evil and villainy, shows up to implement the socialist education movement. She is shocked to find the former poor peasant activist Wang Qiushe still living in poverty, while the private entrepreneur Hu Yuyin, who nourishes the people with her noodles and smiles, is celebrating the completion of a new house. "The rich get richer," she hisses, "while the poor get poorer."

All the local people are forced to attend a mass political meeting one dark night. Li Guoxiang frightens everyone by charging that the folksy old cadres, loved and respected by the common people, have neglected class struggle. Crazy Qin, an innocuous local bookworm who was branded as a rightist in 1957, is brought up on stage and publicly humiliated. There are only two choices, she rants: either this class enemy "stinks" or he is "fragrant." There can be no middle ground.

To save himself, the young Party secretary betrays his former lover, Hu Yuyin. "In this world," he moans, "you've got to get others or they'll get you!" In rapid succession, Hu is declared a new rich peasant, her home and money are confiscated (though she has done nothing illegal), and her husband dies after attempting to kill the wicked Li Guoxiang. For the next three years Hu works alongside the other political lepers who are forced to sweep the streets before dawn every day.

When the disastrous Cultural Revolution strikes in 1966, local despot Li Guoxiang falls from power for a brief time and is made to stand alongside unsavory "bad elements." Before long, however, she is cleared and immediately forges a dirty political and sexual alliance with Wang Qiushe, the worthless, poor peasant buffoon.

Meanwhile, a spiritually healthy bond of respect and love develops between the still-radiant Hu Yuyin and Crazy Qin, the compassionate rightist who turns out not to be crazy at all. But their chance for happiness is crushed when Hu becomes pregnant. First, the sadistic leaders torment the couple by denying their request to get married, and then Crazy Qin is sentenced to ten years in prison. The torture continues as Hu Yuyin, late in her pregnancy, is still forced to sweep snow off the frozen streets. Finally, a sexually impotent but kindly old cadre who hates the dastardly (and childless) Li Guoxiang rushes pitiful Hu Yuyin to a military hospital, where she gives birth to a healthy son she calls Jun (army).

Ten years later, in 1979, it appears that evil has been vanquished, although the process by which it has been confronted and driven out is never revealed. Hu Yuyin's house and money are returned to her, Qin (now her husband) is released from prison, and the family is united. Naturally, they reopen her lively and popular bean-curd

The virtuous (and pregnant) Hu Yuyin, a fragrant blossom that attracts hornets as well as butterflies, is cruelly tormented by vicious Communist operatives in *Hibiscus Town* (*Furongzhen*, d. Xie Jin, 1987, China Film Studio, Shanghai). Photo: China Film Import and Export (L.A.), Inc.

stall. But, at the same time, the degenerate Li Guoxiang has some-how been promoted to a higher office. Wang Qiushe, reduced to the status of village idiot, runs about ominously shouting, "A movement is starting! A movement is starting!" People of virtue, we are warned, must remain on guard.

In technical terms Xie Jin is every bit as careful as his Hollywood counterparts. *Hibiscus Town* is a slick production that meets and in some respects surpasses international standards. But at heart it is still a melodrama that is linked to the classic nonleftist and leftist melo-dramas that were so popular in the Republican era. The prerelease publicity for *Hibiscus Town* could have been written in the thirties for films like *Small Toys*. For example, *Shanghai Film Studio Pictorial*, mak-ing unabashed use of the rhetoric of excess, told its readers: "Hu Yuyin, a natural and fragrant hibiscus flower rooted in the good earth of Furongzhen, attracts many beautiful butterflies, but she also attracts ferocious and evil hornets. Battered by countless storms and icy chills, the petals of the hibiscus blossom wither and fall. For what seems like an eternity, this beautiful and kind-hearted rural lass endures an unjust fate of ridicule and devastation."[45]

Like *Small Toys*, *Hibiscus Town* is located in the vibrant rural heart-land of China and involves a pure, innocent, and defenseless woman (the symbol of China) whose family is ruthlessly persecuted by a source of evil that is alien to everything that is Chinese. The polar-ization between virtue and villainy is absolute; no middle course is allowed. Pain and suffering are inflicted with sadistic pleasure and endured by their victims in a passive, even masochistic, fashion. The narrative is condensed, heightened, and exaggerated in a way that converts the banalities of daily family life into dramatic and highly significant events that symbolize the central moral confrontation of the era. The unspeakably sinister Li Guoxiang arrives in Furongzhen at precisely the moment when the innocent Hu Yuyin is celebrating the completion of her new house. The heavens open and torrential rains fall to earth at precisely the moment her defenseless husband is sentenced to ten years. A deeply rooted system of melodramatic signification is used by Xie Jin to identify the difference between darkness and light and thereby ease the anxieties of a mass audience that has been severely shaken and thrown into profound moral confusion by various cultural calamities. The melodramatic mode provides easy and comforting answers to difficult and complex questions. It offers moral clarity at a time when nothing seems clear. But by personalizing evil, the film leaves the impression that everything would be fine if only the "evil" people were removed from power and replaced by people of "virtue."

In spite of Shao Mujun's assertion that Xie Jin's post–Cultural Revolution melodramas are a "contemporary expression" of the "fine tradition" of critical filmmaking in the thirties and forties, it is clear that Xie Jin's recent work departs from the leftist "May Fourth" tradition in one highly significant way. To the extent that the social and political sources of evil and villainy are established at all in "May Fourth" melodramas, they are associated with the agents of feudalism, capitalism, and imperialism. Similarly, virtue and innocence are invariably associated with the poor and oppressed classes of workers and peasants. The unspoken assumption of many of these classic films was that an anticapitalist, working people's socialist revolution would expel evil and save China. In Xie Jin's *Hibiscus Town*, however, this familiar conception is turned on its head. It is the demonic agents of the Communist Party and their poor peasant running dogs who represent evil, whereas hard-working entrepreneurs and "counterrevolutionary rightists" represent virtue and purity. Thus "May Fourth"–type melodramas were originally designed in the thirties and forties to introduce simplified socialist politics, but Xie Jin's films are, in some important ways, designed to raise serious questions about the type of socialism that unfolded in China after 1949.

Chinese melodramatists like Xie Jin could get away with this type of blasphemous representation in the eighties because it was consistent with the Party's own self-serving desire to identify the Cultural Revolution as an aberration. But Xie Jin's melodramas pushed far beyond the officially sanctioned condemnation of the Cultural Revolution. Xie and other melodramatists often begin with the Cultural Revolution in their films, but go on to lambaste the forced collectivization of agriculture, the antirightist movement, the Great Leap Forward, and the socialist education movement. Xie Jin never says that the Communist Party is hopeless and must be overthrown, but the viewer is left wondering whether the Party did anything right after 1949. It is for this reason that Xie Jin, a veteran Party member himself, is so disliked and distrusted by such Party elders as Deng Liqun and Hu Qiaomu.

Once Xie Jin and other loyal Party members began to use the popular melodramatic format to review the record of the Party in the entire post-1949 period, they became prisoners of the genre. The logic of melodramatic sensationalism dictates that the Party must be viewed as either good or evil. No matter how many unjustly persecuted and kindly old cadres and Party members are worked into the story and no matter how many happy endings are tacked on at the end, as they are in *The Legend of Tianyun Mountain* and *The Herdsman,* Xie Jin's films still assign the villain's role to the Party and thereby seriously subvert its prestige and repution—just as such "May Fourth" films as *Small Toys* and *Heavenly Spring Dream* subverted Guomindang authority.

But there is another, and more important, sense in which Xie Jin is trapped by the melodramatic mode.[46] Melodrama may be appealing because it reveals to the audience the highly personalized human faces of virtue and evil and allows the audience to observe both the depraved intrigues of villainy and the pathetic suffering of its innocent and helpless victims. But aside from arousing righteous indignation, melodrama simply does not take its fanatically loyal audience very far. *Hibiscus Town* and Xie Jin's other melodramas, like their forerunners in the thirties and forties, never tell the audience what motivates evil; they never explain why evil is evil. Evil simply exists and must be struggled against. Furongzhen, like the village portrayed in *Small Toys,* is a happy and tranquil place. Suddenly, and without explanation, the vile Li Guoxiang comes along to inflict pain and misery. Just as suddenly, the Cultural Revolution ends, Hu Yuyin's property and husband are returned, and the town seems tranquil once again. The role of the victims of evil is to suffer and sacrifice rather than resist. The victims do not seem to have a hand in their own salvation. Because Xie Jin's political melodramas, like "May Fourth" melodramas of the Republican period, focus so narrowly on the family unit, it is impossible for him to say anything significant about social and political forces that are at work outside the family.[47] This is why some scholars regard the family melodrama as an essentially petit-bourgeois form of art. Evil gets the attention of the audience when it can be observed bringing pain to the individuals who constitute a family unit. It is not necessary to know precisely why evil has appeared on the scene and why it works the way it does; neither is it necessary to know precisely how evil will be vanquished.

Xie Jin's films do a great deal to undermine the moral legitimacy of the Communist Party. To use the words of Shao Mujun, they "arouse emotions."[48] But it is exactly for this reason that Xie Jin has been attacked so vigorously by younger filmmakers who insist that it is time to move beyond sensational, melodramatic representation. Life is just not as simple as it appears in Xie Jin's films. One does not learn much about how the system "really" works by viewing films like *Hibiscus Town*. Chen Kaige's *Yellow Earth* (*Huang tudi*, 1984) demolishes the myth of the idyllic and harmonious rural village that is consistently portrayed in melodramas of the thirties, forties, and eighties. Huang Jianxin's *Black Cannon Incident* (*Hei pao shijian*, 1986) and *Transmigration* (*Lunhui*, 1989) forcefully reject the notion that absolute good and absolute evil exist anywhere in China. Where Xie Jin's melodramas deny the middle ground, Huang Jianxin's postsocialist films insist that the Chinese social and political arena is composed of nothing but middle ground. No one is pure or innocent.[49] The young filmmakers are interested in subtlety, nuance, and ambiguity, and that is why Western scholars are attracted by their works. Xie Jin is interested in the confrontation between clear moral absolutes. Western observers prefer Fifth Generation directors, but the undeniable fact is they have practically no audience in China. This is why the authorities never felt politically threatened by them. Xie Jin, the veteran melodramatist who sees the Chinese world in basic Manichaean terms of darkness and light, is the one who has the audience. "When people watch Xie Jin's films," Shao Mujun observed, "they don't have to rack their brains to think."[50]

It is highly ironic that backward-looking officials in the Chinese government have spent so much time hounding Xie Jin and subjecting his films to political censorship. The Communist Party comes off badly in his films because he insists upon using the exaggerated melodramatic format. In reality, Xie Jin is no dissident. He is a loyal

Party member allied to an entity we might loosely define as the reform wing of the Party. There is no way to know right now if the massacres of June 1989 caused Xie to rethink his political views. The films he made before the massacres reveal that he advocates a fairly thorough reform of the Communist Party and socialist system, but not their overthrow. His films reject the idea that the Cultural Revolution was an aberration. To save itself and to save China, the Party must abandon the Stalinist and Maoist modes of operation that caused so much needless suffering in the 1949–1979 period.

More specifically, what Xie Jin opposes more than anything else is class struggle and mass mobilization politics. When one looks beyond the rhetoric of *Hibiscus Town*, the most politically daring of all Xie Jin's family melodramas, one does not find a plea for multiparty or pluralistic politics. Xie Jin's critics (and some of his defenders!) say that he is a Confucian Marxist. That is, he believes there is nothing wrong with a one-party state, so long as it is an enlightened, benevolent despotism that renounces cruel class-struggle politics. Xie Jin disputes the view that there were significant numbers of class enemies of socialism in China after 1949. Entrepreneurs like Hu Yuyin and intellectuals like Crazy Qin are valued members of society. The Party, Xie believes, should be worrying more about allowing the various social classes to play their proper role and fostering multi-class harmony in China than about creating a classless utopia.

Reflections on the "May Fourth" Tradition of Chinese Filmmaking

This essay began by asking whether one can speak of a "May Fourth" tradition of Chinese filmmaking and whether Chinese films of the post–Cultural Revolution eighties have anything in common with that tradition. My view is that we can, indeed, speak of a "May Fourth" tradition, so long as we carefully define it to mean the marriage between classic melodrama and elementary Marxism that took place in the 1932–1937 period and resurfaced in the 1946–1949 period. The union resulted in the birth of a popular tradition of critical and independent cinema that saw the crisis of contemporary China in terms of a spectacular moral struggle between the forces of darkness and light. But the partners in this marriage were not equal. The genre dominated the relationship and distorted the "May Fourth" politics. Still, the result was acceptable to the left. Whereas the political implications of classical film melodramas were, at best, unclear, "May Fourth" films implicitly subverted Nationalist rule and embraced the often vaguely defined cause of revolution.

The "May Fourth" tradition of filmmaking disappeared in the years between 1949 and 1979. This powerful "mode of excessive representation," which specialized in identifying degenerate villains who were responsible for the suffering of the innocent in contemporary society, was not tolerated by the architects of the new socialist China. Measured and friendly criticism was one thing, but melodramatic representation was anything but measured.

The Cultural Revolution catastrophe opened the door for the phenomenal revival of the forgotten "May Fourth" tradition of critical melodramatic filmmaking. It was finally possible not only to talk about socialist society in terms of darkness and light, but to identify the Party as the agent of darkness. But, once again, the genre overwhelmed and ultimately distorted the well-intentioned reform Marxism of popular melodramatists like Xie Jin. A cinema that represents Hu Yuyin, the heroine of *Hibiscus Town*, as a radiant flower that attracts both butterflies and hornets can provide opportunities for mass catharsis and thereby ease mass anxieties, but cannot hope to unravel the confusing complexities and frustrating ambiguities of Chinese life.

Still, the melodramatic imagination is deeply rooted in Chinese life. It is a politically flexible mode that somehow manages to adapt and endure. This became apparent in the aftermath of June 4, 1989, the latest in a long series of modern Chinese political and cultural crises. It is obvious that the battered socialist state has no intention in the foreseeable future of allowing loyal but reform-minded artists like Xie Jin to continue to make critical films that subject the Party and class struggle to the glaring light of melodramatic representation. It is equally clear that Deng Xiaoping and his followers have decided to make the melodramatic mode serve their own political purposes. As they tell the story, "a tiny handful" of thugs, hooligans, rioters, and bourgeois parasites, all of them traitors in league with foreign imperialism, instigated a violent and immoral rebellion.

Using the melodramatic rhetoric of excess that has become so common in twentieth-century Chinese political and social discourse, Deng Xiaoping told martial law troops that "We should never forget how cruel our enemies are. For them we should not have an iota of forgiveness." The "dregs of society" were opposed, of course, by virtuous and selfless Party loyalists and the heroes of the People's Liberation Army. Using concise language to refer specifically to the polar extremes of right and wrong, Deng said, "The PLA losses were great, but this enabled us to win the support of the people and made those who cannot tell right from wrong *(shi fei bu qing)* change their viewpoint." "If tanks were used to roll over people," Deng explained, "this would have created a confusion between right and wrong *(shi fei bu ming)* among the people nationwide."[51] In the aftermath of the massacres Chinese publications scrambled to reveal the "true" nature of the saboteurs. Fang Lizhi was described as shameless "scum," Yan Jiaqi as a "contemptible scoundrel," and Wuer Kaixi as an unprincipled "pariah."[52]

By referring to such patently absurd characterizations, I do not mean to trivialize the tragedy that struck China in 1989. This type of melodramatic sensationalism is a familiar ingredient of what Joseph Esherick has referred to as Chinese political theater.[53] Jiang Qing, Lin Biao, Liu Shaoqi, and Deng Xiaoping himself have all been cast, in turn, as agents of darkness. The names change, but the melodramatic conception of the workings of the Chinese universe remains the same.

The problem with Xie Jin's popular melodramas is that they are hostages of a genre that severely limits the imagination. One can easily believe that Xie Jin is sickened by Deng Xiaoping's interpretation of recent Chinese history. Sooner or later Xie, or someone like him, will have a chance to tell the "true" story of the savage confrontation between darkness and light that occurred in spring 1989. Millions of distraught viewers will weep tears of blood as they observe the suffering of the innocent. And they will express boundless joy when the agents of evil are suddenly and miraculously routed on screen and replaced by leaders of "true" virtue.

12 | Male Narcissism and National Culture: Subjectivity in Chen Kaige's *King of the Children*

The Detour

How many [teachers] (the majority) do not even begin to suspect the "work" the system (which is bigger than they are and crushes them) forces them to do, or worse, put all their heart and ingenuity into performing it with the most advanced awareness . . . So little do they suspect it that their own devotion contributes to the maintenance and nourishment of this ideological representation of the School.
Louis Althusser

The history of the "educated" ought to be materialistically presented as a function of and in close relation to a "history of uneducation."
Walter Benjamin

Like living things, words and phrases undergo fates inconceivable at their moments of birth. In contemporary Chinese writings, especially of the kind that we encounter in the media—newspaper articles, reviews in nonacademic journals, and popular political discourses—we run, from time to time, across this phrase, which is used to suggest the determinacy of hope: *lu shi ren zou chu lai de* (roads are made by men). Because of the phrase's popularized nature, I have no need to cite specific examples. Those who read regularly in Chinese would recognize what I am saying immediately. The by now idiomatic nature of this phrase shows us how an expression of hope can be standardized through mass usage.

The phrase originated in a passage from the ending of Lu Xun's "Guxiang" (My Old Home, 1921). Among other things, this is a story that tells of the changed relationship between the narrator and his childhood friend, Runtu, a member of the servant class. Once equals in the world of children's play, the two adult men's reencounter is shaped by a class consciousness that becomes painful for the narrator. Even though, on first seeing Runtu again, the narrator keeps to the old familial appellation *Runtu ge* (older brother Runtu), Runtu addresses him from the place of a servant: *laoye* (old master). As in all of Lu Xun's fiction, the gap between the intellectual narrator, who belongs to the educated class, and the oppressed "others" who make up the contents of his storytelling intensifies as the narrative progresses. In "My Old Home," this gap is "filled" at the end by a reflection on hope. Thinking of hope, the narrator becomes aware of its idolatrous nature. Doesn't his reliance on "hope" make him more similar to Runtu than he first imagined? The difference, he writes, is perhaps simply that between an accessible idol and an intangible one:

> The access of hope made me suddenly afraid. When Runtu had asked for the incense-burner and candlesticks I had laughed up my sleeve at him, to think that he was still worshipping idols and would never put them out of his mind. Yet what I now called hope was no more than an idol I had created myself. The only difference was that what he desired was close at hand, while what I desired was less easily realized.[1]

After asserting the equality between himself and a member of the lower class at the point of his departure from the place in which Runtu is probably stuck for life, the narrator concludes his tale with the passage on hope that subsequently gave rise to the idiomatic phrase "roads are made by men": "I thought: hope cannot be said to exist, nor can it be said not to exist. It is just like roads across the earth. For actually the earth had no roads to begin with, but when many men pass one way, a road is made."[2]

Why is Lu Xun's passage instructive for a discussion of the connections between early-twentieth-century Chinese literature and contemporary Chinese culture? Thematically, Lu Xun's works stage the problems that continue to haunt Chinese intellectuals: the impossibility of effective social change, the unbridgeable gap between the educated class and the "people," and the fantastical nature of any form of "hope." What comes across in this passage is the awareness that hope is at best a form of wager. Hope is, by nature, indeterminate, but people can, if there are large numbers of them, consciously steer it in one direction. Lu Xun's text itself, however, does not do that. Instead it remains, in a way that is ironic with respect to the positive interpretation that has been imposed upon it since, in a state that can be referred to in Chinese as *wuke naihe, wuke wubuke, wuning liangke.* The text's originary indeterminacy, in other words, is what *enables* its subsequent politicized appropriation. The interpretive production of the affirmative phrase "roads are made by men" is thus itself a historical materialization of the arbitrary process of road making that Lu Xun describes: as more people pass one way, a road is made.

A return to the relationship between the elusiveness of an "originary" textual moment and its eventual honed version indicates a way of understanding the notion of the "people" and the "mass" in political processes. One could say that the power of the people or the mass lies in the form of an indeterminacy. Precisely because they are undecided, they can go one way or another. For something—history—to happen, it would take a forcing—an accident perhaps—in a definite direction. The new direction as such, however, always retains its originally arbitrary character.

Lu Xun's tactical understanding of the arbitrary nature of politics, though not directly stated, is implied in the way "hope" always appears as an enigmatic figure in his fictional texts.[3] Because it is always *to be* decided—or arbitrated—hope cannot be known for certain in the present. We can now understand why there are often what appear to be inexplicable shifts in narrative moods in his stories. Marston Anderson comments that such narrative shifts have led his critics to classify his work in two apparently contradictory fashions, as satiric realist or as reminiscent and lyrical.[4] This contradiction is a politically truthful one. In the subsequent reappraisals and criticisms of the writings from the 1920s and 1930s launched by the Chinese Communists, such political truthfulness was threatening because it did not cooperate or conform with the absolute clarity of direction laid down by the Party. One could say that the orthodox Communist criticism of textual elusiveness such as Lu Xun's implies this question: If there is hope, why aren't you writers more assertive? A more programmatic, indeed official, representation of the people and of hope therefore increasingly came to replace the uncompromised incisiveness in Lu Xun's perception. However, the issues embedded in the "making of roads" do not disappear. Although the short-story form became impermissible with the new social orthodoxy in the decades after Lu Xun's death, the problems it poses, precisely because they pertain to fundamental questions of morality, "raise their head every time there is a political thaw."[5]

As a figure of wager, hope can, I think, be redefined through subjectivity. *Subjectivity* is one of those "politically incorrect" words that conjure up notions of "bourgeois idealism" for orthodox Marxist critics. Terry Eagleton, for instance, disapproves of it from the viewpoint of a Western European, supposedly post–Althusserian Marxist literary criticism, as a category tainted with "intransigent individualism": "it remains the case that the subject of semiotic/psychoanalytic theory is essentially the *nuclear* subject."[6] While I disagree with Eagleton, I find his statement useful in helping to clarify the Chinese situation. In Chinese communist scholarship, it is common to hear the same kind of ideological objection to the "subjective," which is mapped onto such expressions as *zhuguan, weixin zhuyi,* and so on. In a period in which cognition is intertwined with issues of politics, and in which creative energies have to be channeled toward fighting for the national cause, the literary forms that can be viewed as paradigms of explorations of subjectivity, such as biographies, autobiographies, diaries, first-person narratives, and narratives that deal explicitly with issues of sexuality, tend to live brief lives and remain subordinated to the more conventionally "public" concerns of history and realism.

If, on the other hand, we dislodge subjectivity from the narrow "nuclear" mode in which Eagleton puts it, and instead understand it in terms of the material relationships among human beings as participants in a society—relationships that are in turn mediated by the collective cultural activities of speaking, reading, and writing—then it is an issue that is as forcefully present in modern Chinese literature and culture as it is in the West, even if it is not named as such.

I suggest that the predominant subjectivity that surfaces in the May Fourth period (mid-1910s to around 1930) is not so much a dense psychic "self," impenetrable and solipsistic, as it is a relationship among the writer, his or her object of narration, and the reader. In political terms, this is the relationship among Chinese intellectuals, the Chinese national culture, and "the people." In the writing of fiction, this relationship always presents itself as a question rather than a solution: How do we write (construct images of our culture) in order to relate to "the people"—*especially those who are socially inferior and powerless, since they are the ones who constitute the "mass" of the nation?* As such, subjectivity, even when it appears in the most "subjective" or "privatized" forms (as, for instance, in Yü Dafu's writings), is incomprehensible apart from its fundamental implication in the question of national culture. At the same time, it is also this tenacious relation with national culture that makes the differences between intellectuals and the masses (differences generated by the activity of literary production) a continual source of tension between Chinese intellectuals and the Party state, as both hold claims to the indeterminate "mass," for whom they both want to speak.[7]

If we rethink the history of modern Chinese literature along these lines, that is, if we regard "history" as a matter of the contending claims made by the state and Chinese intellectuals on "the Chinese people"—a figure as enigmatic as hope itself—then it becomes necessary to ask how "the Chinese people" are represented. Through what kinds of aesthetic displacements and idealizations are they "constituted"?

Typically, "the Chinese people" are displaced onto figures of the powerless. Hence, I think, the large numbers of social inferiors who appear in the texts of modern Chinese literature. Literature is no longer, in the modern world, about the lives of emperors; rather, it is about the oppressed classes—the wretched of the earth. Other than the positivistic view that these are "realistic portrayals" of mod-

ern history, what else can we say about such frequent—indeed epochal—representations of the unprivileged? In other words, why do
the conception and construction of a modern national culture—if
writing in the postimperialistic Third World is in part about that—
take the form of an *aesthetic* preoccupation with the figures of the
powerless? What does it say in terms of the things that we have been
talking about—hope, the making of roads, and subjectivity?

Of all the figures of the powerless, the child is at center stage. One
would need to include here not only stories about children, whether
from the lower or the upper classes, but also the autobiographical
narratives in which Chinese writers look back to their childhood as
a source for their current literary production. (The list of writers
here is long: Lu Xun, Ba Jin, Bing Xin, Ding Ling, Ye Shengtao, Guo
Moruo, Xiao Hong, Shen Congwen, Ling Shuhua, Luo Shu, Zhu
Ziqing, Xu Dishan, and many others.) It is as if adult thinking about
China and the Chinese people always takes the route of memory in
which the writing self connects with the culture at large through a
specific form of "othering"—the presumably not-yet-acculturated figure of the child. In this light, the continuity among Chinese intellectuals from the May Fourth period to the present could be traced in
another one of Lu Xun's enigmatic narrative endings, that of
"Kuangren riji" (The Diary of a Madman, 1918): "*Jiujiu haizi . . .*"
(Save the children . . .). At Yan'an in 1942, Mao Zedong would end
a speech on art and literature with a couplet about children from
Lu Xun, to which he supplied his own politicized interpretation:

> This couplet from a poem by Lu Hsun should be our motto:
>
> > Fierce-browed, I coolly defy a thousand pointing fingers,
> > Head-bowed, like a willing ox I serve the children.
>
> The "thousand pointing fingers" are our enemies, and we will never
> yield to them, no matter how ferocious they are. The "children"
> here symbolize the proletariat and the masses. All Communists, all
> revolutionaries, all revolutionary literary and art workers should
> learn from the example of Lu Xun and be "oxen" for the proletar-
> iat and the masses, bending their backs to the task until their dying
> day.[8]

Mao's interpretation empowers the figure of the powerless child by renaming it as the proletariat and the masses. Ultimately, it is by giving this enigmatic figure, "the Chinese people," a specific politicized shape that the Party state succeeded in mobilizing popular sympathies. The "powerless" is thus turned around representationally, and becomes the means to construct national culture on a "concrete" basis. The utilitarian nature of this process of empowerment is familiar to all of us. The "masses," because they are "powerless," should, ideally speaking, be users of intellectuals, who are now at their *service*.

But service here clusters around another figure—the ox/cow. Lu Xun uses this figure in a such a way as to recall not only China's agrarian origins, but also the familiar and familial process, traceable to images in classical art and poetry, of the affectionate playing between adults and children in which adults act as toy cows on which children ride. The image of "intellectuals becoming oxen for the masses" is thus intertwined with the realm of meanings associated with children, parents, kinship, and genealogy—a realm of meanings that Mao removed—or at least shifted away—from Lu Xun's couplet in order to consolidate his own analysis of Chinese society and its need for revolution in terms of "class" and "class struggle."[9] In ways that exceed Mao's restrictive political purpose, however, Lu Xun's image stages the philosophical struggles between the state and intellectuals over the "Chinese people" in terms of *reproduction* that continue to this day.

The components of this image—intellectuals, oxen, the masses—are what make up Chen Kaige's *Haizi wang* (King of the Children; Xian Film Studio, 1987), a film based on the novel of the same title by Ah Cheng (1984).[10] The story of *King of the Children* takes place in the post–Cultural Revolution period in a rural area. Lao Gan, the narrator and protagonist, is posted to a school after spending years in a production unit. Ah Cheng's story focuses on Lao Gan's relationship with his young students and the changes he introduces in their methods of learning. Before he came, the students had "learned" by copying texts their former teachers had copied onto the blackboard. Seeing how futile this is, Lao Gan teaches them how to read, character by character, and then proceeds to teach them composition. One student, Wang Fu, gradually emerges as the most outstanding one through his hard work. His special relationship with Lao Gan prompts the latter, as he is dismissed from the school at the end, to leave behind for Wang Fu the only available Chinese dictionary, which the students revere as "the teacher of the teacher."

Both the novel and the film draw attention to children as that class of social inferiors that continues to fascinate modern Chinese intellectuals. What distinguishes the children in *King of the Children* is that they pose a specific question about national culture: the status of education. They are thus not simply members—to use the psychoanalytic categories of Jacques Lacan—of a presymbolic infantile state, but already participants in a major social institution, what for Louis Althusser is the major "ideological state apparatus" of the school.[11] At the same time, the children are powerless, their future as yet undecided. This future raises the question of hope, and hope seems dismal in the aftermath of the Cultural Revolution. Although in his novel Ah Cheng never directly describes the Cultural Revolution as such, we feel its destructive effects unmistakably, through the impoverished state in which the Chinese education system now finds itself. What kind of a road can be made for these children? This is, I think, the primary issue in Ah Cheng's text; its force is a pedagogical one. As a socially powerless figure, the schoolchild becomes the site for cultural (re)production and its various levels of arbitration. In Ah Cheng, Lao Gan acts as the agent who steers these schoolchildren away from the reproduction of a destructive culture. By training them to read and write from scratch, we are given to think, it might be possible to regenerate national culture in a positive manner. Instead of being associated with a particular political system, communism, this national culture would now be rooted in the humanistic principles of learning.[12]

For me, what makes Chen Kaige's film interesting to watch is not its faithfulness to Ah Cheng's novel, but the way in which it departs from the novel through its translation into the film medium. This is not a translation in the sense of producing a "filmic version" of the same story. Rather, in the translation that is *filming*, we witness a significant shift from Ah Cheng's *script*. What this means is that, first, the translation from writing into film removes the story from the terrain of words into a realm in which verbal language is merely one among many levels of expression. Second, and more important, the shift from script to film is also a shift *away from* the primacy of writing. Because writing occupies the central position among representational forms in the Chinese culture (in which to draw or paint, for instance, is referred to as *xiehua,* literally "to write a picture"), and also because the content of the story itself is about the acquisition of the use of the written word, the translation into film, in which nonverbal cultural signifiers such as visual images and sounds play a primary role, poses all the questions about literature and national culture we have raised so far—questions that are condensed in Ah Cheng's story into the relationship between teacher and children in the school—in entirely different ways.

In an account of the relationship between literature and film, the Russian formalist critic Boris Eikhenbaum writes:

> The cinema audience is placed in completely new conditions of perception, which are to an extent opposite to those of the reading process. Whereas the reader moved from the printed word to visualisation of the subject, the viewer goes in the opposite direction: he moves from the subject, from comparison of the moving frames to their comprehension, to naming them; in short, to the construction of internal speech. The success of film is partially connected to this new and heretofore undeveloped kind of intellectual exercise.[13]

What Eikhenbaum calls "internal speech" is interchangeable with what I have been referring to as subjectivity, namely, the relationship between the individual as participant in social activity (for instance, film watching) and that which transcends the boundaries of his individualized physical apparatus—his own bodily vision/look. This is a relationship that is always *to be* articulated. The difference between responding to the printed word and responding to film that Eikhenbaum mentions is particularly relevant here because we are dealing with the translation of a novel into a filmic text. Whereas words have provided the clues to a possible relationship between Lao Gan and the world at large (he is, after all, the narrating subject in Ah Cheng's story), how are we to understand that relationship in the film? What is the subjectivity or internal speech that reveals itself in the *King of the Children* by Chen?

One specific *filmic* feature that departs from the novel is the way Chen uses Lao Gan's look to reopen the question of pedagogy.[14] Throughout the film, we see shots of Lao Gan staring into the distance, sometimes as if surprised, other times as if in a daydream. For instance, after he has settled down in his lodgings at the beginning, we have a scene in which the camera, taking the shot from outside his cottage, shows him sitting inside by a window, with his hands hanging out leisurely. As he unconsciously touches himself by crossing his long, graceful fingers, his eyes look into the distance. Following his look, we ask: What does he see? If the individual look is a response to a collective gaze, to what does his look respond? What is the larger realm that connects with this look? In the language of contemporary film criticism, this is a question about suturing—that process of subjective activation and reactivation through complex transactions between symbolic and imaginary significations, transactions that give rise to an illusory sense of unity with the field of the other and to coherence in narrative meaning. How is Lao Gan's stare sutured? In other words, with what does his look cohere?

The School

By following Ah Cheng's *script,* Chen shows that Lao Gan's look seeks its connection in the schoolchildren whose education constitutes his "appointment." The protagonist's look here is the specific device through which the issue of pedagogy is addressed *filmically.* "How does one teach in the aftermath of the Cultural Revolution?" becomes "How does one look into the eyes of China's future generation?" But because the question is now asked specifically in the form of vision, it leaves "subjectivity" a matter of construction, offering us that "new and heretofore undeveloped kind of intellectual exercise" that Eikhenbaum mentions.

Lao Gan's discomfort at the question about pedagogy is evident from the time he arrives at the school. First, he discovers to his surprise that he has been assigned to a higher grade than he thought he was qualified to teach. Then, on arriving at the door of the classroom, he drops his books. As if in a confrontation, he greets with great unease the little faces that await him. This mutually responsive relationship, back and forth between teacher and schoolchildren, directs the narrative development of the story.

When Lao Gan realizes that all he can do is to copy, a deep sense of frustration arises in him. With his back to the children, he copies standardized communist texts onto the blackboard, day in and day out. The children, on their part, copy everything mechanically into their notebooks. The sounds of chalk on the blackboard and pencils on notebooks fill many scenes. As this "collective" activity intensifies, we are forced to ask: What kind of cultural production is taking place here, with what future for these rural children? This series of copying scenes is followed by one in which Lao Gan goes home one night, holds a candle to his broken mirror, and spits at his own image. I will return to the significance of this violent act of self-degradation later.

Things change when Lao Gan begins to teach the copied texts. One of the students, Wang Fu, boldly reprimanding him for his incompetence, proclaims the principles of correct teaching. At this—which appears in every sense a public humiliation by a student, a member of the lower class in the school system—Lao Gan breaks into a laugh, as if he has finally made a connection with the schoolchildren. From then on, he proceeds to teach the students how to read and write, and slowly, each student learns to produce his or her own original thoughts in composition.

Wang Fu's persistence in copying the dictionary and his eventual "success" in producing a piece of coherent writing are the symptoms of the child who has been properly "interpellated" into the system of learning—to use the term from Althusser. Wang Fu's perseverance, seriousness, and ability to work hard are all part of the process by which the school as an apparatus of ideology solicits the voluntary cooperation of its participants.[15] The reproduction of a society, writes Althusser, is not only the reproduction of its skills but also "a reproduction of its submission to the rules of the established order, i.e., a reproduction of submission to the ruling ideology"[16] for those who are exploited.

Precisely because he is sensitive to how ideology works effectively not only through coercion (by the powerful) but more often through consent (from the powerless), Chen's film departs from the more straightforwardly humanistic direction of Ah Cheng's story. We see this in the way Chen handles the episode of copying. Whereas in Ah Cheng's novel Lao Gan leaves behind the dictionary for Wang Fu as a gift, in the film he departs with these words on the table: "Wang Fu, don't copy anymore, not even the dictionary."

What Chen's film makes clear is that even though Ah Cheng's text is radical (since it asserts proper learning against the destructiveness of the Cultural Revolution), it leaves unasked the entire question of what it means to base culture on the act of copying. In reading Ah Cheng's text, one feels that it is not the act of copying that is really the problem; rather it is a matter of finding the right source from which to copy. The protest Ah Cheng makes, accordingly, is that the Cultural Revolution has destroyed such sources. Against such destruction, Ah Cheng shows how one should always write *after* (one has done) something (i.e., one should copy from "life"), or else one may, as Wang Fu does, copy from the dictionary. Chen, on the other hand, does not attach to copying the value of a positive meaning as in Ah Cheng; rather, in it he sees a revelation of the deconstructive meanings of contemporary Chinese culture. For Chen, the destructiveness of the Cultural Revolution is not an accident but the summation of Chinese civilization, and the act of copying, to which the students are reduced, signifies the emptiness of culture itself. This is why he says: "Culture is precisely this: it's a matter of copying."[17] Because Chen's understanding of copying is much more drastic, he also constructs his *King of the Children* in such a way that the success of the child-as-copyist is being scrutinized and challenged through a juxtaposition with other forms of subjectivity. While Ah Cheng's narrative offers a more or less completed circuit of suturing between Lao Gan and the schoolchildren, especially through his special relationship with Wang Fu, this process of suturing is only one of several crucial elements in the film.

The drastic questioning of the traditional authority of the written word (and thus of the primacy of verbal language) is, I would contend, not a questioning of a moralistic kind. As I argue in a discussion of Chen's first film, *Yellow Earth* (1984),[18] the film medium allows Chen to explore the much larger issue of technological reproduction in a modern Third World culture. Although a substantial discussion of this point is beyond the scope of this essay, a brief reference to Martin Heidegger's understanding of technology helps clarify the issues somewhat.[19] In his work, Heidegger dissociates the word *technology* from its more popular associations with instrumentality. Instead, he defines the essence of technology as the bringing forth of being—a process of revealing truth and a mode of knowing. He locates this essence of technology in the Greek word *techne*, which for him does not mean mere technique or craft, but the "bringing forth" of that which "presences" into appearance. For Heidegger, modern machine technology does not depart in essence from the ancient concept of *techne*. Rather, modernity's mechanized, regulating, gigantic, and indeed dangerous apparatuses reveal *techne* as an "enframing" and a "setting upon" of nature in ways hitherto concealed from human apprehension. Because of this, Heidegger says, "modern technology, which for chronological reckoning is the later, is, from the point of view of the essence holding sway within it, the historically earlier."[20] Having shown this about modernity, Heidegger also asks: Is there a time when it is not technology (as we now know it) alone that reveals the meaning of *techne?* He finds his answer in art and especially in poetry.

In many ways, Chen's work (the three films he directed in China prior to 1989) can be seen as an exploration of the question of *techne* in the context of a devastated Third World culture that is at the same time one of the most sophisticated ancient civilizations. The intense challenge posed by Chen's *King of the Children* to the written word is a challenge to the cultured origins of Chinese history. The written script with its stable, permanent cast points to that "enframing" of being that Heidegger suggests as the essence of *techne*. Central to the power—indeed the violence—of writing is its ability to repeat itself. In China, where writing is seldom divorced from history—that is, from the notion of writing as recording and conserving—the written script is *techne* in its most basic form through which the transmission and reproduction of culture are ensured. At the same time, writing is also *modern* technology in the hands of the communist state, which turns it into a pure machine for propaganda and thought-control. These two aspects of writing—first as the cumulative, unbearable burden of the past (history), and then as the technologizing impera-tive to construct, in the modern world, a brand new national culture (revolution)—are brought together succinctly in the mindless *copy-ing* of the post–Cultural Revolution period.

On the night Lao Gan obtains and reads the dictionary for the first time, the scene takes on a surreal feeling as sounds of human voices reciting ancient texts are slowly echoed and magnified, creat-ing a ghostly atmosphere of how tradition impinges upon human consciousness as so many indistinguishably repeating voices. The simple acts of reading and writing, performed here in the rural area, far away from the "centers" of urban civilization, nonetheless partake in this unmistakable sense of culture as copying, echoing, repetition. Rather than concealing it, the impoverished material circumstan-ces help intensify the sheer mechanism of writing as cumulative recording.

In the urban setting, of course, the unstoppable terroristic power of technology is apprehensible in more palpable forms. Chen shows this in his second film, *Da yue bing* (The Big Parade, 1985). In this film, the portrayal of one of the most important bases of Chinese national culture—the People's Liberation Army—combines a fasci-nation with discipline (which suppresses all symptoms of the human body such as crying, fainting, vomiting, or even the physical "defor-mity" of bowed legs) and an ultimate sense of emotional blankness that comes with this technologized discipline. The instrumentaliza-tion of human bodies into a "collective" purpose such as the army, to the point of material impoverishment and deprivation, including deprivation in the form of a restraint of the body's reactions to disciplinary torture, is visible on the screen through the orderliness of soldiers and other production units marching in the "big parade" in front of Tiananmen Square. It is as if the sheer regimentation of human bodies—in uniform, their faces devoid of expression, their movements absolutely identical—provides a kind of pseudo or me-chanical "bridging" of the gap between the irretrievable past and the unknowable future. If this "bridging" indicates modern China's "suc-cessful" achievement of modernization, it is an achievement that, as we sense through the slow motion and funereal music in the last scenes of *The Big Parade*, requires from the individual a submission to the technologized collective goal—to technology as collective goal—in total self-obliteration.

The rural setting of *King of the Children* does not permit the demonstration of the workings of technology in the graphically striking form it takes in *The Big Parade*. In the absence of the industrialized, militarized, and urbanized forms of technology, Chen probes the roots of *techne* in a more basic manner, through the fundamental working of verbal language itself. Here, the power of *techne*, as what brings forth the ordering of being, is demonstrated with frugal means, through a practice of traditional learning—storytelling. One day, the friends from Lao Gan's former production unit come for a visit. Out of sheer playfulness, he has them sit down like students in the classroom, whereupon he proceeds to "teach" them. As he *repeats* his words, it quickly becomes clear that this is one of those narratives that uncover the mechanism of narrating from within, so that "form" and "content" are merged and thus revealed as one: "Once upon a time there was a mountain. In the mountain was a temple. In the temple was a Buddhist monk telling a tale. What is the tale? Once upon a time there was a mountain. In the mountain was a temple. In the temple . . . ."

His friends join him in what immediately becomes an uproar that reproduces the same story over and over again collectively. As they finally come to a stop, the schoolchildren, who have been eavesdropping outside the classroom, pick up from where the adults left off, and run off into the distant hills repeating exactly the same narrative with rhythm. As they disappear on the horizon, the camera returns us to Lao Gan's look. This look is one of surprise, as if he has suddenly "understood" something. What is it that he has understood? What is the content of his sudden awareness? These are questions that the film medium leaves unanswered, and that must be approached through the process of interpretation.

Such a moment of "awareness" is one of the undecidable moments of subjectivity that are crucial for the understanding of modern Chinese culture and literature. Instead of immediately supplying it with a definite meaning, such as "Lao Gan realizes how education is passed on," we should juxtapose it with other components of the film in order to grasp its range of significatory possibilities.

Nature

Side by side with the relationship between teacher and school-children is another set of scenes that revolve around a character who does not exist in Ah Cheng's novel—a cowherd. This is, once again, a child figure, and yet unlike the schoolchildren, the cowherd belongs to "nature." Through him Chen's film creates a discourse that counters the institution of education. What is this counterdiscourse like? In other words, what is the function of the nature child in this film?

"Nature" supplies an alternative form of suturing for Lao Gan's look. Often, as he stares, what he "sees" is the expansiveness of the rural landscape. While some might argue that "nature" as such is the unsuturing of the look and therefore, arguably, a non-Western type of cinematic intervention, I am reluctant to divide "West" and "East" in this facile manner by putting "nature" and "East" in the space of an "outside." There are two reasons for not taking this interpretive step. First, I see the elusiveness and fantasy that are part of nature-as-filmic-signifier as a major *political* means of resisting the over-whelmingly articulate, verbal, indeed verbose machinery of official Chinese communist discourse with its technologies of mass control through propaganda. By presenting a counterdiscourse in the form of a natural muteness, therefore, directors like Chen are not exactly nostalgic about a metaphysical beyond; rather it is a politically en-gaged way of searching for an alternative cultural semiotics—*a detour.* Second, "nature" fulfills the function of being the unconscious side of a male circuit of production. As such, it plays an indispensable role in reinforcing certain patterns of censorship, especially the censorship of the physical body and biological reproduction through woman. This point will become clear in the second part of this essay.

The cowherd first appears in the scenes of Lao Gan's journey to the school. He is dressed in white; a large straw hat covers his face so that we cannot see his features; he is leading a herd of cows on the mountain road. He is mute throughout the film, and his "communication" with Lao Gan takes the opposite form to that of the schoolchildren—the nonverbal.[21] Two scenes demonstrate the significatory power of this nonverbalness.

One day, as Lao Gan is teaching, he sees that the cowherd is doing something on the blackboard in the classroom next door. As he goes and looks, he finds the cowherd has splattered dung on the board; meanwhile he has disappeared into the distance. The second scene shows Lao Gan meeting the cowherd face to face in the fields. He asks: "Where are you from, child? Do you go to school? Why not? I know how to read and write. I can teach you." The cowherd remains mute and goes away.

Why does Chen insert the figure of the mute child in this story about teaching? From the beginning, we feel that the cowherd's existence is a mystery, which belongs to the plane of fantasy rather than to the institutional reality to which Lao Gan is officially appointed. And yet this fantasy intrudes into his path of vision in spite—perhaps because—of its mysterious nature. Here, the use of cinematic image and sound together effects a forceful interplay between the pedagogical and the natural frames of reference. The film begins, after all, with *two* series of sounds—first cowbells, then the sounds of writing with chalk on the blackboard. As Lao Gan travels with his friend Lao Hei to the school, the two men come across things that seem to startle them. Among these things is the cowherd. Typically, we are shown the slightly surprised (?) look of the two male characters, especially Lao Gan; then the camera "sutures" the look by showing a scene from the mountains, a view of rocks falling from a cliff, of trees, and so on. What kind of "suturing" is this? This type of scene, in which Lao Gan's human, individualized look is seen to be actively *looking,* only to be "connected" with something "natural"—that is, something mute, stationary, and uneventful—parallels his actual encounters with the cowherd, who becomes *a personified form of the nonverbal presence of a natural world* that exists side by side (rather than metaphysically beyond) the human institution of learning. Precisely because the cowherd is nonverbal, he belongs more appropriately to the medium that does not rely on verbal language alone to generate its significations. The cowherd's *bodily presence* signifies the challenge of nonpresence, nonparticipation—a form of life and a history of uneducation—that runs parallel but is indifferent to the history of education.

If the pedagogical subjectivity in this film is the circuit that runs between Lao Gan's look and the schoolchildren (which is the dominant narrative in Ah Cheng's novel), then the mute presence of the cowherd alters this subjectivity significantly. Side by side with the pedagogical suturing, especially between Lao Gan and Wang Fu, the inheritor of book culture, is now another one, which is nonverbal *on the child's side*. The nonverbal nature of the cowherd's "response" to Lao Gan forces us to think: What is the use of education? How does it reproduce itself, and for whose benefit?

The status of nature in *King of the Children* carries with it the implications of a counterdiscourse that is situated not in human agency but in fantasy. I mentioned that on the night Lao Gan browses through the dictionary, the film supplies a chorus of muffled voices from the past reciting texts to accompany his reading. At the same time, this "rejoining" with the ancestral voices of education is interrupted by a noise from the outside. It is a cow, standing mysteriously in the dark and walking away as Lao Gan opens the door and discovers it.

If we are to think of subjectivity in terms of the suturing of a perceiving individual and an ambiguous external reality, then Lao Gan's subjectivity that emerges in the film is a bifurcated one. On the one hand, it retains the "good" Chinese tradition of a compassion for children as the socially powerless. His subjectivity directs its own "completion" in the other through the acquisition of the written word. This particular suturing process stands for compliance with a *proper* sense of national culture, as that which has to be built from the most basic technology—writing. Lao Gan's subjectivity takes us toward a determinate and determinable form of hope. If the children are the "masses," then education through literacy represents the hope of a definite and definitive road.

On the other hand, Chen explores Lao Gan's subjectivity through another realm in which the teacher's impulse to reach out to the socially powerless child cannot materialize into an act of pedagogy. Instead, it is met with a defiance that one must describe as at once natural, silent, mysterious, and uncooperative. This other story of subjectivity punctuates Chen's film in the form of scenes that are placed halfway between reality and fantasy—the point is that the audience cannot tell the difference and that it does not matter. What matters is that the figure of the cowherd reappears persistently, as if in a dream, a detour, which swerves from the conscious and straightforward relationship between teacher and schoolchildren.

Along this detour is a nonexistent Chinese character. One day, as Lao Gan is copying texts on the board, he writes down a character that he subsequently erases:

Toward the end of the film, he recalls this episode of mis-writing in his parting words to the students. Cows are stubborn animals, he says; you can scold them and hit them, and they just blink at you. But there are times when cows go wild—that is, when you piss. This is because cows love salt. (In Ah Cheng's novel, Lao Gan also tells us that once you have pissed for a cow, you can make it do anything you want, for it would respect you as if you were its parent.) It was this association of "cow" and "piss," Lao Gan explains, that made him write the imaginary character "cow-water" the other day.

The significatory density of this nonexistent character is, structurally speaking, what counteracts the ferocity of Wang Fu's dedication to verbal language. The "cow-water" fantasy exposes literate culture in a scandalously different manner—as excrement. This exposure takes place at various levels at once. First, the fantasy returns us to the origin of Chinese civilization—peasant knowledge. As such, in a text that is critical of the destructiveness of the Cultural Revolution, tribute is paid to one of Chinese communism's most compelling pedagogical imperatives: intellectuals must learn from peasants. The way cows behave toward urine is an ecological fact that one acquires by being "exiled" in the countryside, not by being in the classroom.

Second, this fantasy is a story about the dialectic of submission and domination. The cows, in spite of their patient and uncomplaining nature, go wild at the rare physical pleasure of salt. Whoever provides this pleasure, in other words, also has the power to dominate them. From the human perspective, this understanding of plea-sure and submission is profoundly disturbing because in it we recog-nize the acts of degradation and humiliation, indeed violence. An act of physical discharge, which eliminates that which stinks—how could this, from the perspective of the properly educated, possibly be a source of pleasure and an inducement to submission? To what can we compare this at the symbolic level? Is this story about animal nature also one about human culture? If so, what kind of blow has been dealt to the dignity of the latter?

The radicalness of "cow-water" lies in the way it reveals the funda-mental violence of culture as a process of production. The success of "culture" is the success of subjugating those who are in need (as, for instance, of salt in the case of cows) for productive purposes. The paradox is that not only would the act of subjugation not make them rebel, but because its violence is at the same time what sustains and nurtures, the dominated respond to it submissively—animalistically. To come back to the making of roads: pissing is, in this light, the act that establishes a path, which is met with pleasure and followed henceforth with loyalty.

If submission as such, transposed onto the human cultural frame, is essential for the formation of "identity," then this fantasy illum-inates the unutterable inequality involved in that process. The silent, fantastical text of this *other* story about Chinese national culture reads: Are not the hard-working, uncomplaining masses of Chinese people like the cows—and is not "tradition," as represented and endorsed by official political orthodoxy, the pissing master? (In the modern economy, "work" is what generates "salary," which etymolog-ically means "payment for one's work in the form of salt.") No matter how abusive this master becomes, the masses succumb to him as the source of their survival. The masses submit even as tradition and national culture crush them. Against this *equivalence* between cows and people, the direct political empowerment of the "masses" that appears in Mao's reading of Lu Xun—a reading that distin-guishes between cows and people by making the former a symbol of those who should serve the latter—is at once a hope, a lie, and the making of a road by force, with blood and tears.

The conception of culture as violence and excrement also returns us to the question of copying and writing-as-reproduction. Unlike Ah Cheng's story, in which one feels that the point of learning is to identify the correct source from which to copy, Chen's film deconstructs cultural production itself as copying. With the insertion of the cowherd, words, texts, dictionaries, and verbal language—summations of the human learning tradition—exist on a par with piss, as the (waste) product of a violently subjugating act to which Chinese individuals, like the intelligent student Wang Fu, have no choice but to submit. The nature of this submission is that of copying and reproducing precisely the source of their subjugation—in other words, cultural violence through institutionalized education itself. It is only when this originary act of violence is completed through the act of submission and voluntary reproduction (since it includes the possibility of pleasure and physical survival) that it becomes fully effective as cultivation and culture. (In Ah Cheng, the hard-working cows are compared to philosophers.) This is why, on first discovering that he cannot teach the students anything except copying—that is, on discovering that he is not, properly speaking, helping to perpetuate culture—Lao Gan expresses physical violence toward *himself*, by spitting at his own image in the broken mirror. Meanwhile, as Wang Fu strikes back in words, Lao Gan is happy: the circuit of teaching that he initiated has been properly completed by this young child's active response and can now regenerate itself.

But if human culture is violent, nature is more so. If the cows in Chen's film are not, as Mao's image suggests, the "intellectual servants" to be used by the proletariat, they are not icons of humanistic benevolence either. The cowherd's (and by implication, nature's) muteness is a form of subjugating presence to which Lao Gan, even though a teacher, submits. In the last scenes of the film, as he departs from the village, we are once again given what look like dream scenes of nature. Chief among these is a field of black stumps, which stand mysteriously and collectively. As these stumps meet our eyes, we hear cowbells and someone pissing. It is the cowherd, who faces the camera and pisses at us directly, his genitals exposed. The camera then shows us his eye under the broken straw hat—is he looking at Lao Gan or at us? With the amplification of cowbells in the wind, the cowherd disappears; we see the black stumps and his hat on one of them. The stumps are magnified and the sounds of the cowbells increase. A moment of quiet. Then the face of the cowherd without the hat: a scruffy country child, turning around, looking at us.

The fantasy of the cowherd returns nature to the cosmic indifference described by the *Dao De Jing: tiandi bu ren, yi wanwu wei chugou* (The cosmos is without/outside human benevolence; it treats everything as mere straw dogs). It is the mute, natural world, forever untamable, which ultimately pisses at us without shame or guilt. Vis-à-vis this nature, human violence itself is, the film says, a mere copy and reproduction.

The Road Not Yet Taken

We have found, especially in persons whose libidinal development has suffered some disturbance, as in perverts and homosexuals, that in the choice of their love-object they have taken as their model not the mother but their own selves. They are plainly seeking themselves as a love-object and their type of object-choice may be termed narcissistic. *[The child] is really to be the center and heart of creation, "His Majesty the Baby," as once we fancied ourselves to be. He is to fulfill those dreams and wishes of his parents which they never carried out . . . At the weakest point of all in the narcissistic position, the immortality of the ego, which is so relentlessly assailed by reality, security is achieved by fleeing to the child.*
Sigmund Freud

Ultimately, a thorough-going feminist revolution would liberate more than women.
Gayle Rubin

It is now possible for me to turn to the issue of "male narcissism" expressed in the title of my essay. While I am sympathetic to the deconstructive reading of culture that Chen Kaige offers through what I have been calling the detour of nature and fantasy, I think such a reading leaves certain forms of human agency that are accountable for such violence unidentified and thus unquestioned. The detour, while it may fundamentally critique the violence of culture as pedagogical suturing, also becomes complicitous with such violence because the alternative it offers, through nature, is *silence*. It is at this point that a social criticism, however partial, of recognizable types of human agency that lurk behind cultural violence is necessary as a way out, even if such criticism does not yet lead to a new road.

By offering a feminist reading as a supplement to my analysis of Chen's bifurcated subjectivity, my point is not to belittle the political subversiveness at work under his direction. It is rather to attempt a mode of reading that, in a way that is not autonomous from but involved with that subversiveness, locates certain excesses that fall outside Chen's detour. These excesses—what to me are possible signs of a new mass and new hope that exist in incomplete forms in the film—are to be found with "woman." By focusing on the question of woman, we will see that the structural interplay between the subjectivities in *King of the Children*—stranded between the pedagogical and the fantastic—is a closed circuit.

A major question results from this supplementary reading based on woman: Is this closed circuit, which I term male narcissism, at bottom a way to resist the reproduction of national culture altogether? If so, why? Why do the male subjectivities in Chen's film seek to connect with the child either through the school or through nature, while bypassing woman? What is the root of this "disturbance" that manifests itself as aesthetic symptom? In other words, does the *passive* role in which Chen casts his male protagonist reflect a response to a larger force of destruction at work, so that the exclusion of woman must be seen not simply as misogyny, but as an effort to cope with what in Lacanian terms we would call symbolic castration?

To deal with these questions, let us now "do a retake" of interpreting *King of the Children.*

If subjectivity is possible only as the result of a certain completion of an individual viewer's look—even if that process of completion is an illusory one—the two types of subjectivity evident in Chen's film, which are held in a contentious relationship with each other, are also held *together* by the absence of women as productive agents. (The girl students are, strictly speaking, recipients, not producers.)

From the beginning, Chen gives us a world of male play. From Lao Gan's former production unit, to the school, to his special relationship with Wang Fu, to the mute cowherd, it is a world of men and men as children at play. In addition, we find several scenes in which Lao Gan is alone against the background of nature, moving his own body around aimlessly and enjoying himself. Between the continuation of human culture through verbal pedagogy and its discontinuation through the fantasy of nature, therefore, what disappears is woman. Moreover, this disappearance of woman occurs as a chiasmus: the woman disappears as the child appears.

We turn, at this point, to Laidi, the woman cook and singer in Lao Gan's production unit. Laidi's entrance is always a disruptive one. Take, for instance, the scene near the beginning in which Lao Gan and his friends gather for a meal before he departs for his new posting. Chen shows us—with what nuanced attention!—the men's comradeship in cooking: first the collective contributions to the menu; then the washing, cutting, and chopping of meat and vegetables; then the setting of rice to be cooked inside a section of bamboo; and finally the sharing of the cooked meal. The power of males in such a group is, as Gayle Rubin would describe it, "not founded on their roles as fathers or patriarchs, but on their collective adult maleness, embodied in secret cults, men's houses, warfare, exchange networks, ritual knowledge, and various initiation procedures."[22] By contrast, although Laidi is a cook, she is never shown to be cooking; instead she strikes one as always bursting onto the scene of male play, bringing with her some kind of disorder. When Laidi enters this first scene of a shared meal, she is announced by her loud voice, her plump body, her broad manners, and a very unfeminine question: "Why don't you ask me for a drink?" Although she is a singer, we never hear her sing; the voice that comes from her is rather always given in a clownish fashion, as shouting and as disharmonious *noise*.

By stripping Laidi of what are conventional feminine (erotic) qualities—submissiveness, shyness, slenderness, and reticence, all of which belong to Lao Gan instead—Chen leaves open the question as to his attitude toward women's role in the production of national culture. To what extent does this exclusion of Laidi from the conventional feminine realm of significations constitute an exclusion of woman in the cultural symbolic realm? And to what extent does her *clowning* become a new type of signification, a feminine power that is in fact stronger than the male because of its libidinally uninhibited nature? Two episodes allow us to negotiate these questions.

Laidi's ambition is to become a teacher of music at the same school where Lao Gan teaches. She wants the men to see that she is more than a cook. But this wish is met with patronizing criticisms from the men, who tease her for not understanding that she has none of the professional qualifications it takes to be a teacher. What she considers to be the most important qualification—her ability to sing and compose in voice—is thus immediately dismissed as irrelevant. Lao Gan, on his part, is honest enough to recognize that he is not properly qualified to teach either. But this understanding of Laidi's *equality* with him does not prompt him to help her.

Meanwhile, Laidi is the one who, among all the people Lao Gan knows, provides him with the Chinese dictionary he needs for teaching. When she comes to his school for a visit, Lao Gan introduces her to Wang Fu as the real owner of the dictionary, whereupon Wang Fu calls her "teacher." In Ah Cheng's novel, Lao Gan writes down Laidi's name as well as his own as donors when he leaves behind the dictionary as a gift. What is interesting about the relationships among Laidi, Lao Gan, and Wang Fu, I think, is that they indicate the potential of a new type of genealogy or reproductive unit. The woman, the man, and the schoolboy form a kind of collective away from the familial reproduction restricted to "blood" and heterosexuality. But as woman is liberated from her erotic and biologically reproductive role, what does she become? What we see in the film is that she has been turned into a comic spectacle whose palpable physical dimensions exceed the closed circuit of male pedagogy and fantasy.

In what sense is this closed circuit narcissistic? I turn now to Freud's argument about narcissism for some definitions. Narcissism, as we understand it in popular usage, is the "love of the self." Freud states that narcissism is not so much a perversion in the pejorative sense as it is a means of self-preservation. He distinguishes between two types of libidinal development in human beings—the anaclitic, which is typified by the search for an object of love external to the subject and which he identifies as active and masculine; and the narcissistic, which is typified by the subject's seeking himself as the love object and which he identifies as passive and feminine. Freud's famous tableau of narcissists follows:

> [Narcissistic] *women* love only themselves with an intensity comparable to that of the man's love for them . . . Such women have the greatest fascination for men, not only for aesthetic reasons . . . but also because of certain interesting psychological constellations. It seems very evident that one person's narcissism has a great attraction for those others who have renounced part of their own narcissism and are seeking after object-love; the charm of a *child* lies to a great extent in his narcissism, his self-sufficiency and inaccessibility, just as does the charm of certain *animals* which seem not to concern themselves about us, such as *cats* and the *large beasts of prey*. In literature, indeed, even the great *criminal* and the *humorist* compel our interest by the narcissistic self-importance with which they manage to keep at arm's length everything which would diminish the importance of their ego. It is as if we envied them their power of retaining a blissful state of mind—an unassailable libido-position which we ourselves have since abandoned.[23]

This passage from Freud clearly reveals his bias, that is, his exclusion of "man" from his tableau of narcissists. But if we disregard this sexual bias (which is obvious), a far more important feature of his argument that is relevant to our present discussion surfaces. We notice that those he identifies as narcissistic share a common status, which is the status of the outsider—marginalized, mute, or powerless—beheld from a distance. Because of this, I would defocus Freud's rigid sexual division between the male and the female as anaclitic and narcissistic, and instead use his argument about narcissism for a *social* analysis that would include men as well as women as narcissists. Narcissism, seen in terms of the "outcast" categories in which Freud locates it, can now be redefined as the effect of a cultural marginalization or even degradation. The narcissist's look of "independence"—a self-absorption to the point of making others feel excluded—to which Freud attributes an aesthetic significance, must therefore receive a new interpretation in the form of a question: Is it the sign of a lack or a plenitude? Is it the sign of insecurity or self-sufficiency? Once we introduce the dialectic of social relation here and understand the "exclusionary look" as a possible result of (or reaction to) being excluded, it becomes necessary to think of certain forms of narcissism not in terms of independence, but as the outward symptoms of a process of cultural devastation, which leaves the self recoiling inward, seeking its connection with itself rather than with external reality.

Freud's argument makes it clear that narcissism is not an intrinsic quality (even though we inevitably attribute it to persons), but a relation produced through the process of observation. In other words, the understanding of narcissism involves a viewing position from which others look narcissistic and exclusionary to us. Narcissism is thus a description of our psychological state in the other—as we feel excluded, the other becomes "narcissistic." In contemporary Chinese cinema, what does the creation of narcissistic male characters tell us about the making of film?—in other words, why is narcissism *conferred upon them*? Why does Chen make his male protagonist self-absorbed, passive, and thus "feminine"? How is this related to the question of national culture?

These questions bring us back to the one I raised at the beginning, namely, why does the writing of national culture in modern China typically take the form of an aesthetic preoccupation with the powerless? If the construction of national culture is a form of empowerment, then the powerless provide a means of aesthetic transaction through which a certain emotional stability arises from *observing* the powerless as a spectacle. In this spectacle, the viewer can invest a great amount of emotional energy in the form of sympathy; at the same time, this sympathy becomes the concrete basis of an affirmative national culture precisely because it *secures the distance from the powerless* per se. The projection of narcissism—an exclusionary self-absorption—onto the other becomes thus a way (as we notice in Freud) of stabilizing, or empowering, the viewing subject's position with an inexplicable aesthetic and emotional pleasure. Such pleasure gives rise, through the illusion of a "solidarity" with the powerless, to the formation of a "unified" community. What distinguishes Chen's film from, say, classical Hollywood narrative films is that it is male, rather than female, figures who make up the spectacle(s) of the powerless. Moreover, it is "maleness" that sutures each point of the aesthetic transaction within the director's control, from (character as) spectacle to (character as) viewer, from feelings of devastation to feelings of solidarity.

According to Freud, a person may love, in the narcissistic manner, the following:

(a) What he is himself (actually himself).
(b) What he once was.
(c) What he would like to be.
(d) Someone who was once part of himself.

These descriptions define the world of male play that provides much pleasure for the men in Chen's film. Laidi, on the other hand, makes it impossible for them to play merely as sexless children; her difference reminds them that there is a world of brute biological reproduction in which they, as the inheritors of Chinese culture, are supposed to participate. Hence, for instance, an attempt at swearing at the beginning of the film is preceded by the question: "Is there any woman around?" If this question is one pertaining to social decorum, then social decorum is an indicator of the functioning of the unconscious. The question points to a shared understanding on the part of the men that swearing, which as a rule alludes to sex or sexual organs, brings out a reality that is on a par with that of woman. As long as women are not present, however, that reality is not materialized and can remain at the level of empty male talk.

On Lao Gan's return visit to the production unit, Laidi touches him. As he refuses such touching, she retorts: "Even if you were to teach for one hundred years, I'd still know what's between your legs!" This reminder of "nature" is as defiant as the trees, the cows, and the cowherd, and yet because it is spoken by a woman—because, shall we say, it comes from a human voice other than that of the male—it cannot be relegated to the realm of fantasy and has the potential of erupting as an alternative symbolic order. Unlike the mute nature child who allows the male "look" to wander in a happy mood of self-exploration and self-projection, the woman's harsh voice keeps calling him back to the world of human culture and the burdens that await him there. For Chen, it is as if these burdens cannot be shaken off unless one becomes perverse—by taking off for the world of fantasy.

Instead of following the road opened up by the female voice, then, Chen's work follows a detour that is, seen in a feminist analysis, a well-trodden philosophical one. This detour heads for the child, voiced or voiceless, a stand-in for culture or nature, who becomes the recipient of what in psychoanalytic language is the process of idealization.

If Lu Xun's call to "save the children" provides the continuity through modern Chinese literature and culture, we need to ask whether the emotional insistence behind such a call is not at the same time an insistence on forgetting and excluding women. While the child occupies a position in modern Chinese literature and culture similar to other figures of social oppression, because of his association with infancy he also offers the illusion that he is "freer" and more originary than the others. By contrast, woman, as the recipient of every type of social construction, is a heavily "corrupted" space—a densely written script—that offers no such illusion of freedom. Because of this, it is much easier to project onto the child the wishes that cannot be fulfilled precisely because of the oppression of culture, through the illusion that the child occupies a kind of beyond-culture status that is superior because outside. The extreme form of this projection, as we see in Chen's film, is achieved by using the child to personify nature's original, amoral violence. The mute, pissing cowherd is, in this light, Chen's supreme invention of a *doubled* narcissistic relation. He is the silent beast confronting the feminine man, the ultimate narcissist—nature—beheld by the human narcissist.

The idealization of the child contains in itself a violence that is self-directed. This violence disguises itself as love of the self, as "narcissism." As Freud says, "At the weakest point of all in the narcissistic position, the immortality of the ego, . . . security is achieved by *fleeing to the child*" (my emphasis). Fleeing to the child—what this means is that what appears to be a love of the self, which generates the look of complete self-absorption, is actually a desperate flight to another figure, who is powerless, inferior, but therefore safest for the realization of otherwise unenactable fantasies. In the Chinese context especially, this process of flight is a complex one. The child onto whom cultural hope is projected is not simply a figure of Chinese sentimentalism. Rather, it is the formation of an ideal, and, as Freud says, "the formation of an ideal would be the condition of repression."[24]

What is repressed, and why does it need to be? The answer to this question must be sought historically and collectively rather than within the space of one essay. For now, I can only point to the visible avoidance of physical sexuality as embodied by woman, an avoidance that aesthetically intersects with the acceptance and idealization of the child. This is, as I have already mentioned, not misogyny *tout court*, but symptomatic of a more profound disturbance.

In the sexual economy, "woman" represents that place in which man is to find his mating other in order to procreate and perpetuate the culture of which he is the current inheritor. "Woman" therefore serves as a reminder of the duty of genealogical transmission—of *chuanzong jiedai*. The question implied in Chen's film is: Do Chinese men in the post–Cultural Revolution period want to perform this duty?

In the idiomatic Chinese expression for the "mating other," *duixiang*, we find a means of understanding the sexual economy in psychoanalytic terms. *Duixiang*, in contemporary psychoanalytic language, is that mirror image which would correspond to one's self, so that when we are looking for a mate, we literally say *zhao duixiang*— "to look for the corresponding image."

In the narcissistic subjectivity, this *duixiang* is internally directed. The "natural" *duixiang* for Lao Gan would have been Laidi, who loves him and wants to be with him—her aspiration to be a music teacher is, one could say, an expression of her wish to "correspond" to him. And yet in Chen's film, the strong woman's love is presented as now farcical, now threatening. The possibilities it offers—heterosexual love, marriage, reproduction—are refused by the film. Instead, the male subjectivity takes another route, and joins children as figures of idealization. It is the children, then, who have come to take the place of the corresponding image, in a way that bypasses the woman (even though she is kept in an affectionate light, as a mother or sister who tends). In bypassing the woman as the figure of reproduction, what does the film project? It projects, as I said, two types of subjectivity, each of which can now be understood in terms of a narcissistic male circuit of reproduction. Reproduction is either strictly through education or through a submission to the awesome muteness of nature. In each we find a "suturing" between the male protagonist and a male child. The "sublimated" message of the film is: the world is generated in this interplay between pedagogy and fantasy, between "culture" and "nature"—that is, without woman and without the physical body!

In Freud's text, narcissistic gratification, involving repression, can be secured through the ego-ideal, which, besides the individual side, also has a social side, in the form of "the common ideal of a family, a class, or a nation": "The dissatisfaction due to the non-fulfillment of this ideal liberates homosexual libido, which is transformed into sense of guilt (dread of the community). Originally this was a fear of punishment by the parents, or, more correctly, the dread of losing their love; later the parents are replaced by an indefinite number of fellow men."[25]

Would it be far-fetched to say that the narrative of modern Chinese history, culminating in the catastrophe of the Cultural Revolution and more recently in the Tiananmen massacre, represents precisely this "dissatisfaction" of the ego-ideal in the form of the nation? The guilt felt by educated Chinese toward their fellow men generates the massive "censorial institution of conscience"—a feeling of being watched by other men—which makes it difficult, if not impossible, to engage in the conventional procedure of searching for the "corresponding image." Instead, *zhao duixiang* becomes a process not of finding the one who loves one, but of self-observation, self-watching, and self-censorship. The displacement of narcissistic emotion onto "corresponding images" that are not women—difficult partners in biological reproduction—but idealized figures of children is symptomatic of both a dissatisfaction with the failure of culture at large and an attempt nonetheless to continue to bear its burden conscientiously, by *disembodying* the reality of culture's reproduction and displacing that reality onto the purely institutional or fantastic level. Contrary to Freud's way of dividing the sexes, a film like *King of the Children* shows us that it is in male subjectivity that the need to secure emotional stability through narcissism is most evident. We can only speculate that this is in direct proportion to the burden of cultural reproduction that publicly/symbolically falls on men. Ironically, in spite of their obviously oppressed status, women seem more exempt from this desperate route since they are considered superfluous from the outset. In this "ironically" lies what I would call "the road not yet taken."

I understand that by equating Laidi with the physical body, I seem to be going against one of the major lessons we have learned from feminism, namely, that "woman" is not about biological reproduction alone. However, my point in emphasizing the reproductive function of woman in this context is rather to show how a criticism of the cultural violence in Chinese culture cannot be undertaken without vigilance for how the physical aspects of life are as a rule suppressed. Because women are traditionally associated with such physical aspects, the exclusion of women from the symbolic realm becomes a particularly poignant way of exposing this general suppression. My insistence on the biological, therefore, is not an attempt to reify it as such, but a means of interrupting the tendency toward what I would, for lack of a better term, call mentalism in Chinese culture, a mentalism that we witness even in a subversive film such as *King of the Children*. Because the Chinese national culture reproduces itself biologically by means of the machinery that is women's bodies even while continuing to dismiss them on account of their femaleness, and because the Chinese communist state controls the population by controlling women's bodies, upon which forced abortions at advanced stages of pregnancy can be performed as "policy"—I think we must belabor women's reproductive role somewhat, even at the risk of "biologism."

In Laidi, we find the suggestion of a healthy narcissism that comprises an assertiveness, spontaneity, and fearlessness to seek what she wants while at the same time letting the other be. Because of this latter ability to let the other be, Laidi's love for Lao Gan is not expressed in the exclusive form of sexual desire and conquest, but rather in the form of a general affection in which one feels the presence of the caring sister, mother, and fellow worker as well. This alternative form of narcissism does not evade the other's difference (through specularization) in order to achieve its own stability. In it we find a different form of hope, toward which the film, caught in the closed circuit of male narcissism, nonetheless gestures, even though it never materializes into a significant new direction.

King of the Children continues, in the formalist manner of Lu Xun, the exploration of the cluster of issues involving Chinese national culture that has haunted Chinese intellectuals since the beginning of the twentieth century. To the literary incisiveness of Lu Xun's conception of hope—not as a road but as a crossroads—Chen's work brings the complexity of the filmic medium, in which the suggestively specular process of *zhao duixiang*—of finding that which gives us "self-regard" and "self-esteem"—takes on a collective cultural significance. If Chinese intellectuals in the twentieth century have consistently attempted to construct a responsible national culture through an investment in figures of the powerless, Chen's film indicates how such an investment, because it is inscribed in the formation of an ego-ideal in the terms I describe, excludes woman and the physical reality she represents. Chen's film offers a fantastic kind of hope—the hope to rewrite culture without woman and all the limitations she embodies, limitations that are inherent in the processes of cultural, as well as biological, reproduction. The subjectivity that emerges in Chen's film alternates between notions of culture and of nature that are both based on a lineage free of woman's interference. As such, even at its most subversive/deconstructive moments (its staging of the unconscious that is nature's brute violence), it partakes of a narcissistic avoidance of the politics of sexuality and of gendered sociality that we would, in spite of the passive "feminine" form it takes, call masculine. This masculinity is the sign of a vast transindividual oppression whose undoing must become the collective undertaking for all of us who have a claim to modern Chinese culture.

Afterword: Reflections on Change and Continuity in Modern Chinese Fiction

In his classic essay "Change and Continuity in Chinese Fiction," Cyril Birch raises a most intriguing issue concerning the place of May Fourth fiction in the historical schema of Chinese literature. He places what he aptly characterizes as the tragic-ironic mode of May Fourth fiction between the comic-satiric tradition of late Qing writing and the highly didactic political allegory of Hao Ran's novels produced at the height of the Cultural Revolution. Thus sandwiched between two native traditions, the May Fourth phase of realism seems like a brief aberration—a small, though revolutionary, change within mainstream continuity. This is what Birch predicted in 1974, when his essay was written (for the Dedham Conference on Modern Chinese Literature), two years before anyone could predict the Cultural Revolution would soon be over:

These new writers of the People's Republic are engaged in a kind of Great Return. Whatever comparative judgments we may wish to make, we are bound to find the new mainland fiction "more Chinese," and it is demonstrably more popular. In all of Chinese narrative and dramatic literature, there is a strong urge toward the exemplary. We must be prepared to see this urge expressed again and again in writings of the future. There is, after all, no reason why the realist phase, which so dominated the literature of nineteenth-century Europe, should occupy China for any more than the space this paper has indicated, the brief decades subsequent to May 4, 1919.[1]

If we look back over the past fifteen years since Birch's essay was written, it would seem that his prediction about the May Fourth legacy was too pessimistic: not only did the urge toward the exemplary dissipate itself, but shortly after the end of the Cultural Revolution, the May Fourth legacy of realism was restored as a corrective to the Maoist excesses of revolutionary romanticism. Post-Mao literature does not effect a "great return" to native forms of collectivity and populism. Rather, it is the theme of self and its emancipation—surely a May Fourth tenet—that has been celebrated. At the same time, Birch was not entirely wrong about the persistence of the communal impulse and the limited phase of realism; what he did not envision was the far more radical prospect that, a decade after 1974, a younger generation of writers on the mainland would become dissatisfied with both legacies and wish to cast their creative writing in new directions that go beyond the native and realist realms.

Before we explore this new phenomenon, it may be useful at this critical juncture in time to reflect once again on the May Fourth legacy in modern Chinese literature and to reconsider Birch's realist paradigm.

That the concept of realism was invested from the very beginning with a high seriousness is common knowledge. It may be recalled that in Chen Duxiu's famous 1917 article proclaiming the Literary Revolution, realism was one of the three central principles on the banner of his "revolutionary army."[2] In Chen's original formulation, the word was placed in a semantic context in which a "fresh and sincere literature of realism" was opposed to "the stereotyped, ornamental literature of classicism" in the same way that the other two tenets—a "simple, expressive literature of the people" and a "plain-speaking and popular literature of society"—were made to oppose and replace the pedantic, obscure, and ornamental literature of the traditional elite. In other words, realism was regarded as a mode of direct, untrammeled expression of popular society. Insofar as this injunction was followed in the fictional works of early May Fourth writers, the practice of realism nevertheless presented a number of problems, both normative and technical. How do we define such terms as "fresh and sincere," "simple and expressive," and "plain-speaking and popular"? It seems that some of the subsequent literary debates—on the use of dialects, on popularization and proletarian-ization, on the "Europeanization" of the May Fourth vernacular—harked back to these unclear initial tenets. At the same time, how-ever, the literary controversies in the early 1930s became dominated by an increasingly doctrinaire view of language that in its excessive emphasis on the need of the mass audience left out certain crucial epistemological and technical questions: What constitutes reality from the May Fourth perspective? How can the Real be represented in a literary—particularly fictional—text? How is it possible to make the literary text "speak" the voices of popular society?

In a recent book, Marston Anderson subjects these complex ques-tions to a nuanced and masterful analysis by drawing upon the fictional works of half a dozen May Fourth writers.[3] Basing his anal-ysis on matters of fictional form, Anderson sees May Fourth realism as derived from an essentially Western epistemology. Western real-ism, which is part of a mimetic tradition, rests on the assumption that a fundamental schism exists between word and reality, and "the exploration of this divide is realism's hidden agenda."[4] In the case of May Fourth fiction, the task of bridging this paradoxical gap—as "realist works are at once distinct from and dependent on the world they describe"[5]—became all but impossible. The realization of its limitations—its formal incapacity to either "mirror" or "frame" the totality of the Real—coupled with an increasingly heightened sense of social activism finally led to the decline of the May Fourth brand of realism: "By the 1930s most saw that critical realism was not the simple tool for social regeneration its advocates had once believed it to be. In working with the mode, Chinese writers and critics had come increasingly to understand that realism did not naturally lend itself to the activism and populism that Chinese radicals felt the times demanded."⁶ Thus increasingly, this awareness of the "social impediments" paved the way for the eruption and triumph of the "crowd," the massification of literature into communal forms of socialist realism in which the "distinction between 'I' and 'they'—between self and society—that had been an indispensable basis for the practice of critical realism" is subsumed in a "collective we."⁷ Thus after much brilliant analysis, Anderson joins Birch in concluding that the journey beyond realism signaled a "great return" to the "communal."

The issues raised by Anderson deserve careful scrutiny. His emphasis on the technical aspect of realism is valid when we recall that the Chinese phrase for "realism" used in the early May Fourth period was indeed *xieshi zhuyi*, which seems to give as much weight to "writing about" reality as to reality itself. In other words, technique becomes an essential component of realism. By the 1930s, however, the phrase had changed to *xianshi zhuyi*, or literally the doctrine of contemporary reality, for which Reality assumes almost an ontological status and the technique of writing is deemphasized At the same time, we must also remember that from the very beginning the early May Fourth practice of realism involved both a formal/technical dimension and a moral intention of the author. Anderson has in fact cited Ye Shaojun to the effect that "true literature originates in the author's deep feelings" and that "the truth of a literary work is dependent on the sincerity of the emotions expressed in it."⁸ That is to say, what Lionel Trilling calls the virtue of "sincerity"—or "to thine own self be true"—has much to do with writing about reality. Although Ye's views may have been indebted to the neo-Confucian notion of self-cultivation, it is equally important to note that, as Trilling has reminded us, the virtue of sincerity was also linked historically to the rise of the concept of the individual with a new awareness of his or her "internal space."⁹ In the May Fourth context, this means essentially that realism may in fact have been part of a manifestation of individualism—that the technique of realistic observation and description carries with it a perspectivism anchored in the sense of truthfulness to both external reality and the author's internal self. Simply put, it means that the sincerity of the author must be a precondition of the technique of realism.

This is indeed the argument of a brilliant new book by Rey Chow, who, citing the seminal work of Prusek, sees a close connection between what Prusek calls "subjectivism and individualism"—the lyrical impulse expressed in autobiographical writings and confessional narratives—and the program of nation building and social reform.[10] Prusek saw May Fourth writers as inheritors of two tendencies from traditional literature—what he called the "lyrical" and the "epic." If May Fourth fiction is affiliated with the "epic" narrative tradition, which in turn provides the formal ground for the social ethos of nationalism and reform or revolution, this does not mean that the lyrical tendency was entirely taken over: in fact "the emphasis on individual emancipation . . . gives to the prominence of lyricism a *revolutionary* significance."[11] Thus both epic and lyrical forms can be made to cohere with the demands of "reality." From Prusek's insight, Chow also sees in the May Fourth preoccupation with "reality" an inheritance from classical Chinese notions of "truthfulness" *(zhen)* and "fullness" *(shi),* according to which "'good' literature is by necessity morally sound writing, which is considered 'truthful' because 'full,' whereas 'fictional' works, which often foreground the vicissitudes of language, are idiomatically associated with 'emptiness' and 'falsehood.'"[12] As Chow aptly puts it, this is indeed the dilemma of realism in the May Fourth period—a "recurrent obsession with 'reality' which sees itself as revolutionary and defines 'truth' as personal and historical *at once.*"[13] In my view, this morally tinged conjunction of individualism and collectivism, reality and fiction, cannot be fully understood, its underlying tensions and contradictions resolved, purely in linguistic or formal terms. If one should dare to reverse the current poststructuralist injunction and resurrect the status of the author as both a textual and an external agent, it would seem that sincerity in the self-perception of the May Fourth author enters directly into the production of the literary text as a crucial factor governing its formal operation.

To put the argument in the form of a generic question: How do we explain the fact that the primary genre for the operation of the early May Fourth realistic mode was the short story and *not* the long novel? How then do we account for the obvious rise of the novel form after 1930? (Not to mention the equally obvious issue that the

long novel never attained the kind of literary privilege and preva-
lence once accorded the *sida qishu,* or the four great "novel" books,
of the late Ming or the "four great novels" of the late Qing?) Following Birch, are we ready to assign a more prominent place to the long
novel—instead of the May Fourth short story—as the exemplary
communal form in Chinese fiction, past and present? Insofar as
these generic distinctions make both formal and "moral" sense, I
would like to argue, somewhat contrary to Anderson's position, that
instead of its formal "limitations," it was precisely the opposite traits
of the short-story form—freedom, brevity, and a lack of constraints—that appealed to the romantic temper of most early May
Fourth writers. In fact, it has been noted that the short story can be
considered the "romantic prose form" in the West: "Whereas the
conventional nineteenth-century novel normally accommodates the
processes of a dense, ordered society, the short story has been by its
very nature remote from the community—romantic, individualistic,
and intransigent," for "in its normally limited scope and subjective
orientation it corresponds to the lyric poem, as the novel does to the
epic."[14] Accordingly, the modern vernacular *(baihua)* short story, one
could argue, was the appropriate vehicle—a free form that registers
the spontaneous ebb and flow of personal emotions (hence a more
subjective form than the traditional novel) or presents a slice of life
vividly from a subjective angle or an individual focal consciousness—
especially when that consciousness springs from a newly discovered
"gendered self" of the woman writer. One need only mention Ding
Ling's famous story "Diary of Miss Sophie" as a pioneering example,
in which the protagonist seeks to construct her own "subjectivity" by
rewriting herself into a different text—a diary in which she is in the
process of becoming an autonomous subject.[15]

It was only when the technique of realism as an individualistic
mode (*xieshi,* an extension of *xieyi*) was replaced by the more embracing and imposing demand of Reality *(xianshi)* that the problematic of the "great divide" between word and reality was set in motion
and given an enormous ideological burden by its pointed reference
to the ills of contemporary Chinese society. Again, if we consider the
possible role of the (real) author in textual production, not only
does Anderson's formal thesis make eminent sense, but what C. T.

Hsia calls the "obsession with China" takes on a dimension of ontological meaning. That is to say, the external social reality becomes
the only Reality that exists for the writer and that also brings about
artistically the "achieved reality" of the fictional universe. Here the
issues are likewise more complicated than what can be seen from a
purely formal analysis.

With a few exceptions the realistic novel of the 1930s was rural in
the sense that its main "chronotope" was the Chinese village or small
town. Even in such seemingly urban works as Lao She's *Luotuo
Xiangzi* (Rickshaw), the evocation of old Peking has a predominantly
rural character. One can almost make the generalization that the
evolution of modern Chinese fiction is a narrative of urban–rural
transition—from the urban-based subjective short story to the more
objective rural novels of the 1930s. This is in sharp contrast to the
development of English literature, which Raymond Williams has
traced as a shift from the pastoral, "knowable communities" of the
countryside to the "cities of darkness and light."[16] How might we
account for this contrary development? In my view, extraliterary
factors—the historical situation in the first half of the twentieth
century—did indeed intrude upon both the collective consciousness
of writers and their fictional worlds—so much so that the real and
the fictional became closely intertwined.

It was at this juncture that the Soviet Marxist notion of "reflectionism" began to exert a powerful impact by its injunction that
literature must reflect the reality of social life. In its Chinese formulation introduced by leftist theoreticians such as Zhou Yang, reflectionism assumed both a passive and a positive role: the fictional text
was seen as a reflecting mirror at the same time as the act of writing
was assigned the function of active critique of societal evils. In other
words, the problem of realism took on an ideological dimension in
which the fictional form—particularly the novel—was made not only
to reproduce a broad mosaic of life but also to articulate a wide
range of societal discontent. As evidenced in the polemical essays by
Qu Qiubai and a host of leftists, popularity of language became
increasingly a populist matter in which the issue of the mass audi-

ence was considered more vital than the creative intention of the author.

This more ideological mode of realism demands a more "committed" interpretive strategy than is given in Anderson's rather formal and negative appraisal. If we take an author-oriented approach, it would seem that in their eagerness to have their fictional canvas encompass a totality of social life, the socially committed writers of the 1930s were caught in the very chaos and disarray of reality itself—to the extent that just as real life itself continued to unfold and baffle the author, its fictional representation likewise led to no neat closure. Some of the long novels written in the 1930s and 1940s are sprawling narratives, forming (sometimes incomplete) trilogies or tetralogies, such as Ba Jin's trilogy *Jiliu* (Torrent) or Lao She's *Sishi tongtang* (Four Generations under One Roof). It seems as if these fictional narratives strove to approximate the process of modern Chinese history by highlighting some of its important moments in the spatial frames of a village or a family. In fact, this narrative "imitation" of history became a significant creative ethos. Even Lin Yutang, an otherwise apolitical author, wrote his only novel "of contemporary Chinese life," *Moment in Peking*[17] (rendered in Chinese as *Jinghua yanyun*), as a narrative of family history.

Thus Chinese literary practice in the 1930s tended to make a dual demand upon author and text—for both sincerity and authenticity—in order to realize the cathartic effect of an imagined sharing of experience between author and reader(s). In this context of sharing, the literary text becomes ill-defined: its language tends to refer as much to what lies outside—that is, the real external world— as to the literary elements within it. In sum, literary or formalistic consciousness is cut through by reality and emotion in the raw. It is this "hybrid" quality that has served for Chinese readers and critics as the general yardstick by which to judge the artistic quality of modern Chinese fiction. We may consider this stance as the "realism of conscience": it "confesses that it owes a duty, some kind of reparation, to the real world—a real world to which it submits itself unquestioningly."[18] It compels the reader to become involved emotionally in the fictional world to the point of total identification with its authentic reality because it is thought to stem from "authentic reality." The sheer length of the novel, therefore, becomes an advantage as it serves to build up an accumulated impact, and in its sprawling "structure" some segments can be more gripping than others. This is what Lao She rather humorously calls "stealing a hand" *(toushou)* to allow a degree of flexibility and freedom in the long novel that is more difficult to achieve in the short story.[19] To this extent, we may push Lao She's argument a step further by stating that the modern Chinese realistic novel does not seem to fulfill what one Western scholar calls "the coherence theory of realism," in which the effect of realism is achieved "not by imitation, but by creation; a creation which, working with the materials of life, absolves these by the intercession of the imagination from mere factuality and translates them into a higher order."[20]

There is no need, of course, to draw a clear line between these two superficial stances—realism of conscience and realism of coherence—and categorize modern Chinese fiction accordingly as belonging predominantly to the former. What complicates the matter further is the obvious issue of intention versus realization. For all its manifested sincerity of intention, a literary text of social conscience depends nevertheless on its formal properties in order to realize its didactic content or its external "ambition." What needs to be (re)emphasized is that what Anderson regards as the "eruption of the crowd" represents both a reconfiguration of voices in the text (in which the hitherto silenced collective takes on a commanding presence) and a conscious authorial reorientation concerning the social purpose of fiction. If this reorientation from self to society can no longer be contained (as Anderson would argue) by the realist form of the May Fourth story, it does not follow that it would lead inevitably to the demise of the realist form itself. In other words, as it often happens when we read the novels of the 1930s, different texts of realism, even if animated by similar social impulses, are enriched in different ways by the uses of language. Here we are not merely talking about regional dialects or the other populist concerns raised by leftist critics. Indeed we must be concerned with the literary uses of narrative language (in such matters as plot, character, tone, voice, etc.). In a work like Xiao Hong's "short" novel *Shengsi chang* (Field of Life and Death), for example, we can argue that a sincere impulse of social conscience is translated into an authentic art of evocation in which the materials of her familiar life are absolved by the intercession of the author's unique imagination and language. Another of her novels, *Hulanhe zhuan* (Tales of Hulan River), does not even read like an average novel, in the opinion of Mao Dun: "It is a narrative poem, a colorful genre painting, a haunting song."[21] One should also add that in this work of "disconnected fragments" the most conscience-ridden moment—the episode about the child-bride—is also structurally and symbolically the most significant, as it brings a purposely intrusive feminist perspective to bear on a narrative of remembrance of her "native soil" *(xiangtu).*

In fact, those works of realist fiction that have endured are precisely those that combine conscience with imagination, social content with formal consciousness. Recent mainland Chinese scholars are beginning to differentiate several varieties of realism in the regional fiction of the 1930s. More specifically, they have seen fit to recover a more "cultured" variety of fiction known as the "Beijing School," consisting of such writers as Fei Ming, Shen Congwen, Ling Shuhua, Xiao Qian, and Wang Zengqi.[22] Among them, the name of Shen Congwen enjoys an exalted position as a writer whose visions of rural reality do not fall into the same revolutionary mode. Interestingly, it is also Shen's more lyrical type of regional fiction that proved to be particularly inspiring to the young generation of writers associated with the "search for roots" *(xungen)* movement in the mid-1980s than the more politically conscientious realism of Wu Zuxiang, Zhang Tianyi, Sha Ting, and Ai Wu.

What distinguishes the "homeland" fiction of Shen Congwen from the usual mode of critical realism is its treatment of the rural locality not merely as critical leverage for dramatizing a social message. According to David Wang's analysis, West Hunan, Shen's homeland, is both a barbarous country and a landscape rich with literary allusions, in particular to the two great masterpieces of classical Chinese literature: Qu Yuan's *Chuci* (Songs of the South) and Tao Qian's "Taohua yuan ji" (Peach Blossom Spring). Shen is fully aware that he is writing within this illustrious tradition. Thus his native soil fiction comprises both a biographical attachment and an imaginative tie to the literary place. But Shen also knows only too well that the present reality of his native land is anything but idyllic. The inevitable tension generated by the "dialogic" relationship between past and present becomes the source of a unique vision of reality. Unlike other writers concerned only with contemporary social injustice and suffering, Shen projects a pastoral world that is based on what Wang calls the "poetics of imaginary nostalgia," a paradox of authentic loss and imagined retrieval that characterizes this specific "tragic-ironic" mode of writing rooted in the conscience of homeland or native soil.

> Native soil literature is literally and rhetorically a "rootless" literature, a kind of literature whose meaning hinges on the simultaneous (re)discovery and erasure of the treasured image of the homeland. Native soil writers come forth to write out what they fail to experience in reality. Their imagination plays just as important a role as their lived experience, and their "gesture" of remembering is no less important than the things remembered. Insofar as the lost past can only be regained through the act of writing, the "form" of remembrance may become itself the content of what is remembered . . . Insofar as the "real" native soil and homeland can only be recapitulated in the form of continuous regression, native soil literature always appears as a "belated" form of writing, nurtured ironically on the "imagination" of loss that calls itself nostalgia.[23]

This paradigm of "nostalgia" not only provides an apt characterization of the work of Shen Congwen and Xiao Hong; it has also had an unintended bearing on the *xungen* fiction of the 1980s. For unlike the fiction of critical realism that emphasizes the immediate linkage between the reality depicted within the text and the Reality without, Shen's evocative powers rise beyond the demands of narrow reflectionism—so much so that his homeland becomes both realistic and allegorical: it refers to both the actual place of his birth and "a textual locus where his discourse 'about' the homeland has germinated, and through which he transports his social/political ideas. In its textual transcription, West Hunan is as much a 'homeland' for Shen Congwen as it is for his readers, wherever their actual homelands are."[24] In this regard, we can also redefine Shen's imaginary nostalgia as a discourse on the paradox of modernity, as he himself made explicit in *Xiangxing sanji* (Random Sketches of a Trip to Hunan), or even something of a national allegory viewed from a schizophrenic perspective. That is to say, Shen's "homeland" represents a displaced "communal" world alienated and uprooted, ironically, by the rootless native soil writer's impulse to construct a coherent narrative about it—an "external" impulse derived from a belief in a new Chinese nationhood as a product of modernity. Whether or not we have stretched his "imaginary" boundaries too far afield, there can be no doubt that Shen Congwen's fiction has enriched the artistic resources and expanded the cultural horizons of modern Chinese realism.

When we think about the post-Mao literature of the 1980s, the immediate background against which we should measure its achievements must be the literature produced during the Cultural Revolution—not Shen Congwen, but Hao Ran and the "mass style" of revolutionary romanticism: what Birch extolled as the great return of the "communal" in the mode of heroic hagiography. In this regard, Birch's many insights are still valid: the renewed sense of social order, the return of didacticism, the formula writing, the popular desire to entertain, and the appearance of the positive hero as either peasant or cadre. Above all, Birch argues that with this great return to the comic-satiric mode, realism of the May Fourth variety becomes all but impossible:

> The post-1942 work of fiction can be assigned to the realist mode only if we accept the arrival of the millennium on the mainland . . . We would have to believe that human nature itself has been fundamentally changed there before we could find realism in fiction where all behavior patterns are dictated by class origin, where the motivation of positive types can be paralleled only by the lives of epic heroes or saints in other literatures, and where the happy ending is mandatory, a formal requirement. What Hao Ran offers us is allegory.[25]

Birch's ironic doubt is apposite because, as he remarks, with the changed definition of human nature there is no room in the fictional text for "the implied author as an individual taking an independent stand."[26] However, the ethos of "taking an individual stand" was not entirely dead: from Ding Ling, Wang Shiwei, and Xiao Jun in the 1940s to Hu Feng, Qian Gurong, Feng Xuefeng, Qin Zhaoyang, Wang Meng, and Liu Binyan in the 1950s and early 1960s, the history of political campaigns has been "littered" with "fallen" heroes who in different ways continued to demand an individual voice without challenging entirely the Party's collective goals. It is not surprising, therefore, that we have witnessed, after Mao's death, "another return"—on the part of these dedicated Party or non-Party "individualists" who were castigated as "rightists." Their mental journey is vividly portrayed in Wang Meng's story "Buli" (Bolshevik Salute).[27] And as the story's title clearly reveals, the intellectual outlook of this entire generation born after May Fourth had been shaped most significantly by Soviet revolutionary literature and thought.

This is not the place to enter into a lengthy discussion of the tradition of Soviet socialist realism. Suffice it to say that it by no means can be reduced to a fictional mode of hagiography about Stakhanovite heroes. To be sure, Chinese writers, like Ai Wu and Xiao Jun, had consciously imitated the Soviet model—with disastrous political consequences: in particular, Xiao Jun's novel, *Wuyue de kuangshan* (Coal Mines in May) received severe criticism for its "unrealistic" portrait of superheroes. But the central Soviet legacy bequeathed to a generation of Party intellectuals and writers in China, especially from the early 1950s to the early 1960s, was a cluster of literary works translated into Chinese and published primarily in *Yiwen*, the translation journal that was instrumental in introducing not only the new crop of Soviet literature after Stalin's death but also a mental attitude and a way of personal behavior that served as model for the intellectuals who blossomed during the Hundred Flowers movement and soon faded into the countryside as "rightists."[28] To put it simplistically, this mental outlook is grounded in a romantic *ressentiment* centering on the conflict between revolutionary commitment to collective goals on the one hand and personal yearning for romantic love and fulfillment on the other. Compared with the Chinese model—the "combination of revolutionary realism and revolutionary romanticism" first proclaimed during the

Great Leap Forward campaign in 1958—the Soviet model still retains a "bourgeois" edge in its insistence on the sincerity of individual feeling and perception. In the case of Hao Ran's *Jinguang dadao*
(The Golden Great Way), however, the heroism of Gao Daquan
contains no residual individualism but the personification of purely
ideological traits: a heroic figure, so to speak, in a new collective
allegorical tale.

It is intriguing to note that in the first crop of works published
after Mao's death, known as *shanghen wenxue* (literature of the
wounded), a striking feature is the portrait of a committed Party
cadre who has suffered unjustly as a victim of the wrongdoing of the
Gang of Four. Whereas the ideological gloss comes clearly from the
Party's new policy, both in characterization and in "sentiment" they
are reminiscent of the Soviet model. In a work such as Zhang Jie's
"Love Must Not Be Forgotten," blatant intertextual references to
Soviet and Russian literature become the central clue to understanding the past of the heroine's mother, whose romance with another
cadre is the focal point of the plot. The real "didactic" agenda of the
story is to restore the sacredness of this "Bolshevik" revolutionary
sentiment. And to the extent that the rehabilitated writers of the
1950s—Liu Binyan, Wang Meng, Qin Zhaoyang, Liu Shaotang,
among others—once again found themselves in a dominant position, we can chart a different course of return, a return both to a
Soviet style of revolutionary romanticism that privileges the individualism of the wronged Party cadre and to a mode of critical realism
focusing once again on the ills of socialist society. The reportage of
Liu Binyan exemplifies this trend.

It would be an easy task to follow the trend and seek out its
obvious affinities with the critical realism of the 1930s—a further
"return" that would provide an alternative line of "change and continuity" to Birch's thesis. With the demise of Hao Ran's communal
utopia, post–Cultural Revolution literature seems to bring us back
not to a "more Chinese" and popular route of exemplary didacticism
(as Birch prophesied) but directly to the May Fourth tradition of
critical realism. In some ways, this is precisely the argument of a
large number of Chinese scholars and Western observers, especially
with regard to the renewed emphasis on individualism and its atten-

dant stance on literature as a form of subjective critique of society. But I would like to differ from this assessment and agree with Birch's and Anderson's position (though for different reasons) that for all its past literary glory, realism as a technical mode and as a May Fourth legacy is found indeed to be deficient—this time by another, and much younger, generation of writers who emerged after the Cultural Revolution.

During the mid-1980s, two creative and controversial trends on the literary scene captured considerable attention: the movement known as "search for roots" and the related phenomenon of "modernistic" experimentalism. I have written elsewhere in general terms about both.[29] In this essay I will merely single out a few issues in order to look at Birch's thesis in a new light.

The impetus for a modernist mode of writing certainly grows out of a sense of deep-seated frustration of the self in its dealings with the external world, a world so enveloped by the Party's frequent shifts of ideological policy that socialist Reality as defined by the Party ceases to command any belief. The reaction of the younger generation, therefore, is not only to recover a sense of selfhood in writing but to "deconstruct" the Party's vision by renouncing its very ideological "master-narrative" through which reality is constituted. Thus the need to experiment with a new fictional language and vision becomes the new "revolutionary" credo. As the critic Li Tuo has argued, the initial step had been taken in the late 1970s by the young poets associated with the unofficial literary journal *Jintian* (Today), and what followed from its example of "obscure poetry" was a mode of writing that ran counter to the "mainstream" of post-Mao realism—from the "literature of the wounded" and "reform literature" (such as Jiang Zilong's "Manager Qiao Assumes Office" and Ke Yunlu's "New Star") and critical reportage.[30] Interestingly, Li Tuo includes both the *xungen* and experimental fiction *(shiyan xiaoshuo)* in the counterrealist trend and traces their origins to the initial position of *Today* magazine—a stance that defines literature as a purely aesthetic endeavor to be separated from politics. Since realism in the socialist mode has been so heavily politicized, the writers of this countermovement have also embarked upon another task—a purposeful deconstruction of the Chinese realist paradigm by stripping away its most sacred tenets: its reflectionism, its linear narrative and "present" time frame, its lifelike or positive characters, and above all its close and critical linkage with external social reality. Their primary "tool" is an invented "poetic" language that owes an intellectual debt to such diverse sources as Baudelaire, Kafka, García Márquez, and Shen Congwen.

That the fiction of Shen Congwen should have attained such an exalted status in their minds is not hard to explain. He was discovered for a practical purpose by the writers from Hunan—Gu Hua, He Liwei, and Han Shaogong—who consciously imitated his lyrical style (He Liwei) or turned his imaginary landscape into a land of political turmoil (Gu Hua's *Fuyong zhen*, or *A Town Called Hibiscus*) or mythic chaos (Han Shaogong's "Ba Ba Ba"). But more important, Shen Congwen's fiction as analyzed above opens up new possibilities for reinventing reality. If for Shen (as David Wang argues) writing fiction about the "native soil" is an act of nostalgic retrieval and artistic re-presentation, the young writers of the 1980s have replaced Shen's "poetics of imaginary nostalgia" with a poetics of cultural reinvention. In Han Shaogong's story "Gui qulai" (The Homecoming), for instance, the plot is clearly embedded in the "Peach Blossom Spring" tale, thus harking back to a regional literary heritage, but the time frame is the "present" of the Cultural Revolution. The juxtaposition of past and present creates a different kind of tension from that found in Shen's stories: instead of overcoming the power of time by the imaginary reconstruction of memory, the "present" reality of the Cultural Revolution is ruptured by the foregrounded "presence" of a mythic past that claims belief. In a way, this mythic voice of the Other reality, reinvented from cultural memory, becomes in Han's other fictional stories even more significant. For, as Han and the other *xungen* writers would argue, the present reality as defined by the Party culture is but a dead "crust" overlaid on the seedbed of a vibrant mixture of several ancient and unorthodox cultures.

And this is precisely the gist of the *xungen* writers' argument: that they have been cut off from the deeper layers, the dormant "lava," of Chinese culture. Their search for "roots" cannot be a nostalgic act but an active effort of imaginary reinvention, so as to revitalize these long absent cultural resources as a way to reconstruct a more meaningful reality (in terms of art) and as a countermyth to the Party's master allegory of revolutionary history. Here I see their project—still ongoing—to be twofold, having to do with their own creative resources of language and their mythic uses of reality and history.

When we examine the works of *xungen* fiction in geographical terms, it would seem that they betray both a regional association and a "marginal" position. Like Shen Congwen, most writers purposefully paint a "border town" landscape by situating their fictional settings in the peripheral regions: the Xing'an mountains in Heilongjiang (Zheng Wanlong), the southwest province of Yunnan (Ah Cheng), northern Shanxi and Shenxi (Shi Tiesheng), and Tibet (Zhaxi Dawa). There is an evident fascination with the minority ethnic cultures of these remote regions that provide an exotic contrast to the dominant Han culture. But if we bear in mind the somewhat ironic fact that most *xungen* writers reside in the urban centers, it is not surprising that they, too, are strangers to these peripheral regions that they wish to uncover as authentic "centers" of Chinese civilization. Herein lies their paradox (somewhat reminiscent of Shen Congwen once again): like exiles returning home after a long absence, they have found the "homeland" of their own culture foreign, and the journey to their "roots" becomes one of increasing "defamiliarization." However, what matters is precisely their attempt to set up by various narrative devices an imaginary boundary between the familiar real world, which continues to be dominated by the ideologies of the Party center, and the unfamiliar "other" world they imagine to have existed. To this extent, their imagined "roots" pose a direct cultural challenge—from the real or imagined margins—to the political center.

At the same time, after separating their "marginal" world from the central sphere of the Party, some writers have become more "localized," using fiction to construct a genealogy of their own region as a more authentic form of history that threatens to substitute for the Party's own hegemonic, but false, History. Jia Pingwa, a writer from Shanxi, wrote a series of fictional sketches of his hometown, Shangzhou, in a reinvented traditional *biji* style. Mo Yan, a writer from

Shandong (a region geographically rather close to the Party center in Beijing), produced his most celebrated novel, *Hong gaoliang* (Red Sorghum), as a familial and "tribal" record *(zupu)* in which the implied author takes painstaking steps to "reconstruct" the heroic feats of his grandparents' generation during the Sino-Japanese War. The novel becomes a double narrative framed by seemingly meticulous research: the more the implied author throws in fragments of documents from the local gazetteers and other historical sources (a clever meta-fictional device), the more the story gains authenticity and plausibility, and the more the reader is made aware of the distance that separates that past world from present reality. Certainly for Mo Yan, familial and local history is the only history that counts.

It can be argued that this desire to (re)construct a family or regional history is itself the result of an obsession with history, which is certainly a dominant Chinese cultural trait. In modern Chinese literature, that obsession is expressed by fictional narratives in which history presents itself not only as the background of reality but as a governing structural principle. Thus it is common to construct fictional trilogies or tetralogies about several generations in one family as something of a microcosm of the historical process. Some works by Ba Jin and Lao She, mentioned earlier, are famous examples. It was only when modern Chinese history was appropriated by the Chinese Communist Party and turned into revolutionary canon and sanctified as the only History that recent fiction departed from its ideological grip and sought to attain a "history" of its own. One finds such a new historical move in Mo Yan's novel—a family chronicle that ironically replicates the same historical moments as in the Party's History. The Party's glorious revolutionary past in guerrilla warfare during the Sino-Japanese War has been a recurrent *topos* for a large number of revolutionary novels and operas produced before and during the Cultural Revolution. In Mo Yan's *Red Sorghum*, the war becomes a family saga in which the "real" heroes and heroines are family ancestors and their bandit friends, thus edging out the Party's commanding role. At the same time, the novel does not merely offer a new version of history; more significantly it lays bare a realm of desire and violence that has never existed in the Party's canonical literature—as if releasing from long repression certain primordial libidinous forces that clamor for narrative recognition. Lurking in the family saga is a subtext of the "collective unconscious" of Chinese life, a record of totems and taboos. This has become increasingly the new "obsession" of a number of writers: Liu Heng's "Fuxi Fuxi," a story of a sexual obsession between aunt and nephew, ends with a blatant reference to the size of the dead nephew's sexual organ. Male sexual prowess thus becomes a new "totemic" force governing the regional universe of peasant life—a far cry from Hao Ran's world of the "golden way" in which the physical power of the tall, big, and perfect hero (Gao Daquan) reveals no trace of sexual energy, only abundant ideological fervor.[31]

It seems that in searching for the "roots" of Chinese culture, *xungen* fiction has unveiled several "realities"—mythic, historical, sexual—that combine to form a new "regional" universe encased in a radically different narrative structure in which the old revolutionary formula no longer holds. Reading such texts as Han Shaogong's "Ba Ba Ba," Mo Yan's *Hong Gaoliang*, Liu Heng's "Fuxi Fuxi," and Ge Fei's "Danian," not to mention the works of Can Xue and Yu Hua, I am reminded, ironically, of what Cyril Birch said about the tragic-ironic mode of May Fourth fiction: "The old feeling of order disrupted and restored is gone; order itself is gone, the world is in chaos, any kind of happy ending unthinkable."[32] And instead of the formulaic closure in pointing to the shining vista of the "correct" way toward communism, the plot of the *xungen* works seems only to lead to a clash of some primordial and irrational forces out of human control and beyond the realm of any bright reality. Tragedy and the "supernatural" (in terms of the ironic workings of nature and fate) wait in the wings—wait for liberation via fiction. It is fair to say that, whatever its intentions, Chinese "roots" fiction has not only pushed old realism to new frontiers; it has gone beyond realism.

The key issue for this transformation of realism is language—and a new consciousness of the function of language in fiction. As Li Tuo has remarked, the theory of realism had attained great popularity in China because it "recognizes the transparency of language; it recognizes that language is indeed capable of reaching the reality it depicts." But the writers of "obscure poetry" began to emphasize just the opposite—"the subjectivity of poetry": "They focus on the self-completeness of language itself and the feasibility of treating the literary text as a system of signs. It does not need to have any corresponding relation with the real world."[33] This new conception of literary language becomes the starting point of experimental fiction. According to Li Tuo, this experimental trend began with Ma Yuan, who constantly seeks to subvert and deconstruct the narrative process itself—hence meta-fiction—and Can Xue, who expands the visual and imagistic properties of the Chinese language so as to render "narration into an endless accumulative process"[34]—piling up rows of distorted images to create a nightmarish landscape of decay and death. It reaches a height in the recent works of Yu Hua, whose experiments take on another macabre dimension by subverting the conventional reading habits of Chinese readers. Aside from these three, a host of younger experimentalists crowded the literary scene in 1987 and 1988—Ye Zhaoyan, Ge Fei, Su Tong, Sun Ganlu, among others—so much so that Li Tuo (in his preface to a collection of Yu Hua's stories) ceremoniously announces the end of the Party's "worker-peasant-soldier" literature.[35]

It may be too early to assess the implications of this new "linguistic turn" for creative writing. If we place it side by side with *xungen* fiction and treat it as two complementary aspects of the same phenomenon (in another, more unilinear division, the *xungen* trend is said to have ended around 1987 to be "followed" by experimental fiction), it would seem that the writers associated with these trends are terribly ambitious: they would like to go back to the "roots" of the *baihua* language itself, together with its repository of dialects, in order to recover its potential "allure," thereby fashioning a prose unsullied by the present ideological language of the "Mao discourse" (*Mao wenti,* in Li Tuo's phraseology). A few of the practitioners have presumably returned to the "purity" of the personal prose tradition of the Ming dynasty (Wang Zengqi) or scaled down modern prose's vocabulary to its bare essentials in order to sharpen its oral quality (as in Ah Cheng's most recent "*biji* stories," for which the reading process should be both intellectual and verbal, as if reading aloud in one's mind). Most writers, however, experiment by reinventing their own language and fictional form.

Interestingly, the generic form found most useful is neither the short story nor the long novel, but the in-between form of "medium-length" novella (*zhongpian xiaoshuo,* consisting of anywhere between fifty thousand and eighty thousand Chinese characters). No critic seems to have studied the origins and evolution of the form or accounted for its privileged position in the writings of "roots" and experimental fiction. To recall a quote about Western realistic genres used earlier in this essay: "Whereas the conventional nineteenth-century novel normally accommodates the processes of a dense, ordered society, the short story has been by its very nature remote from the community—romantic, individualistic, and intransigent." If this statement still holds any relevance, it would seem that at one level the new writers are still negotiating uneasily within the formal constraints of the fictional narrative—undecided, as it were, between conformity and intransigence. On the other hand, the brevity of the short-story form obviously cannot accommodate the process of constructing an alternative history or myth. The novella becomes, therefore, the fitting form that offers sufficient freedom for exploration without imposing an overall structure or "order." The technical problem becomes, therefore, not so much whether the fictional form is adequate to frame a full range of social reality as whether it can give some shape to the unformed workings of a fertile imagination. To some extent, as Han Shaogong's novella "Ba Ba Ba" has shown, the thematic material is too copious to be contained in a short story; at the same time, however, the conceptual structure of the story has the pretension of being a long novel, for which Han's narrative language cannot fully sustain itself. In other words, there remains a gap—not necessarily between word and reality, but between intention and realization. In some cases, the scope of a vision is undercut by the limitations of the language; in others, the inventive flourishes of language all but saturate the text and submerge the vision.

The case of Yu Hua's fiction again offers a revealing example. Several kinds of language experiment are undertaken—a violent parody of a Ming *sanyan* story ("Gudian aiqing," or "Classical Romance") written in imitation classical vernacular; a melodrama about fratricide ("Xianshi yizhong," or "A Kind of Reality") with an ornate "overworked" naturalistic language that depicts torture and killing in minute detail as if to test the reader's endurance of cruelty; a "semiotic" story ("Shishi ruyan," or "A World of Affairs like Smoke") in which human characters become nameless numbers and the fragmented plot brings no cohesion or sequence of time. It is certainly true, as Li Tuo argues, that Yu Hua's language constantly subverts the typical reading expectations of the Chinese readership who wishes to be either entertained or instructed.[36] Instead, Yu Hua's narrative proceeds coldly and cruelly, using the visual capacities of the language to give the most frightening spectacles of violence and death. In so doing, the narrative challenges the reader either to give up reading altogether or to change old reading habits in order to accommodate to the text. Despite its brilliant surfaces, which make the first reading an equally violent experience of shock and dismay, the effect of the challenge gradually wears off, and one finds that the fictional text resembles rather a chessboard on which showy linguistic moves are made to win a language game. (One would not be surprised to detect traces of Alain Robbe-Grillet.) In this sense, Yu Hua's experimental fiction is a bold exercise, but not in my view a mature work of art.

These avant-garde ventures in language do not necessarily entail a journey into High Modernism. One is yet to find any experiment in the vein of Joyce's *Ulysses* or *Finnegan's Wake,* where fictional language becomes a labyrinthean unfolding of a highly subjective "focal consciousness" from an individual character. (In this connection, the modernist writer from Taiwan, Wang Wen-hsing, is much closer to Joyce than is any mainland writer.) On the contrary, what Birch might call the "communal" impulses—from the more traditional attitude of norm sharing and communal celebration that is clearly evident in communist fiction, to the 1930s mode of rural fiction that seeks to represent the whole world of a village or town— are not entirely dead in current mainland Chinese writing. (In the case of Taiwanese fiction, one might add, this communal impulse is expressed by the native soil writers in their strong reaction against the excesses of urban individualism and alienation.) Even in Yu Hua's linguistic universe, one nevertheless detects a vaguely "communal" space that is shared by all the "characters." One wonders if the Chinese attraction to García Márquez's *One Hundred Years of*

Solitude may not have something to do with his "magic" evocation of a mythic/historical village, Macondo, which represents his homeland—or even with Faulkner's Yoknapatawpha. Perhaps there has always been in contemporary Chinese writing, hidden behind all the avant-gardist displays of language and distortions of reality, an "imaginary nostalgia" about China after all.

Notes

1. Visitation of the Past in Han Shaogong's Post-1985 Fiction

This paper is for C. T. Hsia.

1. W. J. F. Jenner, "Is a Modern Chinese Literature Possible?" in *Essays in Modern Chinese Literature and Literary Criticism*, ed. Wolfgang Kubin and Rudolf G. Wagner (Bochum: Brockmeyer, 1982), p. 225.

2. See Deng Xiaoping, "Congratulatory Message to the Fourth Congress of Chinese Writers and Artists," in *Chinese Literature for the 1980s: The Fourth Congress of Writers and Artists*, ed. Howard Goldblatt (Armonk: M. E. Sharpe, 1982), pp. 7–14.

3. Malcolm Bradbury and James McFarlane, "The Name and Nature of Modernism," in *Modernism*, ed. Bradbury and McFarlane (Harmondsworth: Penguin, 1976), p. 25.

4. Li Tuo, "Zhongguo dangdai wenxuede 'xianfeng' yu 'xungen'" ('Avant-Gardism' and 'Root Seeking' in Contemporary Chinese Literature), in *Shijie zhongwen xiaoshuoxuan* (The Commonwealth of Modern Chinese Fiction), ed. Liu Shaoming (Joseph S. M. Lau) and Ma Hanmao (Helmut Martin); Taipei: Shibao, 1987), I, p. 261.

5. Liu Zaifu, "Jinshiniande Zhongguo wenxue jingshen yu wenxue daolu" (The Spirit and Direction of Chinese Literature in the Past Decade), in *Liu Zaifu ji* (The Collected Works of Liu Zaifu; Harbin: Heilongjiang Educational Press, 1988), p. 253.

6. See Zheng Shusen's editorial note to Liu Heng's selection "Gouride liangshi" (Dog Shit Food), in *Bayue jiaoyang* (The Scorching Sun; Taipei: Hongfan, 1988), p. 124.

7. Lei Da, "Dongdangde diju" (The Vibrating Lower Valleys), *Xiaoshuo xuankan* (Fiction Selections), p. 107 (February 1989).

8. Wang Dewei, "Jirenxing: Dangdai dalu xiaoshuode zhongsheng 'guai' xiang" (Pantheon of the Deformed: The 'Bizarre' Visage of Life as Seen in Contemporary PRC Fiction), *Zhongsheng xuanhua* (Heteroglossia; Taipei: Yuanliu, 1988), p. 209.

9. "Root seeking" is *xungen*. It acquired its currency in PRC literary discourse from an essay by Han Shaogong called "Wenxuede gen" (The Roots of Literature). The response from Han's fellow writers was immediate and voluminous. Not counting academic papers, it is estimated that more than fifty essays of various length were published in newspapers and magazines within a year after Han's piece appeared in the April 1985 issue of *Zuojia* (Writers). See Huang Jichi, "Zhongguo dangdai wenxuede wenhua 'xungen' taolun shuping" (Comments on the Cultural 'Root Seeking' in Contemporary Chinese Literature), in his *Wenxuede chuantong yu xiandai* (Literary Tradition and Modernity; Hong Kong: Huahan, 1988), pp. 173–187.

10. Han Shaogong, "Xuebu huigu: Daiba" (My First Steps Recollected: In Lieu of an Afterword), *Yuelan* (Guangdong: Renmin chubanshe, 1981), pp. 265–266.

11. *Urbling* is a word invented by Rachel May. "The Chinese term [*zhiqing*] means literally 'educated youth' . . . In the late 1950s and early 1960s, when the Chinese economy failed to create sufficient job opportunities for them, Urblings were strongly encouraged to go to the countryside supposedly to live and work with their country cousins." See *Seeds of Fire: Chinese Voices of Conscience*, ed. Geremie Barmé and John Minford (New York: Hill and Wang, 1988), p. 102. For a critical study of *zhiqing* literature, see Kam Louie, "Educated Youth Literature: Self Discovery in the Chinese Village," in his *Between Fact and Fiction: Essays on Post-Mao Chinese Literature and Society* (Sydney: Wild Peony, 1989), pp. 91–102.

12. "Juhui" is translated as "The Get-Together" in *Mao's Harvest: Voices from China's New Generation*, ed. Helen F. Siu and Zelda Stern (New York and Oxford: Oxford University Press, 1983), pp. 198–207. Titled "Urbling Winter," the first act of *WM (Wo'Men)* is in English translation in *Seeds of Fire*, pp. 103–116.

13. I have discussed the limitations of PRC "topical" literature in my article "Text and Context: Toward a Commonwealth of Modern Chinese Literature," in *Worlds Apart: Recent Chinese Writing and Its Audiences*, ed. Howard Goldblatt (Armonk: M. E. Sharpe, 1990), pp. 11–28.

14. For a discussion of "Banzhuren" (The Schoolmaster), "Shanghen" (The Scar), and other representative works in the *shanghen* genre, see my essay "The Wounded and the Fatigued: Reflections on Post-1976 Chinese Fiction," *Journal of Oriental Studies* 20:128–142 (1982).

15. *Commonwealth*, I, 261.

16. Cyril Birch, "Change and Continuity in Chinese Fiction," in *Modern Chinese Literature in the May Fourth Era*, ed. Merle Goldman (Cambridge, Mass.: Harvard University Press, 1977), p. 386.

17. Han, "Roots," *Zuojia*, 4:2 (1985).

18. Readers interested in ancient Chu culture can consult Wen Chongyi, *Chu wenhua yanjiu* (A Study of Chu Culture; Nangang: Academia Sinica, 1967); Zhang Zhengming, *Chu wenhuashi* (A History of Chu Culture; Shanghai: Renmin chubanshe, 1987). An interesting study in English, with modern linkages, is Lawrence A. Schneider, *A Madman of Chu* (Berkeley: University of California Press, 1980).

19. "Guiqulai," in *Commonwealth*, I, p. 274; this story is translated as "The Homecoming" in Jeanne Tai's *Spring Bamboo: A Collection of Contemporary Short Stories* (New York: Random House, 1989), pp. 22–40; as "Déjà vu" by Margaret H. Decker, in *Furrows: Peasants, Intellectuals, and the State*, ed. Helen F. Siu (Stanford: Stanford University Press, 1990), pp. 223–237. For stylistic reasons I prefer my own translation.

20. It is impossible to give in the space of a note an account of how the *zhiguai* motif has prevailed in traditional Chinese fiction up to the late Qing. Indeed, as H. C. Chang has claimed: "The supernatural was always part of Chinese life." "General Introduction," *Chinese Literature 3: Tales of the Supernatural* (New York: Columbia University Press, 1984), p. 1. Chang's forty-page introduction gives an excellent survey of this genre of fiction from the earliest times to the Ming dynasty.

21. C. T. Hsia, "Obsession with China: The Moral Burden of Modern Chinese Literature," Appendix I, in *A History of Modern Chinese Fiction*, 2nd ed. (New Haven: Yale University Press, 1971), pp. 533–534.

22. Shi Shuqing, *Wentan fansi yu qianzhan: Shi Shuqing yu dalu zuojia duihua* (Reflections and Prospects: Shi Shuqing's Dialogues with PRC Writers; Hong Kong: Mingbao chubanshe, 1989), p. 128.

23. *Lu Xun quanji* (Complete Works of Lu Xun; Hong Kong: Wenxue yanjiushe, n.d.), VI, p. 483.

24. "Ba Ba Ba," in *Tansuo xiaoshuoji* (Exploratory Fiction: A Collection; Shanghai: Shanghai wenyi chubanshe, 1986), p. 5.

25. Michael Duke, "Reinventing China: Cultural Exploration in Contemporary Chinese Fiction," *Issues and Studies: A Journal of China Studies and International Affairs* 25:41 (August 1989).

26. Jeffrey C. Kinkley, *The Odyssey of Shen Congwen* (Stanford: Stanford University Press, 1987), p. 111.

27. "Hsiao-hsiao" (Xiao-xiao), trans. Eugene Eoyang, in *Modern Chinese Stories and Novellas: 1919–1949*, ed. Joseph S. M. Lau, C. T. Hsia, and Leo Ou-fan Lee (New York: Columbia University Press, 1981), p. 235.

28. Liu Zaifu, "Lun Bing Zai" (On Bing Zai), *Guangming ribao* (Guangming

Daily), November 4, 1988; reprinted in *Fuyin baokan ziliao* (Newspapers and Magazines Research Materials Reproductions), p. 170, (November 1988).

29. Yan Wenjing, "Wo shibushi shangle nianjide Bing Zai?" (Am I an Aging Bing Zai?) *Zuopin yu zhengming* (Works and Polemics) 2:66 (1986).

30. Leo Ou-fan Lee, *Voices from the Iron House: A Study of Lu Xun* (Bloomington: Indiana University Press, 1987), p. 77.

31. For a discussion of Ah Cheng's discovery or rediscovery of traditional Chinese virtues, see Du Maike (Michael Duke), "Zhonghua zhidao bijing butui: Ping Ah Cheng de 'Qiwang'" (The Chinese Way Has Not Declined After All: A Critique of Ah Cheng's "The Chess Master") *Jiushi niandai* (The Nineties), pp. 82–85 (August 1985); Kam Louie, "The Short Stories of Ah Cheng: Daoism, Confucianism and Life," in *Between Fact and Fiction,* pp. 76–91.

32. As Han Shaogong informed Shi Shuqing in the interview, *Reflections and Prospects,* p. 136.

33. Angel Flores, "Magical Realism in Spanish-American Fiction," *Hispania* 38:190 (1955); of related interest, Floyd Merrell, "The Ideal World in Search of Its Reference: An Inquiry into the Underlying Nature of Magical Realism," *Chasqui* 4:6 (February 1975); Scott Simpkins, "Magical Strategies: The Supplement of Realism," *Twentieth-Century Literature* 34:140–154 (Summer 1988).

34. The translation is David Hawkes's; *The Story of the Stone* (Bloomington: Indiana University Press, 1979), I, p. 55.

35. "Nü Nü Nü," in *Diliu bumen* (The Sixth Compartment), ed. Xi Xi (Taipei: Hongfan, 1988), p. 159.

36. Tsai Yuanhuang, for one, has chosen to see, inter alia, the interpersonal relationships between Aunt Shu and her nephew and sworn sister in terms of "limits of kindness and patience." See "Lun Han Shaogong de zhongpian xiaoshuo 'Ba Ba Ba,' 'Nü Nü Nü,' 'Huozhai'" (On Han Shaogong's Novellas "Ba Ba Ba," "Nü Nü Nü," "Fire House"), in his *Haixia liangan xiaoshuode fengmao* (Aspects of Fiction in the PRC and Taiwan; Taipei: Yadian, 1989), p. 178.

37. Sun Longji, "The Deep Structure of Chinese Culture," in *Seeds of Fire,* p. 31.

38. Joseph S. M. Lau, "Duty, Reputation, and Selfhood in Traditional Chinese Narratives," in *Expressions of Self in Chinese Literature,* ed. Robert E. Hegel and Richard C. Hessney (New York: Columbia University Press, 1985), pp. 363–383.

39. Aldous Huxley, *The Devils of Loudon* (New York: Harper and Row, 1952), quoted by Anne F. Thurston, "Urban Violence during the Cultural Revolution: Who Is to Blame?" in *Violence in China: Essays in Culture and Counterculture,* ed. Jonathan N. Lipman and Stevan Harrell (Albany: State University of New York Press, 1990), pp. 150–151.

2. Past, Present, and Future in Mo Yan's Fiction of the 1980s

1. New York: Free Press, 1975. Page numbers given in text.
2. Peasants' "speak[ing] for themselves" in modern times seems to me to put a rather too populistic interpretation on the stormy events of twentieth-century Chinese history. Although every person, even an illiterate peasant, has his or her own individual personality, I think the faces in a mob are still "faceless," just as are the characters depicted in scenes of revolutionary peasant uprising such as, for example, in Ding Ling's *Taiyang zhao zai Sanggan he shang* (The Sun Shines over the Sanggan River; Beijing, 1952), trans. Xianyi and Gladys Yang (Peking: Foreign Languages Press [FLP hereafter], 1954). See note 4.
3. Louis Althusser, "Ideology and Ideological State Apparatuses (Notes towards an Investigation)," in *Lenin and Philosophy and Other Essays*, trans. Ben Brewster (New York: Monthly Review Press, 1971), and Edward Shils, "Ideology," in *The Constitution of Society* (Chicago: University of Chicago Press, 1972–1982), pp. 202–223. Shils's "ideology" is more properly termed "utopia" in the sense given in Karl Mannheim, *Ideology and Utopia* (London: Routledge and Keegan Paul, 1936 [1929]). My thanks to Robert Kramer for this suggestion.
4. As depicted in much post-Mao fiction, the interminable cadre-organized meetings during the past forty years in which peasants were invited to "speak for themselves" (and often denied the freedom not to speak) were highly subject to manipulation by "their superiors" in the Communist Party hierarchy, both peasant cadres and visitors from higher up.
5. The Maoist image of the peasants as the group whose interests writers should think of first was repeatedly propagated by the Dengist Party leadership (and even more conservative elements) throughout the reform period of 1978–1989 in order to criticize writers and works that have offended against Party-defined socialist ideology or limits on stylistic innovations.
6. Leo Ou-fan Lee, "Modern Chinese Fiction: An Interpretive Overview," unpublished conference paper, p. 10.
7. Ibid., p. 19.
8. Lin Yü-sheng, *The Crisis of Chinese Consciousness* (Madison: University of Wisconsin Press, 1979), chap. 6. Leo Ou-fan Lee, *Voices from the Iron House* (Bloomington: Indiana University Press, 1987). *Diary of a Madman and Other Stories*, trans. William A. Lyell (Honolulu: University of Hawaii Press, 1990), contains Lu Xun's short-story collections *Na han* and *Pang huang;* the originals are in *Lu Xun quanji* (Beijing: Renmin wenxue chubanshe, 1981), vols. 1 and 2, respectively.

9. Quoted in C. T. Hsia, *A History of Modern Chinese Fiction* (New Haven: Yale University Press, 1971), p. 198.

10. For the stories mentioned here, see Joseph S. M. Lau, C. T. Hsia, and Leo Ou-fan Lee, eds., *Modern Chinese Stories and Novellas, 1919–1949* (New York: Columbia University Press, 1981). The Chinese texts for this fine anthology of May Fourth short fiction are in Liu Shao-ming and Wong Wai-leung, eds., *Zhongguo xiandai zhongduanpian xiaoshuo xuan (1919–1949)*, 2 vols. (Hong Kong, 1984 [vol. 1] and 1987 [vol. 2]).

11. "Lao She is temperamentally disposed to the rural values of 'old China'— simplicity, decency, honesty, generosity . . . [and thus he] transformed his beloved city into essentially a rural habitat that encompassed the very best elements of traditional China." Leo Ou-fan Lee, "Overview."

12. Lao She, *Luotuo xiangzi* (Peiping: Wenhua shenghuo chubanshe, 1941 [written in 1936]) or (Beijing: Renmin wenxue chubanshe, 1981). Translated by Jean M. James as *Rickshaw: The Novel Lo-t'o Hsiang Tzu* (Honolulu: University of Hawaii Press, 1979).

13. Mao Dun, *Ziye* (Shanghai: Kaiming shudian, 1933). Translated by Hsu Meng-hsiung and A. C. Barnes as *Midnight* (Peking: FLP, 1957).

14. *Touming de hong luobo* (The Crystal Carrot and Other Stories; Beijing: Zuojia chubanshe, 1986) contains "Touming de hong luobo" (November 1984); "Ku he" (March 1985); and "Baigou qiuqianjia" (April 1985). "Huanle," *Renmin wenxue* 1–2:6–42 (January-February 1987). "Dry River" is translated in Jeanne Tai, trans. and ed., *Spring Bamboo: A Collection of Contemporary Chinese Short Stories* (New York: Random House, 1989). "White Dog and the Swings" is translated in Michael S. Duke, ed., *Worlds of Modern Chinese Fiction: Short Stories and Novellas from the People's Republic, Taiwan, and Hong Kong,* (Armonk: M. E. Sharpe, 1991).

15. In many areas of north China, Mo Yan told us in July 1987, the cadres are regarded by the bulk of the peasants as "local emperors" *(tu huangdi)*, to be feared and placated. According to Victor Nee and Su Sijin, in Fujian province, where the peasants have become much better off economically, this is not necessarily the case. There many rural cadres have become nearly otiose. See their "Institutional Change and Economic Growth in China: The View from the Villages," *Journal of Asian Studies*, pp. 3–25 (February 1990). According to another private source, peasants in parts of Jiangsu province expect and are willing to put up with a great deal of economic corruption on the part of rural cadres as long as they continue to prosper at the same time.

16. On post-Mao fiction in this vein, see Michael S. Duke, *Blooming and Contending* (Bloomington: Indiana University Press, 1985), esp. chap. 3. Much of this situation had changed for the better from late 1978 through June

1989, but Party Central is now once again trying to bring the peasants (as well as the factory workers) under more-rigid control, and it is difficult to tell how well it will succeed.

17. The protagonist of "Happiness" thinks to himself as he contemplates suicide, "Last summer vacation you silently shouted out in angry indignation: 'I hate the color green,' whoever sings the praises of the color green is an executioner who kills without leaving a trace of blood." *Renmin wenxue* 1–2: 7 (January 1987).

18. In an unpublished conference paper, "In Search of the 'Genuinely Vicious Voice': Lu Xun and Contemporary Mainland Chinese Fiction" (1988), David Der-wei Wang interprets this ending as a Bakhtinian "carnivalization" of Lu Xun's famous "save the children" at the end of "Hometown." His interpretation is thought provoking, but in view of the overall treatment of women in Mo Yan's works and of the simple logic of this particular story, I prefer to read it straight. I think the implied author wants the narrator to save the woman, not the children.

19. Beijing: Zuojia chubanshe, 1988.

20. In *Hong gaoliang jiazu* (The Red Sorghum Clan; Beijing: Jiefangjun wenyi chubanshe, 1987), Mo Yan illustrates his genuine patriotism for the Chinese nation combined with nostalgia for a poor but noble race that he sees as passing away before his eyes in the present era. It goes without saying that his overwhelming concern with the fate of the Chinese nation and race, his continuing obsession with China, is one of the primary motives behind his writing. A discussion of *Red Sorghum* lies outside the scope of this essay. I have written about it in another context in "The Unchanging Image of the Japanese in Modern Chinese Literature," in *The Walls Within: Images of Westerners in Japan and Images of the Japanese Abroad*, ed. Kinya Tsuruta (Vancouver: Institute of Asian Research, University of British Columbia, 1989), pp. 313–346.

21. In the novel the riot takes place on May 28, 1987. In an ironic disclaimer on the last page of this highly realistic work, Mo Yan wrote: "This book is completely fictional in nature. If there are unfortunate similarities to any actual persons or events, they are the result of accidental coincidence. The author cannot take responsibility for either the feelings or the health of anyone who puts on these shoes and finds that they fit."

22. While I accept the Althusserian view of the ideological nature of *Garlic Song* (the implied author certainly wants his Chinese readers to sympathize with and support the peasants in the social project of reform), I also believe in both the knowledge-producing and -transmitting properties of Mo Yan's narrative (he is competent to and he does show us how the peasants think and feel and act).

23. *Suantai* is equivalent to *suanmiao*, "garlic bolt," in *The Chinese-English Dictionary* (1979); it is the long green stem of the garlic plant, similar to the green part of leeks or green onions. Sautéed alone or with pork and eaten as a vegetable dish in northern China, it is one of the staples of the Beijing diet. I will simply call it garlic for convenience.

24. On the use of the word *virtue* to include both good and bad qualities of character, see Wayne Booth, *The Company We Keep: An Ethics of Fiction* (Berkeley: University of California Press, 1988), pp. 8–12.

25. *Tiantang suantai zhi ge*, p. 243. Subsequent page numbers in the text.

26. This is a clear echo of Lu Xun's bitterly satirical remarks on traditional Chinese medicine in the preface to *Nahan*.

27. This is an act of political opposition to Communist Party and government policy, as was Gao Yang's burial of his mother in the 1960s.

28. The bureaucratic mismanagement of this disastrous fire was a scandal of major proportions among the Chinese media who covered the story and were then not allowed to report the truth about it.

29. Ba Jin's story "Gou" is briefly discussed in C. T. Hsia, *History*, p. 256, and translated in Edgar Snow, ed., *Living China: Modern Chinese Short Stories* (London: George G. Harrap, 1936), pp. 174–180. Reference is made in many other parts of *Garlic Song* to the superior food, drink, and housing of the rural Party cadres. This lends support to the overall impression that they have replaced Ba Jin's hated imperialists as the chief oppressors of the masses.

30. My aesthetic values will be implicit and obvious from the aspects of this novel I praise. Thus I shall not argue them here. Neither would I maintain that Mo Yan's ways of telling a story in Chinese are the only successful ones going. Before the Tiananmen massacre of June 4, 1989, Chinese fiction had entered into a period of healthy pluralism, and quite a few good writers were being published. It would be difficult to rank them now, but I believe that Mo Yan stands very high on any "short list" of best writers in Chinese today and that he shows tremendous promise of becoming a truly great writer.

31. The critic Li Tuo, one of Mo Yan's early supporters, writes that Mo Yan's works exhibit a particularly Chinese *yixiang* ("imagery," the dictionary definition, is less than what Li means by this concept; perhaps "ethos" is the right term) by means of which he is "producing a modern Chinese literature that has both a national and an international character." Preface to *The Crystal Carrot and Other Stories*, p. 10.

32. Though eschewing this de rigueur pretense of Maoist era fiction, one can still say that this work is certainly written *for the sake of* the Chinese peasants; it explains their plight more honestly than most works of peasant fiction from 1949 to date.

33. For this distinction between modern and postmodern, see Jean-Francois Lyotard, *The Postmodern Condition* (Minneapolis: University of Minnesota Press, 1984). Following this distinction, one can say that the vast majority of Chinese fiction in the 1980s is similarly modern, some of it is modernist, but very little if any is postmodernist in Lyotard's terms. See also Theo D'haen, "Postmodern Fiction: Form and Function," *Neophilologus* 71:144–153 (1987), where he argues that behind the fragmentation of "modernist" literature (as opposed to the "postmodern") some "remedy" or "reintegration" is provided for the reader.

34. Weaving the plot, a cliché perhaps, but a very complex business nevertheless. (See Wayne Booth, *Company*, p. 52, for this reference.)

    We can schematize the structure of the first nineteen chapters as follows, using the name of the main character in each story thread followed by the page numbers in the text (some of the stories, of course, overlap):

    Gao Yang: 1–10; 38–54; 72; 74–77; 90–110; 164–187; 232–243 (interrogation, recalls going with Aunt Fang and participation in riot); 256–271; 272–286 (the trial of ten peasants); new beginning (going to sell garlic with Uncle Fang) 198–217.

    Gao Ma: 10–13; 152–163; 188–197; 245–255; 272–286 (the trial of ten peasants, though not mentioned again); 14–37; 69–71; 78–89; 115–131.

    Jinju: 23–32; 52–54; 111–115; 146–151 (suicide by hanging); 193 (in death)–197; 132; 55–71; 78–89; 115–131.

    Aunt Fang: 43–54; 73–74; 132–145; 218–231 (in jail, recalls events just after husband's death); 272–286 (the trial of ten peasants, though not mentioned again).

    Fang family: 55–69; 147 (recalled by Jinju)–149; (recalled by Aunt Fang, Gao Ma also with them) 218–231.

    Uncle Fang: 143 (recalled by Aunt Fang, 132–segment)–145; 198–217 (killed in hit-and-run); 221–231 (burial).

    Young PLA officer: 212–213; 281–286 (a Liu Binyan–style critique of socialism from inside socialist army; dangerous for character and creator).

35. Jane E. Lewin's translation of Gérard Genette's 1972 work *Discours du récit* (Ithaca: Cornell University Press, 1980).

36. Genette eliminates the terms *anticipation* and *retrospective*, "designating as *prolepsis* any narrative maneuver that consists of narrating or evoking in advance an event that will take place later, [and] designating as *analepsis* any evocation after the fact of an event that took place earlier than the point in the story where we are at any given moment." Ibid., p. 40. Prolepses occur in *Tiantang* on pp. 112, 147, 156, 202, and 247; analepses on pp. 143, 147, 158, 165, and 247 (the same bit seems to function as both and should perhaps be called an *anachrony* in Genette's terms).

37. Sheldon Sacks, *Fiction and the Shape of Belief* (Berkeley: University of California Press, 1964).

38. This sentence as well as the reference to Sacks's book is a modified version of a sentence in Wayne Booth, *Company,* p. 64.

39. Mo Yan's use of popular ballads may also be influenced by Zhao Shuli's "Li Youcai banhua" (Rhymes of Li Youcai), but the overall theme and artistic complexity of Mo's work far surpass those of Zhao and other PRC writers of peasant fiction. Mo Yan's use of these ballads constitutes a direct attack on the values of Maoist-era peasant fiction. For "Li Youcai banhua" (1943), see Zhao Shuli, *Zhao Shuli xiaoshuo xuan* (Taiyuan: Shanxi renmin chubanshe, 1980), pp. 17–60, and *Rhymes of Li Youcai and Other Stories,* trans. Sidney Shapiro (Beijing: FLP, 1950, 1980).

40. This idea is part of Leo Ou-fan Lee's interpretation given in *Voices,* p. 55.

41. Ibid., p. 77.

42. Lin Yü-sheng, *Crisis.*

43. Much more needs to be said about the relationship between Lu Xun and contemporary criticism of Chinese culture—that of the *"He shang"* (River Elegy), "cultural exploration" *(wenhua tansuo),* and "nativist: search for roots" *(xungen)* writers—but it cannot be done here.

44. In Beijing in 1987 a well-known literary editor told my wife and me of his experiences in the north China countryside during the Cultural Revolution as a sent-down intellectual. One of the things that moved him very greatly was the realization of how materially and spiritually impoverished the peasants' lives were and how close to an animal existence they lived. He gave two examples: During breaks from work in the fields, thirsty peasants would lap water out of a horse bucket in exactly the same way a horse or a dog would, without using a cup. Peasant couples had very little to say to each other. One peasant even asked him, "What do you and your wife talk about all the time after work? Me and my old lady never have anything to say." He believed this was an accurate measure of the peasants' lack of inner life. This lack of conversation may not be all that typical of younger peasants today, but it is reflected in many post-Mao stories of life in the countryside in the 1970s and is particularly striking in Chen Kaige's film *Yellow Earth* (1985), which concerns the countryside in the 1930s.

45. Leo Ou-fan Lee, *Voices,* pp. 77–78.

3. Shen Congwen's Legacy in Chinese Literature of the 1980s

Research in China for this essay was carried out under a grant from the Committee on Scholarly Communication with the People's Republic of China and the National Endowment for the Humanities.

1. See my *The Odyssey of Shen Congwen* (Stanford: Stanford University Press,

1987). Ling Yu commented in a seminar on Shen Congwen and recent Hunanese writing hosted by Long Haiqing at the Hunan Federation of Literary and Art Circles, Changsha, December 6, 1989. Also present were Cai Cehai, Han Zongshu, He Liwei, Hu Ying, Lin He, Song Wugang, Sun Jiangong, Xiao Jianguo, and Zhao Haizhou.

2. Changsha seminar. Chen Dazhuan, "The Hunan Writers," *Chinese Literature* 2:4–5 (Summer 1989). Chen lists Can Xue as one influenced by Shen. Luo Xingtong of Jishou is a local colorist who has written Miao romances and a saga about Shen's bandit hero Long Yunfei.

3. Shen Congwen claimed he had influenced Sha Ting and He Qifang when I interviewed him on July 24, 1980. Yan Wenjing is one of the young authors Shen Congwen promoted during the Civil War years. See Shen Congwen, "Benkan yinian" (The First Year of This Supplement), *Yishibao*, October 18, 1947. Interviews with Liu Zuchun in Peking, December 17 and 19, 1989.

4. Claudio Guillén, "The Aesthetics of Literary Influence," in his *Literature as System* (Princeton: Princeton University Press, 1973).

5. Stanley Fish, "Literature in the Reader: Affective Stylistics" (1970), in his *Is There a Text in This Class? The Authority of Interpretive Communities* (Cambridge, Mass.: Harvard University Press, 1980), pp. 21–67. Wolfgang Iser, *The Act of Reading* (Baltimore: Johns Hopkins University Press, 1978). The paucity of studies of influence in modern Chinese literature has now been partly made up by the major influence study by Gregory Lee, *Dai Wangshu: The Life and Poetry of a Chinese Modernist* (Hong Kong: The Chinese University Press, 1989).

6. Ye Weilin, "Zai meiyou hangbiao de heliu shang" (On a River without Navigation Markers), in his *Jiu yang* (Premature Death from Drink; Changsha: Hunan wenyi chubanshe, 1987), pp. 105–200.

7. In preparing this essay I came across misstatements to the effect that Shen Congwen had wooed Zhang Zhaohe at Peking University, that Fei Ming influenced He Liwei—for the facts, see Wang Zengqi, preface to He Liwei, *Xiao cheng wu gushi* (No Story in This Little Town; Beijing: Zuojia chubanshe, 1986), pp. 1–8—and that Han Shaogong was rusticated to West Hunan.

8. Fish, pp. 303–371.

9. Changsha seminar.

10. Classic studies are J. Livingston Lowes, *The Road to Xanadu* (Boston: Houghton, 1927), and Richard H. Brodhead, *Hawthorne, Melville, and the Novel* (Chicago: University of Chicago Press, 1976).

11. Changsha seminar, remark by Long Haiqing.

12. Participants at the Changsha seminar said that *Xiang Jun* can refer to all contemporary Hunanese writers, or to just the young and middle-aged.

13. Wang Zengqi, preface to He Liwei, *Xiao cheng wu gushi.*

14. Exploration of "traditions," as a way out of the dilemmas of searching for "influence," was notably advocated by Ihab H. Hassan, "The Problem of Influence in Literary History: Notes Towards a Definition," *Journal of Aesthetics and Art Criticism* 14:66–76 (1955).
15. Can Xue, conversation in Changsha, December 8, 1989.
16. Wang Zengqi, preface to He Liwei, *Xiao cheng wu gushi.*
17. Changsha seminar.
18. Eva Müller of Humboldt University, Berlin, is a scholar of this subject. Zhang Xingjin, "Fang Wang Zengqi shilu" (Transcript of an Interview with Wang Zengqi), *Beijing wenxue* 317:69 (January 1989).
19. Ying Pingshu, "Fang Gu Hua tan *Rulinyuan*" (Interview with Gu Hua about *The Scholars' Garden*), *Zhonghua ribao,* May 29, 1989.
20. Gu Hua, "Na bi de juren" (A Giant among Writers), *Zheng ming* 129:50–55 (July 1988) and 130:51–55 (August 1988); quotation, 130:53.
21. Gladys Yang, "Translator's Preface," *Pagoda Ridge and Other Stories* (Beijing: Panda Books, 1985), p. 6. Gu Hua, "Na bi de juren," 129:52.
22. Gu Hua, "Na bi de juren," 130:53.
23. This term, which also means "genre painting," has been applied to the stories of Wang Zengqi. See Wang Zengqi, "Tantan fengsu hua" (A Chat about Portraits of Local Folkways), in his *Wancui wentan* (Literary Talks from My Late Blooming; Hangzhou: Zhejiang wenyi chubanshe, 1988), pp. 106–114.
24. Guo Rencheng and Tan Wei, "'Furongguo' zhong de 'furong' zhi shenma?" (What Does the "Furong" Mean in "Furongguo"?), *Qiusuo* 7:91–92 (June 1982). Mao Zedong, "Reply to a Friend," *Mao Tsetung Poems* (Beijing: Shangwu yinshuguan, 1976), pp. 78–79. Citations are from Gu Hua, *A Small Town Called Hibiscus,* trans. Gladys Yang (Beijing: Panda Books, 1983).
25. Gu Hua, *Zhen nü* (Chaste Women; Hong Kong: Xiangjiang chuban gongsi, 1987). Gu Hua, *Rulinyuan* (Taipei: Haifeng, 1990).
26. Jeffrey C. Kinkley, "Echoes of Maxim Gorky in the Works of Ding Ling and Shen Congwen," *Republican China* 15.1:56–64 (November 1989).
27. Gu Hua, "Postscript," in his *A Small Town Called Hibiscus,* pp. 258–260; Gu Hua, "About *Pagoda Ridge,*" in his *Pagoda Ridge,* pp. 256–260.
28. Gu Hua, *Furongzhen* (Beijing: Renmin wenxue chubanshe, 1984), p. 2. Translation (slightly modified) by Gladys Yang, pp. 14–15.
29. Translation from Kinkley, *The Odyssey of Shen Congwen,* pp. 176–177.
30. See Lin Qing, "*Furongzhen* he *Bian cheng* yishu fengge de bijiao yanjiu" (A Comparative Study of the Art of *Hibiscus Town* and *Border Town*), *Wenyi luncong* 20:333–346 (June 1984).
31. Zhang Xingjin, p. 69. Annie Curien, "Préface," p. 6, in Wang Zengqi, *Les trois amis de l'hiver* (Arles: Philippe Picquier, 1989). Shi Shuqing and Wang

Zengqi, "Yu pingdanchu xian zhenyun" (Truth and Depth amid the Plainness), *Wenxuebao*, March 10, 1988.

32. So the Institute of Literature told me when I asked to see Wang in June 1980.

33. Wang Zengqi, "Shen Congwen he ta de *Bian cheng*" (Shen Congwen and His *Border Town*), and "Shen Congwen de jimo" (The Loneliness of Shen Congwen), in his *Wancui wentan*, pp. 136–171. Wang Zengqi, "Guanyu 'Shoujie'" (About "Ordination"), *Wancui wentan*, p. 4.

34. Ten of Wang's nineteen essays over a page long about his own writing in *Wancui wentan* mention Shen Congwen.

35. *Wancui wentan*, preface, p. 4, and main text, p. 26. Huang Ziping, "Wang Zengqi de yiyi" (The Significance of Wang Zengqi), *Beijing wenxue* 317:48, 52 (January 1989).

36. Harold Bloom, *The Anxiety of Influence* (New York: Oxford University Press, 1973).

37. *Wancui wentan*, pp. 156, 159; Wang Zengqi, "Yi ge aiguo de zuojia" (A Patriotic Writer), in his *Puqiao ji* (Puqiao Collection; Beijing: Zuojia chubanshe, 1989), pp. 53–55. Wang did publish a second memorial article about Shen (collected in *Puqiao ji*, pp. 56–68).

38. *Wancui wentan*, p. 29.

39. Göran Hermerén, *Influence in Art and Literature* (Princeton: Princeton University Press, 1975), p. 23.

40. *Wancui wentan*, p. 38.

41. Ibid., p. 62. The two stories are in *Wang Zengqi zixuan ji* (Wang Zengqi's Own Selection of His Works; Guilin: Li Jiang chubanshe, 1987), pp. 223–242, 267–286.

42. Wang Zengqi, "Da Nao jishi," in his *Wang Zengqi zixuan ji*, p. 269. English translation by Kuang Wendong in *Chinese Literature* 10:9 (October 1981). Page references to "A Tale of Big Nur" in the text refer to this translation.

43. Shen Congwen, *The Border Town and Other Stories*, trans. Gladys Yang (Beijing: Panda Books, 1981), p. 14.

44. *Wang Zengqi zixuan ji*, p. 230. Cf. Shen Congwen, "Yu hou" (After Rain), in his *Shen Congwen xiaoshuo xuan* (Selected Short Stories by Shen Congwen; Beijing: Renmin wenxue chubanshe, 1982), I, p. 37 (bottom two lines). This is song no. 1 in Shen Congwen, "Ganren yaoqu" (Songs of the Zhen'gan Folk), *Chenbao fukan* 1499:63 (December 1926).

45. *Wancui wentan*, pp. 52–55, 128–129. Mikhail M. Bakhtin, *The Dialogic Imagination* (Austin: University of Texas Press, 1981), p. 324.

46. This is Wang's own example, in his *Wancui wentan*, pp. 92–95.

47. Comments by David Pollard at the Harvard conference.

48. Brevity: *Wancui wentan*, pp. 50, 115–118 ("Shuo duan" [On Brevity]). Dis-

cursive plots: p. 57. Planning ahead: p. 74. Theme *(zhuti)*: pp. 34, 36–37. Wang on tight plots in Shen Congwen: p. 151. Wang Zengqi, "Chen Xiaoshou" (Small-Hands Chen), in his *Wang Zengqi zixuan ji*, pp. 430–432. Translated by Howard Goldblatt in *Fiction* 8.2/3:142–145 (1987).

49. Comments by David Pollard at the Harvard conference.

50. *Wancui wentan*, pp. 129, 158.

51. Kinkley, *The Odyssey of Shen Congwen*, pp. 254–258.

52. *Wancui wentan*, pp. 15, 20, 22–23, 31, 104. Wang Zengqi, "Fuchou" (Revenge), in his *Wang Zengqi zixuan ji*, pp. 109–118.

53. Terminology as in William Tay, "Wang Meng, Stream-of-Consciousness, and the Controversy over Modernism," *Modern Chinese Literature* 1.1:7–24 (September 1984).

54. He Liwei himself brought up the fact that he was indebted to Shen Congwen when I visited him in New York with Jon Solomon, May 22, 1988.

55. Changsha seminar. Shen Congwen said that human events consisted equally of "social phenomena" and "dream phenomena," in "Duanpian xiaoshuo" (The Short Story; 1941), *Shen Congwen wen ji* 12:114.

56. He Liwei, "Taojin ren" (Panning for Gold), in his *Xiao cheng wu gushi*, pp. 15–28. Quotations are from He Liwei, "Gold Prospectors," trans. Alice Childs, *Chinese Literature* 2:114–125 (Summer 1989).

57. He Liwei, "Xiao cheng wu gushi," in his *Xiao cheng wu gushi*, p. 29.

58. He Liwei, "Baise niao" (The White Birds), in his *Xiao cheng wu gushi*, pp. 126–132. (Emphasis added.)

59. He Liwei, "Haoqing haoqing de Shamu He" (How Clear How Clear the Fir Tree River), in his *Xiao cheng wu gushi*, p. 37.

60. "Baise niao," p. 127.

61. Han Shaogong, "Shi yi san lu" (Three Records Passed Down from History), in his *Youhuo* (Lure; Changsha: Hunan wenyi chubanshe, 1986), p. 81.

62. Han Shaogong, letters to Kinkley, March 1, 1989, and July 3, 1989.

63. Zeng Zhennan, "Heise de hun yu lanse de meng" (Black Souls and Blue Dreams), *Wenyibao*, September 21, 1985. Han Shaogong, "Kefu xiaoshuo yuyan zhong de 'xueshengqiang'" (Overcome the Conventions of Schoolboy Talk in the Language of Fiction), *Beifang wenxue* 1:69 (January 1983). Han Shaogong, "Lan gaizi" (Blue Bottlecap), in his *Youhuo*, p. 24.

64. Han Shaogong, "Wenxue de 'gen'" (Literary "Roots"), *Zuojia* 4:2–5 (April 1985), written in January 1985, as were all three stories by Han mentioned in this essay. Xia Yun (Helen Hsia), "Zhimian beilun de Han Shaogong" (The Frank and Unconventional Han Shaogong), *Meizhou Huaqiao ribao*, February 27, 1987. See also Ling Yu, "Chongjian Chu wenxue de shenhua xitong" (Rebuilding the Myth System of Chu Literature), in *Hunan shiyan*

xiaoshuo xuan (Selected Hunanese Experimental Fiction), ed. Mo Yingfeng (Changsha: Hunan wenyi chubanshe, 1987), p. 347.

65. Changsha seminar, on the trip to West Hunan. Qiuquan, "Xun 'gen' de husheng yu dui qi yiyi de kending" (The Call to Seek "Roots" and the Affirmation of Their Significance), *Zuopin yu zhengming* 6:77 (June 1986). Ji Hongzhen, "Wenhua 'xungen' yu dangdai wenxue" ("Searching for Cultural Roots" and Contemporary Literature), *Wenyi yanjiu* 60:69 (March 1989). Wang Xiaoming, "Bu xiangxin de he bu yuanyi xiangxin de" (What One Doesn't Believe and Doesn't Want to Believe), *Wenxue pinglun* 4:35n9 (July 1988). Ling Yu, Changsha seminar. Fan Wenlan, *Zhongguo tongshi* (Comprehensive History of China; Beijing: Renmin chubanshe, 1978), I, pp. 19–28, 116–117. Zhang Zhengming, ed., *Chu shi luncong* (Articles on Chu History; Wuhan: Hubei renmin chubanshe, 1984), followed by Zhang's *Chu wenhua shi* (History of Chu Culture; Shanghai: Shanghai renmin chubanshe, 1987).

66. Han Shaogong, "Xunzhao dongfang wenhua de siwei he shenmei youshi" (Seek Out the Intellectual and Aesthetic Strengths of Eastern Culture), *Wenxue yuebao* 6:53–54 (June 1986).

67. Han Shaogong, "Guiqulai" (Return), in his *Youhuo*, pp. 1–18.

68. Han Shaogong, "Ba Ba Ba" (Da Da Da), in his *Youhuo*, pp. 155–199.

69. Xia Yun, "Zhimian beilun de Han Shaogong."

70. Wang Xiaoming, pp. 24–28.

71. Ling Yu, Changsha seminar.

72. Xia Yun, "Zhimian beilun de Han Shaogong."

73. Han Shaogong's prefatory remarks to his "Ba Ba Ba," in Mo Yingfeng, p. 10.

74. On Lu Xun and Qu Yuan, see Leo Ou-fan Lee, ed., *Lu Xun and His Legacy* (Berkeley: University of California Press, 1985), pp. 20–23.

4. Imaginary Nostalgia

The first segment of this essay appears in a different form in my book *Fictional Realism in Twentieth-Century China: Mao Dun, Lao She, Shen Congwen* (New York: Columbia University Press, 1992), chap. 7.

1. Jeffrey Kinkley, "Shen Congwen and the Uses of Regionalism in Modern Chinese Literature," *Modern Chinese Literature* 1.2:157–183 (1985).

2. Lu Xun, introduction to *Zhongguo xinwenxue daxi* (Compendium of Modern Chinese Literature), ed. Zhao Jiabi (Shanghai: Liangyou, 1935–1936), II, p. 9.

3. Shen Congwen, "Taoyuan yu Chenzhou" (Taoyuan and Chenzhou), *Xiangxing sanji* (Random Sketches on a Trip to Hunan), in *Shen Congwen wenji*

(The Works of Shen Congwen), ed. Shao Huaqiang and Ling Yu (Hong Kong: Sanlian shudian, 1984), IX, pp. 234–241.

4. See, for example, Shen Congwen, "Yige dai shuitapi maozi de pengyou" (A Friend in an Otterskin Hat), *Xiangxing sanji*, pp. 226–227, and "Taoyuan yu Chenzhou," pp. 234–241. See also Ling Yu, *Cong biacheng zouxiang shijie* (From the Border Town to the World; Taipei: Luotuo chubanshe, 1987), pp. 392–393, 410.

5. Ibid., p. 226.

6. Ibid., p. 227.

7. Shen Congwen, "Taoyuan yu Chenzhou," p. 234.

8. Tao Qian, p. 168.

9. Leo Ou-fan Lee, "The Solitary Traveler: Images of the Self in Modern Chinese Literature," in *Expressions of Self in Chinese Literature*, ed. Robert Hegel and Richard C. Hessney (New York: Columbia University Press, 1985), p. 296.

10. My concept of the aesthetics of residue and fragment is partially derived from Stephen Owen's discussion of classical Chinese poetry in *Remembrances: The Experience of the Past in Classical Chinese Poetry* (Cambridge, Mass.: Harvard University Press, 1986), esp. pp. 66–79.

11. Song Zelai, *Penglai zhiyi* (Bizarre Stories about Formosa; Taipei: Qianwei chubanshe, 1988).

12. Ibid., pp. 18–19.

13. See Shi Shuqing's interview with Wang Zengqi, in Shi Shuqing, *Duitanlu: miandui dangdai dalu wenxue xinling* (Conversations: Facing the Literary Minds of Mainland China; Taipei: Shibao chuban gongsi, 1989), pp. 164–180; also see Wang Zengqi, "Shen Congwen Xiansheng zai Xinanlianda" (Mr. Shen Congwen at Southwestern Union University), *Lianhe wenxue* (Unitas) 27:160–164 (1987).

14. See, for example, Shi Shuqing's interview with Ah Cheng in *Duitanlu*, p. 110. In my interview with him, Jia Pingwa said that he was inspired by Shen Congwen's fiction as early as the late seventies, when he was a college student. The interview took place at Columbia University on October 15, 1991.

15. Mo Yan, *Honggaoliang jiazu* (The Red Sorghum Family; Beijing: Jiefangjun wenyi chubanshe, 1988), p. 2.

16. Zhou Yingxiong, "Honggaoliang jiazu yanyi" (The Saga of the Red Sorghum Family), *Xiaoshuo, lishi, xinli, renwu* (Fiction, History, Psychoanalysis, and Characters; Taipei: Dongda tushu, 1989), pp. 61–81.

17. Zhou Yingxiong, pp. 72–75.

18. Yu Guangzhong, preface to *Jiling chunchiu* (Taipei: Hongfan, 1986), pp. 1–9; Joseph Lau, "Shanzai xuwu piaomiaojian" (Mountains in the Midst of

Misty Void), literary supplement, *Lianhebao* (United Daily), January 11, 1984; Long Yingtai, "Yige zhongguo xiaozhen de zuxiang" (A Sculpture of a Small Chinese Town), *Dangdai* (Contemporary) 2:166 (1986); Cao Shujuan, "Duoluo de taohuayuan" (A Fallen Peach Blossom Spring), *Zhonghua xiandai wenxue daxi* (A Comprehensive Anthology of Contemporary Chinese Literature in Taiwan; Taipei: Jiuge, 1989), pp. 614–637.

19. See Joseph Lau, "The Tropics Mythopoetized: The Extraterritorial Writing of Li Yung-p'ing in the Context of the Hsiang-t'u Movement," *Tamkang Review* 12.1:26 (1981).

5. Urban Exoticism in Modern and Contemporary Chinese Literature

1. See especially Leo Ou-fan Lee, *The Romantic Generation of Modern Chinese Writers* (Cambridge, Mass.: Harvard University Press, 1973).

2. Peter Li, *Tseng P'u* (Boston: Twayne, 1980), p. 69.

3. See Pierre Citron, *La poésie de Paris dans la littérature française de Rousseau à Baudelaire* (Paris: Minuit, 1961), II, p. 274.

4. Nicholas R. Clifford, *Shanghai 1925: Urban Nationalism and the Defense of Foreign Privilege* (Ann Arbor: Michigan Papers in Chinese Studies, 1979), p. 1.

5. Georges Soulié de Morant, *Ce qui ne s'avoue pas, même a Shanghaï, ville de plaisirs* (Paris: Flammarion, 1927), p. 53.

6. Fu Yanchang, "Zhonghua minzu you yishu wenhua de shihou" (When the Chinese People Will Have an Artful Civilization), in Fu Yanchang, Zhu Yingpeng, and Zhang Ruogu, *Yishu sanjia yan* (Three Personal Views on Art; Shanghai: Liangyou, 1927), pp. 3–6.

7. Fu in a letter to his colleague Zhang Ruogu, in ibid., p. 358.

8. Zhu Yingpeng, "Zhengtong dipai de yishu sixiang" (The Artistic Agenda of Orthodox Greek Art), in ibid., p. 127.

9. See Zhang Ruogu, "Dao minjian qu" (Let's Go among the People; essay on Tian Han's homonymous screenplay), in Zhang, *Zhanzheng yinshi nannü* (On War, Gluttony, and Desire; Shanghai: Liangyou, 1933), pp. 96–107.

10. Fu Yanchang, "Yishu zhi biaozhun" (On the Standards of Art), in Fu, Zhu, and Zhang, *Yishu sanjia yan*, pp. 1–2.

11. Fu Yanchang, "Yi miao wei zhongxin de dushi" (The City Surrounding a Temple), in Fu, *Shiliunian zhi zasui* (Shreds from Sixteen Years; Shanghai: Jinwu, 1928), p. 102.

12. Fu Yanchang, "Yishu yu chengshi" (Art and the City), in Fu, Zhu, and Zhang, *Yishu sanjia yan*, p. 37.

13. See Fu's preface to Lu Mengshu, *Achuan jie* (My Sister Achuan; Shanghai: Zhenmeishan, 1928), p. 2.

14. See Zhang Ruogu, "Teijiaqingu xiaozuo ji" (A Leisure Break at the Tiko-chenko), in Zhang, *Yiguo qingdiao* (Exotic Atmospheres; Shanghai: Shijie shuju, 1929), p. 3.

15. Ibid., p. 4.

16. See Dongya Bingfu (Zeng Pu), "Dongya Bingfu xu" (A Preface by Dongya Bingfu), in ibid., p. 5; words that are capitalized throughout mark expressions that appear in "exotic" Latin letters in the Chinese original.

17. Zeng Xubai, "Zeng Xubai zizhuan" (Zeng Xubai: My Life), unpublished manuscript presented to me by the author in Taipei in 1987.

18. Zeng Pu, "Dongya Bingfu xu," pp. 9–10.

19. Zeng Xubai, "Zeng Xubai zizhuan."

20. Zhang Ruogu, "Chuci jian Dongya Bingfu" (My First Encounter with Zeng Pu), in Zhang, *Yiguo qingdiao*, pp. 21–22.

21. See Zhang Ruogu, "Yiguo qingdiao" (L'amour exotique), in ibid., p. 1.

22. Li, *Zeng P'u*, p. 118.

23. See Zhang Ruogu, "Chuci jian Dongya Bingfu," p. 6.

24. Ibid., p. 4.

25. Zhang Ruogu, "Duhui jiaoxiangqu" (Urban Symphony), in Zhang, *Duhui jiaoxiangqu* (Urban Symphonies; Shanghai: Zhenmeishan, 1929), pp. 13–14.

26. Zhang Kebiao, "Haishang caizi gao chuban: Ji Shao Xunmei" (A Shanghai Prodigy Takes Up Publishing: Remembering Shao Xunmei), *Shanghai wenshi* 2:8 (April 1989).

27. See esp. Heinrich Fruehauf, "Urban Exoticism in Modern Chinese Literature, 1910–1933" (Ph.D. dissertation, University of Chicago, 1990).

28. Shao Xunmei, "The Soul of Shanghai," trans. Kai-yu Hsu, in *Twentieth-Century Chinese Poetry: An Anthology* (Ithaca: Cornell University Press, 1983), pp. 127–128.

29. Tian Huiguang, "Ditie" (Subway), *Chengshi wenxue* 16:55 (October 1985).

30. Wang Qi, "Zhoumo wuhui" (Weekend Dance), *Chengshi wenxue* 16:56 (October 1985).

31. See Guo Yuyi, "Zai xuanzhuan de renliu zhong" (Among Spiraling Dancers), *Chengshi wenxue* 11:21–26 (May 1985).

32. See Hang Ying, "Weinasu de kanjian" (A Short-Sleeve Jacket for Venus), *Guangzhou wenyi* 1:54–55 (January 1985).

33. Huang Jinhong, "Xunzhao wutai" (Searching for Stages), *Guangzhou wenyi* 4:34 (April 1990).

34. See Wu Liang, "Chengshi ren: Ta de shengtai yu xintai" (The Urban Type: His Élan Vital and His Way of Life), *Shanghai wenxue* 1:79–83 (January 1986), and "Chengshi yu women" (The City and Us), *Shanghai wenxue* 11:82–87 (November 1986).

35. Gao Erpin, *Dushi de nüer* (City Daughters; Changsha: Hunan renmin, 1988), pp. 123–124.

36. Luo Jianyi, "Dishigao" (Disco), *Guangzhou wenyi* 9:11 (September 1987).

37. Ibid., p. 20.

38. See Huang Jinhong, "Nanzihan, ah, nanzihan" (Strong Man, Oh, Strong Man), *Guangzhou wenyi* 9:2–17 (September 1986).

39. Liao Xiaomian, "Heise bijini" (Black Bikini), *Guangzhou wenyi* 6:6 (June 1990).

40. Guo Xiaodong, "Dushi de fengya: Tianyuanshi shidai de zhongjie" (Urban Poetry: The End of the Era of Pastoral Verse), *Guangzhou wenyi* 4:45 (April 1990).

41. Lü Shuhuai, "Zhoumo Kafeiwu" (Weekend Café), *Guangzhou wenyi* 1:39 (January 1991).

42. Editor's preface to Zhang Aolie, "Dushi qingjie he dushi yishi" (Urban Consciousness and the Density of Urban Atmosphere), *Guangzhou wenyi* 2:40 (February 1990).

43. See Sun Xiaogang et al., *Chengshi ren* (City People; Shanghai: Xuelin, 1987).

44. Guo Xiaodong, "Dushi de fengya," p. 43.

45. See Huang Jinhong, "Xunzhao wutai," p. 34.

6. Text, Intertext, and the Representation of the Writing Self in Lu Xun, Yu Dafu, and Wang Meng

An earlier version of this essay was presented at the Symposium on Representation of the Self in Modern Chinese Literature, UCLA Center for Chinese Studies, in conjunction with the Southern California China Colloquium, January 12, 1991. I am grateful to the participants of that lively symposium for their comments and criticisms. I wish also to express my appreciation to Kenneth DeWoskin and Ross Chambers for reading the essay and raising thoughtful questions that helped me clarify some of my ideas.

1. Lu Xun, "Kuangren riji" (Diary of a Madman), in *Nahan* (Call to Arms; Beijing: Renmin wenxue chubanshe, 1979), p. 4. I have slightly revised the translations by Yang Xianyi and Gladys Yang to bring out the more literal meanings of the original text. *The Complete Stories of Lu Xun*, trans. Yang Xianyi and Gladys Yang (Bloomington: Indiana University Press, 1981), pp. 1–12. I have also benefited from consulting William A. Lyell's translation in his *Diary of a Madman and Other Stories* (Honolulu: University of Hawaii Press, 1990), pp. 29–41.

2. Leo Ou-fan Lee, *Voices from the Iron House: A Study of Lu Xun* (Bloomington: Indiana University Press, 1987), p. 53.

3. Important studies of the influence of Gogol's 1835 story on Lu Xun include

Douwe W. Fokkema, "Lu Xun: The Impact of Russian Literature," in *Modern Chinese Literature in the May Fourth Era*, ed. Merle Goldman (Cambridge, Mass.: Harvard University Press, 1977), pp. 89–101 (see esp. pp. 96–98); Patrick Hanan, "The Technique of Lu Hsun's Fiction," *Harvard Journal of Asiatic Studies* 34:55–96 (1974); J. D. Chinnery, "The Influence of Western Literature on Lu Xun's 'Diary of a Madman,'" *Bulletin of the School of Oriental and African Studies* 23.1:309–322 (1960).

4. This major concept of poststructuralism is one that can be productively applied to the Chinese literary tradition, as I hope this essay demonstrates. Barthes's notion of the text as "a multidimensional space in which a variety of writings, none of them original, blend and clash," as "a tissue of quotations drawn from innumerable centres of culture," is particularly useful when examining modern Chinese texts, existing as they do at various fracture points of literary history. See his "The Death of the Author," in Roland Barthes, *Image-Music-Text*, trans. Stephen Heath (New York: Hill and Wang, 1977), p. 146. But since I believe it necessary to situate these texts within their specific historical, political, and ideological contexts, I am stopping short of going all the way into that "Barthesian space of infinite and anonymous citations," where any verbal construct, including the *I* that approaches the text, is itself already a plurality of other texts, of infinite or, more precisely, lost codes. Does poststructuralism, if followed through to its logical extremes, tend to self-destruct? If that is the case, it may be a condition that studies of Chinese literature might wish to circumvent or postpone. In the meantime I believe that we should avail ourselves of poststructuralist concepts whenever useful for our analysis. For a discussion of the range of meanings covered by intertextuality, see Jonathan Culler, "Presupposition and Intertextuality," *The Pursuit of Signs: Semiotics, Literature, Deconstruction* (Ithaca: Cornell University Press, 1981), pp. 100–118.

5. Andrew Plaks has demonstrated, for example, how sixteenth-century novels adapted and often radically revised preexisting source materials or antecedent versions to produce a "singularly original literary creation" like the *Jin Ping Mei*. Andrew H. Plaks, *The Four Masterworks of the Ming Novel: Ssu ta ch'i shu* (Princeton: Princeton University Press, 1987), p. 71.

6. Yu Dafu, *Zhongguo xinwenxue daxi: Sanwen erji daoyan* (Introduction to New Chinese Literature Series: Essays, vol. 2; Hong Kong: Xianggang wenxue yanjiushe, 1963), p. 2887. Yu Dafu's introduction is dated April 1935. There has been much debate on the meaning of "individual" *(geren)* in Yu Dafu's statement or in any Chinese statement. What is the Chinese notion of individual? For the purposes of this essay, "individual" will be taken to mean the single human being as a distinct, identifiable entity; it does not necessarily encompass such modern European values as "uniqueness, privacy,

autonomy, and dignity." For the source of the above phrase and a comparison between Western and Chinese notions of "individualism," see Donald J. Munro's introduction to *Individualism and Holism: Studies in Confucian and Taoist Values*, ed. Donald J. Munro, Michigan Monographs in Chinese Studies, no. 52 (Ann Arbor: Center for Chinese Studies, University of Michigan, 1985), pp. 1–16.

7. Liu Zaifu, *Xinge zuhe lun* (Theory of the Composite Character; Shanghai: Shanghai wenyi chuban she, 1986), p. 29.

8. See Emile Benveniste, "Subjectivity in Language," *Problems in General Linguistics*, trans. Mary Elizabeth Meek (Coral Gables: University of Miami Press, 1971), p. 224. For a discussion of Benveniste and the inseparability of language, discourse, and subjectivity, see Kaja Silverman, *The Subject of Semiotics* (Oxford: Oxford University Press, 1983), esp. pp. 43–53. Other works of literary criticism that have applied or discussed the notion of the subject as a textual production include Paul Jay, *Being in the Text: Self-Representation from Wordsworth to Roland Barthes* (Ithaca: Cornell University Press, 1984), esp. pp. 18, 28ff.; Paul Smith, *Discerning the Subject* (Minneapolis: University of Minnesota Press, 1988), chap. 2, "Text."

9. See, for example, Terry Eagleton, *Literary Theory: An Introduction* (Minneapolis: University of Minnesota Press, 1983), esp. pp. 83, 92–93, 141.

10. The effect of this literary device has been much discussed. See Leo Ou-fan Lee, "Tradition and Modernity in the Writings of Lu Xun," *Lu Xun and His Legacy*, edited with an introduction by Leo Ou-fan Lee (Berkeley: University of California Press, 1985), pp. 3–31. William A. Lyell, Jr., *Lu Hsun's Vision of Reality* (Berkeley: University of California Press, 1976), contains a delightful translation of the preface into "rather stilted English" to emphasize the contrast in language with the diary that follows; see p. 270. A fuller and even more delightfully stilted version can be found in Lyell, *Diary of a Madman and Other Stories*, p. 29.

11. Patrick Hanan's useful and now widely adopted phrase for describing the narratorial situation of traditional vernacular fiction. Patrick Hanan, *The Chinese Vernacular Story* (Cambridge, Mass.: Harvard University Press, 1981), p. 215.

12. Lu Xun, "Wo zenme zuoqi xiaoshuo lai" (How I Came to Write Fiction), in *Lu Xun quanji* (Complete Works of Lu Xun; Beijing: Renmin chubanshe, 1957), IV, p. 39.

13. *Analects* 18.5.

14. Milena Dolezelova-Velingerova has argued that what makes Lu Xun's story distinctively modern is not his imitation of Gogol, the writing of a second "Diary of a Madman," but his "establishing a specific, original link between the form of the diary and the figure of the madman." Her paper "Lu Xun's

'Diary of a Madman': The Language of Modernity" was given at a Workshop on Critical Approaches to Modern Chinese Short Stories, December 11–19, 1982, East-West Center, Honolulu. What is particularly interesting for my purposes is how Lu Xun then goes on to use the link as a device for presenting his story.

15. Marie Maclean, *Narrative as Performance: The Baudelairean Experiment* (London and New York: Routledge, 1988), p. 26.

16. Jaroslav Prusek, "The Changing Role of the Narrator in Chinese Novels at the Beginning of the Twentieth Century," in his *The Lyrical and the Epic: Studies of Modern Chinese Literature*, ed. Leo Ou-fan Lee (Bloomington: Indiana University Press, 1980), pp. 110–120; Milena Dolezelova-Velingerova, *The Chinese Novel at the Turn of the Century* (Toronto: University of Toronto Press, 1980). Wu Woyao's *Ershi nian muduzhi guai xianzhuang* (Strange Events Seen in the Past Twenty Years; 1903–1910) achieves its coherence through the use of a first-person protagonist as a formal unifying principle, but there is not a trace of the "typical Western search for self" (Dolezelova-Velingerova, p.71), and the personal feelings and emotions of the narrator are almost absent. A little-known example of first-person narration from 1906 is discussed in Yang Yi, *Zhongguo xiandai xiaoshuoshi* (History of Modern Chinese Fiction; Beijing: Renmin wenxue chubanshe, 1986), I, p. 29.

17. David Der-wei Wang, "Storytelling Context in Chinese Fiction: A Preliminary Examination of It as a Mode of Narrative Discourse," *Tamkang Review* 15.1–4:131–150 (1984–85).

18. See Andrew H. Plaks, "Full-length *Hsiao-shuo* and the Western Novel: A Generic Reappraisal," *China and the West: Comparative Literature Studies*, ed. William Tay, Ying-hsiung Chou, and Heh-hsiang Yuan (Hong Kong: The Chinese University Press, 1980), pp. 163–176, esp. pp. 171ff.

19. Published in 1923 and 1924, revised in 1931 and 1935. Anthologies of fiction compiled by Lu Xun include *Gu xiaoshuo gouchen* (Ancient Anecdotes Recovered; 1938) and *Tang Song chuanqi ji* (A Collection of Tales of Tang and Song; 1927), followed by a second volume in 1928. For a discussion of these works, see John C. Y. Wang, "Lu Xun as a Scholar of Traditional Chinese Literature," *Lu Xun and His Legacy*, pp. 90–103.

20. Ross Chambers, *Story and Situation: Narrative Seduction and the Power of Fiction*, Theory and History of Literature (Minneapolis: University of Minnesota Press, 1984), XII, p. 4.

21. See his *Lu Xun's Vision of Reality*, p. 270.

22. Yu Dafu, "Chenlun," *Yu Dafu daibiao zuo* (Representative Works of Yu Dafu), ed. Liu Jiaming (Zhengzhou: Huanghe wenyi chubanshe, 1989), pp. 1–39. My quotations from this story will be drawn from the translation by Joseph S. M. Lau and C. T. Hsia, with some occasional revisions to underscore the

literal meaning of the text. See C. T. Hsia and Joseph S. M. Lau, eds., *Twentieth-Century Chinese Stories* (New York and London: Columbia University Press, 1971), pp. 3–33.

23. Perhaps more than twenty thousand copies over the following two or three years; see Chen Pingyuan's meticulous study of Chinese fiction from 1898 to 1927, *Zhongguo xiaoshuo xushi moshide zhuanbian* (The Changes in Narrative Form in Chinese Fiction; Shanghai: Shanghai renmin chubanshe, 1988), p. 278.

24. See introduction to the story in Hsia and Lau, *Twentieth-Century Chinese Stories*, p. 1.

25. Guo Moruo, "Lun Yu Dafu (On Yu Dafu), *Moruo wenji* (Collected Works of Moruo; Beijing: Renmin wenxue chubanshe, 1959), XII, p. 547.

26. Jaroslav Prusek, "Introduction to *Studies in Modern Chinese Literature*," in *The Lyrical and the Epic: Studies of Modern Chinese Literature*, ed. Leo Ou-fan Lee (Bloomington: Indiana University Press, 1980), p. 72.

27. Yu Dafu, "Wuliu nian lai chuangzuo shenghuo de huigu" (Looking Back at My Life in Creative Writing of the Past Five or Six Years), *Zhongguo xiandai zuojia tan chuangzuo jingyan* (Modern Chinese Writers Talk about Their Experiences in Writing), ed. Shandong Shifan Xueyuan, Zhongwenxi, Wenyi Lilun Jiaoyanshi (Teaching and Research Section on Literary Theory, Department of Chinese, Shandong Normal College; Jinan: Shandong renmin chubanshe, 1980), p. 112.

28. See Leo Ou-fan Lee, *The Romantic Generation of Modern Chinese Writers* (Cambridge, Mass.: Harvard University Press, 1973), p. 110.

29. The Yu Dafu hero is a rich mixture indeed. Mau-sang Ng discusses the typology of the hero in Yu Dafu's short stories of the 1920s in terms of his relationship with the Western European romantic hero, the *caizi* (profligate littérateur) and *mingshi* (honorable nonserving scholars) of the Chinese tradition, the Japanese *watakushi-shōsetsu* ("I-novel"), and most particularly the influence of the downtrodden and superfluous heroes of nineteenth-century Russian literature. See Mau-sang Ng, "Yu Dafu's Superfluous Hero," in his *The Russian Hero in Modern Chinese Fiction* (Hong Kong: The Chinese University Press; New York: State University of New York Press, 1988), pp. 83–127. My focus in this essay is on the more evident intertextual "tags" that are in dialogue within the text.

30. *Shiji huizhu kaozheng* (*Shiji:* Assembled Commentaries and Annotations; Beijing: Wenxue guji kanxingshe, 1955), X, p. 5207. For a discussion of the "assimilation of personal identity into tradition" in Sima Qian, see Stephen W. Durrant, "Self as the Intersection of Traditions: The Autobiographical Writings of Ssu-ma Ch'ien," *Journal of the American Oriental Society* 106.1:33–40 (January–March 1986).

31. "The Nameless Self: A Paradoxical Stereotype in Traditional Chinese Autobiographical Literature," talk by Wolfgang Bauer, Center for Chinese Studies Humanities Seminar, University of Michigan, Ann Arbor, April 7, 1990.

32. The central character of "Sinking," who writes poems in exile, laments his lonely fate, and ends his life by drowning, suggests many parallels with the life and legend of Qu Yuan. But a shadowy and mythical figure to begin with, the Qu Yuan who became increasingly prominent during the twentieth century was in large part one who had been significantly transformed by New Culture values. See Lawrence A. Schneider, "Man and Superman in Republican China," *A Madman of Ch'u: The Chinese Myth of Loyalty and Dissent* (Berkeley: University of California Press, 1980), pp. 87–124. Qu Yuan was not, in other words, a clearly ideologized autobiographical self with an established textual tradition that could be "discarded."

33. One can find echoes from early Chinese "dropout" literature in Yu Dafu's autobiographical writings, versions of poverty, love of nature, drunkenness, indifference to worldly affairs, and so on. Still his basic self-pitying pose, indeed the very term itself, as a *lingyu zhe* (a superfluous man), is repeatedly acknowledged to be inspired by Western literature. See "Lingyu zhe," *Yu Dafu daibiao zuo*, pp. 334–340. For a full discussion of the various strands of influence on Yu Dafu, see Mau-sang Ng, "Yu Dafu's Superfluous Hero."

34. Chen Pingyuan, *Zhongguo xiaoshuo xushu xingshide zhuanbian*, p. 134.

35. Kang Lin, "Lun 'wusi' shiqi zhishi fenzi ticai xiaoshuode zhongxin chongtu" (The Central Conflict in Fiction about Intellectuals during the "May Fourth" Period), *Zhongguo shehui kexue* (Chinese Social Science) 6.130 (1985).

36. This poem may have been first published in the story, but there is another version in which the last two lines read quite differently. Most telling is the absence of the phrase *shenzhou*, a poetic name for China, thus suggesting that the poem was written for another occasion, when he was not "looking homeward," or "weeping for his beloved country." The other classic poem inserted into the story had been published earlier, on October 6, 1915, in the Shanghai *Shenzhou ribao* (Shanghai Shenzhou Daily). See *Yu Dafu wenji* (Yu Dafu's Literary Works; Hong Kong: Sanlian Book Company, 1982), vol. 10, *Shici* (Poetry), pp. 88, 21.

37. For an example of how events in Yu Dafu's fiction and "life" may parallel yet diverge from each other, we may compare this story with the account he gives of a visit to a brothel in Tokyo when he was a student at a preparatory school in Nagoya. He sheds hot tears the morning after over what this short night has done to his ideals, his ambitions, his warm feelings for his country. But he survives and takes the train back to school; other-

wise there would have been no story. See "Xueye—zizhuan zhi yizhang" (Snowy Night—a Chapter in My Autobiography), *Yu Dafu wenji* (Collected Works of Yu Dafu; Hong Kong: Huacheng chubanshe, 1982), IV, p. 96.

38. Michael Egan, "Yu Dafu and the Transition to Modern Chinese Literature," *Modern Chinese Literature in the May Fourth Era*, ed. Merle Goldman, p. 312.

39. From Matthew Arnold's 1855 poem "Stanzas from the Grande Chartreuse," lamenting the passing of the age of faith: "Wandering between two worlds, one dead,/The other powerless to be born,/With nowhere yet to rest my head,/Like these, on earth I wait forlorn." *Victorian and Later English Poets,* ed. James Stephens, Edwin L. Beck, and Royall H. Snow (New York: American Book Company, 1949), p. 560.

40. Wang Meng, "Bu li" (Bolshevik Salute), in *Wang Meng xiaoshuo baogao wenxue xuan* (Selected Works of Fiction and Reportage by Wang Meng; Beijing: Beijing chubanshe, 1981), pp. 222–308. Page numbers in parentheses refer to this text. To demonstrate the relationship between individual identity on the one hand and the use and understanding of texts on the other, it will be necessary to quote extensively from the story, for reasons that I hope will become obvious. I have benefited by consulting Wendy Larson's translation, but try for a more literal version when necessary for textual analysis. *Bolshevik Salute: A Modernist Chinese Novel,* trans. (with introduction and critical essay) Wendy Larson (Seattle: University of Washington Press), 1989.

41. Robert E. Hegel, "An Exploration of the Chinese Literary Self," *Expressions of Self in Chinese Literature,* ed. Robert E. Hegel and Richard C. Hessney (New York: Columbia University Press, 1985), p. 13.

42. See Wendy Larson, *Bolshevik Salute: A Modernist Chinese Novel,* p. 4. The poem is also translated in Yue Daiyun, *Intellectuals in Chinese Fiction* (Berkeley: Institute of East Asian Studies, University of California, 1988), p. 119. Yue Daiyun's study includes a detailed analysis of "Bu li," to assess the "weaknesses and worth of this generation of intellectuals." See chap. 5, "Chinese Intellectuals of the 1950s as Seen in Wang Meng's *Bu li,*" pp. 108–133.

43. Zhong Yicheng's struggle to see if the self can be affirmed or reclaimed as a distinct, continuing individual entity may be seen as an attempt to reverse the process described by Althusser: "all ideology hails or interpellates concrete individuals as concrete subjects." See his "Ideology and Ideological State Apparatuses (Notes towards an Investigation)," in Louis Althusser, *Lenin and Philosophy and Other Essays,* trans. Ben Brewster (London: New Left Books, 1971), p. 162.

44. For an account of the controversy, as well as a useful discussion of the

410 | Notes to Pages 189-195

meaning of the critical term "stream-of-consciousness," see William Tay, "Wang Meng, Stream-of-Consciousness, and the Controversy over Modernism," *Modern Chinese Literature* 1.1:7–24 (September 1984).

45. Wendy Larson, *Bolshevik Salute: A Modernist Chinese Novel;* see pp. 142–149, "Language and Negativity."

46. This is of course the "language trap" that deconstructionists see in all texts, not just those caught in radical shifts of political ideology. My attempt is to see how useful this concept might be when applied in an analysis that is specific to this particular text and its operations.

7. Invention and Intervention

An earlier and different version of this essay appeared in *Genders* 12 (Winter 1991) under the title "The Female Tradition in Modern Chinese Literature: Negotiating Feminisms across East/West Boundaries." The author wishes to thank *Genders* and the University of Texas Press for allowing this revision to be published.

1. As Wendy Larson points out in her essay, "The End of 'Funü Wenxue': Women's Literature from 1925 to 1935," *Modern Chinese Literature* 4.1–2:39–54 (Spring and Fall 1988), the term *nüxing wenxue* appeared as early as in May Fourth criticism and was interchangeable with *funü wenxue* (women's literature). In the 1980s, however, the latter more or less dropped out of women critics' vocabulary, whereas the former acquired a new historical dimension and became extremely popular. Most contemporary critics now regard *nüxing wenxue* as a literary tradition that has its origins in May Fourth criticism.

2. Zhao Mei, "Zhishi nüxing de kunhuo yu zhuiqiu: Nüxing wenxue zai xin shiqi shinian zhong" (The Dilemma and Quest of Female Intellectuals: Female Literature in the Decade of the New Era), *Dangdai zuojia pinglun* (Studies in Contemporary Writers) 6:30 (1986). Translation mine.

3. Li Ziyun, "Nüzuojia zai dangdai wenxue zhongde xianfeng zuoyong" (The Vanguard Role of Women Writers in Contemporary Literature), *Dangdai Zuojia pinglun* 6:4 (1987). Translation mine.

4. Also see Li Xiaojiang, *Xiawa de tansuo* (Eve's Pursuit; Zhengzhou: Henan renmin chuban she, 1988), and her *Nüxing shenmei yishi tanwei* (A Preliminary Inquiry into the Female Aesthetic; Zhengzhou: Henan renmin chuban she, 1989).

5. Meng Yue and Dai Jinhua, *Fuchu lishi dibiao* (Emerging from the Horizon of History; Zhengzhou: Henan renmin chuban she, 1989), p. 14.

6. For further reference, see Wu Daiying, "Nüxing shijie he nüxing wenxue" (The Female World and Female Literature), *Wenyi pinglun* (Art and Liter-

ary Criticism) 1:61–65 (1986); Jin Yanyu, "Lun nüzuojia qun: Xin shiqi
zuojia qun kaocha zhi san" (On Women Writers as a Group Phenomenon:
A Study of Contemporary Writer Groups), *Dangdai zuojia pinglun* 3:25–31
(1986); Ma E'ru, "Dui 'liangge shijie' guanzhao zhong de xin shiqi nüxing
wenxue: Jianlun zhongguo nü zuojia shijie de lishi bianhua" (Contemporary Female Literature and Its Conception of the "Two Worlds": A History
of the Changing Perspective of Chinese Women Writers), *Dangdai wenyi
sichao* (Current Trends in Art and Literature) 5:91–95 (1987); and also see
Ren Yiming, "Nüxing wenxue de xiandai xing yanjin" (The Evolution of
Female Literature in a Modern Age), *Xiaoshuo pinglun* (Fiction Studies)
3:17–22 (1988).

7. Mao's binary opposition of equality and difference on gender issues inca-
pacitated Chinese women more than it empowered them. It served the
interest of the state through exploiting women's labor power. Whenever a
labor shortage occurred, women's participation in productive activity was
encouraged as a form of gender equality. See Hongjun Su's "Feminist Study
on Mao Zedong's Theory of Women and the Policy of the Chinese Communist Party Toward Women Through a Study on the Party Organ *Hongqi*,"
Chinese Historian 3.2:21–35 (July 1990).

8. Meng Yue theorizes gender politics in the literature of socialist realism in
"Nüxing biaoxiang yu minzu shenhua" (Female Images and the Myth of
the Nation), *Ershi yi shiji* (Twenty-first Century) 4:103–112 (1991). Briefly,
she perceives three dominant female images that serve to eliminate female
subjectivity and uphold the authority of the Party. They are represented
respectively by the liberated rural woman Xi'er in *Baimao nü* (The White-
haired Girl); the intellectual woman Lin Daojing in *Qingchun zhige* (The
Song of Youth), who becomes a Bildungsroman heroine under the guidance of the Party; and the strong Party leader such as Jiangjie in *Hongyan*
(Red Cliff) or Ke Xiang in *Dujuan Shan* (Mount Azalea).

9. Tani Barlow, "Theorizing Woman: *Funü, guojia, jiating*," *Genders* 10:146
(Spring 1991).

10. Zhang Kangkang, "Women xuyao liangge shijie" (We Need Two Worlds),
Wenyi pinglun (Art and Literary Criticism) 1:57 (1986). The speech was
given earlier at an international symposium on women authors in West
Germany.

11. In a published interview by Wang Zheng ("Three Interviews: Wang Anyi,
Zhu Lin, Dai Qing," *Modern Chinese Literature* 4.1–2:99–119 [Spring and Fall
1988; Summer 1990]), Wang Anyi speaks rather disparagingly of women
and feminism. To gauge Wang's complex view on the issue, see, for example, Wang's 1986 essay "Nanren he nüren, nüren he chengshi" (Man and
Woman, Woman and City), *Dangdai zuojia pinglun* 5:66 (1986). Of course,

a work of fiction always speaks for itself, and what it says does not necessarily coincide with the author's private opinion.

12. Yu Qing, "Kunan de shenghua: Lun nüxing wenxue nüxing yishi de lishi fazhan guiji" (The Sublimation of Suffering: Tracing the Historical Development of Female Literature and Female Consciousness), *Dangdai wenyi sichao* 6:55 (1987). The English translation is mine.

13. Interestingly enough, Elaine Showalter's name is mentioned in her writing. In fact, the names of Virginia Woolf, Simone de Beauvoir, and other Western feminists are frequently brought up in the writings of Chinese women critics in the eighties who refuse to call themselves "feminists."

14. Li Xiaojiang, a university teacher who initiated women's studies programs in post-Mao China, did at first try to obtain support from the Fulian, but she did not get even a single response to the letters she sent out. In frustration, she decided to rely on herself and rally the support of her fellow female scholars. Their independent efforts have been very successful. Zhengzhou University, where Li teaches Chinese literature, became the first university to offer courses on women writers in China. See Li Xiaojiang, "Zouxiang nüren" (In Search of Woman), *Nüxing ren* (The Female Person), September 4, 1990, p. 260.

15. I am indebted to Wendy Larson for calling my attention to this problem when commenting on an earlier version of this essay.

16. "The All-China Women's Federation" is unpopular among Chinese men and women for different reasons, which indicates the subtle ambivalence even in official feminism. The idea of getting women organized empowers women on a symbolic level, if not in the real sense of the word, and poses a threat to the traditional male strategy of isolating the female gender to render it powerless. To Chinese women, however, the organization never truly represents them. It obeys the Party just as much as do other mass organizations in China. For related studies in English, see Tani Barlow, "Theorizing Woman: *Funü, guojia, jiating*," and Xiaolan Bao, "Integrating Women into Chinese History—Reflecting on Historical Scholarship on Women in China," *Chinese Historian* 3.2:3–20 (July 1990).

17. All four journals come from outlying cities rather than from Beijing or Shanghai (*Dangdai zuojia pinglun* from Shenyang, *Wenyi pinglun* from Harbin, *Dangdai wenyi sichao* from Lanzhou, and *Xiaoshuo pinglun* from Xi'an), which indicates the rise of the periphery against the centered ideology. This situation is compared to siege warfare by some, parodying Mao's famous saying: "Nongcun baowei chengshi" (Besiege the city from the countryside).

18. Zong Pu attracted a good deal of attention as early as 1956, when she had her "Hongdou" (Red Pea) published, for which she was persecuted. "Wo

shi shui?" (Who Am I?) came out twenty-three years later and is called "the first psychological fiction after Mao" by Li Ziyun.

19. Yi Zhen, "Ding Ling nüshi" (Miss Ding Ling), in *Ding Ling Yanjiu ziliao* (Research Material on Ding Ling), ed. Yuan Liangjun (Tianjin, 1982), p. 223.

20. Mao Dun, "Nü zuojia Ding Ling" (Ding Ling the Female Writer), in Yuan Liangjun, p. 253.

21. Qian Qianwu, "Ding Ling," in Yuan Liangjun, p. 226.

22. Xiao Lin, "Shitan 'Ai shi bu neng wangji de' de gediao wenti" (On the Moral Legitimacy of "Love Must Not Be Forgotten"), *Guangming Daily*, May 14, 1980, p. 4. Note that the reviewer favors the authorial point of view in fiction as opposed to the first-person voice used in Zhang Jie's story.

23. Dai Qing, "Bu neng yong yizhong secai miaohui shenghuo: Yu Xiao Lin tongzhi shangque" (Life Should Not Be Portrayed in a Single Color: A Response to Comrade Xiao Lin), *Guangming Daily*, May 28, 1980, p. 4.

24. Zhang Xinxin, whom I have not included in this study, deserves mention here. Like Zhang Jie, her debut in literature also caused a major controversy. Her novella "Zai tongyi dipingxian shang" (On the Same Horizon), *Shouhuo* (Harvest) 6:172–233 (1981), published while she was a student of drama, shocked some critics, who later condemned her in the official press. For that reason she was unable to find employment after graduation. Accusing the author of "bourgeois individualism" and "social Darwinism," her critics ignored the fact that she was actually criticizing male egotism and exploring the identity of self and gender in its complexity. For a survey of Zhang's career and works in English, see Carolyn Wakeman and Yue Daiyun, "Fiction's End: Zhang Xinxin's New Approaches to Creativity," in *Modern Chinese Women Writers: Critical Appraisals*, ed. Michael S. Duke (Armonk and London: M. E. Sharpe, 1989), pp. 196–216.

25. The "Three Themes on Love" consist of "Huangshan zhi lian" (Love in a Wild Mountain), *Shiyue* (October) 4(1986); "Xiaocheng zhi lian" (Love in a Small Town), *Shanghai Wenxue* (Shanghai Literature) 8(1986); and "Jinxiugu zhi lian" (Love in the Valley of Splendor), *Zhongshan* (Bell Mountain) 1 (1987).

26. Ding Ling, "Shafei nüshi de riji" (The Diary of Miss Sophia), in *Ding Ling duanpian xiaoshuo xuan*, (Ding Ling's Short Stories; Beijing, 1981), p. 73. The English version used is that translated by Tani E. Barlow, with minor modifications, in Tani E. Barlow and Gary J. Bjorge, eds., *I Myself Am a Woman: Selected Writings of Ding Ling* (Boston: Beacon Press, 1989). Further references to this work will be included in the text.

27. Zhang Jie, *Ai shi buneng wangji de* (Love Must Not Be Forgotten; Guangzhou, 1980), p. 109. The English version used is as translated by

414 | Notes to Pages 203–213

William Crawford in Perry Link, ed., *Roses and Thorns: The Second Blooming of the Hundred Flowers in Chinese Fiction, 1979–1980* (Berkeley: University of California Press, 1984), with minor modifications. Further references will be included in the text.

28. Most reviewers read this story as a romantic tragedy and overlook the important role that the narrator plays here. See Zeng Zhennan, Kou Shan, and Wang He's reviews in *Guangming Daily*, July 2, 1980, p. 4. Translation mine. Further references will be included in the text.

29. Wang Anyi, "Jinxiugu zhi lian" (Love in the Valley of Splendor), *Zhong Shan* (Bell Mountain) 1:4 (1987). Translation mine.

30. I am not interested in applying the Lacanian theory of subjectivity or any other psychoanalytical theory to the works under discussion. My immediate concern is to describe some of the specific tropes or textual strategies such as mirroring that literally allow the female subject to confront herself in the text.

31. Ding Ling, "Meng Ke," *Ding Ling duanpian xiaoshuo xuan*, pp. 37–38. Translation mine.

32. Ding Ling, "Shafei nüshi de riji" (The Diary of Miss Sophia), p. 44.

33. Yi-tsi Mei Feuerwerker, *Ding Ling's Fiction* (Cambridge, Mass.: Harvard University Press, 1982), p. 46.

34. Zhang Jie, *Fang zhou* (The Ark; Beijing, 1983), p. 23. Translation mine. Further references will be included in the text.

35. See the epigraph to *Fang zhou*, which quotes from *Hou han shu* (The History of the Latter Han): "Fang zhou bing wu, fu yang jile" (Two boats race along side by side, enjoying the full pleasure of diving and climbing).

36. See Alison Bailey, "Traveling Together: Narrative Technique in Zhang Jie's 'The Ark,'" in Duke, *Modern Chinese Women Writers: Critical Appraisals*, pp. 96–111.

37. Zhang Jie, *Fang zhou* (The Ark), p. 1.

38. "Zumu Lü" (Emerald), *Huacheng* (Flower City) 3:87 (1984). Translation mine.

39. Wang Anyi, "Jinxiugu zhi lian" (Love in the Valley of Splendor), p. 16.

40. Since the heroine's pursuit takes the form of a romantic adventure, the imagery of mists and clouds also retains its erotic connotations. The consummation of her love, for example, is depicted thus: "Finally, they stepped into the wall of clouds and, sure enough, before them lay another world" (p. 26).

41. Zhang Xinxin's novella "Zai tongyi dipingxian shang" (On the Same Horizon) is another good example of a work in which female subjectivity is pitted directly against marriage and male egotism.

42. Ding Ling, "Shafei nüshi de riji" (The Diary of Miss Sophia), p. 79.

43. When we recall the author's own life, it is not surprising that she eventually became a dedicated communist. See Tani Barlow's introduction to *I Myself Am a Woman*.

44. The allusion to the "pale-faced lover" is reminiscent of the stereotyped image of the romantic scholar-lover, or *xiaosheng*, popularized in traditional fiction and drama, such as *Peony Pavilion*.

45. The term "female bonding," rather than homosexuality, is used here to describe the range of female relationships explored by the three authors. In choosing not to pin down the meaning of those relationships, I intend to emphasize the fact that identity politics, which seems to be the main thrust of the current debate on homosexuality in the United States, is not the way in which my Chinese authors deal with sexual relationships in their works, and I see no reason why I should fix identities (gay, lesbian, bisexual, or straight) on their characters.

46. Zhang Jie, *Fang zhou* (The Ark), p. 87.

47. "Dixiongmen" (Brothers), *Shouhuo* (Harvest) 3:4 (1989). Translation mine. Further references will be included in the text.

8. Living in Sin

1. *Lu Xun quanji* (The Complete Works of Lu Xun; Beijing: People's Literature Press, 1982), II, pp. 110–131. Translation with title "Regret for the Past," available in Lu Xun, *Wandering* (Beijing: Foreign Languages Press, 1981), pp. 102–121.

2. *Shouhuo* (Harvest) 3:255–267 (June 1958). Translation available in Hsu, Kai-yu, ed., *Literature of the People's Republic of China* (Bloomington: Indiana University Press, 1980), pp. 282–303.

3. *Cuiyuan* (Verdant Garden of Letters) 2:4–11 (February 1990).

4. *Lu Xun*, I, pp. 158–166. For discussion of this, see William A. Lyell, *Lu Hsün's Vision of Reality* (Berkeley: University of California Press, 1976); Mau-sang Ng, *The Russian Hero in Modern Fiction* (Hong Kong: Chinese University Press, 1988), pp. 227–228; and Chen Minte, "Aiqing ticai de lishixing tupo: Lun 'Shangshi' zhong de aiqing beiju" (A Historical Breakthrough in the Subject of Love: On the Love Tragedy in "Remorse"), *Zhongguo shehui kexue* (China Social Sciences) 2:165–179 (1983).

5. Translation of text from Lyell, p. 208.

6. Leo Ou-fan Lee, *Voices from the Iron House: A Study of Lu Xun* (Bloomington: Indiana University Press, 1987), p. 63.

7. Marston Anderson also discusses the problem of how to read the narrators who mediate the stories in Lu Xun's fiction in *The Limits of Realism: Chinese*

Fiction in the Revolutionary Period (Berkeley: University of California Press, 1990), pp. 90–92.

8. Whose burden is greater here fluctuates: Juansheng's emptiness, selfishness, and weakness, or Zijun's limited revolutionary consciousness.
9. Chen, p. 174 (emphasis mine).
10. Lee, p. 63. See also Ng, pp. 232–234.
11. Lyell, p.135. Since the story is related in the first person by a male narrator and was published soon after Lu Xun first met the young woman who would become his common law wife, a sympathetic identification between Juansheng and Lu Xun is somewhat irresistible. What this identification emphasizes, though, is that the story is a masculine expression or representation of the love. The thoughts and feelings of the woman are never directly expressed.
12. This is Lyell's term, p. 203.
13. "Shangshi," p. 112.
14. "Regret," pp. 105–106.
15. "Shangshi," p. 114.
16. *Lu Xun*, II, pp. 44–56.
17. "Regret," p. 113.
18. Ibid., p. 104.
19. Ibid., p. 107.
20. Ibid., p. 114.
21. Ibid.
22. Ibid., pp. 111–112.
23. Ibid., p. 112.
24. Many Chinese critics have noted this; c.f. Chen, p. 169, and Liu Zaifu, *Xingge zuhe lun* (On Character Composition; Shanghai: Shanghai Literary Press, 1986), p. 29.
25. Marston Anderson has also noted the attention to eyes in other stories by Lu Xun, particularly in connection with the cannibalistic impulse expressed in "A Madman's Diary" or in "The True Story of Ah Q." See Anderson, pp. 82–83.
26. "Shangshi," p. 124.
27. Ibid., p. 126.
28. "Regret," p. 102.
29. Ibid., p. 104 (emphasis mine).
30. "Shangshi," p. 111.
31. "Regret," p. 115.
32. Chen, p. 166.
33. See Bonnie S. McDougall, *Mao Zedong's "Talks at the Yan'an Conference on*

Literature and Art": *A Translation of the 1943 Text with Commentary* (Ann Arbor: Michigan Papers in Chinese Studies, 1980).

34. Jeffrey Kinkley, "Fang Chi (1919–)," in Hsu Kai-yu, pp. 281–282. William Jenner, "Is a Modern Chinese Literature Possible?" in *Essays in Modern Chinese Literature and Literary Criticism,* ed. Kubin and Wagner, (Bochum: Herausgeber Chinathem, 1982), pp. 223–224.

35. "Laifangzhe," p. 255.

36. "Visitor," 302.

37. Ibid., p. 302.

38. Ibid., p. 286.

39. Ibid., p. 288.

40. Ibid., p. 285.

41. Ibid., p. 290.

42. Ibid.

43. Ibid., p. 285.

44. Ibid., p. 296.

45. Ibid., p. 291.

46. Ibid., p. 285.

47. Ibid.

48. "Laifangzhe," p. 266.

49. Ibid.

50. Ibid., pp. 266–267.

51. Ibid., p. 267 (emphasis mine).

52. Noted in Kinkley, p. 281.

53. "Cunzi," p. 4.

54. Ibid., p. 6.

55. Ibid., p. 7.

56. Ibid.

57. Ibid., p. 10.

58. Ibid., (emphasis in original text).

59. Ibid., p. 5.

60. Ibid., p. 6.

61. It should be noted that I assign the masculine pronoun to the narrator here not arbitrarily or simply because the author is male, but rather specifically because he observes and keeps Aidi at a distance (she literally is not there for most of the story) while evaluating the intellectual and moral make-up of Yonghe and the other men in the story.

62. "Cunzi," p. 11.

63. In his call for more contemporary works that express a realization of guilt and a sense of repentance, the contemporary critic Liu Zaifu has also demonstrated a concern with the same character weaknesses that Gao

describes in this story. Liu states, "As a people who frequently display [the infirmities of] 'amnesia,' and 'love of face,' we can forget many things and cover up many things, but this period of calamity [i.e., the Cultural Revolution] must not be forgotten and must not be covered up." Liu Zaifu, "Zuojia de liangzhi he wenxue de chanhui yishi—Tan Ba Jin de *Suixianglu*" (Author's Conscience and the Sense of Repentance in Literature—Discussing Ba Jin's *Random Notes*), in *Liu Zaifu lunwen ji* (Collected Essays of Liu Zaifu), p. 316. While Liu attributes the view expressed in this statement to Ba Jin, it is clear from the article that he is in complete sympathy with it.

64. In fact, when Liu Zaifu discusses such weaknesses as arising from a culture's psychological structure and as requiring recognition and admission of guilt, he uses both the masculine and the feminine pronouns. "Zuojia," p. 322.

9. Lu Xun's Facetious Muse

1. Zhang Xinxin, "Biyao de huida" (A Necessary Response), *Wenyi bao* (Literary Gazette; June 1983); as quoted in the introduction to Edward Gunn, Donna Jung, and Patricia Farr, eds., *The Dreams of Our Generation and Selections from Beijing's People* (Ithaca: Cornell University East Asia Papers, 1986), no. 41, p. 2.

2. See the analysis by Carolyn Wakeman and Yue Daiyun, "Fiction's End: Zhang Xinxin's New Approaches to Creativity," in *Modern Chinese Women Writers*, ed. Michael S. Duke (Armonk: M. E. Sharpe, 1989).

3. Zhang Xinxin, "Women zhe ge nianji de meng" (Dreams of Our Generation; Chengdu: Sichuan wenyi chubanshe, 1985), p. 188.

4. Ibid., p. 244.

5. Han Shaogong, "Nü Nü Nü" (Woman Woman Woman), in *Youhuo* (The Lure; Changsha: Hunan wenyi chubanshe, 1986), pp. 200–258; here p. 252.

6. Ibid., pp. 253–254.

7. Han Shaogong, "Wenxue de gen" (The Roots of Literature), *Zuojia*, pp. 2–5 (April 1985); here p. 4.

8. Han Shaogong, "Nü Nü Nü," p. 258.

9. Liu Heng, "Fuxi Fuxi," in *Dong xi nan bei feng* (Winds from All Directions; Beijing: Zuojia chubanshe, 1989), pp. 152–256; here p. 250.

10. Ibid., p. 255.

11. Yu Zheng, "Shenhua chonggou de xiandai jueze—manshuo 'Fuxi Fuxi'" (The Modern Option of Myth Restructuring—a Casual Discussion of "Fuxi Fuxi"), *Wenxue ziyou tan* 4:113–118 (1989); here p. 115.

12. Cheng Fangwu, "*Nahan* de pinglun" (Critique of *The Outcry*), *Chuangzao jikan* 2:2 (February 1924).

13. Lu Xun, "*Gushi xinbian* xuyan" (Preface to *Old Tales Retold*), *Lu Xun quanji* (Beijing: Renmin wenxue chubanshe, 1981), II, pp. 341–342; here p. 341.

14. See the discussion of "genius" in "Ren zhi lishi" (A History of Man; in *Lu Xun quan ji*, I, pp. 8–24) and the discussion of the "warrior of the spirit" in "Moluo shi li shuo" (The Power of Mara Poetry; in *Lu Xun quan ji*, I, pp. 63–115). Christine M. Pfeil has discussed the development of Lu Xun's thought in depth in the unpublished article "Lu Xun: The Early Essays, 1903–1908," to which I am indebted.

15. Lu Xun, "Wei you tiancai zhi qian" (Waiting for a Genius), *Lu Xun quanji*, I, pp. 166–70; here p. 166.

16. Lu Xun, "Xiao zagan" (Odd Fancy), *Lu Xun quanji*, III, pp. 530–534; here p. 532. Yang Zhu, a contemporary of Mencius, was famous for advocating egotism.

17. "*Gushi xinbian* xuyan," pp. 341–342. I have used the translation of Yang Hsien-yi and Gladys Yang, *Old Tales Retold* (Beijing: Foreign Languages Press, 1972), pp. 1–2.

18. Wu Ying, "Ruhe lijie *Gushi xinbian* de sixiang yiyi" (How to Understand the Ideological Content of *Old Tales Retold*), *Wenyi yuebao* 9(1956); reprinted in Meng Guanglai and Han Rixin, eds., "*Gushi xinbian*" *yanjiu ziliao* (Research Materials on *Old Tales Retold;* Jinan: Shandong wenyi chubanshe, 1984), pp. 191–207; here p. 198.

19. Li Sangwu, "*Gushi xinbian* zhong de zhuyao zuopin shi zhendui xianshi de fengci zuopin, haishi lishi zuopin?" (Are the Major Works in *Old Tales Retold* Reality-oriented Satirical Fiction or Historical Fiction?), *Wenyi yuebao* 11(1956); reprinted in "*Gushi xinbian*" *yanjiu ziliao*, pp. 208–219.

20. *Old Tales Retold*, p. 3.

21. Among the uncontested examples of *roman-à-clef* references in *Old Tales Retold* are those to Lu Xun's renegade student Gao Changhong (who appears as Lord Fengmeng in "Escape to the Moon") and to the historian Gu Jiegang (Lord Birdhead in "Curbing the Flood"). See Lin Chen's article "Lu Xun yu Kuangpiao she" (Lu Xun and the Hurricane Society), in "*Gushi xinbian*" *yanjiu ziliao*, pp. 481–487, for an account of Lu Xun's relationship with Gao Changhong, and Dong Rui, *Lu Xun* "*Gushi xianbian*" *qianxi* (A Cursory Analysis of Lu Xun's *Old Tales Retold;* Hong Kong: Zhongliu chubanshe, 1979), pp. 78–80, for a discussion of Lu Xun's relationship with Gu Jiegang. Lu Xun apparently feared that too much emphasis on such references in *Old Tales Retold* risked trivializing the work and limiting its audience. He would surely have argued, in defense of these passages, that recognition of the specific models for Lord Fengmeng and Lord Birdhead is not necessary for a full appreciation of the stories in which they appear; what matters is that the reader recognize in these characters prevalent types

420 | Notes to Pages 259–266

on the Chinese literary or political scene (i.e., the young opportunist and the stuffy pedant). That is to say, he expected these characters to be interpreted differently by different audiences: his personal acquaintances (and particularly his enemies) would recognize the personal allegory, whereas the general readership would see these characters as belonging to the larger political or cultural allegory that runs throughout *Old Tales Retold*.

22. Thomas M. Greene has identified five varieties of anachronism, which he labels naive, abusive, serendipitous, creative, and pathetic (or tragic). Lu Xun's use of anachronism meets the definition of "creative anachronism," which "involves a deliberate dramatization of historical passage, bringing a concrete present into relation with a specific past and playing with the distance between them" ("History and Anachronism," in *Literature and History: Theoretical Problems and Russian Case Studies*, ed. Gary Saul Morson, Stanford: Stanford University Press, pp. 205–220; here p. 210).

23. Lu Xun, "Fei gong" (Opposing Aggression), *Lu Xun quanji*, II, p. 460. I have slightly revised the translation in *Old Tales Retold*, p. 118.

24. Lu Xun, "Cai wei" (Eating Vetch), *Lu Xun quanji*, II, p. 404.

25. Lu Xun, "Li shui" (Curbing the Floods), *Lu Xun quanji*, II, p. 376.

26. Northrop Frye, "Allegory," in *Princeton Encyclopedia of Poetry and Poetics*, ed. Alex Preminger (Princeton: Princeton University Press, 1965), p. 12.

27. Lu Xun himself vehemently objected to one critic's suggestion that the character Laozi in "Leaving the Pass" was the author's self-portrait. See "Chuguan de 'guan'" (The Key to "Leaving the Pass"), in *"Gushi xinbian" yanjiu ziliao*, pp. 57–61. Lu Xun's objection to autoallegorical readings of the later stories may represent a retrospective attempt to police the interpretation of his fiction; even if his comments faithfully reflect his intention at the time of the story's composition, they do not, of course, rule out a subconscious process of allegorization.

28. *Old Tales Retold*, p. 3. The foreword to *Wild Grasses* begins with a similar conceit: "When I am silent, I feel replete; when I open my mouth to speak, I feel empty" ("Tici," *Lu Xun quanji*, II, p. 159).

29. *Old Tales Retold*, p. 4.

30. Lu Xun follows the account in the Tang writer Sima Zhen's *Bu shi ji*, according to which Gong Gong and Zhuan Xu's war making topples Heaven and makes necessary Nü Wa's repair of Heaven. In earlier versions of the story in *Shanhai jing* and *Liezi*, the repair of Heaven occurs prior to the battle of Gong Gong and Zhuan Xu.

31. Greene, "History and Anachronism," p. 209.

32. Guo Moruo, "Zhuangzi yu Lu Xun" (Zhuangzi and Lu Xun), in *"Gushi xinbian" yanjiu ziliao*, pp. 648–668.

33. Lu Xun, "Qi si" (Raising the Dead), *Lu Xun quanji*, II, p. 471.
34. For a discussion of the relation between mythopoesis and the "numinous," see Eric Gould, *Mythical Intentions in Modern Literature* (Princeton: Princeton University Press, 1981), esp. pp. 171–182.

10. Lives in Profile

1. Hsia's idea that modern Chinese literature as a whole has been negatively affected by a preoccupation with social and political concerns can be found in "Obsession with China: The Moral Burden of Modern Chinese Literature," an appendix to *A History of Modern Chinese Fiction*, 2nd ed. (New Haven: Yale University Press, 1971), pp. 533–554.
2. M. M. Bakhtin, *The Dialogical Imagination: Four Essays*, ed. Michael Holquist, trans. Caryl Emerson and Michael Holquist (Austin: University of Texas Press, 1981), p. 267.
3. These categories are, of course, those made famous by Wayne Booth in *The Rhetoric of Fiction* (Chicago: University of Chicago Press, 1961). They are based on an autonomy of text that has generally not been recognized either by modern Chinese critics or by authors.
4. Examples of the commanding, authorial, manipulating voice are so numerous, particularly in post-1942 fiction, that they hardly need rehearsing. Perhaps most extreme among these is Hao Ran's authorial voice in his three-volume novel dating from 1964–65, *Yanyang tian* (Bright, Sunny Skies). This text goes to extreme lengths to manipulate the knowledge meted out to character and reader alike in a titanic effort designed to show the extent to which the "class enemy" can hide himself among the myriad of everyday phenomena.
5. One of the best examples of this is Dai Houying's *Ren A! Ren*, a novel completed in 1980. Clearly wishing to depart from the enforced uniformity of Cultural Revolution fiction, the author goes to some trouble to create her text in the form of a series of depositions narrated by different characters. While this works at first in giving the reader a sense that a number of authentically different voices are involved, as the novel moves on, it becomes increasingly clear that all the characters have been enlisted in the cause of demonstrating that some of them are part of the solution and others are part of the problem. In the end, we are left with each character having retreated to a familiar stereotype.
6. The definitive translation and commentary on the important documents produced by Mao at Yan'an in 1942 are contained in Bonnie S. McDougall, *Mao Zedong's "Talks at the Yan'an Conference on Literature and Art": A Transla-*

tion of the 1943 Text with Commentary (Ann Arbor: Michigan Center for Chinese Studies, 1980).

7. An English translation of Yu's story by George Kennedy, "Intoxicating Spring Nights," can be found in *Straw Sandals: Chinese Short Stories, 1918–1933*, ed. Harold R. Isaacs (Cambridge, Mass.: MIT Press, 1974), pp. 68–83. For an alternative view of Yu Dafu's writing that makes a case for Yu's ironic detachment from the narrator in his stories, see Michael Eagan, "Yu Dafu and the Transition to Modern Chinese Literature," in *Modern Chinese Literature in the May Fourth Era*, ed. Merle Goldman (Cambridge, Mass.: Harvard University Press, 1977), pp. 309–324.

8. See C. T. Hsia's *History*, p. 22, where the idea appears in the following invidious formulation: "This didactic concern engenders by and large an attitude of indifference toward art."

9. Among the things that Leo Lee demonstrates with his perceptive discussion of Wang Meng's writing in "The Politics of Technique: Perspectives of Literary Dissidence in Contemporary Chinese Fiction," in *After Mao: Chinese Literature and Society, 1978–1981*, ed. Jeffrey C. Kinkley (Cambridge, Mass.: Council on East Asian Studies, Harvard University, 1985), pp. 159–190, is that a transformation of the surface political views of an author does not imply change in the structure of literary texts he may produce. See esp. p. 182.

10. Shen Yanbing, "Xiaoshuo xin chao lan xuanyan" (Declaration of the "New Tide in Fiction" Column), *Xiaoshuo yuebao* (Fiction Monthly) 11.1 (January 1920), reprinted in *Mao Dun wenyi zalun ji* (A Collection of Mao Dun's Essays on Literature and Art; Shanghai: Shanghai wenyi chubanshe, 1981), I, p. 8. See also Bonnie S. McDougall, *The Introduction of Western Literary Theories into Modern China* (Tokyo: Centre for East Asian Cultural Studies, 1971), p. 148: "Ch'en Tu-hsiu tried to apply the same method to Chinese literature, describing the traditional literature as both classical and romantic, and prophesying a trend towards realism in the new literature. This interpretation of the past and the future of Chinese literature became the standard one for many years."

11. Shen Yanbing, *"Ziran zhuyi yu Zhongguo xiandai xiaoshuo"* (Naturalism and the Modern Chinese Novel), in *Zhongguo xin wenxue daxi* (Compendium of Modern Chinese Literature), ed. Zhao Jiabi (reprint, Hong Kong: Wenxue yanjiushe, 1972), II, pp. 386–387. Originally published in *Xiaoshuo yuebao* 13.7 (July 10, 1922).

12. The notion that a heedless subjectivity is at the root of the problems with Chinese literature is one that Shen mentions a number of times. See, for instance, *"Shemma shi wenxue?"* (What Is Literature?), a 1924 essay in which he focused his critique of subjectivity on the *mingshi pai*—the celebrity writers. *Daxi*, II, p. 170.

Rey Chow, in her recently published *Women and Chinese Modernity: The Politics of Reading between West and East* (Minneapolis: University of Minnesota Press, 1991), has made a similar observation about the narrative voice in Ba Jin's *Jia* (The Family): "Ironically, precisely because we are shown the 'inner thoughts' of different characters in the same meditative manner, they all become facets of the same narrative voice, the voice that in this way turns 'autobiographical,' writing about itself and no one else" (p. 99).

13. Shen Yanbing, *"Wenxue he rende guanxi ji Zhongguo gulai duiyu wenxuezhe shenfende wuren"* (The Relationship of People to Literature and the Traditional Misperception of the Status of the Writer in China), *Xiaoshuo yuebao* 12.1:9 (January 1921) reprinted in *Mao Dun wenyi zalun ji* I.23.

14. The story can be found in *Lu Xun quanji* (Complete Works of Lu Xun; Beijing: Renmin wenxue chubanshe, 1981), I, pp. 422–433. The standard translation by Yang Xianyi and Gladys Yang is in *Selected Works of Lu Hsun* (Peking: Foreign Languages Press, 1956), I, pp. 8–21.

15. Bakhtin, *Dialogic Imagination*, p. 412.

16. David Carroll, "Narrative, Heterogeneity, and the Question of the Political: Bakhtin and Lyotard," in *The Aims of Representation: Subject/Text/History*, ed. Murray Krieger (New York: Columbia University Press, 1987), p. 81. (Emphasis in original.)

17. On Barthes's codes, see *S/Z*, trans. Richard Howard (New York, 1974), pp. 19–21.

18. This denial of Lao Kang a space in the narrator's memory is particularly striking in the context of Chinese literature, where memory has always been a preeminent theme. See Stephen Owen, *Remembrances: The Experience of the Past in Classical Chinese Literature* (Cambridge, Mass.: Harvard University Press, 1986).

19. Wang Anyi, "Lao Kang huilai," in *Haishang fanhua meng* (Bustling Dreams at Sea; Guangzhou: Huacheng chubanshe, 1989), p. 227. The translation is by Jeanne Tai, "Lao Kang Came Back," in *Spring Bamboo* (New York: Random House, 1989), p. 45.

20. *"Zhufu"* is in *Lu Xun quanji*, II, pp. 5–23. "The New Year's Sacrifice" is in *Selected Works of Lu Hsun*, I, pp. 150–173.

21. *Lu Xun quanji*, II, p. 10.

22. For a treatment of this issue in the context of a number of recent theories on how to read narrative, see David Carroll, *The Subject in Question* (Chicago: University of Chicago Press, 1982).

23. See Marston Anderson's discussion of the manner of reading Chinese literature: "Where an interpretive disturbance was recognized [in a text], it was imputed not to a representational inadequacy inherent in the text

but to the inability of the interpreter to fully apprehend the significance of an abundantly sufficient text." *The Limits of Realism: Chinese Fiction in the Revolutionary Period* (Berkeley: University of California Press, 1989), p. 21.

24. For a closer analysis of Lu Xun's use of the first-person voice, see my "Blossoms in the Snow: Lu Xun and the Dilemma of Modern Chinese Literature," *Modern China* 10.1:49–77 (January 1984).

25. For the most insightful discussion of this theme, see Marston Anderson, "The Barred View: On the Enigmatic Narrator in Xiao Jun's 'Goats,'" in *Reading the Modern Chinese Short Story*, ed. Theodore Huters (Armonk: M. E. Sharpe, 1990), pp. 37–50.

26. See Liu Xiaobo, *"Wu fa huibi de fansi"* (Unavoidable Reflection), *Zhongguo* 4:103–111 (April 1986).

27. For an enumeration of some of these devices, see my "Speaking of Many Things: Food, Kings, and the National Tradition in Ah Cheng's 'The Chess King,'" *Modern China* 14:388–418 (October 1988). Looking at the rhetoric of confounding expectation within the stories opens up new sets of interpretive possibilities. Such an approach, for instance, does not rule out the Daoist interpretation of Ah Cheng that has been one of the most popular approaches to his stories. It simply moves that Daoist interpretation in the direction of play with the arbitrariness of language rather than toward a notion of mystical union with the universe.

28. For a summary of the background information, see Jeffrey C. Kinkley, "The Cultural Choices of Zhang Xinxin, a Young Writer of the 1980s," in *Ideas across Cultures: Essays on Chinese Thought in Honor of Benjamin I. Schwartz*, ed. Paul Cohen and Merle Goldman (Cambridge, Mass.: Harvard University Press, 1990), pp. 151–153. Zhang Xinxin and Sang Ye's own accounts can be found in *Beijing ren*. See note 29 below for bibliographical information.

29. The full title of the first Chinese edition is *Beijing ren: Yibaige putong ren de zishu* (Peking Man: The Self-Narratives of 100 Ordinary People; Shanghai, 1986). The second printing (also done in August) records a total of 18,750 volumes in print. The Taipei printing is divided into two volumes that were printed over a year apart and contains a total of 108 segments. The first half was published in October 1987 by Linbai chubanshe and edited by Wong Tak-wai (Huang Dewei). The second half, *Beijing ren (xia)*, was published in January 1989 by the same press and with the same editor. Each volume contains 54 segments. Citations to the Chinese originals in the pages to follow will refer to both the Shanghai and the Taipei editions, with the reference to the Shanghai edition given first in italics.

The first collection of English translations, *Chinese Profiles*, was published in Beijing by Panda Books in 1986 and contains 39 segments, with the translations including everything in the Chinese originals. The second collection of translations, *Chinese Lives: An Oral History of Contemporary China*, was published in New York by Pantheon in 1987 and edited by W. J. F. Jenner and Delia Davin. It must be said that *Chinese Lives* takes what I consider to be unacceptable liberties in the editorial process, with certain segments being shortened and with the marks of the authorial voice being removed in most instances.

30. "The 'implied author' chooses, consciously or unconsciously, what we read; we infer him as an ideal, literary, created version of the real man; he is the sum of his own choices." Booth, *The Rhetoric of Fiction*, pp. 74–75.

31. This segment is the second one included in the volume; pp. 7/38. Further references to this work will be given parenthetically in the text.

11. Melodramatic Representation and the "May Fourth" Tradition of Chinese Cinema

1. Examples of both approaches can be found in Nick Browne, Donald Gibbs, Paul G. Pickowicz, and Vivian Sobchack, eds., *Cinema and Social Change in Contemporary China* (forthcoming).

2. For a discussion of the attitude of May Fourth literary intellectuals toward commercial filmmaking, see Paul G. Pickowicz, *Marxist Literary Thought in China: The Influence of Ch'ü Ch'iu-pai* (Berkeley: University of California Press, 1981).

3. See Cheng Jihua, Li Shaobai, and Xing Zuwen, eds., *Zhongguo dianying fazhan shi* (Beijing: Zhongguo dianying chuban she, 1963), I, pp. 3–49.

4. See Sun Yu, "Cinema in the 1930s under the Influence of the May Fourth Movement," in *Electric Shadows: 45 Years of Chinese Cinema*, ed. Tony Rayns and Scott Meek (London: British Film Institute, 1980), p. T3.

5. See Li Xiao, Li Kezhen, and Li Jiansheng, "Zhongguo dianying zong mulu (1905–1937)," and Wang Yongfang and Jiang Hongtao, "Zai Hua faxing waiguo yingpian mulu (1896–1924)," *Zhongguo dianying yanjiu* 1.1:184–259, 260–282 (December 1983).

6. For a biography of Luo, see Zhongguo dianyingjia xiehui dianying shi yanjiubu, ed., *Zhongguo dianyingjia liezhuan* (Beijing: Zhongguo dianying chuban she, 1982–1986), I, pp. 183–190. (Hereafter this multivolume source will be referred to as *ZDL*.)

7. For biographies of Shi and Cai, see *ZDL*, I, pp. 15–23, 338–349. For a discussion of Zhu, see Lin Nien-tung, "Zhu Shi-lin," in *A Comparative Study of Post-War Mandarin and Cantonese Cinema: The Films of Zhu Shi-lin, Qin Jian and Other Directors*, ed. Shu Kei (Hong Kong: Hai Kwong Printing Company, 1983), pp. 22–25.

8. Wang Yongfang and Jiang Hongtao, "Zai Hua faxing waiguo yingpian mulu," p. 260.

9. For information on Qian (who was known as A Ying), Xia, Zheng, and Hong, see *ZDL*, I, pp. 76–83, 261–277, 196–201, 214–221; for Yang and Tian, see *ZDL*, II, pp. 115–130, 55–66. See Paul G. Pickowicz, *Marxist Literary Thought in China*, for a discussion of the Sun Society romantic Marxists.

10. See Zhongguo dianying yishu yanjiu zhongxin, Zhongguo dianyingjia xie hui, and Beijing dianying xueyuan, eds., *Xia Yan de dianying daolu* (Beijing: Zhongguo dianying chuban she, 1985), pp. 6–7.

11. Ke Ling argues that it did. See "Shiwei 'Wusi' yu dianying hua yi lunkuo," *Zhongguo dianying yanjiu* 1.1:4–19 (December 1983).

12. For an argument that stresses censorship, see Jay Leyda, *Dianying: An Account of Films and the Film Audience in China* (Cambridge, Mass.: MIT Press, 1972), pp. 88–89.

13. This is the basic view put forward in Cheng Jihua, Li Shaobai, and Xing Zuwen, eds., *Zhongguo dianying fazhan shi*.

14. Sun Yu, p. T6.

15. The term *melodrama* is used here in its broadest possible sense. I recognize, of course, that there are many different types of melodramas and that each has its own characteristics. By referring to the direct impact of American film melodrama on Chinese cinema, I do not mean to suggest that Chinese film melodramas did not have their own national characteristics or that they were not influenced by Chinese traditions of narrative and stagecraft. For recent applications of melodrama theory to contemporary Chinese filmmaking, see E. Ann Kaplan, "Melodrama/Subjectivity/Ideology: The Relevance of Western Melodrama Theories to Recent Chinese Cinema," *East-West Film Journal* 5.1:6–27 (January 1991), and Stephanie Alison Hoare, "Melodrama and Innovation: Literary Adaptation in Contemporary Chinese Film" (Ph.D. dissertation, Cornell University, 1989).

16. The following discussion of melodrama draws heavily on Peter Brooks, *The Melodramatic Imagination: Balzac, Henry James, Melodrama, and the Mode of Excess* (New York: Columbia University Press, 1985).

17. Ibid., p. 5. These words were used by Theodora Bosanquet to characterize the way in which Henry James viewed the world outside his study.

18. Ibid., p. 40.

19. Perry Link, *Mandarin Ducks and Butterflies: Popular Fiction in Early Twentieth-Century Chinese Cities* (Berkeley: University of California Press, 1981).

20. Brooks, p. 20.

21. Ibid., p. 17.

22. For biographical sketches, see *ZDL:* Wang Chenwu (I, pp. 4–9), Shi Linghe (I, pp. 47–52), Situ Huimin (I, pp. 53–64), Sun Yu (II, pp. 81–87), Wu

Yonggang (II, pp. 156–163), Shen Xiling (I, pp. 84–91), Ying Yunwei (I, pp. 102–110).

23. For a detailed Red Guard denunciation of Xia Yan and the thirties "Communist film group," see Shanghai hong qi dianying zhipianchang hong qi geming zaofan bingtuan, ed., *Dianying xiju sishinian liang tiao luxian douzheng jishi* (Shanghai, 1967).

24. The most important pre–Cultural Revolution book that presented this point of view (Cheng Jihua, Li Shaobai, and Xing Zuwen, eds., *Zhongguo dianying fazhan shi*) was reprinted without revision in 1980.

25. Cai Shusheng [Xia Yan], "Kan le 'Xiao wanyi' zhi Sun Yu xiansheng," *Shen bao*, October 10, 1933.

26. The text of *Small Toys* is contained in Sun Yu, *Sun Yu dianying xuanji* (Beijing: Zhongguo dianying chuban she, 1981), pp. 91–126.

27. For a discussion of Bu Wancang, see Paul G. Pickowicz, "The Theme of Spiritual Pollution in Chinese Films of the 1930s," *Modern China* 17.1:40–44 (January 1991).

28. See Zhongguo dianyingjia xiehui dianying shi yanjiu bu, ed., *Ruan Lingyu* (Beijing: Zhongguo dianying chuban she, 1985), and Liu Guojun, *Cong xiao yatou dao mingxing: Ruan Lingyu zhuan* (Chengdu: Sichuan wenyi chuban she, 1986).

29. Brooks, p. 88.

30. Sun Yu places the emphasis on the class solidarity of the poor, but it is clear that the unity of the people portrayed in *Small Toys* is also related to the fact that they are from the same hometown in rural Jiangsu. Emily Honig argues that native-place identity was far more important to many women factory workers than their class identity. See *Sisters and Strangers: Women in the Shanghai Cotton Mills, 1919–1949* (Stanford: Stanford University Press, 1986).

31. For a sketch of Tang Xiaodan see *ZDL*, II, pp. 100–109.

32. *Shen bao*, February 26-March 9, 1947.

33. Tang Xiaodan, "Jituo yu xiwang—daoyanzhe de hua," in *Tiantang chun meng* (Shanghai, 1947).

34. Robert Lang, *American Film Melodrama: Griffith, Vidor, Minnelli* (Princeton: Princeton University Press, 1989), pp. 47, 24.

35. See Leo Ou-fan Lee, "The Tradition of Modern Chinese Cinema: Some Preliminary Explorations and Hypotheses," in *Perspectives on Chinese Cinema*, ed. Chris Berry (Ithaca: Cornell University East Asia Papers, 1985), pp. 1–20, for a discussion of late-forties cinema that emphasizes its "social realism."

36. Brooks, p. 33.

37. See *ZDL*, VI, pp. 481–495.

38. For a discussion of the works of Xie Jin and others in the early sixties, see Paul G. Pickowicz, "The Limits of Cultural Thaw: Chinese Cinema in the Early 1960s," in *Perspectives on Chinese Cinema*, ed. Chris Berry (Ithaca: Cornell University East Asia Papers, 1985), pp. 97–148.

39. See Paul Clark, *Chinese Cinema: Culture and Politics since 1949* (Cambridge: Cambridge University Press, 1987).

40. Shao Mujun, "Chinese Films: 1979–1989," *China Screen* 3:11 (1989).

41. *Beijing Review* 33.8:46 (February 19–25, 1990).

42. For a discussion of works by Xie Jin and others in the early eighties, see Paul G. Pickowicz, "Popular Cinema and Political Thought in Post-Mao China: Reflections on Official Pronouncements, Film, and the Film Audience," in *Unofficial China: Popular Culture and Thought in the People's Republic*, ed. Perry Link, Richard Madsen, and Paul G. Pickowicz (Boulder: Westview Press, 1989), pp. 37–53.

43. *China Screen* 2:33 (1988).

44. For a discussion of early eighties melodramas, see Ma Ning, "Symbolic Representation and Symbolic Violence: Chinese Family Melodrama of the Early 1980s," *East-West Film Journal* 4.1:79–112 (December 1989).

45. See *Shang ying huabao* 1:1 (January 1987). Similar advertising can be found in *Dazhong dianying* 4 (April 1987).

46. For another discussion of *Hibiscus Town*, see Nick Browne, "Society and Subjectivity: The Political Economy of Chinese Melodrama," in Browne et al., *Cinema and Social Change in Contemporary China*.

47. Another analysis of Xie Jin's melodramas is contained in Ma Ning, "Spatiality and Subjectivity in Xie Jin's Film Melodrama of the New Period," in Browne et al., *Cinema and Social Change in Contemporary China*.

48. Shao Mujun, p. 11.

49. See Paul G. Pickowicz, "Huang Jianxin and the Notion of Postsocialism," in Browne et al., *Cinema and Social Change in Contemporary China*.

50. Shao Mujun, p. 11.

51. *Zhong gong shisan jie si zhong quan hui* (Beijing: Xin xing chuban she, 1989), pp. 11–13.

52. *Beijing Review* 32.49:23–26 (December 4–10, 1989).

53. Joseph W. Esherick and Jefferey N. Wasserstrom, "Acting Out Democracy: Political Theater in Modern China," *The Journal of Asian Studies* 49.4:835–865 (November 1990).

12. Male Narcissism and National Culture

A modified version of this essay was published in *Camera Obscura* 25/26 (1991).

1. *The Complete Stories of Lu Xun*, trans. Yang Xianyi and Gladys Yang (Beijing:

Foreign Languages Press; Bloomington: Indiana University Press, 1981), p. 65.

2. Ibid., p. 65.

3. In an essay called "Xiwang," Lu Xun follows the Hungarian poet and revolutionary Petöfi Sándor to say that the unfoundedness of hopelessness is similar to that of hope itself. In a poem called "Hope," Sándor compares hope to a prostitute, implying by that traditional "metaphor" its faithlessness and mystery to men. See "Xiwang," *Yecao, Lu Xun chuanji,* vol. 2 (Beijing: Renmin wenxue chubanshe, 1981).

4. Marston Anderson, "The Morality of Form: Lu Xun and the Modern Chinese Short Story," *Lu Xun and His Legacy,* edited and with an introduction by Leo Ou-fan Lee (Berkeley: University of California Press, 1985), pp. 32–53. Anderson's arguments are further elaborated in his *The Limits of Realism: Chinese Fiction in the Revolutionary Period* (Berkeley: University of California Press, 1990).

5. Anderson, "The Morality of Form," p. 52.

6. Terry Eagleton, "Ideology, Fiction, Narrative," *Social Text* 2:71 (Summer 1979); emphasis in the original.

7. A good example of this tension in the pre-1949 period is found in Mao Dun's essay "From Guling to Tokyo" (1928), in which he scrutinizes the question of what constitutes "proletarian literature." See "From Guling to Tokyo," trans. Yu-shih Chen, *Bulletin of Concerned Asian Scholars,* pp. 38–44, (January–March 1976).

8. "Talks at the Yan'an Forum on Literature and Art," *Mao Tse-tung on Literature and Art* (Beijing: Foreign Languages Press, 1960, 1977), pp. 39–40. The couplet is from Lu Xun's "Zizhao" (Self-mockery), *Ji wai ji, Lu Xun chuanji,* vol. 7 (Beijing: Renmin wenxue chubanshe, 1981).

9. For a helpful discussion of how to interpret this image, I am grateful to the students who took my course "Introduction to Literary Theory for Students of Modern Chinese Literature," Winter 1990, at the University of Minnesota.

10. See *A Cheng xiaoshuo: qi wang, shu wang, haizi wang* (Taipei: Haifeng chubanshe, 1988), pp. 163–213.

11. See Louis Althusser, "Ideology and Ideology State Apparatuses: Notes towards an Investigation," *Lenin and Philosophy and Other Essays* (New York: Monthly Review Press, 1971), pp. 127–186.

12. Since I have already analyzed Ah Cheng's story at length elsewhere, my discussion of it here is brief. Interested readers are asked to see "Pedagogy, Trust, Chinese Intellectuals in the 1990s—Fragments of a Post-Catastrophic Discourse," *Dialectical Anthropology* 16:3 (Special Issue on Post-Mao China), in press.

13. Boris Eikhenbaum, "Literature and Cinema (1926)," in *Russian Formalism: A Collection of Articles and Texts in Translation,* ed. Stephen Bann and John E. Bowlt (New York: Harper and Row, 1973), p. 123. For an extended version of Eikhenbaum's views on cinema, see his "Problems of Cinema Stylistics," in *Russian Formalist Film Theory,* ed. Herbert Eagle (Ann Arbor: University of Michigan Slavic Publications, 1981), pp. 55–80.

14. In a recent article, Kaja Silverman distinguishes the look, which is individualized and has a human bearer, and the gaze, which is external and collective. She argues that in Hollywood cinema, the male look is always exchangeable with the gaze because it is disburdened of lack. See "Fassbinder and Lacan: A Reconsideration of Gaze, Look, and Image," *Camera Obscura* 19:54–84 (January 1989). While making use of these terms, I want to emphasize that the distribution of "male" and "female" characteristics in *King of the Children* reverses the Hollywood paradigm. The male look in Chen's film is the bearer of a lack; it is the male who occupies the passive (classically "feminine") position. The question is: why? As I argue in the second half of my essay, this is a question of symbolic castration, or cultural violence, which is particularly germane to the understanding of the contemporary Chinese situation.

15. See my account of the humanistic and patriarchal meanings of Wang Fu's "success" in "Pedagogy, Trust, Chinese Intellectuals in the 1990s," *Dialectical Anthropology* 16:191–207 (1991).

16. Althusser, "Ideology and Ideology State Apparatuses," p. 132.

17. Chen Wanying, "Interview with Chen Kaige, Director of *King of the Children* and *Yellow Earth,*" *Playboy,* Chinese edition, May 1988, p. 48.

18. Rey Chow, "Silent Is the Ancient Plain: Music, Film-Making, and the Conception of Reform in China's New Cinema," *Discourse* 12.2:82–109 (Spring–Summer 1990).

19. See Martin Heidegger, "The Origin of the Work of Art," *Poetry, Language, Thought,* trans. Albert Hofstadter (New York: Harper Colophon Books, 1971), pp. 15–87; "The Question Concerning Technology," *The Question Concerning Technology and Other Essays,* translated and with an introduction by William Lovitt (New York: Harper Colophon Books, 1977), pp. 3–35.

20. "The Question Concerning Technology," p. 22.

21. Chen's fascination with the inarticulate or verbally clumsy child is evident in his other films as well—for instance, Han Han in *Yellow Earth* and the young soldier Hou, who stutters, in *The Big Parade.*

22. Gayle Rubin, "The Traffic in Women: Notes on the 'Political Economy' of Sex," in *Toward an Anthropology of Women,* ed. Rayna Reiter (New York: Monthly Review Press, 1975), p. 168.

23. Sigmund Freud, "On Narcissism: An Introduction" (1914), *A General Selec-*

tion from the Works of Sigmund Freud, ed. John Rickman (New York: Double-day, 1957), p. 113; my emphases.

24. Ibid., p. 116. A perfect example of the massive destructiveness that results from the idealization of children, who are used to enact otherwise unrealizable fantasies, was Mao's mobilization of the Red Guards during the Cultural Revolution.

25. Ibid., p. 123.

Afterword

1. Cyril Birch, "Change and Continuity in Chinese Fiction," in *Modern Chinese Literature in the May Fourth Era*, ed. Merle Goldman (Cambridge, Mass.: Harvard University Press, 1977), p. 404.

2. Chow Tse-tsung, *The May Fourth Movement* (Cambridge, Mass.: Harvard University Press, 1960), p. 276.

3. Marston Anderson, *The Limits of Realism: Chinese Fiction in the Revolutionary Period* (Berkeley: University of California Press, 1990), esp. chaps. 1 and 2.

4. Ibid., p. 200.

5. Ibid., pp. 200–201.

6. Ibid., p. 200.

7. Ibid., p. 202.

8. Ibid., pp. 40–41.

9. Lionel Trilling, *Sincerity and Authenticity* (Cambridge, Mass.: Harvard University Press, 1972), p. 24.

10. Rey Chow, *Women and Chinese Modernity: The Politics of Reading between West and East* (Minneapolis: University of Minnesota Press, 1991), pp. 92–95. See also Jaroslav Prusek, *The Lyrical and the Epic: Studies of Modern Chinese Literature*, ed. Leo Ou-fan Lee (Bloomington: Indiana University Press, 1980).

11. Chow, p. 93.

12. Ibid., p. 94.

13. Ibid., p. 95.

14. Ian Reid, *The Short Story* (London: Methuen, 1977), pp. 27–28.

15. See Lydia Liu's essay in this volume.

16. Raymond Williams, *The Country and the City* (New York: Oxford University Press, 1973), chap. 14.

17. Lin Yutang, *Moment in Peking: A Novel of Contemporary Life* (New York: John Day, 1939).

18. Damian Grant, *Realism* (London: Methuen, 1970; reprinted 1981), p. 14.

19. Lao She, "Wo zenyang xie duanpian xiaoshuo" (How I Wrote Short Stories), *Laoniu poche* (Old Ox and Broken Cart; Hong Kong, reprint, 1961), p. 53.

20. Grant, p. 15.

21. Hsiao Hung, *The Field of Life and Death and Tales of Hulan River*, trans. Howard Goldblatt (Bloomington: Indiana University Press, 1979), appendix, pp. 288–289.

22. Yan Jiayan, *Zhongguo xiandai xiaoshuo liupai shi* (History of Schools in Modern Chinese Fiction; Beijing: Renmin wenxue chubanshe, 1989), chap. 6.

23. David Der-wei Wang, *Mao Dun, Lao She, Shen Congwen: Chinese Fiction in the Twentieth Century* (New York: Columbia University Press, 1992), chap. 7, pp. 8, 13; quoted with the author's permission. The paragraph is also quoted in Wang's essay in this volume.

24. Ibid., p. 11.

25. Birch, pp. 403–404.

26. Ibid., p. 403.

27. See the essay by Yi-tsi Feuerwerker in this volume.

28. See Rudolph Wagner's paper for the Harvard conference, "Life as a Quote from a Foreign Book: Love, Paul, and Rita" (not included in this volume), esp. pp. 10–12.

29. See Leo Ou-fan Lee, "Beyond Realism: Thoughts on Modernist Experiments in Contemporary Chinese Writing," in *Worlds Apart: Recent Chinese Writing and Its Audiences*, ed. Howard Goldblatt (Armonk: M. E. Sharpe, 1990), pp. 64–77. For a brief introduction to *xungen* fiction, see my introduction to Jeanne Tai, ed., *Spring Bamboo: A Collection of Contemporary Chinese Short Stories* (New York: Random House, 1989).

30. Li Tuo, Talks at the Symposium of Overseas Chinese Writers (Oslo), *Jintian* (Today) 2:94 (1990).

31. By contrast, when sexuality is depicted by Wang Anyi, a female writer, repression and desire spring from a more human life-world, in which consuming or obsessive love replaces the flaunting of male physical prowess. A good example is her novella "Xiaocheng zhilian" (Love in a Small Town). The issue of male narcissism—certainly a prevalent hallmark of works by a number of male authors, particularly Zhang Xianliang—awaits more critical study. Rey Chow finds such a symptom even in the works of film director Chen Kaige (see her essay in this volume).

32. Birch, p. 391.

33. Li Tuo, p. 97.

34. Ibid., p. 98.

35. I am obviously indebted to Li Tuo for having introduced me to the works of these new writers and for sharing with me his insights and papers such as his introduction to Yu Hua's fiction.

36. Li Tuo, p. 98.

Contributors

Marston Anderson taught Chinese literature at Yale University. He is the author of *The Limits of Realism: Chinese Fiction of the Revolutionary Period* (1990).

Rey Chow teaches in the Department of Comparative Literature at the University of Minnesota. She is the author of *Woman and Chinese Modernity: The Politics of Reading between West and East* (1991) and *Writing Diaspora: Tactics of Intervention* (1992).

Margaret H. Decker is Assistant Professor of Chinese language and literature at the University of Minnesota. She has published several translations of contemporary Chinese short stories and is currently working on a book-length study of Gao Xiaosheng.

Michael S. Duke is Professor of Chinese in the Department of Asian Studies at the University of British Columbia. He is the author of *Blooming and Contending: Chinese Literature in the Post-Mao Era* (1985) and *The Iron House: A Memoir of the Chinese Democracy Movement and the Tiananmen Massacre* (1990). He is the editor of numerous anthologies, most recently *Worlds of Modern Chinese Fiction: Short Stories and Novellas from the People's Republic, Taiwan, and Hong Kong* (1991).

Yi-tsi Mei Feuerwerker (Mei Yici) teaches modern Chinese literature and comparative literature at the University of Michigan. She is the author of *Ding Ling's Fiction: Ideology and Narrative in Modern Chinese*

Literature (1982) and is currently working on the changing representation of the writer/intellectual self and the peasant other in modern Chinese fiction.

Heinrich Fruehauf studied East Asian languages and civilizations at the University of Tübingen, Fudan University, Hamburg University, Waseda University, and the University of Chicago, where he completed his doctorate in 1990. His areas of expertise are modern Chinese literature and, more recently, traditional Chinese medicine.

Theodore Huters is a member of the Department of East Asian Languages and Literatures at the University of California, Irvine. He has published a number of books and articles in the field of modern Chinese literature and literary history.

Jeffrey C. Kinkley is Associate Professor of history at St. John's University in New York and Assistant Editor (China) of *The Journal of Asian Studies*. He is the author of *The Odyssey of Shen Congwen* (1987) and many critical studies and translations of contemporary fiction from China and Taiwan.

Joseph S. M. Lau was born in Hong Kong and educated at National Taiwan University and Indiana University. He is at present Professor of Chinese at the University of Wisconsin, Madison. He has translated Malamud, Bellow, and Orwell. His two anthologies, *Chinese Literature: The Classical Tradition* (coedited with John Minford) and *Chinese Literature: The Modern Tradition* (with Howard Goldblatt), are forthcoming.

Leo Ou-fan Lee teaches in the Department of East Asian Languages and Cultures at the University of California, Los Angeles. His major books are *The Romantic Generation of Modern Chinese Writers* (1973) and *Voices from the Iron House: A Study of Lu Xun* (1987).

Lydia H. Liu received her Ph.D. degree in Comparative Literature at Harvard University in 1990. She is Assistant Professor of Chinese and comparative literature at the University of California, Berkeley. Her forthcoming book is on selfhood, nationhood, and literary practice in modern China.

Paul G. Pickowicz is Professor of history and Chinese studies at the University of California, San Diego. He is the author of *Marxist Literary Thought in China: The Influence of Ch'ü Ch'iu-pai* (1981), the coauthor of *Chinese Village, Socialist State* (1991), and the coeditor of *Unofficial China: Popular Culture and Thought in the People's Republic* (1989). He is at present writing a book on cinema and society in late Republican China.

David Der-wei Wang is currently Associate Professor of Chinese literature in the Department of East Asian Languages and Cultures at Columbia University. He has published three books in Chinese: *From Liu E to Wang Zhenhe: Critical Essays on Modern Chinese Realist Fiction* (1986), *Heteroglossia: Modern Chinese Fiction of the Thirties and Eighties* (1988), and *Reading Contemporary Chinese Fiction: Taiwan, Mainland, Hong Kong, and Overseas* (1991). He is also the author of *Fictional Realism in Twentieth-Century China: Mao Dun, Lao She, Shen Congwen* (1992).

Ellen Widmer teaches Chinese literature and East Asian studies at Wesleyan University. A specialist in Ming and Qing fiction, she is the author of *The Margins of Utopia: Shui-hu hou-chuan and the Literature of Ming Loyalism* (1987).

Harvard Contemporary China Series

Chinese Society on the Eve of Tiananmen:
The Impact of Reform
Edited and with an Introduction by Deborah Davis
and Ezra F. Vogel

New Perspectives on the Cultural Revolution
Edited and with an Introduction by William A. Joseph,
Christine P. W. Wong, and David Zweig